TAXATION, TECHNOLOGY
AND THE USER COST OF CAPITAL

CONTRIBUTIONS
TO
ECONOMIC ANALYSIS

182

Honorary Editor:
J. TINBERGEN

Editors:
D.W. JORGENSON
J. WAELBROECK

NORTH-HOLLAND
AMSTERDAM • NEW YORK • OXFORD • TOKYO

TAXATION, TECHNOLOGY AND THE USER COST OF CAPITAL

E. BIØRN

Department of Economics
University of Oslo
Norway

1989

NORTH-HOLLAND
AMSTERDAM • NEW YORK • OXFORD • TOKYO

ISBN: 0 444 87490 9

Publishers:
ELSEVIER SCIENCE PUBLISHERS B.V.
Sara Burgerhartstraat 25
P.O. Box 211, 1000 AE Amsterdam
The Netherlands

Distributors for the United States and Canada:
ELSEVIER SCIENCE PUBLISHING COMPANY, INC.
655 Avenue of the Americas
New York, N.Y. 10010
U.S.A.

PRINTED IN THE NETHERLANDS

INTRODUCTION TO THE SERIES

This series consists of a number of hitherto unpublished studies, which are introduced by the editors in the belief that they represent fresh contributions to economic science.

The term "economic analysis" as used in the title of the series has been adopted because it covers both the activities of the theoretical economist and the research worker.

Although the analytical methods used by the various contributors are not the same, they are nevertheless conditioned by the common origin of their studies, namely theoretical problems encountered in practical research. Since for this reason, business cycle research and national accounting, research work on behalf of economic policy, and problems of planning are the main sources of the subjects dealt with, they necessarily determine the manner of approach adopted by the authors. Their methods tend to be "practical" in the sense of not being too far remote from application to actual economic conditions. In additon they are quantitative.

It is the hope of the editors that the publication of these studies will help to stimulate the exchange of scientific information and to reinforce international cooperation in the field of economics.

The Editors

PREFACE

This study attempts to give a unified treatment of the cost of capital services and its relationship to the corporate income tax system on the one hand and to the production technology of the firm on the other. In recent decades, quantitative information on this cost has become useful for several purposes in applied economic research, in particular in macroeconomic and econometric model building and public economics.

The study relates the measurement of the price of capital services to the measurement of the capital stock of the firm, and gives a parallel treatment of the neo-classical technology with malleable capital and the putty-clay technology with vintage specific input coefficients. It further discusses and unifies various concepts of neutrality of corporate income taxation. Empirical illustrations based on Norwegian data are given. The study is intended to serve as a reference for researchers in econometric model building, corporate investment behaviour, tax analysis, and national accounting.

Thanks are due to several persons who have contributed, in various ways, at several stages during the work with this monograph. First, I want to express my gratitude to Dale W. Jorgenson for his encouragement, advice, and kind interest in the project. I have also received several helpful comments from colleagues who have read, partly or entirely, previous versions of the manuscript, and I want in particular to thank Petter Frenger and Kåre Petter Hagen for a substantial number of comments, as well as good advice, on the complete manuscript. My appreciation also goes to Sigbjørn Atle Berg, Erling Holmøy, Tor Jakob Klette, Karl Ove Moene, Erik Offerdal, Øystein Olsen, and Agnar Sandmo for useful comments on specific points, to Jørgen Ouren for help and advice with the programming of the numerical calculations, to Elisa Holm, Hanne Rambøl, Anne Skoglund, Anne Thorstensen, and Solveig Wiig for excellent typing and word-processing of several versions of the manuscript, and to Bruce Wolman who, with impressive skill, set the final camera-ready version in the computer type-setting system T$_E$X. Of course, I have the only responsibility for any remaining errors and shortcomings.

Finally, I gratefully acknowledge financial support from the Norwegian Research Council for Science and the Humanities.

Oslo, November 1988

Erik Biørn

CONTENTS

CHAPTER 1

INTRODUCTION

1.1   General background

The capital accumulation process plays a crucial role in economic growth. This study is concerned with the concept and measurement of one of the basic determinants of capital accumulation and factor allocation, and hence of efficiency and growth, in a market economy, namely the cost of using real capital as an input in production. This topic, like the problem of measuring capital input itself, has been much discussed among economists. The definition and measurement of the cost of using real capital input has been approached in several ways in the public finance, the macroeconomic, and the econometric literature. In business economics, investment criteria based on the present value of an 'investment project' or on its internal rate of return have had predominance. In empirical econometrics, a measure of the cost of capital services may be essential for the modelling of capital accumulation and the estimation of relations explaining corporate investment behaviour.

In recent decades, the effect of the *tax system* on the efficiency of capital allocation, through its distortionary effects on the incentives to save and invest and the discrimination between different types of capital assets it creates, has become an issue of increasing importance not only in the economic and econometric literature, but also in the tax policy debate. In several western countries, major reforms of the capital taxation have been accomplished or are under way. A close examination of the literature shows, however, a substantial diversity in approach when analyzing such tax reforms.

The present study attempts to provide a unified treatment of the cost of capital services, with emphasis on its relation to the corporate income tax system on the one hand, and to the production technology of the firm on the other. In the greater part of the study, the cost of capital services will be considered an input price which, loosely speaking, has a similar relationship to capital input as the wage rate has to labour input. It is a rental price, representing the cost of using one unit of capital input per unit of time in the same way as the wage rate is a rental price for labour input. But unlike the wage rate, the capital service price cannot — with some exceptions — be observed directly in the market. From an econometric point of view, this limited observability of the capital service price raises particular problems.

The tax imposed on corporate income, or net profit, and the tax on corporate wealth (if the tax system includes such a tax), are essentially taxes on the capital stock of the firm. This is the reason why the corporate tax system may affect the cost of using capital services as perceived by the firm, and may lead to a distortion of its input and output decisions. Capital, unlike for instance labour services and energy, is a *durable* input. Each capital good invested "produces" services to its user over a period which is longer than the conventional accounting period, usually one year, which underlies the corporate income (and wealth) taxation. Since capital is durable, the tax code — *inter alia* via the rules for deduction of financial costs, the depreciation rules, and the rules for taxation of capital gains — usually gives a prescription of how the firm's real investment expenditures should be accounted over time. This "periodization" of the investment cost imposed by the tax code may be different from the "periodization" which would be "correct" if the purpose is to define the true net profit of the firm. There may be several reasons why such differences arise between the tax accounted income and the true income. Measurement problems is one such reason. The tax system will then affect the shadow value of capital services for an optimizing firm. The textbook conclusion that a profit tax does not distort the producer's input and output decisions is valid in a stylized world of static profit maximization and with a particular definition of taxable profit only.

Analytic expressions for the cost of capital services which reflect the effect of the tax system are needed for numerous purposes in macroeconomic model building, public economics, and econometrics. Such expressions may be defined, interpreted, and measured in several ways depending on the specific features of the tax system, the purpose of the investigation, and the availability of data. Seminal contributions to this literature were given by Jorgenson (1963, 1967), Jorgenson and Stephenson (1967), and Hall and Jorgenson (1967, 1971). They defined the *user cost of capital* as the opportunity cost of using real capital input in the presence of an income tax and depreciation rules, and incorporated it into a neo-classical model of producer behaviour. Since the term 'user cost of capital' over the years has become familiar in the literature, we shall use it, or its abbreviated form the 'user cost', in this monograph. The term 'user price (of capital)' would perhaps have been more appropriate, since the variable is essentially a price variable, whereas the word cost is commonly referring to the product of a price and a quantity variable. The work of Jorgenson on the impact of the corporate tax system on the user cost of capital in a neo-classical setting will be one of the starting points for this study.

The problems encountered in defining and measuring the cost of capital services are closely related to those that arise when measuring the real capital stock, or the flow of capital services. They are in a sense dual problems. The capital measurement problem has for a long time been recognized as a complex and controversial problem in economic research. Indeed, Hicks has described it as "one of the nastiest jobs that economists has set to statisticians" [Hicks (1969, p. 253)]. At the core of the problem lies the fact that 'the capital stock' is a multi-dimensional economic concept. First, it is a *capacity* measure, representing the (potential) flow of services which can currently be "produced" by a production unit by means of the stock of capital goods existing at the time. Second, capital has a *wealth* characteristic. The value of a capital good reflects its ability to produce capital services today and in the future. From this it follows that capital goods which are equivalent in terms of *current* capacity may be widely different when characterized by their *future* usefulness in the production process. While the capacity dimension of the capital stock is in focus when specifying the production technology, its wealth dimension is the relevant dimension to consider when defining corporate income, depreciation, taxes assessed on income and wealth, and hence income after taxes. As a consequence, both the capacity and the wealth dimension of the capital will be involved in the measurement of the cost of capital services in the presence of a corporate tax system. The incorporation of the two-dimensional nature of corporate capital is a distinctive feature of the approach to be taken in this study. The problem of measuring the cost of capital services then becomes no less complicated than the capital measurement problem. In fact, at some stages in our analysis, *three capital concepts* will be involved, one related to capacity, one related to wealth, and one related to the way in which capital is accounted by the tax system. The duality between the measurement of the capital stock and the measurement of its service price is a second starting point for the present study.

A basic consequence of this duality is that the measurement of the cost of capital services and the measurement of the capital stock should utilize the same representation of the production technology. The specification of the technology has two aspects, one related to the *deterioration* of the capital input, the other related to *input substitution*. First, assume that a measure of (the capacity dimension of) the capital stock can be constructed by cumulating a weighted sum of past investment flows, i.e. the so-called 'perpetual inventory method'. The deterioration and retirement of capital goods over time will then be represented by the form of the weighting function used. The deterioration process is an equally important component in the user cost of capital as it is in the capital stock itself. It follows from the duality that this weighting function, to be denoted as the *survival function* of capital in this study, should be represented in exactly the same way when constructing capital stocks as when constructing their user costs. Second, the specification of factor substitution — notably between capital and other inputs — should be the same. We get one user cost of capital concept if the description of the technology is based on the *neo-classical model*, with malleable capital and perfect substitutability between different vintages of capital after installation. This is different from the concept which we get when assuming a vintage technology characterized by imperfect substitutability between different capital vintages after installation, for instance the *putty-clay* technology, with fixed input coefficients ex post.

The large majority of theoretical and applied works in this field — following Jorgenson's seminal contributions from the 1960's — have been based on a neo-classical description of the technology and on a particular parametric form of the survival function, namely the *exponential decay specification*. Under this assumption, the retirement will be a constant, time invariant share of the volume of the capital stock. This implies that the rate of retirement is independent of the age distribution of the capital stock. Over the years, this has become the standard representation of the retirement process not only in the literature on capital measurement, but also in the growing literature on the neutrality or lack of neutrality of the corporate income tax system.

Several objections can, however, be raised against this approach. First, the assumption of an exponentially declining survival function has been empirically contested by several authors [e.g. Griliches (1963), Feldstein and Foot (1971), Eisner (1972), Feldstein and Rothschild (1974), and Hulten and Wykoff (1981b)], although the issue is still open. Second, even if exponential decay may be an acceptable simplifying *approximation* for long-term analysis, for instance in modelling economic growth [confer Jorgenson (1963, p. 251) (1965, pp. 50–51)], it may give an inadequate description of the deterioration process in the short run. Econometricians working with quarterly or annual data and short-term models as well as researchers in empirical tax analysis may feel it as a strait-jacket. Third, taking exponential decay as a maintained hypothesis, places strong restrictions on the class of tax systems which can be analyzed from the point of view of neutrality. It is hardly an accident that the literature on this topic has so far been almost exclusively confined to considering the declining balance method of calculating depreciation allowances for tax purposes. This is probably due to the formal similarity which exists between this depreciation schedule and the exponential decay retirement process since it implies that a constant share of the book value of the firm's capital stock is written off in its tax accounts each year regardless of its age distribution. The neutrality properties of other depreciation schedules which are in use in several countries and for which the depreciation allowances depend on the age distribution of the capital stock, e.g. straight-line depreciation, straight-line with accelerated depreciation in some form, and the sum-of-the-year-digits schedule, then cannot be properly handled within this framework. The empirical relevance of non-exponential survival functions is a third starting point for the study.

1.2 Outline of the monograph

The content of the monograph is organized as follows. Chapter 2 describes investment criteria based on present value calculations related to an investment project, including the internal rate of return criterion. Its purpose is to show that a cost of capital concept can be defined without using a quantity representation of capital and to discuss the role of the corporate tax system in that context. Chapters 3 and 4 are preliminaries to the two following chapters. The basic capital concepts are introduced in chapter 3. They are termed the gross capital stock and the net capital stock — referring to the capacity and the wealth dimension of the capital, respectively. The chapter also introduces the retirement, depreciation, and other variables related to gross and net capital. Chapter 4 is concerned with the user cost of capital corresponding to a neo-classical representation of the technology in a taxless economy. Two interpretations of the user cost, a service price interpretation and a shadow value interpretation, are given. A formalization of the corporate tax system which is convenient for analyzing, under different tax regimes, the relationship between the taxation of corporate income and wealth, and the user cost of capital it implies, is given in chapter 5. The specification includes the rules for deduction of financial costs, the depreciation rules, and the rules for taxation of capital gains in the income tax base, as well as a tax on the value of the capital stock of the firm. The resulting generalization of the user cost of capital and its properties are then discussed in chapter 6.

The next two chapters are concerned with the user cost of capital when the neo-classical assumption of perfect substitutability between different capital vintages, i.e. the malleability assumption, is replaced by a vintage model assuming a putty-clay technology. Chapter 7 deals with the taxless case, and in chapter 8, a generalization allowing for taxes is discussed. We focus in particular on the differences between the user cost of capital implied by the different assumptions about factor substitution under the two technologies and the role of the scrapping decisions for capital under the putty-clay technology.

Next, in chapter 9, issues related to the *neutrality* of the corporate tax system are discussed. Alternative ways of characterizing neutrality by means of the user cost representation of the tax system and alternative ways of measuring 'tax wedges' describing departures from this situation, are presented. Empirical applications are discussed in the following two chapters. Chapter 10 presents and discusses an extensive set of estimated time series of user costs and neutrality indicators based on Norwegian tax rules, and tax and investment data for Norwegian manufacturing for the years 1965–1984. Both actual systems and more or less hypothetical tax reforms — *inter alia*, systems in which the components of the income tax base are indexed — and alternative forms of survival functions are considered. In chapter 11, different aspects of the duality between the measurement of the capital stock and of its service price are illustrated empirically. Finally, some concluding remarks are given in chapter 12.

Only the part of the tax system which relates to the firm will be considered in this study. Capital is used as synonymous with corporate capital. We will therefore, to a modest degree, unlike for instance Stiglitz (1973), King (1977), and Auerbach (1983a,1983b), be concerned with problems at the interface between the personal and the corporate sector. Such problems include the impact of the personal tax system on the user cost of capital in the corporate sector, via, *inter alia*, the financial decisions of the firm and its shareholders and the effect of international capital flows. In our analysis of the user cost, all financial decisions will be regarded as having been determined prior to the decisions about real investment. Consequently, when discussing the neutrality of the tax system, our aim is not to investigate the *overall* departure from neutrality, but only the part which relates to the corporate taxation. Throughout the study, focus is, as already declared, on the way in which the user cost of capital and its properties are related to the corporate tax system and to the technology of the firm.

CHAPTER 2

BASIC INVESTMENT CRITERIA AND THE COST OF CAPITAL

2.1 Introduction

A concept often used in the economic analysis of corporate investment decisions is the *investment project*. It may represent the purchase and operation
of a machine for a specific purpose, the construction of a factory building,
an advertising campaign etc. This is a standard terminology in business
economics [cf. e.g. Bierman and Smidt (1980)] and also occurs frequently
in macroeconomic textbooks [see e.g. Ackley (1961, chapter 18) and Allen
(1967, chapter 4)]. Decisions about whether or not to invest in a project
are commonly based on a comparison of the present value of its expected
revenues with its costs, these revenues and costs being treated as exogenous
variables. The most familiar of these *investment criteria* are the internal
rate of return criterion and the present value criterion [cf. e.g. Bierman and
Smidt (1980, chapters 2 and 3)]. Such investment criteria involve no 'stock
of capital' or 'flow of capital services'. They therefore appear as basically
different from decision rules for capital accumulation derived from theo-
ries of producer behaviour specifying capital among several substitutable
inputs and assuming a separation of revenues and costs into price and quantity components, including a separation of the cost of using capital into a
quantity of capital services and a price of such services.

  The purpose of this chapter is to show that a cost of capital concept for
an investment project can be established without using a quantity representation of capital. The chapter is intended to serve as a "bridge" between
investment criteria based on the rate of return and the user cost of capital
concepts which will be our main concern in this study. These concepts are
the cost of capital services for a firm whose production process can be represented by a *neo-classical* technology (chapter 4) and for a firm for which
a *putty-clay* vintage technology is relevant (chapter 7). It is difficult to
give the notion of an investment project a precise meaning with reference
to neo-classical theory, since this theory assumes that capital goods can

be transferred from one production process to another without frictions of any kind; capital goods do not "belong" to specific production processes from the time of investment until the scrapping time. This property of the neo-classical model will be elaborated in chapter 3. On the other hand, if the technology has a vintage characteristic, so that capital cannot be transferred without costs or frictions from one production process to another, a 'project' in the terminology of business economics can be associated more or less directly with the 'vintage'. The relationship between a 'project' and a 'vintage' will be elaborated for a putty-clay model in chapter 7.

Let us now consider an investment project in the terminology of business economics. The value of the project and its rate of return are defined in section 2.2, and three equivalent investment criteria are then derived, in section 2.3. From one of them, we can establish a cost of capital concept, which will be shown in section 2.4. Two examples are discussed in some detail in section 2.5, and section 2.6 is concerned with generalisations of the rate of return and the cost of capital which take the income tax into account. Some concluding remarks follow in section 2.7.

2.2   The value and the rate of return of an investment project

Consider a firm in the process of deciding whether or not to invest in a given project. The project has a fixed scale, which can not be altered by the firm. Its *cost*, A, is incurred instantaneously, at time $s = 0$, and its *revenue* is the payment stream $\{y(s), \ s \geq 0\}$, $y(s)$ denoting the (intensity of the) payment at time s. These variables are assumed to be known with certainty at the time of investment. We assume that $y(s)$ is *non-negative* for all $s \geq 0$, which will be satisfied if no outlays are due after the initial purchase cost. The project is thus described by $\{A; y(s), s \geq 0\}$. Time is considered as continuous and, for simplicity, we let $y(s)$ be defined for all non-negative s, assuming it to be zero in periods when the project earns no revenue.

The *value of the project*, or more precisely, its initial value, is defined as the present value of its revenue over the life cycle, discounted at the current nominal interest rate, i, i.e.

$$(2.1) \qquad\qquad V(0) = \int_0^\infty e^{-is} y(s) \, ds \, .$$

The subscript 0 indicates that this value refers to age $s = 0$, to distinguish it from the more general age specific concept to be defined below. Since $y(s)$ is non-negative, the value of the project will be positive for all interest rates $i < \infty$. The *total profit* over the project's life cycle, the *life cycle profit* for short, is the present value of its net payment stream, i.e. its value minus its cost,

$$(2.2) \qquad \Pi = V(0) - A = \int_0^\infty e^{-is} y(s)\, ds - A\,.$$

It is convenient to consider the revenue function normalized against its initial value, i.e.

$$(2.3) \qquad x(s) = \frac{y(s)}{y(0)}\,, \qquad s \geq 0\,.$$

The present value of this normalized revenue function is

$$(2.4) \qquad w(i) = \int_0^\infty e^{-is} x(s)\, ds\,,$$

which is formally the Laplace transform of $x(s)$.[1] Since this function is decreasing in i when $x(s)$ is non-negative and strictly positive for at least some $s > 0$, we know that $w'(i) < 0$ for all i, and that $w(-\infty) = \infty$, and $w(\infty) = 0$. We can then express the value of the project and its life cycle profit compactly as

$$(2.5) \qquad V(0) = y(0)w(i)\,,$$

$$(2.6) \qquad \Pi = y(0)w(i) - A\,,$$

and we know that

$$(2.7) \qquad \frac{\partial V(0)}{\partial i} = \frac{\partial \Pi}{\partial i} = y(0)w'(i) < 0\,,$$

so that $V(0)$ and Π *decrease monotonically* from ∞ to 0 and from ∞ to $-A$, respectively, as i increases from $-\infty$ to ∞.[2]

---

[1] Cf. e.g. Bartle (1964, pp. 372–373). See also section 3.3.

[2] Monotonicity of $w(i)$ and $V(0)$ in i, which is stated as a Fundamental Theorem in Hicks (1973, p. 19), relies strongly on the assumptions that the revenue function $x(s)$ is *non-negative* and that *truncation* of the process is not possible. Conditions under which similar results hold in the more general cases where the revenue may change between positive and negative values, where arbitrary truncation is possible,

The *(internal) rate of return* of the project is defined as the value of the interest rate, $i = i^*$, which equates the value of the project and its cost. Formally, i^* is determined from $y(0)w(i^*) = A$, which implies

(2.8) $$i^* = w^{-1}[A/y(0)].$$

Since $w(i)$ is monotonically decreasing in i, from infinity to zero, a unique (positive or negative) solution, i^*, for a given $x(s)$ will exist for any positive (and finite) values of A and $y(0)$.

2.3   Three equivalent investment criteria

The investment project under consideration will be carried out if its value exceeds its cost, i.e. if its life cycle profit is positive. The investment criterion based on present values is thus [cf. e.g. Bierman and Smidt (1980, p. 51)]

(2.9) $$y(0)w(i) - A \overset{\displaystyle >}{\underset{\displaystyle <}{=}} 0 \iff \begin{bmatrix} \text{Invest} \\ \text{Indifferent} \\ \text{Do not invest} \end{bmatrix}.$$

This basic investment criterion can be translated into criteria expressed in terms of critical values of the cost of the project A, the interest rate i, and the initial yield $y(0)$, as follows:

(2.9.a) $$\begin{bmatrix} \text{Invest} \\ \text{Indifferent} \\ \text{Do not invest} \end{bmatrix} \iff A \overset{\displaystyle <}{\underset{\displaystyle >}{=}} A^* = y(0)w(i),$$

or

(2.9.b) $$\begin{bmatrix} \text{Invest} \\ \text{Indifferent} \\ \text{Do not invest} \end{bmatrix} \iff i \overset{\displaystyle <}{\underset{\displaystyle >}{=}} i^* = w^{-1}[A/y(0)],$$

or

(2.9.c) $$\begin{bmatrix} \text{Invest} \\ \text{Indifferent} \\ \text{Do not invest} \end{bmatrix} \iff y(0) \overset{\displaystyle >}{\underset{\displaystyle <}{=}} y^* = A/w(i).$$

---

or where the interest rate is time varying, are discussed in Arrow and Levhari (1969), Sen (1975) and Ross, Spatt, and Dybvig (1980).

The equivalence of (2.9.a)–(2.9.c) follows from the fact that $w(i)$ is monotonically decreasing in i. Here (a) A^* has the interpretation of the largest investment cost for which the project would be profitable, given i, $x(s)$, and $y(0)$, (b) i^* denotes the largest interest rate which the project could sustain, given A, $x(s)$, and $y(0)$, and (c) y^* denotes the smallest initial yield which would make the project profitable, given A, $x(s)$, and i. This can also be seen from the following three equivalent expressions for the life cycle profit:

$$(2.10) \qquad \Pi = A^* - A = y(0) \int_0^\infty [e^{-is} - e^{-i^*s}] x(s)\, ds$$

$$= [y(0) - y^*] \int_0^\infty e^{-is} x(s)\, ds.$$

2.4 The cost of capital interpreted as the yield from a marginal project

We now use the third of the investment criteria above, i.e. (2.9.c), to derive a cost of capital concept. Assume that a project with an instantaneous cost A is financed by a loan at the current interest rate i. If the yield of the project had started at $y(0) = y^* = A/w(i)$ and had been declining as $x(s)$, and if the firm had used this yield flow, i.e. $y^*x(s)$, to repay the loan, then it would have been indifferent between investing and not investing in the project. The flow $\{y^*x(s),\ s \geq 0\}$ thus is the yield necessary to repay the loan, i.e. the project $\{A; y^*x(s),\ s \geq 0\}$ is a *marginal project*.

Then, instead of saying that the project has a cost A as an instantaneous initial outlay, we could say that it has a cost

$$(2.11) \qquad c(s) = y^*x(s) = \frac{Ax(s)}{w(i)}, \qquad s \geq 0,$$

at age s, the present value of which over the life cycle of the project is the total cost. In other words, $c(s)$ converts the total cost A into a flow of costs over its life cycle. We shall denote $c(s)$ as the *annual cost* at age s. Using (2.4) and (2.11), the life cycle profit (2.6) can be written as

$$(2.12) \qquad \Pi = [y(0) - c(0)] \int_0^\infty e^{-is} x(s)\, ds = \int_0^\infty e^{-is} \pi(s)\, ds,$$

where

$$(2.13) \qquad \pi(s) = [y(0) - c(0)]x(s) = y(s) - c(s), \qquad s \geq 0,$$

can be interpreted as the profit at age s. Thus, deducting the cost at age s, $c(s)$, from the yield flow, $y(s)$, gives a profit flow, $\pi(s)$, the present value of which over the life cycle of the project is the life cycle profit Π. We shall denote $\pi(s)$ as the *annual profit* at age s. This is our *first* way of motivating the interpretation of $c(s)$, defined in (2.11), as the cost of capital for the investment project $\{A; y(s), \ s \geq 0\}$.

An alternative way of motivating the cost of capital interpretation of (2.11) is the following. Consider the project at age s, and define its value as the present value of its remaining yield, i.e.[3]

$$(2.14) \quad V(s) = \int_s^\infty e^{-i(\theta - s)} y(\theta)\, d\theta = y(0)e^{is} \int_s^\infty e^{-i\theta} x(\theta)\, d\theta, \quad s \geq 0,$$

which generalizes the definition (2.1). Differentiation with respect to s gives $V'(s) = iV(s) - y(s)$. Hence, using (2.13), we can write the yield at age s as

$$(2.15) \qquad y(s) = iV(s) + [-V'(s)] = c(s) + \pi(s), \qquad s \geq 0,$$

which can be interpreted as follows. *The yield of a project at age s equals the sum of the interest on the value of the project at age s, $iV(s)$, and its (instantaneous) loss of value at this age, $-V'(s)$ (first equality).* Interpreting this yield, in general, as a cost plus a profit (second equality), we see that *for a marginal project*, for which $\pi(s) = 0$ for all s, *the cost should cover the imputed interest on the project value and the instantaneous loss of value (depreciation) exactly.* Hence, for a marginal project, the annual cost $c(s)$ at any age s is determined once the value of the project at this age, its instantaneous rate of decline, and the rate of interest are known. This is our *second* way of motivating the cost of capital interpretation of $c(s)$.

---

[3] This is a special case of a more general principle for capital valuation, cf. Hotelling (1925), Dorfman (1969), and Hicks (1973, chapter II).

2.5 Examples

Let us illustrate the concepts and results presented above by means of two examples.

2.5.1 Example 1: Constant yield

Assume that the project gives a constant payment flow $y(0)$ up to age N, when its yield drops to zero. We then have from (2.3)

$$(2.16) \qquad x(s) = \begin{cases} 1 & \text{for } 0 \le s \le N, \\ 0 & \text{for } s > N, \end{cases}$$

which, when inserted into (2.4) and (2.14), gives a present value of the normalized revenue function equal to

$$(2.17) \qquad w(i) = \frac{1}{i}\left[1 - e^{-iN}\right]$$

and a value of the project at age s equal to

$$(2.18) \qquad V(s) = y(0)\frac{1}{i}[1 - e^{-i(N-s)}], \qquad 0 \le s \le N.$$

In this case, $w(i)$ is simply the value of a constant annuity of 1 discounted over N years at the rate i, and the value of the project at age s, $V(s)$ is its annual yield times the value of a constant annuity of 1 discounted over the number of service years remaining, $N - s$, at the rate i.

The basic investment criterion, (2.9), now takes the form

$$(2.19) \qquad y(0)\left[1 - e^{-iN}\right] \begin{array}{c} > \\ = \\ < \end{array} iA \iff \begin{bmatrix} \text{Invest} \\ \text{Indifferent} \\ \text{Do not invest} \end{bmatrix},$$

so that the rate of return is implicitly determined by [cf. (2.8)]

$$(2.20) \qquad 1 - e^{-i^*N} = i^*\frac{A}{y(0)}.$$

The annual cost of capital, like the yield flow, is constant and is given by [cf. (2.11)]

$$(2.21) \qquad c(s) = \frac{A\,i}{1 - e^{-iN}}, \qquad 0 \le s \le N.$$

This is the familiar formula

$$cost\ of\ capital = \frac{project\ cost}{annuity\ factor}.$$

Eqs. (2.20) and (2.21), after elimination of A, define the following relationship between the cost of capital, the interest rate, and the rate of return

$$(2.22) \qquad \frac{c(0)}{y(0)} = \frac{c(s)}{y(s)} = \frac{i}{i^*} \frac{1 - e^{-i^* N}}{1 - e^{-iN}}.$$

This formula can be used to translate any value of i^* into an equivalent value of $c(s)$ and vice versa. If the life time N is infinitely large, $c(s)$ is proportional to i and inversely proportional to i^*.

From (2.13) and (2.21), it follows that the annual profit flow, like the yield and the annual cost of capital, is constant and equal to

$$(2.23) \qquad \pi(s) = y(0) - \frac{A\,i}{1 - e^{-iN}}, \qquad 0 \le s \le N.$$

The implicit interest and depreciation components of the yield are not, however, constants in this case. The interest component is [cf. (2.15) and (2.18)]

$$iV(s) = y(0)\left[1 - e^{-i(N-s)}\right], \qquad 0 \le s \le N,$$

while the depreciation component is

$$-V'(s) = y(0)e^{-i(N-s)}, \qquad 0 \le s \le N.$$

If $i > 0$, the former is decreasing with the age of the project and the latter is increasing, in such a way that their sum is constant and equal to $y(0)$. Furthermore, the interest component is an increasing function and the depreciation component is a decreasing function of the interest rate. The rate of depreciation $[-V'(s)/V(s)]$ also depends on the interest rate and is an increasing function of the age of the project.

2.5.2 Example 2: Exponentially declining yield

In the second example, we assume that the yield from the project is exponentially declining at the rate δ, starting at $y(0)$, i.e.

$$(2.24) \qquad x(s) = e^{-\delta s}, \qquad s \geq 0,$$

where the maximal life time may, in principle, be infinite. Substituting (2.24) into (2.4) and (2.14), we find a present value of the relative revenue function equal to

$$(2.25) \qquad w(i) = \frac{1}{i + \delta},$$

and a value of the project at age s

$$(2.26) \qquad V(s) - y(0) \frac{e^{-\delta s}}{i + \delta}, \qquad s \geq 0.$$

This value starts at $y(0)/(i + \delta)$ and declines at the same rate as the yield flow.

The basic investment criterion, (2.9), now becomes

$$(2.27) \qquad y(0) \overset{>}{\underset{<}{=}} A(i + \delta) \Longleftrightarrow \begin{bmatrix} \text{Invest} \\ \text{Indifferent} \\ \text{Do not invest} \end{bmatrix}.$$

From (2.8) and (2.25) it follows that the rate of return on the project can be written explicitly as

$$(2.28) \qquad i^* = \frac{y(0)}{A} - \delta,$$

i.e. it is simply the difference between the initial yield/cost ratio, $y(0)/A$, and the rate of decline of the yield. The associated cost of capital is [cf. (2.11)]

$$(2.29) \qquad c(s) = A(i + \delta)e^{-\delta s}, \qquad s \geq 0.$$

The cost of capital for this project starts at $c(0) = A(i + \delta)$ and declines at the same rate, δ, as the yield flow and the value of the project. Eliminating

A from (2.28) and (2.29), we get the following relationship between the cost of capital, the market interest rate, and the internal rate of return

(2.30) $$\frac{c(0)}{y(0)} = \frac{c(s)}{y(s)} = \frac{i+\delta}{i^*+\delta}.$$

For given values of $y(s)$, i, and δ, the values of $c(s)$ and $i^* + \delta$ vary in inverse proportion.

The profit flow, like the yield and the cost of capital, is also declining at the rate δ, since (2.13), (2.24), and (2.29) imply

(2.31) $$\pi(s) = [y(0) - A(i+\delta)]e^{-\delta s} = \pi(0)e^{-\delta s}, \qquad s \geq 0.$$

It follows directly from (2.26) that the interest component is the share $i/(i+\delta)$ of the yield, i.e.

$$iV(s) = y(0)\frac{i\,e^{-\delta s}}{i+\delta},$$

and the depreciation component is the complementary share, $\delta/(i+\delta)$, i.e.

$$-V'(s) = y(0)\frac{\delta e^{-\delta s}}{i+\delta} = \delta V(s).$$

A basic characteristic of a project with an exponentially declining yield thus is that its value declines with age at a constant rate $-V'(s)/V(s) = \delta$, so that δ can be interpreted as the *rate of depreciation* of the project. In this case, we thus have the familiar relationship

initial cost of capital = project cost × (interest rate + depreciation rate)

2.6   The rate of return and the cost of capital in the presence of an income tax

So far, we have paid no attention to the effect of the income tax and the prescription given in the tax code for deduction of the cost of the project. This prescription includes the *depreciation rules* and the *rules for interest deduction*. Assume now that the yield of the project is subject to an income tax at the (constant) rate u, the tax base at age s being the yield $y(s)$ after deduction of depreciation allowances and interest costs. The depreciation allowances are constructed in such a way that a share k of the investment cost ($0 \leq k \leq 1$) is *immediately deductible* against income and the rest, i.e. the share $1 - k$ of the cost, is subject to *'ordinary' depreciation*. The profile of the latter part of the depreciation allowances reflects the time profile of the yield flow. The interest cost is defined as the interest rate i times the value of the project net of the (tax-accounted) depreciation. To preserve a certain generality, a share m of the interest cost ($0 \leq m \leq 1$) is assumed to be deductible in the income tax base.[4]

How will the introduction of this kind of tax system affect the rate of return of the project and its cost of capital? Let us again consider the examples with constant yield and with exponential yield, discussed in section 2.5. For each example, two alternative assumptions with respect to the *financing* of the investment will be considered:

Case a: The firm finances the full cost of the project by a loan, the "tax saving" implied by the initial depreciation allowances is disposed by the owner of the firm.

Case b: The firm finances the cost of the project, net of the initial depreciation allowances, by a loan, i.e. the implied "tax saving" is retained by the firm.[5]

2.6.1 Example 1: Constant yield, linear depreciation

Assume, as in example 1 in section 2.5, that the project gives a constant yield $y(0)$ over N years and then the yield drops to zero. Accordingly, linear depreciation over the same period is allowed in the firm's tax accounts as 'ordinary' depreciation. The initial depreciation allowance (at age 0) then is kA. Assuming that this is deductible against other income, this implies a net acquisition cost to the firm equal to $(1 - uk)A$. The ordinary depreciation allowance at age s is constant and equal to the acquisition cost net of the initial allowance, divided by the life time of the project, i.e. $(1 - k)A/N$, $0 < s \leq N$, so that the depreciation allowances add to A over the project's life time.

Case a: Loan equal to full cost A

In this case, the initial debt of the firm is A. The debt is repaid in accordance with the linear depreciation profile, so that the debt remaining

---

[4] A similar assumption is made in King (1975, p. 274).

[5] This is the assumption about the financing of the investment made by King (1975, p. 275), and Atkinson and Stiglitz (1980, p. 145).

at age s is $(1 - s/N)\,A$. The interest cost on this debt is $i(1 - s/N)A$, of which the share m is deductible. The tax base at age s is then

$$y(0) - (1 - k)\frac{A}{N} - mi\left(1 - \frac{s}{N}\right)A, \qquad 0 \leq s \leq N,$$

which gives a net after tax cash-flow equal to

$$y(0) - u\left\{y(0) - (1 - k)\frac{A}{N} - mi\left(1 - \frac{s}{N}\right)A\right\}, \qquad 0 \leq s \leq N.$$

The after tax life cycle profit is the present value of this cash-flow less the net acquisition cost, i.e.

$$(2.32) \quad \Pi = \int_0^N e^{-is}\left[y(0) - u\left\{y(0) - (1 - k)\frac{A}{N} - mi\left(1 - \frac{s}{N}\right)A\right\}\right]ds$$
$$- (1 - uk)A.$$

Since it can be shown, by using integration by parts, that

$$\int_0^N e^{-is}\left(1 - \frac{s}{N}\right)ds = \frac{1}{i}\left[1 - \frac{1}{iN}\left(1 - e^{-iN}\right)\right],$$

this expression can be simplified to

$$\Pi = (1 - u)y(0)w(i) + u(1 - k)\frac{w(i)}{N}A + um\left(1 - \frac{w(i)}{N}\right)A - (1 - uk)A,$$

where $w(i)$ is the annuity factor defined in (2.17). Rearranging terms, we can write the after tax profit as

$$(2.33) \quad \Pi = (1 - u)\left[y(0)w(i) - A\left\{1 + \frac{u(1 - k - m)}{1 - u}\left(1 - \frac{w(i)}{N}\right)\right\}\right].$$

The project under consideration will be profitable, give a zero profit, or be non-profitable in the presence of the income tax if the expression in the square bracket of (2.33) is positive, zero, or negative, respectively. This leads to the investment criterion

$$(2.34) \quad y(0)w(i) \overset{\geq}{\underset{<}{=}} A\left[1 + \frac{u(1 - k - m)}{1 - u}\left(1 - \frac{w(i)}{N}\right)\right]$$
$$\Longleftrightarrow \begin{bmatrix} \text{Invest} \\ \text{Indifferent} \\ \text{Do not invest} \end{bmatrix}.$$

This investment criterion generalizes (2.19) and coincides with it if either

(i) the tax rate is zero: $u = 0$, or

(ii) the interest rate is zero: $i = 0$, since $w(0) = N$, or

(iii) the sum of the share of the investment cost allowed as an initial depreciation allowance and the share of the interest cost deductible in the tax base is unity: $k + m = 1$.

An alternative interpretation of the after tax life cycle profit (2.33) is the following: Defining

$$A \left[1 + \frac{u(1 - k - m)}{1 - u} \left(1 - \frac{w(i)}{N} \right) \right]$$

as a tax corrected project cost — the correction factor in the square bracket representing the effect of the depreciation and interest deduction rules — eq. (2.33) says that

after-tax life cycle profit $= (1 - \text{tax rule}) \times (\text{pre-tax life cycle yield}$

$- \text{tax corrected project cost}).$

The tax corrected project cost thus defined will be smaller than, equal to, or larger than the actual project cost, according as $k + m \gtrless 1$, i.e. according as the sum of the share of the project cost deductible as an initial allowance and the share of the interest cost deductible against current income is greater than, equal to, or less than unity.

The rate of return on the project in the presence of an income tax is, as in the no-tax case, the value of the interest rate, $i = i^*$, which makes the life cycle profit equal to zero. Formally, it is obtained from

$$(2.35) \qquad y(0)\, w(i^*) = A \left[1 + \frac{u(1 - k - m)}{1 - u} \left(1 - \frac{w(i^*)}{N} \right) \right],$$

which defines i^* as a function of the yield/cost ratio $y(0)/A$, the life time N, and the tax parameters u, k, and m.

Likewise, as in the zero-tax case, the cost of capital is the value of the (constant) yield $y(0)$ for which a zero life cycle profit would be obtained. Formally, it is given by

$$(2.36) \qquad c = \frac{A}{w(i)} \left[1 + \frac{u(1 - k - m)}{1 - u} \left(1 - \frac{w(i)}{N} \right) \right],$$

which is simply the ratio between the tax corrected investment cost and the annuity factor $w(i)$. It thus generalizes (2.21).

It is informative to consider the case where the life time goes to infinity, i.e. $N \to \infty$ and hence $w(i) \to 1/i$. Eqs. (2.35) and (2.36) then give a rate of return and a cost of capital equal to

$$i^* = \frac{y(0)}{A} \frac{1-u}{1-u(k+m)}, \qquad (N \to \infty),$$

$$c = A i \frac{1-u(k+m)}{1-u}, \qquad (N \to \infty),$$

respectively. From this we directly obtain

$$i^* \underset{<}{\overset{>}{=}} \frac{y(0)}{A} \iff c \underset{>}{\overset{<}{=}} Ai \iff k+m \underset{<}{\overset{>}{=}} 1 \qquad (N \to \infty).$$

Case b: Loan equal to net cost $A(1 - uk)$

In this case, the initial debt is $(1 - uk)A$. Assuming that the debt is repaid in accordance with the linear depreciation schedule, the debt remaining at age s is $(1 - s/N)(1 - uk)A$, so that the net after tax cash-flow from the project is

$$y(0) - u \left\{ y(0) - (1-k)\frac{A}{N} - mi\left(1 - \frac{s}{N}\right)(1-uk)A \right\}, \qquad 0 \le s \le N.$$

If $m > 0$, $k > 0$, this cash-flow is smaller than in case a, since the firm is allowed a smaller interest deduction and hence its tax payment is larger. The after-tax life cycle profit now becomes

(2.37)
$$\Pi = \int_0^N e^{-is} \left[y(0) - u\left\{ y(0) - (1-k)\frac{A}{N} \right.\right.$$
$$\left.\left. - mi\left(1 - \frac{s}{N}\right)(1-uk)A \right\} \right] ds - (1-uk)A,$$

which can be simplified to

$$\Pi = (1-u)y(0)w(i) + u(1-k)\frac{w(i)}{N}A + um\left(1 - \frac{w(i)}{N}\right)(1-uk)A - (1-uk)A,$$

with $w(i)$ still defined as in (2.17). Rearranging terms, this gives

(2.38)

$$\Pi = (1 - u)\left[y(0)w(i)\right.$$
$$\left. - A\left\{1 + \frac{u(1 - k - m + ukm)}{1 - u}\left(1 - \frac{w(i)}{N}\right)\right\}\right].$$

As before, the project will be profitable, give a zero profit, and be non-profitable according as the expression in the square bracket is positive, zero, or negative. Hence, the basic investment criterion reads

(2.39)

$$y(0)w(i) \gtreqless A\left[1 + \frac{u(1 - k - m + ukm)}{1 - u}\left(1 - \frac{w(i)}{N}\right)\right]$$

$$\Longleftrightarrow \begin{bmatrix} \text{Invest} \\ \text{Indifferent} \\ \text{Do not invest} \end{bmatrix}.$$

The formal difference between this and the investment criterion in case a, (2.34), is that the term ukm has been added in the numerator of the fractional expression in the square bracket. This reflects the different assumptions about the financing of the project, and hence about the interest payment. We note that (2.39) coincides with the investment criterion in the zero-tax case, (2.19), if either

(i) the tax rate is zero: $u = 0$, or

(ii) the interest rate is zero: $i = 0$, or

(iii) immediate deduction of the cost of the project ($k = 1$) and no deduction of debt interests ($m = 0$) is allowed, or

(iv) no initial depreciation ($k = 0$) and full deduction of debt interests ($m = 1$) is allowed.

Case (iii) is the case with a 100 per cent instantaneous depreciation, case (iv) is the case with a 100 per cent true economic depreciation. Thus, $k + m = 1$ will not be a necessary and sufficient condition for the tax system to be non-distorting in this case as it is in case a: $k = 1$, $m = 0$, and $k = 0$, $m = 1$ are non-distorting in both cases, whereas $k = 1 - m$, $0 < m < 1$, is non-distorting in case a, but will distort the ranking of different projects, and hence affect the investment decisions in case b.

Table 2.1: Project specific cost of capital. Constant yield and infinite life time.

Financing of the project	$k = 0$ $m = 0$	$k = 0$ $m = 1$	$k = 1$ $m = 0$	$k = 1$ $m = 1$
a: Loan equal to full cost	$\frac{Ai}{1-u}$	$\cdot\ Ai$	Ai	$Ai\frac{1-2u}{1-u}$
b: Loan equal to net cost	$\frac{Ai}{1-u}$	Ai	Ai	$Ai(1-u)$

The tax corrected rate of return is implicitly determined by

$$(2.40) \qquad y(0)w(i^*) = A\left[1 + \frac{u(1-k-m+ukm)}{1-u}\left(1 - \frac{w(i^*)}{N}\right)\right]$$

and the cost of capital is equal to

$$(2.41) \qquad c = \frac{A}{w(i)}\left[1 + \frac{u(1-k-m+ukm)}{1-u}\left(1 - \frac{w(i)}{N}\right)\right].$$

Again, it is informative to consider a project with an infinite life time. Setting $N \to \infty$ in (2.40) and (2.41), we obtain

$$i^* = \frac{y(0)}{A}\frac{1-u}{(1-uk)(1-um)}, \qquad (N \to \infty),$$

$$c = Ai\frac{(1-uk)(1-um)}{1-u}, \qquad (N \to \infty),$$

which imply

$$i^* \begin{array}{c}\geq\\<\end{array} \frac{y(0)}{A} \iff c \begin{array}{c}\leq\\>\end{array} Ai \iff (1-uk)(1-um) \begin{array}{c}\leq\\>\end{array} 1-u \quad (N \to \infty).$$

The resulting expressions for the cost of capital for the boundary values of k and m, with an infinite life time, are given in table 2.1. The cost of capital is the same in the two cases if either k or m is zero. If $k = m = 1$, i.e. if both a 100 per cent instantaneous depreciation and full interest deductibility is allowed, there is a difference. In the case where the loan is equal to the full cost, the cost of capital will be negative if $u > 0.5$. This can never occur when the loan is equal to the net cost, provided the tax rate does not exceed 100 per cent.

2.6.2 Example 2: Exponentially declining yield, depreciation according to declining balance

In the second example, the yield of the project is exponentially declining, being $y(0) e^{-\delta s}$ at age s. Accordingly, the depreciation rates permitted for tax purposes as ordinary depreciation decline as $\delta e^{-\delta s}$. This corresponds to the declining balance schedule of depreciation allowances. As in example 1, the initial depreciation allowance is kA, which implies a net acquisition cost equal to $(1 - uk)A$. The allowance at age s is $(1 - k)\delta e^{-\delta s} A$ $(s > 0)$, so that the depreciation allowances add to the project cost over the life time, since

$$kA + \int_0^\infty (1 - k)\delta e^{-\delta s} A\, ds = A.$$

Case a: Loan equal to full cost A

In this case, the initial debt is A. It is repaid in accordance with the declining balance schedule, so that the debt remaining at age s is $e^{-\delta s} A$. The tax base at age s is then

$$y(0)e^{-\delta s} - (1 - k)\delta e^{-\delta s} A - mie^{-\delta s} A,$$

which gives a net after tax cash-flow

$$[y(0) - u\{y(0) - (1 - k)\delta A - miA\}] e^{-\delta s}$$

and a life cycle profit equal to

$$(2.42) \quad \Pi = \int_0^\infty e^{-is} [y(0) - u\{y(0) - (1-k)\delta A - miA\}] e^{-\delta s}\, ds - (1-uk)A.$$

After some rearranging, this can be written as

$$(2.43) \qquad \Pi = (1 - u) \left[\frac{y(0)}{i + \delta} - A \left(1 + \frac{u(1 - k - m)}{1 - u} \frac{i}{i + \delta} \right) \right].$$

From this we derive the investment criterion

$$(2.44) \quad \frac{y(0)}{i + \delta} \gtreqless A \left(1 + \frac{u(1 - k - m)}{1 - u} \frac{i}{i + \delta} \right) \iff \begin{bmatrix} \text{Invest} \\ \text{Indifferent} \\ \text{Do not invest} \end{bmatrix}.$$

As before, the rate of return of the project is obtained by setting $\Pi = 0$ and solving for i. In this case, we find from (2.43) the following explicit solution

$$(2.45) \qquad i^* = \left[\frac{y(0)}{A} - \delta\right] \frac{1-u}{1-u(k+m)} .$$

To get the tax corrected rate of return, we only have to multiply the pre-tax rate of return, i.e. the initial yield/cost ratio minus the depreciation rate (2.28), by $(1-u)/(1-u(k+m))$. This factor is larger than, equal to, or smaller than unity according as the share of the cost of the project deductible as an initial allowance and the share of the interest cost deductible is greater then, equal to, or smaller than one, i.e. $k+m \gtreqless 1$.

The cost of capital is obtained by setting $\Pi = 0$ and solving for $y(0)$. This gives

$$c(0) = A\left[i + \delta + \frac{u(1-k-m)}{1-u}i\right] = A\left[i\frac{1-u(k+m)}{1-u} + \delta\right] ,$$

for the initial age and in general for age s,

$$(2.46) \qquad c(s) = A\left[i\frac{1-u(k+m)}{1-u} + \delta\right]e^{-\delta s} , \qquad s \geq 0 .$$

The latter formula is simply the one we would obtain by "correcting" the market interest rate in the pre-tax cost of capital formula, (2.29), by the factor $(1-u(k+m))/(1-u)$ and keeping the depreciation rate unchanged.

Case b: Loan equal to net cost $A(1-uk)$

In this case, the initial debt is $(1-uk)A$ [cf. case b of example 1], and assuming that it is repaid in accordance with the declining balance depreciation schedule, the debt remaining at age s is $e^{-\delta s}(1-uk)A$. This gives an after tax cash-flow equal to

$$[y(0) - u\{y(0) - (1-k)\delta A - mi(1-uk)A\}]e^{-\delta s} ,$$

so that the life cycle profit becomes

$$(2.47) \qquad \Pi = \int_0^\infty e^{-is} [y(0) - u\{y(0) - (1-k)\delta A - mi(1-uk)A\}]e^{-\delta s} \, ds$$
$$- (1-uk)A .$$

After some rearranging, this can be written as

$$(2.48) \qquad \Pi = (1-u)\left[\frac{y(0)}{i+\delta} - A\left(1 + \frac{u(1-k-m+ukm)}{1-u}\frac{i}{i+\delta}\right)\right].$$

This gives the investment criterion

$$\frac{y(0)}{i+\delta} \gtrless A\left(1 + \frac{u(1-k-m+ukm)}{1-u}\frac{i}{i+\delta}\right)$$

$$(2.49)$$

$$\Longleftrightarrow \begin{bmatrix} \text{Invest} \\ \text{Indifferent} \\ \text{Do not invest} \end{bmatrix}.$$

The rate of return obtained from (2.48) is

$$(2.50) \qquad i^* = \left[\frac{y(0)}{A} - \delta\right]\frac{1-u}{(1-uk)(1-um)}.$$

To get the tax corrected rate of return, we only have to multiply the pre-tax rate, (2.28), by a simple function of the tax parameters, $(1-u)/\{(1-uk)(1-um)\}$.

Setting $\Pi = 0$ in (2.48) and solving for $y(0)$, we get the corresponding initial cost of capital,

$$c(0) = A\left[i\frac{(1-uk)(1-um)}{1-u} + \delta\right],$$

and in general for age s,

$$(2.51) \qquad c(s) = A\left[i\frac{(1-uk)(1-um)}{1-u} + \delta\right]e^{-\delta s}, \qquad s \geq 0.$$

Again, we only have to multiply the interest term in the pre-tax capital cost formulae, (2.29), by a simple function of the tax parameters.

The cost of capital formulae for the boundary values of k and m, with $s = 0$, are given in table 2.2.[6]

---

[6] The bottom line of this table corresponds to table 1 in King (1975, p. 277) and table 5.1 in Atkinson and Stiglitz (1980, p. 147).

Table 2.2: Project specific cost of capital. Exponential yield. $s = 0$.

Financing of the project	$k = 0$ $m = 0$	$k = 0$ $m = 1$	$k = 1$ $m = 0$	$k = 1$ $m = 1$
a: Loan equal to full cost	$A(\frac{i}{1-u} + \delta)$	$A(i + \delta)$	$A(i + \delta)$	$A(i\frac{1-2u}{1-u} + \delta)$
b: Loan equal to net cost	$A(\frac{i}{1-u} + \delta)$	$A(i + \delta)$	$A(i + \delta)$	$A(i(1 - u) + \delta)$

2.7   Concluding remarks

This chapter has shown how it is possible to derive from investment criteria related to the present value of an investment project a cost of capital
concept. The derivation of this concept did not involve a quantity representation of capital. In all cases considered there is a simple relationship
between the cost of capital, the present value the project, and its internal
rate of return. The standard investment criteria in business economics,
based on the two latter kind of concepts, can therefore be equivalently
expressed in terms of the cost of capital as defined in this chapter. This
also holds when the effect of an income tax, via the rules for deduction
of depreciation allowances and interest payments as well as the financing
of the investment are taken into account. The investment criteria can be
expressed in terms of a tax corrected cost of capital.

So far, simplifying assumptions on crucial points have been made. The
first is, as already declared, that no quantity representation of capital has
been involved. Second, in specifying the tax structure, the 'ordinary' depreciation allowances are assumed to agree with the form of the revenue
function. In practice, this assumption will not be satisfied. Third, *inflation* is disregarded. In specifying the yield flow $y(s)$, no distinction is made
between its quantity and price component. Fourth, *perfect foresight* is assumed, and no distinction is made between *ex ante* and *ex post* concepts.

These assumptions will be relaxed or modified in the following chapters.

CHAPTER 3

BASIC CAPITAL CONCEPTS: GROSS AND NET CAPITAL

3.1 Introduction

This and the next three chapters will be concerned with a producer with a *neo-classical* technology. As stated in chapter 1, the problems arising in defining and measuring the cost of capital services are closely related to those that arise when defining and measuring the real capital stock. In this chapter, we define the basic capital concepts corresponding to a neo-classical production technology. Some derived concepts will also be discussed.

We shall be concerned with two capital concepts, to be denoted as *gross capital* and *net capital*, in this study. These terms are used, with varying meaning, in the literature. Gross capital, as the term will be used here, is, loosely speaking, the variable which measures the *instantaneous* flow of services from the stock of capital existing at a certain point of time. It is the capital concept used in a static neo-classical production function. The user cost of capital is the cost per unit of capital services, or equivalently, a measure of the cost of using the productive capacity of the capital stock at a given point of time. Net capital represents, loosely speaking, the capital's wealth dimension and measures its *prospective* flow of services. It will not be directly involved in the description of the production technology, but it will be needed in the definition of the user cost of capital, since the capital's wealth dimension is relevant to the definition of corporate income, true depreciation, depreciation for tax purposes, and hence taxable income and the net income after taxes. Net capital also represents the market value if a market for used capital goods is assumed to exist.[1]

---

[1] This distinction between the volume of capital as a measure of productive capacity and the volume of capital as a measure of the real value of capital is made more or less explicit by several authors. See for instance, Haavelmo (1960, chapter XVIII), Johansen (1960, p. 28), and Hicks (1973, chapter XIII).

The chapter is organized as follows. The capacity dimension of the capital stock — represented by the gross capital stock and the related variable retirement — is discussed in section 3.2. Two useful transformations of the weighting function used in the definition of gross capital — the survival function — are discussed in section 3.3. In section 3.4, we consider some consequences of adopting a probabilistic interpretation of the retirement process for capital goods. The wealth dimension of the capital — represented by the net capital stock and the related variable depreciation, is discussed in section 3.5 — and finally, in section 3.6, we consider two examples with parametric survival functions, which illustrate the main results.

3.2 Capital as a capacity concept

3.2.1 The survival function

Let $J(t)$ denote the quantity of capital invested at time t, where time is considered as continuous. This investment results in an increase in the production capacity at time t. To characterize the retirement of the capital units over time and the loss of efficiency of the remaining units, we introduce the function $B(s)$. It indicates the proportion of an investment made s years (periods) ago which still exists as productive capital. Hence, it represents both the *loss of efficiency* of existing capital units and the *physical disappearance* of old capital goods.[2] This function, which we call the *(technical) survival function*, or the *survival profile*, has the following properties:

$$0 \le B(s) \le 1, \qquad B'(s) \le 0, \qquad s \ge 0,$$

(3.1)

$$B(0) = 1, \qquad \lim_{s \to \infty} B(s) = 0.$$

We assume that the stock of capital and the flow of services from this stock are measured in such a way that *one (efficiency) unit of capital produces one unit of capital services per unit of time*. This normalization

---

[2] We may, in principle, consider $B(s)$ as the product of two factors, one indicating the relative number of capital units surviving at age s (the survival curve), the other indicating the relative decline in efficiency of each remaining unit (the efficiency curve). Since we shall make no use of such a decomposition in the following, we do not specify it here. But for the purpose of measuring capital stocks from market data, the distinction between the survival curve and the efficiency curve is highly important.

implies that

$$(3.2) \qquad K(t,s) = B(s)J(t-s), \qquad s \geq 0,$$

can be given the joint interpretation as the number of capital (efficiency) units which are s years old at time t (i.e. the capacity of vintage $t-s$ which still remains at time t) and the instantaneous flow of services produced at time t by capital of age s.

3.2.2 Gross capital

Let us make the basic neo-classical assumption that capital units belonging to different vintages, i.e. invested at different points of time, are perfect substitutes in the production process. We can then aggregate (3.2) across vintages to get an expression for the total volume of capital at time t,

$$(3.3) \qquad K(t) - \int_0^\infty K(t,s)\,ds = \int_0^\infty B(s)J(t-s)\,ds.$$

This variable can be used to represent the input of capital services in a (static) neo-classical production function. It is a *technical* concept: $K(t)$ has the joint interpretation as the total number of capital efficiency units at time t and the instantaneous flow of services produced by these units at time t. We call it the *gross capital stock*.[3]

---

[3] An expression for the gross capital stock similar to (3.3) can be found in e.g. Jorgenson (1974, pp. 191–192) and Hulten and Wykoff (1980, p. 100). The terminology, however, is not consistent in the literature. Some authors (e.g. Steele (1980)) define gross capital as the cumulated volume of past gross investment over a period of length N, the capital's life time. In our notation, this corresponds to

$$K(t) = \int_0^N J(t-s)\,ds.$$

Others, like Young and Musgrave (1980), use gross capital as synonymous with the capital measure derived from the 'perpetual inventory method', in stating that "gross capital stock for a given year [is obtained] by cumulating past investment and deducting the cumulated value of the investment that has been discarded" (Young and Musgrave (1980, pp. 23–24)). This definition coincides with (3.3) if $B(s)$ represents the retirement of capital goods and takes no account of the loss of efficiency of the remaining goods. It is also used by Johansen and Sørsveen (1967, p. 182). Our definition, with $B(s)$ representing jointly the survival curve and the decline in efficiency, corresponds to the 'efficiency corrected capital stock' in the Johansen-Sørsveen terminology.

3.2.3 Retirement

We now turn to the related variable retirement. The flow of capital goods retired or scrapped at time t is, by definition, the part of the gross investment which does not contribute to an increase in the gross capital stock. Formally, it is the difference between the gross investment, $J(t)$, and the increase in the gross capital stock, $\dot{K}(t)$. From (3.3) we find, by using integration by parts, that the *volume of retirement* at time t can be expressed in terms of the previous investment flow as follows:

$$(3.4) \qquad D(t) = J(t) - \dot{K}(t) = \int_0^\infty b(s) J(t-s)\, ds\,,$$

where the "dot" indicates the derivative with respect to time and

$$(3.5) \qquad b(s) = -B'(s)\,, \qquad s \geq 0\,.$$

The function $b(s)$, to be called the *(relative) retirement function*, indicates the structure of the retirement process: $b(s)\, ds$ is the share of (the efficiency of) an *initial* investment of one unit which disappears from s to $s+ds$ years after installation. From (3.1) and (3.5) it follows that $b(s)$ is non-negative and satisfies

$$(3.6) \qquad \int_0^\infty b(s)\, ds = 1\,.$$

The volume of retirement at time t can be decomposed by vintages in the following way: Let

$$(3.7) \qquad D(t,s) = b(s) J(t-s)$$

denote the retirement of capital of age s at time t. Then the total retirement can be written as

$$(3.8) \qquad D(t) = \int_0^\infty D(t,s)\, ds\,.$$

From (3.2) and (3.7) we find that the *age specific retirement rates* can be expressed as

$$(3.9) \qquad \frac{D(t,s)}{K(t,s)} = b^*(s)\,, \qquad s \geq 0\,,$$

where

$$(3.10) \qquad b^*(s) = \frac{b(s)}{B(s)} = -\frac{d \ln B(s)}{ds}, \qquad s \geq 0.$$

The difference between $b(s)$ and $b^*(s)$ reflects their different normalization. The former is normalized against the *initial* investment at age 0, the latter against the capital *remaining* at age s. The overall retirement rate,

$$(3.11) \qquad \frac{D(t)}{K(t)} = \frac{\int_0^\infty b^*(s) K(t, s) \, ds}{\int_0^\infty K(t, s) \, ds},$$

is a weighted average of the age specific retirement rates with the age specific gross capital stock used as weights. It thus depends on the age distribution of the capital, and will therefore (in general) be a time varying parameter.[4]

3.3 Two auxiliary functions

Two transformations of the survival function $B(s)$ will be extensively used in the following. In this section, we define these transformations, comment on their interpretation, and present some of their properties.

3.3.1 The discounted per unit service flow function

The first transformation of $B(s)$ is

$$(3.12) \qquad \Phi_\rho(s) = \frac{\int_s^\infty e^{-\rho(z-s)} B(z) \, dz}{B(s)}, \qquad s \geq 0,$$

where ρ is a constant. The numerator of this expression can be interpreted as the value of the total flow of capital services produced by one *new* capital unit from the time it is s years old until it is scrapped, discounted to the time when it attains age s with a rate of discount equal to ρ. Since the denominator represents the share of the initial investment which attains age s, the function $\Phi_\rho(s)$ can be interpreted simply as *the discounted*

---

[4] Confer Nickell (1978, pp. 117–119).

future service flow per unit of capital which is s years of age. It thus is a *conditional* per unit service flow function. In particular,

$$\Phi_\rho(0) = \int_0^\infty e^{-\rho z} B(z)\, dz$$

is the present value of the total service flow from one *new* capital unit. Mathematically, $\Phi_\rho(0)$ is the *Laplace transform* of $B(s)$.[5] Obviously, since $B(s)$ is non-negative for all s,

(3.13) $$\frac{\partial \Phi_\rho(s)}{\partial \rho} < 0, \qquad s \geq 0.$$

3.3.2 The discounted per unit retirement flow function

The second transformation of $B(s)$ is

(3.14) $$\Psi_\rho(s) = \frac{\int_s^\infty e^{-\rho(z-s)} b(z)\, dz}{B(s)}, \qquad s \geq 0,$$

where ρ is a constant and $b(s)$ is defined as in eq. (3.5). The numerator of this expression represents the retirement flow of one new capital unit which occurs after age s, discounted to the time when the unit attains age s. Since $B(s)$ represents the share of one unit which attains age s, the function $\Psi_\rho(s)$ can be interpreted as *the present value of the remaining retirement flow per capital unit which is s years of age.* It is a *conditional* per unit retirement flow function. In particular,

$$\Psi_\rho(0) = \int_0^\infty e^{-\rho z} b(z)\, dz$$

is the present value of the total retirement flow related to one *new* capital unit. Mathematically, $\Psi_\rho(0)$ is the Laplace transform of $b(s)$. Obviously, since $B(s)$ is non-negative for all s,

(3.15) $$\frac{\partial \Psi_\rho(s)}{\partial \rho} < 0, \qquad s \geq 0,$$

---

[5] Cf. e.g. Bartle (1964, p. 372). Confer also the analogous expression (2.4) in chapter 2, $B(s)$ corresponding to $x(s)$.

i.e. the function is, like $\Phi_\rho(s)$, monotonically decreasing in ρ for any age s, with a value for a zero discounting rate equal to

$$\Psi_0(s) = \frac{\int_s^\infty b(z)\,dz}{B(s)} = 1, \qquad s \geq 0.$$

If $\rho \neq 0$, it is easy to show from the definitions (3.12) and (3.14), by using integration by parts, that

$$(3.16) \qquad\qquad \Psi_\rho(s) + \rho\Phi_\rho(s) = 1, \qquad s \geq 0.$$

Any relationship which can be expressed in terms of the per unit retirement flow function Ψ can thus be expressed in terms of the per unit service flow function Φ, except when the rate of discount ρ is zero.

3.4 A probabilistic interpretation

So far, we have interpreted the deterioration and retirement of capital as a deterministic process. Both the life time and the decline in efficiency with the age of the capital have been treated as completely known in advance. For an "average" capital unit in a large population of units, this may be a useful simplification. But for a specific capital good, e.g. a specific machine, a specific building or — to take a most familiar example — a specific light bulb, it may be questionable. The actual life time of a specific capital good is usually unknown when it is installed. It may be subject to random events which cannot be predicted by the investor in advance. *Ex ante* the life time of the good, or rather of any of its efficiency units, may be considered a stochastic variable S, with a given, time-invariant probability distribution. The functions $B(s)$, $b(s)$, $b^*(s)$, $\Phi_\rho(s)$, and $\Psi_\rho(s)$, which we defined and interpreted in sections 3.2 and 3.3 by treating the retirement and deterioration of capital as a deterministic process, will then get a different meaning. To put the results from the deterministic version of the model into perspective, we discuss briefly this probabilistic interpretation.

3.4.1 The survival probability function and the failure rate.

Instead of saying that $B(s)$ is the share of the capital good, measured in efficiency units, which remains at age s, we say that it represents the probability that a new capital good (or, more precisely, any of its efficiency units) will survive for at least s years, i.e.

$$(3.17) \qquad B(s) = P(S \geq s), \qquad s \geq 0.$$

Then $b(s) = -B'(s)$ [cf. (3.5)] will be the *probability density function* of the life time and $b^*(s) = b(s)/B(s)$ [cf. (3.10)] is the function called the *failure rate function* (or hazard rate function, force of mortality) in statistical theory of reliability [cf. Barlow and Proschan (1975, section 3.1) or Kalbfleisch and Prentice (1980, subsection 1.2.1)]. The relative retirement function in the deterministic interpretation of the model thus corresponds to the density function of the life time in the probabilistic interpretation, and the age specific retirement rate function, deterministically interpreted, corresponds to the failure rate function, probabilistically interpreted.

3.4.2 The functions $\Psi_\rho(s)$ and $\Phi_\rho(s)$ and the moment generating function of the remaining life time

Let T be the *remaining* life time of a capital unit which has already attained age s, i.e. $T = S - s$. The probability that the unit will still survive for at least τ years, given that it has attained age s can, by using (3.17), be expressed as

$$(3.18) \qquad P(T \geq \tau | S \geq s) = \frac{B(\tau + s)}{B(s)} = B(\tau | s), \qquad s \geq 0, \ \tau \geq 0,$$

where $B(\tau | s)$ is defined by the last equality. It then follows that the conditional density function of the remaining life time at age s can be expressed as

$$(3.19) \qquad b(\tau | s) = \frac{d}{d\tau} \left[1 - B(\tau | s)\right] = \frac{b(\tau + s)}{B(s)}, \qquad s \geq 0, \ \tau \geq 0.$$

Substituting $z = \tau + s$ in (3.14) and using (3.19), we find that $\Psi_\rho(s)$ can be written as

$$(3.20) \qquad \Psi_\rho(s) = \int_0^\infty e^{-\rho\tau} b(\tau | s) \, d\tau = E(e^{-\rho T} | s), \qquad s \geq 0.$$

This function has the interpretation as the *Laplace transform of the density function of the remaining life time T at age s.*[6] Its deterministic interpretation, given in subsection 3.3.2, is the present value of the remaining retirement flow per capital unit which is s years old.

Expanding $e^{-\rho T}$ in (3.20) by Taylor's formula, we obtain

$$(3.21) \qquad \Psi_\rho(s) = 1 + \sum_{i=1}^{\infty}(-1)^i \frac{\rho^i}{i!} E(T^i|s), \qquad s \geq 0.$$

This is the *moment generating function of the remaining life time T at age s.* Combining this expression with (3.16), we find that $\Phi_\rho(s)$ also is a moment generating function of the remaining life time, since it can be expressed in terms of the moments of the distribution of T as follows:

$$(3.22) \qquad \Phi_\rho(s) = E(T|s) + \sum_{i=2}^{\infty}(-1)^{i-1} \frac{\rho^{i-1}}{i!} E(T^i|s), \qquad s \geq 0.$$

3.4.3 The expected life time

If $\rho = 0$, all terms of second and higher order in (3.22) vanish, and we get simply

$$(3.23) \qquad \Phi_0(s) = \frac{1}{B(s)} \int_s^{\infty} B(z)\,dz = E(T|s), \qquad s \geq 0.$$

This expression shows that there is an interesting analogy between the deterministic and the probabilistic interpretation of the retirement process. The undiscounted future service flow from one capital unit of age s over its remaining service life according to the former interpretation corresponds to the expected remaining life time of a capital unit which has attained age s according to the latter interpretation.[7]

---

[6] Cf. e.g. Feller (1966, Chapter XIII.1).

[7] By successively differentiating $\Phi_\rho(s)$ with respect to ρ and setting $\rho = 0$, the second and higher order moments of the distribution of T can be obtained.

3.5   Capital as a wealth concept

3.5.1 *The capital value*

So far, we have only been concerned with the capital's capacity dimension, i.e. capital as a technical concept. We now turn to its value dimension, i.e. capital as an economic concept. Let $q(t)$ denote the investment price, i.e. the price of one new capital unit, at time t. The value of the investment in new equipment at time t is $V(t,0) = q(t)J(t) = q(t)K(t,0)$. The value of an old capital unit — i.e. the price at which it could be sold in a competitive market (if such a market exists) — does not, in general, reflect its historic cost, but rather the service flow that it is likely to produce during its remaining life time. This *prospective service flow* is the property of interest one to a potential user of the capital.

Let $V(t,s)$ denote the value of the capital stock which is s years old at time t. It can be written as

$$(3.24) \qquad\qquad V(t,s) = q(t,s)K(t,s),$$

where $q(t,s)$ is the price of one capital (efficiency) unit of age s at time t and $K(t,s)$ is the number of such units, defined in (3.2). In particular, $q(t,0) = q(t)$ and $K(t,0) = J(t)$. By aggregating (3.24) across vintages, we get the following expression for the total capital value at time t:

$$(3.25) \qquad V(t) = \int_0^\infty V(t,s)\,ds = \int_0^\infty q(t,s)K(t,s)\,ds.$$

How is the value concept $V(t)$ related to the quantity concept gross capital $K(t)$? The main problem in answering this question is to describe the mechanism determining the vintage prices $q(t,s)$. We will approach this problem in two steps.

3.5.2 *Net capital I: No discounting of future services*

A reasonable implication of the neo-classical assumption that capital units belonging to different vintages are perfect substitutes in the production process, is that all vintage prices $q(t,s)$ are increasing functions of the current investment price $q(t)$, for each given age s. Otherwise, possibilities for arbitrage between the vintages would exist. On the other hand, since in a perfect market the agents consider the prospective, rather than the instantaneous, flow of services from each capital unit, it is reasonable to assume that the vintage prices are decreasing (or at least non-increasing) functions of the age s, at each point of time t.

In the following, we make the specific assumption that the relative prices per unit of capital objects of different ages at any point of time *perfectly reflect the differences in their prospective service flows.* This is the way in which we describe precisely the assumption of a *perfect capital market* with no possibility for arbitrage between vintages. Let us first discuss the implications of this assumption when it is interpreted to hold in terms of *undiscounted* service flows, while considering the more general case based on discounting in subsection 3.5.4 below.

Recalling the (deterministic) interpretation of the function $\Phi_\rho(s)$ given in subsection 3.3.1, this perfect capital market assumption can be expressed as

$$(3.26) \qquad \frac{q(t,s)}{\Phi_0(s)} = \frac{q(t,0)}{\Phi_0(0)} = \frac{q(t)}{\Phi_0(0)} \qquad \text{for all } t \text{ and all } s \geq 0 \,.$$

It says that a "law of indifference" exists between the different capital vintages, in the sense that a firm which buys a capital (efficiency) unit of age s at the price $q(t,s)$ pays the same price per unit of *prospective* capital services as a firm buying a new capital unit at the price $q(t)$. And this equality holds for all ages at any point of time.[8]

Using (3.23), this assumption of a perfect capital market can alternatively be expressed as

$$\frac{q(t,s)}{E(T|s)} = \frac{q(t,0)}{E(T|0)} = \frac{q(t)}{E(S)} \qquad \text{for all } t \text{ and all } s \geq 0 \,,$$

where $E(S) = E(T|0)$ is the expected life time of a new capital good and $E(T|s)$ is the expected remaining life time of a capital good which is s years old. The probabilistic interpretation of the perfect market assumption (3.26) thus is that *the capital price per year of remaining expected life time shall be the same for all vintages at any point of time.*

---

[8] In cases where vintage prices exist as observed market variables — e.g. for autos, offices buildings, and dwellings — a "law of indifference" of this kind has been used for implicit estimation of the survival function. See for instance, Hall (1971), and Hulten and Wykoff (1981a).

Substituting (3.26) in (3.24), while using (3.2), it follows that the vintage specific capital value can be expressed in terms of $q(t)$ and $J(t-s)$ as

$$(3.27) \qquad V(t,s) = q(t)\frac{\Phi_0(s)}{\Phi_0(0)}K(t,s) = q(t)G_0(s)J(t-s)\,,$$

where

$$(3.28) \qquad G_0(s) = \frac{B(s)\Phi_0(s)}{\Phi_0(0)} = \frac{\int_s^\infty B(z)\,dz}{\int_0^\infty B(z)\,dz}\,, \qquad s \geq 0\,.$$

The function $G_0(s)$ represents the share of the total flow of capital services from one new capital unit over its life time which is produced after age s. The value of the capital of age s at time t is obtained by multiplying the replacement value of the capital originally installed, $q(t)J(t-s)$, by this function. The function $G_0(s)$ is a weighting function for gross investment with the same general properties as $B(s)$ [cf. (3.1)], namely,

$$(3.29) \qquad \begin{aligned} 0 \leq G_0(s) \leq 1\,, \qquad & \frac{dG_0(s)}{ds} \leq 0\,, \qquad s \geq 0\,, \\ G_0(0) = 1\,, \qquad & \lim_{s\to\infty} G_0(s) = 0\,. \end{aligned}$$

The total capital value $V(t)$ can now be decomposed into a price component equal to the current investment price $q(t)$ and a quantity component $K_N(t)$ as

$$(3.30) \qquad\qquad\qquad V(t) = q(t)K_N(t)\,,$$

where

$$(3.31) \qquad\qquad K_N(t) = \int_0^\infty G_0(s)J(t-s)\,ds\,.$$

We call $K_N(t)$ the *net capital stock* at time t. It is a quantity concept, but is based on another principle of aggregating the previous investment flow than the gross capital concept $K(t)$, defined in (3.3). The weight assigned to the quantity invested s years ago in $K_N(t)$, i.e. $G_0(s)$, is the share of the total service flow produced by one unit invested *after it is s years old*. The construction of $K(t)$ on the other hand, is based on the survival function $B(s)$, i.e. on the *instantaneous* service flow from each vintage.[9] The distinction between our concepts gross capital and net capital corresponds, broadly, to the distinction between the "backward-looking" and the "forward-looking" measures of capital in Hicks (1973, ch. XIII).[10]

We can decompose the total net capital by vintages by defining net capital of age s at time t as

$$(3.32) \qquad K_N(t,s) = \frac{V(t,s)}{q(t)} = \frac{\Phi_0(s)}{\Phi_0(0)} K(t,s) = G_0(s) J(t-s),$$

and writing (3.31) as an aggregate as

$$(3.33) \qquad K_N(t) = \int_0^\infty K_N(t,s)\, ds.$$

3.5.3 Depreciation I: No discounting of future services.

We now turn to the related variable depreciation. Depreciation has the same relationship to net capital as retirement has to gross capital. Unlike retirement, depreciation can be defined either in volume or in value terms. The *volume of depreciation* is the difference between the volume of the gross investment and the increase in the net capital stock. Using (3.31), it

---

[9] The term net capital is used to some extent, although with a slightly varying meaning, in the literature. Often, it is defined by general statements like "Net capital stock is obtained ... by deducting [from the cumulated past investment] the cumulated value of depreciation" (Young and Musgrave (1980, p. 24)), and "Gross capital stock, less the amount of accrued capital consumption gives net capital stock. Net capital stock is two dimensional in that it reflects not only the capital in current use, but also the unexpired future potential of those assets" (Steele (1980, p. 227)).

[10] Confer the following statements: "At a moment of time ... supply is given; so the marginal valuation determines the price. Such a valuation must be a forward-looking valuation, a capitalization of the marginal stream of net output which disposal over the marginal unit will permit. Market prices, of capital goods, may thus themselves be regarded as forward-looking valuations; so a measure of capital at market prices is itself a forward-looking measure. Thus what we deduce, from rethinking the *value* measure of capital ... is that it is, or should be, substantially equivalent to a capitalization of future net outputs; but such a capitalization is not in principle dependent upon the existence of a market for capital goods ..." (Hicks (1973, pp. 157–158)) and "For a backward-looking measure ... calls for no comparison between physical characteristics of the capital goods which appear in new and old processes respectively. The backward measure is derived by accumulating past net inputs" (Hicks (1973, p. 159)). Confer also Haavelmo (1960, section 31.I).

can be written as

$$(3.34) \qquad D_N(t) = J(t) - \dot{K}_N(t) = \int_0^\infty g_0(s) J(t-s)\, ds\,,$$

where[11]

$$(3.35) \qquad\qquad g_0(s) = -\frac{dG_0(s)}{ds}\,, \qquad s \geq 0\,.$$

The conceptual difference between retirement and depreciation in volume terms reflects the difference between gross and net capital.

The function $g_0(s)$, which, by virtue of (3.29), is non-negative and satisfies

$$(3.36) \qquad\qquad \int_0^\infty g_0(s)\, ds = 1\,,$$

represents the structure of the depreciation (in volume terms), in a similar way as $b(s)$ represents the retirement process. One might say that $g_0(s)$ is the economic counterpart to the technical function $b(s)$, since the former, in contrast to the latter, rests on a specific assumption about the behaviour of the capital market, formalized in (3.26). In the sequel, $g_0(s)$ will be referred to as the *(relative) depreciation function*. From (3.28) and (3.35), we find the following simple relationship between the depreciation function and the survival function

$$(3.37) \qquad\qquad g_0(s) = \frac{B(s)}{\int_0^\infty B(z)dz} = \frac{B(s)}{\Phi_0(0)}\,, \qquad s \geq 0\,.$$

Let us define

$$(3.38) \qquad\qquad D_N(t,s) = g_0(s) J(t-s)\,,$$

which represents the depreciation (in volume terms) of capital of age s at time t. From (3.2), (3.37), and (3.38) it follows that

$$(3.39) \qquad \frac{D_N(t,s)}{K(t,s)} = \frac{g_0(s)}{B(s)} = \frac{1}{\Phi_0(0)} \qquad \text{for all } t \text{ and all } s \geq 0\,.$$

This depreciation rate, defined as the ratio between the volume of *depreciation* and the *gross* capital stock, will thus be the same for all vintages at

---

[11] Confer the equivalent derivation of the expression for retirement, (3.4), from the expression for gross capital, (3.3).

any point of time and equal to the inverse of the *total* service flow from one new capital unit. The perfect market condition (3.26) implies equality between these age specific depreciation rates. Hence, the overall depreciation rate, similarly defined, will be equal to the common value of the age specific rates, i.e.

$$(3.40) \qquad \frac{D_N(t)}{K(t)} = \frac{\int_0^\infty D_N(t, s)\, ds}{\int_0^\infty K(t, s)\, ds} = \frac{1}{\Phi_0(0)}.$$

Note that this relationship rests on the particular definition of depreciation rate adopted: the ratio between the *economic* concept of depreciation and the *technical* concept of *gross* capital. A similar invariance will not hold if depreciation is related to *net* capital, which may be a more common definition of a depreciation rate. From (3.32) and (3.39) we find

$$(3.41) \qquad \frac{D_N(t, s)}{K_N(t, s)} = \frac{1}{\Phi_0(s)}, \qquad s \geq 0,$$

i.e. with this alternative definition, the depreciation rate for capital which is s years old is the inverse of the *remaining* service flow from one capital unit which has attained this age. And this function will, in general, be age dependent. The overall depreciation rate then becomes

$$(3.42) \qquad \frac{D_N(t)}{K_N(t)} = \frac{\int_0^\infty \Phi_0(s)^{-1} K_N(t, s)\, ds}{\int_0^\infty K_N(t, s)\, ds},$$

which is (in general) a time varying parameter.

We next turn to depreciation in value terms. The *(net) value of depreciation* at time t, $E(t)$ is, by definition, the difference between the value of the gross investment at time t and the increase in the capital value, i.e.

$$(3.43) \qquad E(t) = q(t)J(t) - \dot{V}(t) = q(t)J(t) - q(t)\dot{K}_N(t) - \dot{q}(t)K_N(t).$$

Using (3.34), this can be written as

$$(3.44) \qquad E(t) = q(t)D_N(t) - \dot{q}(t)K_N(t),$$

i.e. the net value of depreciation can be interpreted as the difference between the gross value of depreciation, $q(t)D_N(t)$, and the appreciation of the capital stock, $\dot{q}(t)K_N(t)$. Inserting for $K_N(t)$ and $D_N(t)$ from (3.31) and (3.34), we obtain

$$(3.45) \qquad E(t) = \int_0^\infty [q(t)g_0(s) - \dot{q}(t)G_0(s)]J(t-s)\,ds\,.$$

Again, a decomposition by vintages is informative. Let

$$(3.46) \qquad E(t,s) = [q(t)g_0(s) - \dot{q}(t)G_0(s)]J(t-s)$$

be the value of depreciation of capital of age s at time t. Combining this expression with (3.27), (3.28), and (3.37), we find

$$(3.47) \qquad E(t,s) = \left[\frac{1}{\Phi_0(s)} - \frac{\dot{q}(t)}{q(t)}\right]V(t,s)\,, \qquad s \geq 0\,.$$

This shows that the age specific depreciation rate in value terms at age s, $E(t,s)/V(t,s)$, is obtained by simply subtracting the current rate of increase of the investment price from the corresponding depreciation rate in volume terms, given by (3.41). A similar decomposition holds for the aggregate depreciation rate.

3.5.4 Net capital II: Discounting of future services

So far, the law of indifference between the capital vintage prices $q(t,s)$ has been assumed to hold in terms of undiscounted future service flows, cf. (3.26). How should the results be modified when this law of indifference is interpreted to hold in terms of discounted service flows? For a firm operating in a competitive capital market, the latter seems to be a more realistic assumption, since the owners of the capital, under neo-classical assumptions, always have the opportunity to sell a capital good — and its future service flow — and purchase financial assets with a positive rate of return. As a consequence, service flows produced at different future points of time do not have the same "value" to the firm today.

Replace, then, (3.26) by

$$(3.48) \qquad \frac{q(t,s)}{\Phi_\rho(s)} = \frac{q(t,0)}{\Phi_\rho(0)} = \frac{q(t)}{\Phi_\rho(0)}\,, \qquad \text{for all } t \text{ and all } s \geq 0\,,$$

where $\Phi_\rho(s)$ is defined as in (3.12) and ρ is interpreted as the *real* rate of return on financial assets.[12] Substituting this expression in (3.24), we find that the vintage specific expressions for the capital value, (3.27), and for the net capital stock, (3.32), change into

$$(3.49) \qquad V(t,s) = q(t)\frac{\Phi_\rho(s)}{\Phi_\rho(0)}K(t,s) = q(t)G_\rho(s)J(t-s)$$

and

$$(3.50) \qquad K_N(t,s) = \frac{V(t,s)}{q(t)} = \frac{\Phi_\rho(s)}{\Phi_\rho(0)}K(t,s) = G_\rho(s)J(t-s),$$

where the weighting function is now given by

$$(3.51) \qquad G_\rho(s) - \frac{B(s)\Phi_\rho(s)}{\Phi_\rho(0)} - \frac{\int_s^\infty e^{-\rho(z-s)}B(z)\,dz}{\int_0^\infty e^{-\rho z}B(z)\,dz}, \qquad s \geq 0.$$

Obviously, $G_\rho(s)$ has the same general properties as $G_0(s)$, cf. (3.29). The total net capital stock is obtained by aggregation over vintages. This gives

$$(3.52) \qquad K_N(t) = \int_0^\infty K_N(t,s)\,ds = \int_0^\infty G_\rho(s)J(t-s)\,ds.$$

Net capital, thus defined, will, in contrast to gross capital, depend on the rate of discount. In general, the net capital stock will, *ceteris paribus*, increase with increasing rate of discount. The intuitive explanation of this is the following. The calculation of the net capital stock, via the multiplication by $\Phi_\rho(s)/\Phi_\rho(0)$, is a way of "correcting" the gross capital stock for the presence of "old" capital goods when focusing on their market value [cf. (3.50)]. When the rate of discount increases, the weight given to the remaining service flows from both new and old capital units decreases, but the decrease is relatively stronger for the new units, since they have the relatively longer service life. This means that $\Phi_\rho(s)/\Phi_\rho(0)$ will be an increasing function of ρ and will approach 1 as ρ goes to infinity, regardless of the form of the survival function $B(s)$. With a sufficiently high rate of discount, the prospective nature of the net capital stock becomes insignificant since a negligible weight will then be given to the future service flow. As a consequence, $K_N(t)$ approaches $K(t)$ when ρ goes to infinity.

---

[12] Since capital is a real asset and its flow of services is a quantity variable, the appropriate rate of discount will be a real rate of return. For a further discussion of the discounting rate, see section 4.2.

3.5.5 Depreciation II: Discounting of future services

As a consequence of the change in the definition of net capital, the expression for the *volume of depreciation*, (3.34), changes into

$$(3.53) \qquad D_N(t) = J(t) - \dot{K}_N(t) = \int_0^\infty g_\rho(s) J(t-s) \, ds \,,$$

where $g_\rho(s)$, the relative depreciation function, is now defined as

$$(3.54) \qquad\qquad g_\rho(s) = -\frac{dG_\rho(s)}{ds} \,.$$

From (3.12), (3.16), and (3.51) we obtain

$$(3.55) \qquad\qquad g_\rho(s) = \frac{B(s)\Psi_\rho(s)}{\Phi_\rho(0)} \,, \qquad s \geq 0 \,.$$

This expression generalizes (3.37).

Decomposing $D_N(t)$ by vintages in the same way as in subsection 3.5.3, by defining

$$(3.56) \qquad\qquad D_N(t,s) = g_\rho(s) J(t-s) \,,$$

it follows, by using (3.2) and (3.55), that the vintage specific *depreciation rates* normalized against the *gross* capital stock, become

$$(3.57) \qquad\qquad \frac{D_N(t,s)}{K(t,s)} = \frac{\Psi_\rho(s)}{\Phi_\rho(0)} \,, \qquad s \geq 0 \,.$$

This expression generalizes (3.39). It says that the depreciation rate at age s is equal to the ratio between the discounted remaining retirement flow per capital unit which has attained this age, and the total discounted service flow from one *new* capital unit. Since $\Psi_\rho(s)$ is, in general, a function of s, the same will be true for this depreciation rate, and the age invariance noted in subsection 3.5.3 for the no-discounting case no longer holds.

The corresponding generalization of the alternative definition of the depreciation rate, (3.41), obtained from (3.16), (3.50), and (3.57), is

$$(3.58) \qquad\qquad \frac{D_N(t,s)}{K_N(t,s)} = \frac{\Psi_\rho(s)}{\Phi_\rho(s)} = \frac{1}{\Phi_\rho(s)} - \rho \,, \qquad s \geq 0 \,.$$

The share of the net capital stock which depreciates at age s is thus the inverse of the *remaining* discounted service flow per capital unit of age s less the rate of discount. Aggregation across vintages yields

$$(3.59) \qquad \frac{D_N(t)}{K_N(t)} = \frac{\int_0^\infty \Phi_\rho(s)^{-1} K_N(t,s)\,ds}{\int_0^\infty K_N(t,s)\,ds} - \rho.$$

Again, the aggregate depreciation rate depends (in general) on the age composition of the net capital stock and it also depends on the rate of discount.

Finally, we reconsider depreciation in value terms. From (3.49), (3.51), (3.52), (3.53), and (3.55) it follows that the *value of depreciation* at time t is equal to

$$(3.60) \qquad E(t) = q(t)D_N(t) - \dot{q}(t)K_N(t) = \int_0^\infty E(t,s)\,ds,$$

where

$$(3.61) \qquad \begin{aligned} E(t,s) &= [q(t)g_\rho(s) - \dot{q}(t)G_\rho(s)]\,J(t-s) \\ &= \left[\frac{\Psi_\rho(s)}{\Phi_\rho(s)} - \frac{\dot{q}(t)}{q(t)}\right]V(t,s) \\ &= \left[\frac{1}{\Phi_\rho(s)} - \rho - \frac{\dot{q}(t)}{q(t)}\right]V(t,s). \end{aligned}$$

As in the no-discounting case, the age specific depreciation rates in value terms, $E(t,s)/V(t,s)$, can be obtained by subtracting the current rate of increase in the investment price from the corresponding depreciation rates in volume terms, given by (3.58). All information required to compute the complete set of age specific depreciation rates in volume and value terms is contained in the inverse of the per unit discounted service flow function, $1/\Phi_\rho(s)$ and the parameters ρ and $\dot{q}/q$.

3.5.6 A remark on the relationship between gross and net capital

The terms net and gross capital may suggest that the former is *always* less than (or at most equal to) the latter. Will this inequality be satisfied for all ages regardless of the form of the survival function? Unfortunately, the answer is no in general. The inequality will, however, hold for all the *parametric* survival functions with which we shall be concerned in this study. [Cf. sections 11.2–11.5.] This can be shown as follows.

It follows from (3.50) that $K_N(t, s) \leq K(t, s)$ for all s if $\Phi_\rho(s) \leq \Phi_\rho(0)$ for all s. This implies that net capital will not exceed gross capital if

$$\int_s^\infty f(z)\, dz \leq f(s) \int_0^\infty f(z)\, dz$$

holds for all $s > 0$, where

$$f(z) = e^{-\rho z} B(z) \,.$$

This inequality will usually hold, but will not be satisfied if $f(z)$ is declining sufficiently fast at the beginning and then declines at a very slow pace.[13]

3.6   Two examples

Two simple examples with parametric survival functions serve to illustrate the general results obtained above. They will also be used as reference examples in the subsequent chapters. [Confer also section 2.5.]

3.6.1 *Exponentially declining survival function*

By far the most familiar survival function in the literature is the exponential function in which the efficiency of each vintage of capital goods declines at a constant rate δ, i.e.

$$(3.62) \qquad\qquad B(s) = e^{-\delta s}, \qquad s \geq 0 \,,$$

which is often denoted as exponential decay. The corresponding relative retirement function, (3.5), is

$$(3.63) \qquad\qquad b(s) = \delta e^{-\delta s}, \qquad s \geq 0 \,,$$

---

[13] An example of a piecewise linear, convex function which does not satisfy the inequality for all positive s is: $f(z) = 1 - az$ for $0 \leq z \leq n$, $f(z) = (N - z)(1 - an)/(N - n)$ for $n \leq z \leq N$, where $0 < n < N$, $1/N < a < 1/n$, provided n is sufficiently small and a is sufficiently large. Such a situation is, however, unlikely to occur in practice.

i.e. it is also declining at the rate δ. Hence, the age specific retirement rate, (3.10), (or the failure rate function, if interpreted probabilistically; cf. subsection 3.4.1) is constant and equal to δ, i.e.

$$(3.64) \qquad b^*(s) = \delta, \qquad s \geq 0.$$

This is a particular property of the exponentially declining survival function.

The discounted per unit service flow function, (3.12), and the discounted per unit retirement flow function, (3.14), become, respectively,

$$(3.65) \qquad \Phi_\rho(s) = \frac{1}{\rho + \delta}, \qquad s \geq 0,$$

$$(3.66) \qquad \Psi_\rho(s) = \frac{\delta}{\rho + \delta}, \qquad s \geq 0.$$

Thus, both these functions are age invariant in the exponential case. From (3.51) and (3.55) it then follows that

$$(3.67) \qquad G_\rho(s) = B(s), \qquad s \geq 0,$$

$$(3.68) \qquad g_\rho(s) = b(s), \qquad s \geq 0.$$

This equality between the weighting functions for net and gross capital and for depreciation and retirement implies that *net capital is numerically equal to gross capital, and depreciation is numerically equal to retirement, regardless of the time path of the investment and regardless of the rate ρ at which the future service flow is discounted*. This is another remarkable and particular property of the exponentially declining survival function.

Inserting (3.64)–(3.66) in (3.9), (3.57), (3.58), and (3.61), we obtain

$$(3.69) \qquad \frac{D(t,s)}{K(t,s)} = \frac{D_N(t,s)}{K(t,s)} = \frac{D_N(t,s)}{K_N(t,s)} = \delta,$$

$$(3.70) \qquad \frac{E(t,s)}{V(t,s)} = \delta - \frac{\dot{q}(t)}{q(t)},$$

for all t, s, and ρ, regardless of the time path of the investment.

To summarize, then, we can say that the main implications of specifying an exponentially declining survival function is that the following derived functions all become age invariant:

– the per unit discounted service flow function, $\Phi_\rho(s)$,

- the per unit discounted retirement flow function, $\Psi_\rho(s)$,
- the age specific retirement rate, $b^*(s)$,
- the age specific depreciation rate in volume terms, whether defined as D_N/K or as D_N/K_N, and finally
- the age specific depreciation rate in value terms, E/V.

3.6.2 Simultaneous retirement

Consider then the case in which all capital units retain their full efficiency during N periods and then disappear completely (often called "one horse shay" or "sudden death"). This implies

$$(3.71) \qquad\qquad B(s) = \begin{cases} 1 & \text{for } 0 \le s \le N, \\ 0 & \text{for } s > N, \end{cases}$$

$$(3.72) \qquad\qquad b(s) = \begin{cases} 0 & \text{for } s \ne N \\ \text{undefined} & \text{for } s = N. \end{cases}$$

By using (3.12) and (3.16), this implies that the discounted per unit service flow function and the discounted per unit retirement flow function are, respectively,

$$(3.73) \quad \Phi_\rho(s) = H_\rho(N - s) = \frac{1}{\rho}\left[1 - e^{-\rho(N-s)}\right], \quad 0 \le s \le N,$$

$$(3.74) \quad \Psi_\rho(s) = 1 - \rho H_\rho(N - s) = e^{-\rho(N-s)}, \qquad 0 \le s \le N,$$

where $H_a(M) = (1 - e^{-aM})/a$ is the present value of a constant annuity of 1 discounted continuously over M years at the rate a.

The weighting functions for net capital and depreciation now become

$$(3.75) \qquad G_\rho(s) = \frac{H_\rho(N - s)}{H_\rho(N)}$$

$$= \frac{1 - e^{-\rho(N-s)}}{1 - e^{-\rho N}} \xrightarrow[\rho \to 0]{} 1 - \frac{s}{N}, \qquad 0 \le s \le N,$$

$$(3.76) \qquad g_\rho(s) = \frac{\rho e^{-\rho(N-s)}}{1 - e^{-\rho N}} \xrightarrow[\rho \to 0]{} \frac{1}{N}, \qquad\qquad 0 \le s \le N.$$

In this case, the weighting function for net capital is linearly declining at the rate $1/N$ under no discounting, and equal to the ratio between the annuity factors for $N - s$ years and N years if a discounting is performed. Hence, under a simultaneous retirement survival profile, it is of crucial importance to distinguish between the gross and the net capital stock and between retirement and depreciation.

To get a closer understanding of the difference, it is informative to consider the implied retirement and depreciation rates. First, since (3.71) implies that $D(t, s) = 0$ for $s < N$, $D(t, N) = J(t - N)$, and that $K(t, s) = J(t - s)$ for $0 \leq s < N$, the age specific retirement rates are given by

$$(3.77) \qquad \frac{D(t, s)}{K(t, s)} = \begin{cases} 0 & \text{for } 0 \leq s < N, \\ \text{undefined} & \text{for } s = N. \end{cases}$$

Second, inserting (3.73) and (3.74) in (3.57), (3.58), and (3.61), we get

$$(3.78) \qquad \frac{D_N(t, s)}{K(t, s)} = \frac{\rho e^{-\rho(N-s)}}{1 - e^{-\rho N}} \xrightarrow[\rho \to 0]{} \frac{1}{N}, \qquad 0 \leq s < N,$$

$$(3.79) \qquad \frac{D_N(t, s)}{K_N(t, s)} = \frac{1}{H_\rho(N - s)} - \rho \xrightarrow[\rho \to 0]{} \frac{1}{N - s}, \qquad 0 \leq s < N,$$

$$(3.80) \qquad \frac{E(t, s)}{V(t, s)} = \frac{1}{H_\rho(N - s)} - \rho - \frac{\dot{q}(t)}{q(t)} \xrightarrow[\rho \to 0]{} \frac{1}{N - s} - \frac{\dot{q}(t)}{q(t)},$$
$$0 \leq s < N.$$

Obviously, the retirement rates and the two measures of the depreciation rates in volume terms are widely different for all positive (and finite) values of N and s in this case. And they are all age dependent, with one exception: $D_N(t, s)/K(t, s) = 1/N$ for all $s (\leq N)$ when $\rho = 0$, which also follows directly from (3.39).

All these conclusions are strongly different from those obtained when the survival function is exponentially declining.

CHAPTER 4

THE USER COST OF CAPITAL UNDER NEO-CLASSICAL TECHNOLOGY. PART 1. NO TAXES

4.1 Introduction

In chapter 3, we established the quantity concepts gross and net capital and decomposed the capital value into a capital price, equal to the current investment price, and a quantity of capital equal to the net capital stock. On this basis, we now define the user cost of capital. The gross capital stock corresponding to the neo-classical description of the production technology, which represents the instantaneous flow of services from this stock, and the user cost of capital may be regarded as *dual* variables. This price-quantity duality for the durable goods model has been developed by Arrow (1964), Hall (1968), and Jorgenson (1974). A basic implication of the duality is that the price and the quantity variables should be constructed from the same representation of the retirement process, i.e. from the same survival function. [Confer Jorgenson (1974, p. 205).]

The concept of the user cost of capital, unlike the gross capital stock, is not invariant to changes in the corporate income tax system. This system is basically a system for taxation of the *capital* of the firm; the tax code gives a prescription of how the expenditures connected with the acquisition and use of capital should be treated in the income tax base. Although the corporate tax system is a main concern of this study, we shall, for expository convenience, build up our argument gradually, and in this chapter, we disregard taxes altogether. The definition and discussion of the user cost in the presence of a corporate income tax will be postponed until chapter 6, after we have considered, in chapter 5, a wide selection of tax systems and tax codes.

The definition of the user cost of capital in a situation with no taxes may be approached in two alternative ways. The first is a *service price interpretation* derived directly from the law of indifference between vintage prices which underlies the construction of the net capital stock. This interpretation is discussed in section 4.2. The second is a *shadow price inter-*

pretation derived from the optimizing conditions for capital accumulation under a neo-classical technology. It is discussed in section 4.3. Two examples based on parametric survival functions are considered in section 4.4. In the concluding section, section 4.5, a decomposition of the user value of the capital services is discussed. This decomposition, which also is a way of characterizing the price-quantity duality, will be a starting point for much of the subsequent analysis.

4.2 A service price interpretation

In subsection 3.5.4, we postulated — in the spirit of the perfect market assumption of the neo-classical model — a "law of indifference" to hold between the different capital vintages. This "law" expressed that a firm which invests in an old capital good, regardless of its age, should pay the same price per unit of (discounted) capital services today and in the future as a firm buying a new good at the current investment price. This assumption of a perfect capital market is expressed mathematically in (3.26) for the case with no discounting of future capital services and in (3.48) when a discounting of the services is performed. It seems sensible to interpret the common value of the purchase price per unit of capital services under this perfect market condition as the firm's price of capital services. Formally, the service price at time t is then given by

$$(4.1) \qquad c(t) = \frac{q(t)}{\Phi_\rho(0)} = \frac{q(t)}{\int_0^\infty e^{-\rho s} B(s)\, ds},$$

where ρ is the rate at which future capital services are discounted. The rate of discount depends, in general, on the current time, which we might indicate, more precisely, as $\rho = \rho(t)$. This is the service price interpretation of the user cost of capital in the absence of taxes.

To obtain an econometrically relevant representation of (4.1) it remains, however, to interpret the discounting rate ρ in terms of market variables. Since $B(s)$ can be given a quantity interpretation — as the instantaneous flow of capital services from one capital unit s years after installation [cf. subsection 3.2.1] — ρ is a *real* interest rate. Then it can be written as $\rho = r - \gamma$, where $r = r(t)$ is a nominal rate of return on financial assets at time t and $\gamma = \gamma(t)$ is the inflation rate as expected at this time. When rates of price increase differ between commodities an important question is: to which price does γ refer? Since we are assuming a neo-classical technology with malleable capital and a perfect capital market, we interpret γ as the rate of increase of the *investment price*. The reason for this is the following: In (4.1), as in (3.48), ρ is the (net) rate of return forgone by a firm which owns the capital and uses its services rather than purchasing interest-bearing financial assets. With perfect substitutability between different capital vintages, the firm always has the opportunity of transforming real capital, regardless of age, costlessly into financial assets, and the real cost of keeping the real asset is the real interest rate measured against the current investment price.

Eq. (4.1) expresses a relationship between the current values of the service price and the investment price at time t. It can alternatively be formulated as a relationship between the *current* investment price and the time path of the *expected* service price in the following way. For any given value of ρ, i.e. for any value of r and γ at time t, eq. (4.1) will imply $c(t)$ and $q(t)$, as well as their expected values, to move proportionally. Hence, the value of c which at time t is expected to prevail at time $t + s$ will be equal to

$$(4.2) \qquad\qquad c(t + s, t) = c(t)e^{\gamma s}, \qquad\qquad s \geq 0.$$

Combining (4.1) and (4.2), we obtain

$$(4.3) \qquad\qquad q(t) = \int_0^\infty e^{-(\rho+\gamma)s} c(t + s, t) B(s)\, ds.$$

This equation says that the current purchase cost of an investment good at time t shall be equal to the present value of its (expected) future service price, when allowance is made for retirement and decline in efficiency with age. The relationship is stated in the latter form by e.g. Jorgenson and Sullivan (1981, p. 175) for the case with an exponentially declining survival function, $B(s) = e^{-\delta s}$. Confer also Jorgenson (1974, p. 205). The condition (4.3) is called the intertemporal arbitrage relation by Takayama (1985, p. 694), also with reference to the exponential declining survival function.

Eqs. (4.1) and (4.3) are equivalent ways of expressing the relationship between the current investment price and the (current and expected) user cost only when the interest and inflation rates are (expected to be) constant, and then these two prices will have the same rate of increase. Below, we make four supplementary remarks on these relationships. First, (4.1) is far easier to implement econometrically than (4.3), since it expresses the current service price $c(t)$ by means of a closed form relationship which holds regardless of the form of the survival function $B(s)$.

Second, although we have made the auxiliary assumption (4.2) about the expected time path of the service price, eqs. (4.1) and (4.3) admit a *myopic interpretation* of the service price. This is discussed in more detail in appendix A. We show that the current service price implied by (4.3) can be written as [cf. eqs. (A.4) and (A.5) in appendix A]

$$(4.4) \qquad c(t) = q(t)[r(t) + b(0)] - \triangle(t, 0),$$

where $b(0) = -B'(0)$ and $\triangle(t, 0)$ is the derivative of the expected vintage price of capital vintage t with respect to the age of the capital at age 0. Hence, the service price of capital at time t is known once the firm knows the price of a new capital unit, the current interest rate, the age specific retirement rate at age 0, and the price at which a new capital unit can be expected to be sold in a perfect market after an infinitesimal time ds has elapsed. However, this myopic formula, although theoretically important, is of little practical interest, for instance in econometric model building, when markets for used capital goods do not exist or their prices are unobservable. The only role of the assumption of a constant rate of increase of the investment price is to establish a link between the observed market price of new capital goods and the unobserved prices of used goods. Making this assumption, we can express the derivative of the vintage price as [cf. eq. (A.13) in appendix A]

$$
\begin{aligned}
\triangle(t, 0) &= \dot{q}(t) + q(t)\left[\rho(t) + b(0) - \frac{1}{\Phi_\rho(0)}\right] \\
&= q(t)\left[\gamma(t) + \rho(t) + b(0) - \frac{1}{\Phi_\rho(0)}\right].
\end{aligned}
$$

(4.5)

Since $r(t) = \gamma(t) + \rho(t)$, we see that (4.4) and (4.5) imply (4.1) regardless of the form of the survival function $B(s)$.

Third, it is not, *in general*, possible to express $c(t)$ in terms of $q(t)$ and its *instantaneous* rate of increase from the equation

investment price = present value of expected future service costs.

For such a relationship to exist, restrictions will have to be imposed on either the form of the discounting factor, the expected time path of the investment price, or the survival function.[1]

Fourth, eq. (4.1) is *formally* similar to the expressions for the user cost of capital derived and interpreted in chapter 2, alternatively as the implicit cost of an investment project converted to a repayment flow, or as the yield from a marginal project [cf. eqs. (2.11)–(2.13)]: $c(0)$ in chapter 2 corresponding to $c(t)$ above, $\imath$ corresponding to ρ, $w(\imath)$ corresponding to $\Phi_\rho(0)$, A corresponding to $q(t)$, and $B(s)$ corresponding to $x(s)$. The underlying assumptions, however, are substantially different, since in chapter 2 only one vintage (project) is involved and no capital stock concept and no assumption of a perfect capital market is needed.

---

[1] An implicit service price definition of the user cost in the general case is the following:

$$(*) \quad q(t) = \int_0^\infty e^{-r(t+s,t)s} c(t+s,t) B(s)\, ds = \int_t^\infty e^{-r(\theta,t)(\theta-t)} c(\theta,t) B(\theta-t)\, d\theta\,,$$

where $r(t+s,t)$ is the (average) interest rate for the time interval $t, t+s$ as expected at time t and where we in the latter integral have set $\theta = t+s$. Consider two cases.

1. If the *investment price and the discounting factor are both simple exponentials* in time, i.e.

$$q(t+s) = q(t)e^{\gamma s}\,,$$

$$r(t+s,t) = r(t) = \rho(t) + \gamma(t)\,,$$

for all s, then $(*)$ has the same form as (4.3), which can be rearranged to give a closed form expression for $c(t)$, (4.1). This property holds regardless of the form of $B(s)$.

2. If the *survival function is exponential*, i.e.

$$B(s) = e^{-\delta s}\,,$$

with no restrictions imposed on $q(t)$ and $r(t+s,t)$, we can from $(*)$, by differentiation, derive (confer e.g. Boadway (1980, pp. 252–253) and Jorgenson and Sullivan (1981, pp. 175–176))

$$\dot{q}(t) = -c(t) + r(t)q(t) + \delta q(t)\,,$$

i.e.

$$c(t) = q(t)[r(t) - \dot{q}(t)/q(t) + \delta]\,,$$

where $r(t) = r(t,t)$ is the interest rate at time t. In this case, however, c and q will not move proportionally over time unless $\dot{q}(t)/q(t) = \gamma$ and $\dot{r}(t) = 0$, and then the user cost satisfies the textbook formula $c(t) = q(t)(r - \gamma + \delta)$.

Our conclusion, then, is that sufficient conditions for a closed form expression for $c(t)$ to exist are either (1) that the expected investment price and the discounting factor are exponentials in time, or (2) that the survival function is exponential.

4.3   A shadow price interpretation based on optimizing conditions

The shadow price interpretation of the user cost of capital will depart more strongly than the service price interpretation from the interpretation in terms of an investment project that we gave in chapter 2. It will be derived from the first order conditions for maximization of the present value of a firm's cash-flow. Let

$$(4.6) \qquad\qquad X(t) = F\big(K(t)\big)$$

be the profit of the firm for a given capital stock $K(t)$ before deduction of the capital cost, but after it has performed a (partial) maximization with respect to all other inputs. The maximization is subject to a neo-classical production function connecting inputs and output(s). The function (4.6) is thus a *restricted profit function*, and the marginal profit of capital is assumed to be positive and decreasing, i.e. $F' > 0$ and $F'' < 0$.

This formulation could be generalized along two lines. First, we could include time t as a separate argument in F, representing exogenous factors affecting the profit, e.g. changes in the output price(s) or in the noncapital input prices or (Hicks neutral) *technical change*, i.e. shifts in the underlying production function. The following conclusions will not be affected by this extension of the model, so for simplicity, we retain the formulation (4.6).

Second, we could redefine F so as to allow for *uncertainty*. To indicate the nature of this extension, consider the following example. Assume that the firm faces uncertainty with respect to the output and/or the input prices, which can be represented by a probability distribution. The firm's strategy is to maximize the expected value of the utility of its profit, conditional on the capital stock $K(t)$. Then (4.6) could be reinterpreted as representing the expected optimal profit, conditional on the capital stock. The form of F would then reflect not only the production technology of the firm, but also the probability distribution of the prices and the form of the utility function of the firm's owners.

It is the capacity dimension of the capital, i.e. the gross capital stock, which is relevant to the description of the firm's technology, [cf. subsection 3.2.2]. Accordingly, $K(t)$ is the argument in the (restricted) profit function. The user cost of capital to be defined below is the shadow price of using the capacity of one (marginal) capital unit at a given point of time.

The net cash-flow at time t, in the absence of taxes, is defined as the gross operating surplus less the investment cost, i.e.

(4.7) $$R(t) = X(t) - q(t)J(t).$$

The objective of the firm is maximization of the present value of its net cash-flow over the period $(0, \infty)$, i.e.

$$W = \int_0^\infty e^{-rt} R(t) \, dt,$$

where r is the interest rate used in the discounting. This optimization problem is derived from the more basic problem of optimizing the consumption path of the owners of the firm, r representing the rate of discount at which a nominal payment at one point of time can be converted into payments at other points of time.[2] For the present, r is considered a free parameter, which does not necessarily coincide with the market rate of interest. Inserting (4.6) and (4.7), we obtain

(4.8) $$W = \int_0^\infty e^{-rt} [F(K(t)) - q(t)J(t)] \, dt.$$

The maximization of W is subject to (3.3) which connects the capital stock with the previous investment flow. Let $\xi(t)$ be the Lagrange parameter associated with this constraint at time t, so that the Lagrangian of the problem can be written as

$$U = \int_0^\infty e^{-rt} [F(K(t)) - q(t)J(t)] \, dt$$
$$- \int_0^\infty \xi(t) \left[K(t) - \int_0^\infty B(s)J(t-s) \, ds \right] dt.$$

The part of the total capital stock $K(t)$ that it predetermined at the decision time, $t = 0$, is

$$K_0(t) = \int_t^\infty B(s)J(t-s) \, ds.$$

---

[2] This interpretation relies on the Fisher Separation Theorem. See Fisher (1930) and Hirshleifer (1958) for a discussion of this theorem in a two period context.

We can now rewrite the second part of the Lagrangian, i.e. the part which involves the Lagrange parameter,

$$U_2 = \int_0^\infty \xi(t) \left[K(t) - K_0(t) - \int_0^t B(s)J(t-s)\,ds \right] dt \,,$$

in the following way: Changing the integration variables into $\theta = t - s$ and $\tau = s$, we find that

$$\int_0^\infty \xi(t) \int_0^t B(s)J(t-s)\,ds\,dt = \int_0^\infty \int_0^\infty \xi(\theta + \tau)B(\tau)J(\theta)\,d\tau\,d\theta \,,$$

so that U_2 can be written as

$$U_2 = \int_0^\infty \left[\xi(t)\big(K(t) - K_0(t)\big) - J(t)\int_0^\infty \xi(t+s)B(s)\,ds \right] dt \,.$$

Inserting this expression in the Lagrangian, it takes the form

(4.9) $$U = \int_0^\infty \Psi[K(t), J(t), t]\,dt \,,$$

where

(4.10)
$$\Psi[K(t), J(t), t] = e^{-rt}[F\big(K(t)\big) - q(t)J(t)] - \xi(t)[K(t) - K_0(t)]$$
$$+ J(t)\int_0^\infty \xi(t+s)B(s)\,ds \,.$$

The necessary[3] first order conditions for constrained maximization of W subject to (3.3) can now, by using (4.9) – (4.10), be written as

$$\frac{\partial \Psi}{\partial K(t)} = e^{-rt}F'[K(t)] - \xi(t) = 0 \,,$$

$$\frac{\partial \Psi}{\partial J(t)} = -e^{-rt}q(t) + \int_0^\infty \xi(t+s)B(s)\,ds = 0 \,.$$

---

[3] We assume that the initial value of the capital stock, $K(0)$, is optimally adjusted, so that — provided $q(t)$ is a continuous function of time — the integral equation (4.11) will not imply $K(t)$ to show a discrete jump at $t = 0$.

Eliminating the Lagrange parameter, we get

(4.11)
$$\int_0^\infty e^{-rs} F'[K(t+s)]B(s)\,ds$$
$$= \int_t^\infty e^{-r(\theta-t)} F'[K(\theta)]B(\theta-t)\,d\theta = q(t)\,.$$

This equation generates the optimal path of the planned gross capital, for a given expected path of the investment price, a given interest rate, and a given survival function. The term $F'[K(t+s)]B(s)$ represents the increase in profit to be obtained at time $t+s$ by increasing capital at time t by one unit, assuming all other inputs optimally adjusted at any time. The condition (4.11) thus says that the total present value of this marginal profit flow over the capital's life time, discounted at the nominal interest rate, shall be equal to the initial investment price. This condition shall be satisfied at any time in the planning period; it will in particular hold at the decision time $t = 0$.

We now *set the user cost of capital equal to the shadow price of capital services* in this optimization problem,[4] i.e.

(4.12) $\qquad c(t+s,t) = F'\big(K(t+s)\big)\,, \qquad$ for all $s \geq 0$.

This is the shadow price interpretation of the user cost of capital in the absence of taxes. Eqs. (4.11) and (4.12) give the same implicit definition of the user cost of capital as does eq. (4.3) with $r = \rho + \gamma$, under the assumption made about the expected path of the investment price. We have commented upon this assumption above. Since (4.3) is equivalent to (4.1) in this case, this implies that the shadow price interpretation of the user cost, (4.12), is equivalent to the service price interpretation derived in section 4.2.

An alternative way of expressing the marginal condition for capital is the following: Differentiate the second equality in (4.11) with respect to t, while paying regard to (3.5). This gives

(4.13) $\qquad F'[K(t)] = q(t)r - \dot{q}(t) + \int_t^\infty e^{-r(\theta-t)} F'\big(K(\theta)\big)b(\theta-t)\,d\theta\,.$

---

[4] Expressed in terms of the Lagrange multiplier in (4.10), this shadow price is equal to $e^{r(t+s)}\xi(t+s)$.

Since $b(\theta-t)$ is the retirement which at time θ would result from a marginal investment of one unit at time t, $F'(K(\theta))b(\theta - t)$ represents the corresponding loss of profit. Eq. (4.13) thus says that the marginal profit which follows from increasing capital at time t by one unit should be equal to the investment price times the real interest rate, $r - \gamma$, plus the present value of the loss of future profits which corresponds to the retirement of this marginal investment.[5] Substituting $\rho = r - \gamma$, $s = \theta - t$, and the user cost definition (4.12) in (4.13), we obtain

$$(4.14) \qquad c(t) = c(t,t) = q(t)\rho + \int_0^\infty e^{-(\rho+\gamma)s} c(t+s,t)b(s)\,ds\,.$$

Following a similar line of argument as that leading from (4.1) to (4.3) and assuming $\rho \neq 0$, we find that (4.14) is equivalent to the following relationship between the user cost and the investment price

$$(4.15) \qquad c(t) = \frac{q(t)\rho}{1 - \Psi_\rho(0)} = \frac{q(t)\rho}{1 - \int_0^\infty e^{-\rho s} b(s)\,ds}\,.$$

This expression — which says that the user cost at time t equals the investment price at time t times the real interest rate divided by one minus the discounted per unit retirement flow from a new capital unit — is equivalent to (4.1). This follows from (3.16) (provided that $\rho \neq 0$).

4.4   Two examples

Let us consider two examples with parametric survival functions to illustrate the two alternative user cost definitions given above. The examples are the same as in section 3.6.

---

[5] Arrow (1964) shows, formally, that this optimization leads to myopic decision rules; confer his eqs. (8–4), (8–5), and (8–14), and the statement "The rule may be said to be myopic (short-sighted) in that the future movements of the profit function play no role in the determination of the current stock of capital and therefore of current investment." (p. 23). Note that Arrow, as a simplification, sets the capital price equal to one and expresses the constraint on the maximization as a relationship between $J(t)$ and $\dot{K}(t)$ instead of as a relationship between $J(t)$ and $K(t)$ as is done here [confer his eq. (8–9)].

4.4.1 Exponentially declining survival function

In the case where the survival function declines exponentially at the rate δ, i.e. [cf. (3.62)]

$$(4.16) \qquad\qquad B(s) = e^{-\delta s}, \qquad s \geq 0,$$

the service price definition (4.1) leads straightly to

$$(4.17) \qquad\qquad c(t) = q(t)(\rho + \delta) = q(t)(r - \gamma + \delta).$$

This is the familiar textbook formula

$$user\ cost = investment\ price \times (real\ interest\ rate + retirement\ rate),$$

since δ has the interpretation as the retirement rate (and coincides with the depreciation rate) in this case [cf. (3.69)].

The shadow price interpretation (4.11)–(4.12), on the other hand, implies

$$\int_t^\infty e^{-(r+\delta)(\theta-t)} c(\theta, t)\, d\theta = q(t).$$

Differentiating this expression with respect to t and rearranging, we get

$$(4.18) \qquad\qquad c(t) = c(t, t) = q(t)(r - \dot{q}(t)/q(t) + \delta).$$

This equation coincides with (4.17) when $\dot{q}(t)/q(t) = \gamma$ for all t.

Since $b(0) = \delta$, and $\Phi_\rho(0) = 1/(\rho+\delta)$ for an exponential survival function [cf. (3.63) and (3.65)], it follows from (4.5) that

$$(4.19) \qquad\qquad \Delta(t, 0) = \dot{q}(t)$$

in this case. The interpretation of this is that the exponential survival function has the particular property that the derivative of the vintage price with respect to *age* at time t and age 0 is equal to the derivative of the investment price with respect to *time* at time t. Inserting (4.19) in (4.4), we obtain (4.18), which confirms this interpretation.

Perhaps the most remarkable property of the exponential survival function is that it admits an *additive decomposition* of the user cost into a (real) interest component and a retirement component. The former is $q(t)(r - \gamma)$, the latter is $q(t)\delta$. As a consequence, a change in the parameter characterizing retirement, i.e. δ, has the same effect on the user cost regardless of the value of the interest rate. This is a counterpart to the additive relationship which exists between the quantity variables gross investment, the gross capital stock, and its time derivative in this case, i.e. $J(t) = \dot{K}(t) + \delta K(t)$.

4.4.2 Simultaneous retirement

Consider the case where all capital units retain their full efficiency during N periods and then disappear completely, i.e. [cf. (3.71)]

$$(4.20) \qquad B(s) = \begin{cases} 1 & \text{for } 0 \le s \le N, \\ 0 & \text{for } s > N. \end{cases}$$

The service price definition (4.1) leads to

$$(4.21) \qquad c(t) = \frac{q(t)}{H_\rho(N)} = \frac{\rho q(t)}{1 - e^{-\rho N}},$$

where $H_\rho(N) = (1 - e^{-\rho N})/\rho$ is the value of a constant annuity of 1 discounted over N years at the rate ρ. In this case, we thus have the simple relationship

$$\text{user cost} = \frac{\text{investment price}}{\text{annuity factor}}.$$

The shadow price interpretation (4.11)–(4.12) yields

$$\int_t^{t+N} e^{-r(\theta - t)} c(\theta, t)\, d\theta = q(t),$$

which after differentiation with respect to t gives

$$(4.22) \qquad rq(t) - \dot{q}(t) = c(t,t) - e^{-rN} c(t+N,t).$$

This differential equation cannot be solved explicitly for $c(t) = c(t,t)$ in general, but if we make the additional assumption that $q(t)$ follows an exponential growth path with rate γ, it is consistent with a path for $c(\theta, t)$ with the same growth rate. Substituting $\dot{q}(t) = \gamma q(t)$ and $c(t + N, t) = c(t)e^{\gamma N}$ in (4.22), we get $(r - \gamma)q(t) = (1 - e^{-(r-\gamma)N})c(t)$, which is equivalent to (4.21) with $\rho = r - \gamma$. This shows that the equivalence between the service price interpretation and the shadow price interpretation of the user cost holds in this case as well.

What can be said about the myopic interpretation of the user cost in this case? Since $b(0) = 0$ and $\Phi_\rho(0) = H_\rho(N)$ [cf. (3.72) and (3.73)], it follows from (4.5) that the derivative of the vintage price with respect to *age* at time t and age 0 is

(4.23)

$$\Delta(t,0) = \dot{q}(t) + q(t) \left[\rho - \frac{1}{H_\rho(N)}\right]$$

$$= \dot{q}(t) - q(t) \frac{\rho e^{-\rho N}}{1 - e^{-\rho N}} .$$

We see that $\Delta(t,0) < \dot{q}(t)$ as long as $\rho > 0$ and N is finite, i.e. this derivative will be *less than* the derivative of the investment price with respect to time at time t. This property of the vintage price is different from that under exponential decay. Since it can be shown, by means of a first order Taylor expansion, that $1/H_\rho(N) \approx \rho + 1/N$, we have approximately

$$\Delta(t,0) = \dot{q}(t) - \frac{q(t)}{N} ,$$

i.e. the derivative of the vintage price with respect to age is equal to the derivative of the investment price with respect to time less the investment price divided by the service life.

The user cost formula for the simultaneous retirement case, (4.21) — unlike the exponential one — does not admit an additive decomposition into a (real) interest component and a retirement component, since $1/H_\rho(N)$ is a non-linear function of N and ρ. Although $1/H_\rho(N) \approx \rho + 1/N$, to a first order of approximation, so that we may write the user cost *approximately* in additive form as $c(t) \approx q(t)(\rho + 1/N)$, this approximation may give very inaccurate results. If, for instance, $\rho = 0.05$, $N = 50$, and $q(t) = 1$, the approximate formula gives $c(t) = 0.07$, whereas the exact formula gives $c(t) = 0.0545$.[6]

4.5 A decomposition of the user value of capital services

From the definitions of gross and net capital, capital value, and depreciation given in chapter 3, and of the user cost of capital given in the present chapter, the user value of the capital services can be decomposed in an interesting way, which illuminates further the relationship between the quantity and price variables at the heart of our study. Consider vintage $t - s$ at

---

[6] In section 11.4 there is a further discussion of approximation formulae for the user cost under non-exponential survival functions based on Taylor expansions.

time t. From (3.57) and (3.16) we find that the ratio between depreciation (in volume terms) and gross capital can be expressed as follows for any discounting rate and any survival function:

$$(4.24) \qquad \frac{D_N(t,s)}{K(t,s)} = \frac{\Psi_\rho(s)}{\Phi_\rho(0)} = \frac{1}{\Phi_\rho(0)} - \rho\frac{\Phi_\rho(s)}{\Phi_\rho(0)}.$$

Since (4.1) and (3.50) imply that the relative user cost is $c(t)/q(t) = 1/\Phi_\rho(0)$ and that the ratio between the net and the gross capital stock is $K_N(t,s)/K(t,s) = \Phi_\rho(s)/\Phi_\rho(0)$, this ratio can be rewritten as

$$\frac{D_N(t,s)}{K(t,s)} = \frac{c(t)}{q(t)} - \rho\frac{K_N(t,s)}{K(t,s)}.$$

Rearranging, we obtain the following decomposition of the product of the user cost and the gross capital in vintage $t - s$ at time t, which represents the user value of the services from vintage $t - s$ at time t:

$$(4.25) \qquad c(t)K(t,s) = \rho q(t)K_N(t,s) + q(t)D_N(t,s).$$

If we interpret $\rho = r - \gamma$ as the real interest rate and $\rho q(t)K_N(t,s) = \rho V(t,s)$ as the implicit *real* interest cost on the capital value in vintage $t - s$ at time t, this equation says that

$$\begin{aligned} &\quad\;\; \textit{User value of capital services} &(cK) \\ &= \textit{Real interest on capital value} &(\rho q K_N) \\ &+ \textit{Gross value of depreciation} &(q D_N). \end{aligned}$$

Since the price variables $c(t)$ and $q(t)$ are age independent, we can, by integrating (4.25) over s, derive a similar relationship for the aggregate capital stock,

$$(4.26) \qquad c(t)K(t) = \rho q(t)K_N(t) + q(t)D_N(t).$$

An alternative decomposition of the user value can be defined in terms of the *nominal* interest on the capital value and the *net* value of depreciation. From (3.61), with $\dot{q}(t)/q(t) = \gamma$, we get the following expression for the net rate of depreciation in value terms:

$$(4.27) \qquad \frac{E(t,s)}{V(t,s)} = \frac{1}{\Phi_\rho(s)} - \rho - \gamma.$$

Since, from (3.49) and (4.1) we have $V(t, s)/K(t, s) = c(t)\Phi_\rho(s)$, we can rewrite this ratio as

$$\frac{E(t, s)}{V(t, s)} = \frac{c(t)K(t, s)}{V(t, s)} - \rho - \gamma,$$

which yields

(4.28) $$c(t)K(t, s) = (\rho + \gamma)V(t, s) + E(t, s).$$

If we interpret $\rho + \gamma = r$ as the nominal interest rate and $rV(t, s)$ as the implicit nominal interest cost on the capital value, this equation says that

$$
\begin{aligned}
&\textit{User value of capital services} &&(cK) \\
=\ &\textit{Nominal interest on capital value} &&(rV) \\
+\ &\textit{Net value of depreciation} &&(E).
\end{aligned}
$$

The corresponding relationship for the aggregate capital stock is

(4.29) $$c(t)K(t) = (\rho + \gamma)V(t) + E(t).$$

The decompositions of the user value given in (4.25) and (4.28) are valid regardless of the form of the survival function. In case of an *exponential* survival function, where $K_N(t, s) = K(t, s)$, $D_N(t, s) = \delta K(t, s)$, and $E(t, s) = (\delta - \gamma)V(t, s)$ [cf. subsection 3.6.1], the decompositions become particularly simple:

$$
\begin{aligned}
c(t)K(t, s) &= q(t)\rho K(t, s) + q(t)\delta K(t, s) \\
&= (\rho + \gamma)V(t, s) + (\delta - \gamma)V(t, s), \qquad s \geq 0.
\end{aligned}
$$

If the retirement process follows the *simultaneous retirement* pattern, in which case $K_N(t, s)/K(t, s) = H_\rho(N - s)/H_\rho(N)$, $D_N(t, s)/K_N(t, s) =$

$1/H_\rho(N - s) - \rho$, and $E(t,s)/V(t,s) = 1/H_\rho(N - s) - \rho - \gamma$ [cf. subsection 3.6.2], the decompositions are more complicated. Now (4.25) and (4.28) read

$$c(t)K(t,s) = q(t)\rho\frac{H_\rho(N - s)}{H_\rho(N)}K(t,s)$$

$$+ q(t)\left(\frac{1}{H_\rho(N - s)} - \rho\right)\frac{H_\rho(N - s)}{H_\rho(N)}K(t,s)$$

$$= (\rho + \gamma)V(t,s) + \left(\frac{1}{H_\rho(N - s)} - \rho - \gamma\right)V(t,s), \ \ 0 \le s \le N.$$

In the latter case, changes in the interest rate will affect the (gross and net) depreciation value component of the user value of capital services. This is a reflection of the non-linearity of the user cost function [cf. subsection 4.4.2].

This decomposition of the capital service value will be illustrated for a wide variety of survival functions in section 11.5.

CHAPTER 5

THE CORPORATE TAX SYSTEM

5.1 Introduction

In section 2.6, we discussed investment criteria for a single project, characterized by a given cost and a given revenue function, and derived the corresponding rate of return and cost of capital when the effect of an income tax was included in the specification of the revenue function. In this chapter, we give a formalization of the corporate income tax for a neoclassical technology and show how this tax can be described to fit into the framework for analyzing the user cost of capital as developed for the taxless case in chapter 4. In addition to the income tax, a tax on the value of the capital stock of the firm is also included.

The chapter is organized as follows. We start by defining, in addition to gross and net capital previously defined, a third capital stock concept. It is called the accounting capital and is the key variable on which the taxation of the firm's capital is based (section 5.2). Then we focus successively on each of the components of the income tax function and discuss alternative ways of treating — *inter alia*, with regard to indexation — depreciation allowances, interest deductions, and capital gains in the tax base (section 5.3). The depreciation allowances will reflect the form of the accounting capital function prescribed in the tax code. The interest deductions and the taxable capital gains will depend on either the market value of the capital stock, or the accounting capital, or both. The tax on the capital value can be interpreted as a tax imposed on the firm's assets, i.e. as a wealth tax, but it can also be given the interpretation as a tax on the capital input of the firm. From these elements, we define a set of distinct tax systems, and for convenience, we organize them into two broad classes, denoted as class A and class M, respectively (section 5.4). A compact characterization of the net taxable deductions — in terms of present values of the total income deductions per unit of investment cost — ends the chapter (section 5.5).

5.2   Accounting capital and depreciation allowances

A crucial element in the description of any system of corporate income taxation — although it is not often made explicit — is the accounting capital. Briefly, the accounting capital of a firm is the assessment of the value of the production capital used by the firm and the tax authorities in defining the tax base for income (and possibly also capital value) taxation. It is, like the market value of the capital stock, $V(t)$, a value concept and may coincide with it, but will, in general, be different from it. This difference will come into focus several times in the following, for instance when discussing neutrality issues [cf. chapter 9]. For convenience, we shall regard the accounting capital as decomposed into a price and a volume component.

5.2.1 Accounting capital in volume terms

Consider first the volume component of the accounting capital. In analogy with the definition of the survival function, $B(s)$, and its counterpart for net capital, $G_\rho(s)$, we let $A(s)$ denote the proportion of the volume of an investment made s years ago which is still included in the firm's accounting capital. The function $A(s)$, which may be denoted as the *survival function of the accounting capital,* has the same general properties as $B(s)$ and $G_\rho(s)$, i.e. [cf. (3.1) and (3.29)]

$$
\begin{aligned}
0 \le A(s) \le 1, \qquad A'(s) \le 0, \qquad s \ge 0, \\
A(0) = 1, \qquad \lim_{s \to \infty} A(s) = 0.
\end{aligned}
$$

(5.1)

Then,

(5.2)
$$
H(t, s) = A(s)J(t - s)
$$

represents the part of the accounting capital in volume terms which relates to investment made s years ago at time t, and

(5.3)
$$
H(t) = \int_0^\infty H(t, s)\, ds = \int_0^\infty A(s)J(t - s)\, ds
$$

is the total accounting capital in volume terms at time t.

The associated *depreciation allowances in volume terms* is the difference between gross investment and the increase in the accounting capital. From (5.3) we find that the depreciation allowances at time t is

$$(5.4) \qquad D_H(t) = J(t) - \dot{H}(t) = \int_0^\infty a(s)J(t-s)\,ds\,,$$

where

$$(5.5) \qquad a(s) = -A'(s)\,;$$

confer the similar expressions for retirement $D(t)$ and depreciation $D_N(t)$ given in eqs. (3.4)–(3.5) and (3.53)–(3.54).

The function $a(s)$ is non-negative and represents the weights given to capital of age s when calculating accounted depreciation in volume terms: a share $a(s)\,ds$ of the volume of an initial investment is written off from s to $s + ds$ years after installation. We call it the *(relative) depreciation function of the accounting capital*. From (5.1) and (5.5) it follows that $a(s)$ is non-negative and satisfies

$$(5.6) \qquad \int_0^\infty a(s)\,ds = 1\,,$$

i.e. *in volume terms*, any capital good invested is allowed to be written off completely in the firm's accounts over its life cycle. We do not allow for the possibility that the tax system may permit the firm to write off more, or less, than the initial investment. We could, however, take such a possibility into account by replacing $0 \le A(s) \le 1$ and $A(0) = 1$ in (5.1) by $0 \le A(s) \le A_0$ and $A(0) = A_0$, where A_0 is as arbitrary positive constant, representing the share of the volume of investment which is subject to depreciation allowances.

Defining

$$(5.7) \qquad D_H(t,s) = a(s)J(t-s)\,,$$

which is the depreciation allowance for capital of age s at time t in volume terms, we can write $D_H(t)$ as an aggregate of vintage specific depreciation allowances as

$$(5.8) \qquad D_H(t) = \int_0^\infty D_H(t,s)\,ds\,.$$

From (5.2) and (5.7) it follows that the age specific rates of depreciation allowances can be written as

$$(5.9) \qquad \frac{D_H(t,s)}{H(t,s)} = a^*(s), \qquad s \geq 0,$$

where

$$(5.10) \qquad a^*(s) = \frac{a(s)}{A(s)} = -\frac{d\ln A(s)}{ds}, \qquad s \geq 0.$$

These rates are, like the corresponding age specific retirement rates [cf. (3.10)], in general age dependent, but are time invariant. The difference between $a(s)$ and $a^*(s)$ reflects their different normalization. The former is normalized against the *initial* investment at age 0, the latter against the accounting capital *remaining* at age s.

5.2.2 Accounting capital and depreciation in value terms

We now turn to the corresponding concepts in value terms. The tax authorities' assessment of a firm's capital stock for tax purposes can be based either on the original (historic) cost of the investment or on its replacement cost. The value of the accounting capital which is of age s at time t, at *original cost*, is the product of the accounting capital in volume terms and the investment price at time $t - s$, i.e.

$$(5.11) \qquad V_O(t,s) = q(t-s)H(t,s) = A(s)q(t-s)J(t-s),$$

the subscript O denoting 'original'. Aggregation over vintages yields a total accounted capital value at original cost equal to

$$(5.12) \qquad V_O(t) = \int_0^\infty V_O(t,s)\,ds = \int_0^\infty A(s)q(t-s)J(t-s)\,ds.$$

The value of the accounting capital of age s at time t at *replacement cost* is

$$(5.13) \qquad V_R(t,s) = q(t)H(t,s) = A(s)q(t)J(t-s),$$

the subscript R denoting 'replacement', and its total value becomes

$$(5.14) \qquad V_R(t) = \int_0^\infty V_R(t,s)\,ds = \int_0^\infty A(s)q(t)J(t-s)\,ds = q(t)H(t).$$

The accounted replacement value of the capital stock is simply equal to the product of the current investment price and the accounting capital in volume terms.

The difference between the value of gross investment and the increase in the value of the accounting capital is, by definition, the *net value of the depreciation of the accounting capital*. Let $E_O(t)$ and $E_R(t)$ denote this net value evaluated at original cost and at replacement cost, respectively, i.e.

$$(5.15) \qquad\qquad E_O(t) = q(t)J(t) - \dot{V}_O(t),$$

$$(5.16) \qquad\qquad E_R(t) = q(t)J(t) - \dot{V}_R(t).$$

Since (5.12), (5.14), and (5.3)–(5.5) imply

$$\dot{V}_O(t) = q(t)J(t) - \int_0^\infty a(s)q(t-s)J(t-s)\,ds,$$

$$\dot{V}_R(t) = q(t)\left[J(t) - \int_0^\infty a(s)J(t-s)\,ds\right] + \dot{q}(t)\int_0^\infty A(s)J(t-s)\,ds$$

$$= q(t)J(t) - q(t)D_H(t) + \dot{q}(t)H(t),$$

we obtain

$$(5.17) \quad E_O(t) = \int_0^\infty a(s)q(t-s)J(t-s)\,ds,$$

$$(5.18) \quad E_R(t) = \int_0^\infty a(s)q(t)J(t-s)\,ds - \dot{q}(t)\int_0^\infty A(s)J(t-s)\,ds$$

$$= q(t)D_H(t) - \dot{q}(t)H(t).$$

These expressions represent the value counterparts to (5.4).

The interpretation of (5.17) and (5.18) is the following. Evaluating accounting capital at original cost implies a value of depreciation which is a weighted average of the historic investment cost of the different vintages, $q(t-s)J(t-s)$, with weights given by the relative depreciation function $a(s)$. Using replacement cost, the implied net value of depreciation is the difference between $q(t)D_H(t)$, the *gross value of depreciation*, and $\dot{q}(t)H(t)$, i.e. the accounted *appreciation* of the capital stock. The gross value of depreciation in the latter case is obtained as a weighted average of the replacement cost of the different vintages, $q(t)J(t-s)$, with weights given by the relative depreciation function $a(s)$. Eq. (5.18) is — from the point of view of tax accounting — the counterpart to (3.60), which gives the true depreciation based on market values.

We can decompose $E_O(t)$ and $E_R(t)$ by vintages as follows

$$(5.19) \qquad E_O(t) = \int_0^\infty E_O(t, s)\, ds,$$

$$(5.20) \qquad E_R(t) = \int_0^\infty E_R(t, s)\, ds,$$

where

$$(5.21) \qquad E_O(t, s) = a(s)q(t - s)J(t - s) = q(t - s)D_H(t, s)$$
$$= a^*(s)V_O(t, s),$$

$$E_R(t, s) = [a(s)q(t) - \dot{q}(t)A(s)]J(t - s)$$
$$(5.22) \qquad = q(t)D_H(t, s) - \dot{q}(t)H(t, s)$$
$$= \left[a^*(s) - \frac{\dot{q}(t)}{q(t)}\right] V_R(t, s),$$

the last equalities following from (5.7), (5.10), (5.11), and (5.13). The interpretation of (5.21) and (5.22) is simple: Using accounting at *original cost*, the implied vintage specific value of depreciation of vintage $t - s$ at time t, $E_O(t, s)$, is obtained by multiplying the accounted value of this vintage by the age specific rate of depreciation allowances (in volume terms), $a^*(s)$. A similar relationship holds between depreciation and capital values accounted at *replacement cost* if we only reduce the age specific rate of depreciation allowances in volume terms by the rate of increase of the investment price. Eq. (5.22) is — from the point of view of tax accounting — the counterpart to (3.61), which relates to market values.

5.3   The tax function

We assume, as already declared, that two kinds of taxes are imposed on the firm: an *income tax* and a tax on the value of its capital stock, denoted as a *capital value tax*, for short. The income tax is a tax on net profit — defined as the output value minus the current costs of labour, energy, materials, etc., after the tax-permitted net costs related to the purchase, financing, and use of capital have been deducted. The capital value tax may be interpreted in two ways: either as a tax on capital services, imposed on the user, regardless of the ownership of the firm, or — if the firm holds a financial position such that the net value of its financial assets is always zero — as a net wealth tax.

In this section, we consider alternative ways of defining taxable income and taxable capital value on the basis on the capital value concepts introduced above. The focus will be one the following issues:

(i) the treatment of depreciation allowances,

(ii) the treatment of interest deductions (cost of finance),

(iii) the treatment of capital gains, and

(iv) the relationship between the accounting capital concept used in defining depreciation allowances and taxable capital value, on the one hand, and the capital concept which underlies the calculation of interest deductions and capital gains, on the other.

For this purpose, we define

u: income tax rate $(0 \leq u < 1)$,

v: capital value tax rate $(v \geq 0)$,

X: output value minus total current costs of all inputs other than capital, i.e. gross operating surplus [cf. (4.6)],

S_D: depreciation allowances deductible in income tax base,

S_I: interest costs deductible in income tax base,

S_G: capital gains included in income tax base,

V_T: value of accounting capital implicit in depreciation allowances and capital value tax (the subscript T denoting tax-defined).

Following the tax code for joint-stock companies in most countries (including Norway), we specify both taxes as proportional. We assume furthermore that the tax rates u and v are constant over time (or at least expected so by the firm), and that all costs of inputs other than capital (i.e. labour, energy, materials, etc.) are completely and immediately deductible in the income tax base. This means that the tax treatment of these inputs will not distort the firm's decisions. The tax payment at time t can then be written compactly as

$$(5.23) \qquad T(t) = u[X(t) - S_D(t) - S_I(t) + S_G(t)] + vV_T(t).$$

We now proceed by first discussing alternative definitions of V_T, S_D, S_I, and S_G (subsections 5.3.1–5.3.3), and then combine these definitions in different ways to obtain different tax systems (section 5.4).

5.3.1 Treatment of capital value tax and depreciation allowances

Subsection 5.2.2 presented two alternative definitions of the firm's accounted capital value, based on original cost (O) and on replacement cost (R), respectively. The implied definitions of the (taxable) capital value and the (gross) depreciation allowances are, respectively:[1]

Alternative AO. Depreciation allowances based on accounting capital at original cost:

$$V_T(t) = V_O(t),$$

$$S_D(t) = E_O(t),$$

Alternative AR. Depreciation allowances based on accounting capital at replacement cost:

$$V_T(t) = V_R(t),$$

$$S_D(t) = E_R(t) + \dot{q}(t)H(t) = q(t)D_H(t),$$

where V_O, V_R, E_O, and E_R are defined as in eqs. (5.12), (5.14), (5.17), and (5.18).

Again we assume that the investment price increases (or that the producers expect it to increase) at a constant rate γ, i.e. [cf. (4.2)]

(5.24) $$q(t) = q(0)e^{\gamma t} \qquad \text{for all } t.$$

Let now ε be a general *inflation adjustment parameter (indexation parameter)*, defined as the rate at which the original investment cost is allowed to be inflated in the firm's tax reports when calculating accounting capital and depreciation allowances. The two alternatives above can then be expressed compactly as

(5.25) $$V_T(t) = \int_0^\infty A(s)e^{\varepsilon s}q(t-s)J(t-s)\,ds$$

---

[1] We here use $A\,O$ and $A\,R$ as acronyms for accounting + original and accounting + replacement, respectively. Similar acronyms will be used in the sequel.

$$= q(t) \int_0^\infty A(s)e^{(\varepsilon-\gamma)s} J(t-s)\,ds\,,$$

$$(5.26) \qquad S_D(t) = \int_0^\infty a(s)e^{\varepsilon s} q(t-s) J(t-s)\,ds$$

$$= q(t) \int_0^\infty a(s)e^{(\varepsilon-\gamma)s} J(t-s)\,ds\,,$$

where $e^{\varepsilon s}q(t-s)J(t-s)$ is the inflation adjusted investment cost of vintage $t-s$ at time t and

$$\varepsilon = 0 \text{ in alternative } AO\,,$$

$$\varepsilon = \gamma \text{ in alternative } AR\,.$$

These equations can represent any tax code which permits inflation adjustment of the historic investment cost, to a degree which departs from the rate of price increase of the capital category under consideration ($\varepsilon \neq \gamma$). Such tax codes are of substantial practical interest since indexation of a tax base will often in practice, for reasons of administrative convenience etc., be based on an index of the *overall* inflation rate in the economy — for instance an average output price index, an average consumer price index, the GDP deflator, etc. — which may deviate from the rate of increase of the *specific* investment price relevant to the firm. The distinction between general and specific inflation is highly relevant in this case.

5.3.2 Treatment of interest deductions

Next we turn to the interest deduction component of the tax function. Three issues may be raised when constructing rules for deduction of the interest cost, or more generally, the cost of finance of the investment:

(i) Which capital concept should be the basis for these deductions: the *accounting* value of the capital (whether based on original or on replacement cost) or its *market* value?

(ii) Should *complete* or *partial* deductibility of the interest cost (cost of finance) be permitted?

(iii) Should the firm — regardless of the answer given to question (ii) — perform an indexation of the interest cost, i.e. should it be allowed to deduct its *nominal* or its *real* interest cost? And if only the real interest cost is deductible, how should it be defined?

By giving different answers to these questions, we define different codes for interest deductibility. Five alternatives will be discussed below. Two of these are, like the depreciation allowances, based on the accounting capital only, two are based on the market value of the capital only, and the last one is a mixed code.

Let

m: proportion of the (imputed) interest cost (however defined) which is deductible in the income tax base ($0 \leq m \leq 1$), $m = 1$ denoting full deductibility and $m = 0$ denoting no deductibility,

i: nominal market rate of interest (cost of finance).

Two comments on this notation are in order. First, the parameter m is exogenously given. This can be interpreted in several ways, depending on (a) the formal rules for deductibility of debt interest and/or dividend payments in the corporate taxable income, and (b) the way in which the investment is financed. Assume, for instance, that the capital value concept which underlies the tax permitted interest deductions is the market value of the capital stock, V.[2] One interpretation of this assumption is that the firm is completely equity financed, iV is its dividend payments — i being the dividend rate claimed by its share-holders — and m is the proportion of these payments which is deductible in the income tax base. Another (and usually more realistic) interpretation is that the firm is both equity and debt financed. Motivated by e.g. risk considerations, borrowing constraints, etc. it adjusts its debt ratio in such a way that — given the rules for deduction of debt interests and dividend payments in the tax code — a constant proportion m of the imputed interest cost on the value of its capital stock is actually deducted. Since we do not explain the debt structure of the firm, m is exogenously determined.[3] If, in particular, the firm has no retained earnings, if its dividend payments are not deductible in the income tax base — which is the case in several countries[4] — and if nominal debt interests are completely deductible, then m represents the

---

[2] Confer alternative MN below. A similar line of argument may be followed if the accounting capital concept V_T is used.

[3] See section 6.4 for a further discussion of this simplifying assumption.

[4] Norway is an exception, since dividend payments are deductible in the corporate income base when calculating central government tax, but it is not deductible when calculating municipal tax. The converse principle is applied in the taxation of the share-holder: dividends received by persons are subject to central government tax (although at a progressively increasing rate which differs from the proportional rate applied to the firm), but are free from municipal tax.

firm's debt ratio. These examples illustrate that m is not usually a genuine tax parameter, it may also reflect the financial structure of the firm.[5] Second, i, the market interest rate, does not necessarily coincide with the rate of discount r used in defining the present value of net cash-flow [cf. (4.8)], and for the present, we need two different symbols for these variables. The relationship between r and i will be discussed in section 6.4.

The first two alternatives are

Alternative AO. Interest deductions based on accounting capital at original cost:

$$S_I(t) = miV_O(t) = mi \int_0^\infty A(s)q(t-s)J(t-s)\,ds\,,$$

Alternative AR. Interest deductions based on accounting capital at replacement cost:

$$S_I(t) = miV_R(t) = miq(t) \int_0^\infty A(s)J(t-s)\,ds\,.$$

Utilizing, as above, the inflation adjustment parameter ε, AO and AR may be "condensed" into

System A. Interest deductions based on the accounting capital:

$$(5.27) \qquad S_I(t) = miV_T(t) = miq(t) \int_0^\infty A(s)e^{(\varepsilon-\gamma)s}J(t-s)\,ds\,,$$

where V_T is defined as in (5.25) and

$$\varepsilon = 0 \text{ in alternative } AO,$$
$$\varepsilon = \gamma \text{ in alternative } AR.$$

An interest deduction system like this — which forces the firm to use the same capital concept, V_T, when calculating its interest deductions as when calculating its depreciation allowances — may not be widely applied, but it is an interesting alternative to existing systems.

A more familiar alternative is

---

[5] A similar remark applies to the interpretation of v as a rate of net wealth tax. If the firm is subject to a net wealth tax, v will represent not only the tax rules, but also its financial structure, cf. subsection 10.2.3.

Alternative MN. Interest deductions based on the nominal cost of finance at market value

$$S_I(t) = miV(t) = miq(t) \int_0^\infty G(s)J(t-s)\,ds\,,$$

where V is the market value of the capital defined in (3.49). We also consider its modification in which the firm is allowed to deduct (wholly or partly) the "real interest cost" only. It can be formalized as

Alternative MI. Interest deductions based on the inflation adjusted cost of finance at market value

$$S_I(t) = m(i-\varepsilon)V(t) = m(i-\varepsilon)q(t) \int_0^\infty G(s)J(t-s)\,ds\,,$$

where ε is the statutory inflation adjustment parameter, so that $i-\varepsilon$ is the statutory real interest rate. Or stated otherwise, only the share $(i-\varepsilon)/i$ of the actual interest cost is included in the tax base. A share m of this inflation adjusted interest cost is deductible.[6]

Another way of formalizing indexation of the interest deductions is the following. Let the nominal interest cost based on the *market* value of the capital be reduced by the value increase implicit in the *accounting* capital.[7] A share m of this "net interest cost" is deductible. The interpretation of this is that the tax system imposes on the firm an inflation adjustment of its interest cost which is equal to its accounted capital gains. This gives

Alternative MI*. Interest deductions based on nominal cost of finance at market value less accounted capital gains

$$S_I(t) = m[iV(t) - \varepsilon V_T(t)]$$

$$= mq(t) \int_0^\infty [iG(s) - \varepsilon A(s)e^{(\varepsilon-\gamma)s}]J(t-s)\,ds\,.$$

The last three alternatives can be "condensed" into

---

[6]   Indexed tax systems have received much attention in economic policy debate in several countries recently. The Norwegian Tax Commission, for instance, recommended in its report [NOU (1984)] the conversion to a fully indexed system for interest costs for both the corporate and the personal sectors, after a transition period of a few years. For a discussion of the indexation of the income tax base in the 1986 U.S. tax reform, see Fullerton (1987), in particular sections 3.3, 3.5, and 3.7.

[7]   Confer eq. (5.29) below.

System M. Interest deductions based (wholly or partly) on the market capital value

$$S_I(t) = m\{iV(t) - \varepsilon[\alpha_I V(t) + (1 - \alpha_I)V_T(t)]\}$$

(5.28)
$$= mq(t) \int_0^\infty [(i - \varepsilon\alpha_I)G(s)$$

$$- \varepsilon(1 - \alpha_I)A(s)e^{(\varepsilon-\gamma)s}]J(t - s)\,ds\,,$$

where α_I is a constant between zero and one, representing the weight given to the market value when calculating the inflation adjustment. This equation defines a set of interest deduction rules; in particular,

$$\varepsilon = 0 \text{ in alternative } MN,$$

$$\alpha_I = 1 \text{ in alternative } MI,$$

$$\alpha_I = 0 \text{ in alternative } MI^*.$$

Systems A and M, as parametrized in (5.27) and (5.28), represent general codes for interest deductibility in the corporate income tax base. This parametrization is applicable regardless of the value of the indexation parameter ε prescribed by the tax authorities, which facilitates comparison between systems, both with regard to theoretical properties and empirical implications.

We now turn to the last element in the income tax base.

5.3.3 Treatment of capital gains

The construction of a code for taxation of capital gains raises questions of essentially the same kind as those discussed above for the interest deduction component:

(i) Which capital concept should form the basis for calculating capital gains: the *accounting* value of the capital or its *market* value?

(ii) Should *complete* or *partial* taxation of the accrued capital gains be permitted?

(iii) Should the firm — regardless of the answer given to question (ii) — be allowed to perform an indexation of its capital gains; i.e. should full *nominal* or only *real* capital gains be subject to taxation? And in the latter case, how should the real capital gains be defined?

Different answers to these questions define different codes. The five alternatives to be considered below correspond to those for interest deductibility discussed in subsection 5.3.2 above.

Let

n: proportion of the (imputed) capital gains (however defined) which is included in taxable income ($0 \leq n \leq 1$), $n = 1$ denoting full taxation of the gains and $n = 0$ denoting no taxation.

This parameter, like m, is considered as exogenously given and can be interpreted in several ways, depending on (a) the statutory tax rates for capital gains and whether capital gains are taxed on an accrual basis or at the time of realization, and (b) the way in which the firm is financed, and whether the capital gains are considered as "belonging" to the firm or to its owners. For a discussion of the interplay between the corporate and the personal taxation as far as the capital gains taxation is concerned, see Auerbach (1983a, section V.B). In general, n will not be a genuine tax parameter; it also reflects the (exogenously given) financial structure of the firm. Usually, its value is substantially below unity, one reason being that capital gains are normally taxed at the time of realization, which implies that a substantial tax credit may be obtained for this component of the corporate income tax.[8] In some cases — for instance if the firm is a going concern which is able to transform a significant part of its capital gains into (extraordinary) depreciation allowances for new capital goods — it may obtain an almost infinite tax credit, i.e. a value of n close to zero.

Consider first

Alternative AO. Capital gains based on accounting capital at original cost

$$S_G(t) = 0.$$

---

[8] We could have represented the effect of this tax credit by introducing an accrual-equivalent capital gains tax rate u^*, defined as the rate that would give the same terminal after tax wealth when applied to the accrued capital gains as is obtained by applying the statutory income tax rate u to the gains at the time of realization, and letting $n = u^*/u$. Then n would have become a function of the interest rate, the remaining life time, and possibly other financial market variables.

We have this simple relationship since, when accounting capital at historic cost is used, no genuine capital gains emerge: gross depreciation always coincides with net depreciation in this case.[9] Next, we define

Alternative AR. Capital gains based on accounting capital at replacement cost

$$S_G(t) = w\gamma V_R(t) = w\gamma q(t) \int_0^\infty A(s) J(t - s) \, ds \, ,$$

since $\gamma V_R(t)$ is the difference between the gross and the net depreciation of the accounting capital based on replacement value [cf. (5.18)]. These alternatives can be "condensed" into:

System A. Capital gains based on the accounting capital

$$(5.29) \qquad S_G(t) = n\varepsilon V_T(t) = n\varepsilon q(t) \int_0^\infty A(s) e^{(\varepsilon - \gamma)s} J(t - s) \, ds \, ,$$

where ε is the inflation adjustment parameter, defined as above. In particular,

$$\varepsilon = 0 \text{ in alternative } AO \, ,$$
$$\varepsilon = \gamma \text{ in alternative } AR \, .$$

Taxable capital gains can — perhaps more realistically — be defined on the basis of the recorded changes in the market value of the capital stock. This motivates us to consider

Alternative MN. Capital gains based on the nominal market value of the capital stock

$$S_G(t) = n\gamma V(t) = n\gamma q(t) \int_0^\infty G(s) J(t - s) \, ds \, ,$$

and

Alternative MI. Capital gains based on the inflation adjusted market value of the capital stock

$$S_G(t) = n(\gamma - \varepsilon) V(t) = n(\gamma - \varepsilon) q(t) \int_0^\infty G(s) J(t - s) \, ds \, .$$

---

[9] Mathematically, this follows from (5.12) and (5.17).

If, in the last case, the inflation adjustment is "correct", i.e. if $\varepsilon = \gamma$, then no capital gains will be recorded, since the inflation adjustment will exactly exhaust the nominal capital gain. A zero taxable gain is thus a property which alternatives AO and MI have in common, but the reason is different: In the former, the underlying accounting capital does not change its *nominal* value, since it is based on historic cost; in the latter, changes in the nominal value are recorded, but the value change in *real* terms is zero by definition.

Finally, we specify a code which, like MI, permits inflation adjustment of the nominal capital gains. But now the nominal gains based on the *market* value of the capital are reduced by the gains as *accounted* by the tax authorities. This code can be considered the "net" result of combining alternative MN and system A. Formally, it is defined by

Alternative MI*. Capital gains at nominal market value reduced by accounted capital gains

$$S_G(t) = n[\gamma V(t) - \varepsilon V_T(t)]$$

$$= nq(t) \int_0^\infty [\gamma G(s) - \varepsilon A(s)e^{(\varepsilon - \gamma)s}] J(t - s) \, ds \, .$$

The last three alternatives are members of

System M. Capital gains based (wholly or partly) on the market capital value

$$S_G(t) = n\{\gamma V(t) - \varepsilon[\alpha_G V(t) + (1 - \alpha_G)V_T(t)]\}$$

(5.30) $$= nq(t) \int_0^\infty [(\gamma - \varepsilon \alpha_G)G(s)$$

$$- \varepsilon(1 - \alpha_G)A(s)e^{(\varepsilon - \gamma)s}] J(t - s) \, ds \, ,$$

where α_G is a constant between zero and one, representing the weight given to the market value when calculating the inflation adjustment, and ε is the inflation adjustment parameter. This equation defines a set of rules for capital gains taxation; in particular,

$$\varepsilon = 0 \text{ in alternative } MN,$$

$$\alpha_G = 1 \text{ in alternative } MI,$$

$$\alpha_G = 0 \text{ in alternative } MI^*.$$

Systems A and M, as parametrized in (5.29) and (5.30), represent general codes for calculating taxable capital gains on an accrual basis. These parametrizations, like the corresponding ones for depreciation allowances, (5.26), and for interest deductions, (5.27) and (5.28), can be used regardless of the value of the indexation parameter ε. This does not imply, however, that the tax authorities are assumed to impose the same inflation adjustment procedure on all the components of the firm's tax base. On the contrary, the degree of indexation of the interest deductions and the capital gains will often in practice be different from the degree of indexation of the depreciation allowances. This difference may be one of the main reasons for non-neutrality of the tax system. [Cf. chapter 9.] To formalize this, two indexation parameters will be needed.

5.4 Specific tax systems

We have taken the tax function (5.23) to pieces. Let us now, by using the concepts and results in section 5.3, put its elements together in different ways to obtain distinct tax *systems.*

5.4.1 Two main categories: class A and class M

Corresponding to the categorization in section 5.3, the tax systems we shall be concerned with in the following fall into two broad categories (A and M being acronyms for 'accounting' and 'market', respectively):

Class A. Systems in which the calculation of depreciation allowances, interest deductions, capital gains, and the capital value tax are all based on the *accounting* capital as prescribed by the tax authorities.

Class M. Systems in which the calculation of interest deductions and capital gains is based on the *market* value of the capital stock, which is different from the accounting capital underlying the calculation of depreciation allowances and the capital value tax.

Class A

The tax function for this class of systems is obtained by substituting (5.25), (5.26), (5.27), and (5.29) in (5.23). This gives a tax payment flow at time

t equal to

$$(5.31) \qquad T(t) = u \left[X(t) - q(t) \int_0^\infty \mu_A(s) J(t-s) \, ds \right],$$

where

$$(5.32) \qquad \mu_A(s) = a(s) e^{(\varepsilon - \gamma)s} + \left(mi - n\varepsilon - \frac{v}{u} \right) A(s) e^{(\varepsilon - \gamma)s}.$$

As before, $A(s)$ is the weighting function for the accounting capital, $a(s) = -A'(s)$ is the corresponding relative depreciation function, and ε is the indexation parameter for the accounting capital. The other symbols are defined as in section 5.3. The parameters u, v, m, n, and ε, and the function $A(s)$ characterize uniquely this class of tax systems.

Class M

To characterize the M class of tax systems, two indexation parameters will be needed:

ε_1: statutory rate of inflation used in calculating the value of the accounting capital underlying the tax-permitted depreciation allowances and the capital value tax, and

ε_2: statutory rate of inflation implicit in the calculation of the tax deductible interest cost and the taxable capital gains.

The tax function for this rather general class is obtained by substituting (5.25) and (5.26) with $\varepsilon = \varepsilon_1$ and (5.28) and (5.30) with $\varepsilon = \varepsilon_2$ in (5.23). This gives a tax payment flow at time t equal to

$$(5.33) \qquad T(t) = u \left[X(t) - q(t) \int_0^\infty \mu_M(s) J(t-s) \, ds \right],$$

where

$$(5.34) \qquad \begin{aligned} \mu_M(s) = {} & \left[a(s) - \frac{v}{u} A(s) \right] e^{(\varepsilon_1 - \gamma)s} \\ & + [m(i - \alpha_I \varepsilon_2) - n(\gamma - \alpha_G \varepsilon_2)] G(s) \\ & - [m(1 - \alpha_I) - n(1 - \alpha_G)] \varepsilon_2 A(s) e^{(\varepsilon_2 - \gamma)s}. \end{aligned}$$

Here $G(s)$ denotes the weighting function for net capital [cf. (3.51)] — the subscript ρ being, for simplicity, omitted. The other symbols are defined as in section 5.3. By assigning different values to ε_1 and ε_2, we can formalize systems with no indexation, partial indexation, and full indexation, as will be seen below. The parameters u, v, m, n, ε_1, ε_2, α_I, and α_G, and the function $A(s)$ characterize uniquely this class of tax systems.

The functions $\mu_A(s)$ and $\mu_M(s)$ summarize — for class A and M, respectively — the effect of the previous investment decisions on the current income tax base. An increase in the *replacement* value of an investment made s years ago, $q(t)J(t-s)$, by one unit reduces the current tax base by $\mu_A(s)$ and $\mu_M(s)$ units, respectively. These functions will play a key role in much of our subsequent analysis. Equations (5.31)–(5.34) — reflecting the effect of the firm's past purchase and financing of capital on its income tax base today — clearly demonstrate the dynamic structure of the corporate tax system. The tax function is "backward looking"; the tax payment depends, in a fairly complex way, on the previous investment flow, the survival function, the accounting capital function inherent in the tax code, the interest and inflation rates, and the parameters defining the rules for calculating.interest deductions and capital gains in the income tax base.[10]

5.4.2 Five tax systems

Five distinct tax systems will be in focus in the following. The first two of these, to be denoted as systems AO and AR, belong to class A and the last three, systems MNO, MNR, and MI, belong to class M. Their basic characteristics are:[11]

System AO. Accounting capital is evaluated at original cost, and depreciation allowances, interest deductions, capital gains, and capital value tax are all based on this capital value.

---

[10] Moreover, the parametrization may also represent the effect of the firm's ownership and financial position, to the extent that these factors are reflected in m and n. [Confer subsections 5.3.2 and 5.3.3.]

[11] What should be understood by a distinct tax system in the present context is not obvious. In this study, we do not interpret the form of the weighting function $A(s)$ and the values of m and n as characteristics of a tax system, but rather as parameters of a given system. Changing, for instance, m from one to zero does not, in our terminology, give a different tax system, but only another member of the same system. A change in the definition of the indexation parameters ε, ε_1, and ε_2 or in the values of α_I and α_G will, on the other hand, be considered a change in the tax system; cf. table 5.1.

System AR. Accounting capital is evaluated at full replacement cost and depreciation allowances, interest deductions, capital gains, and capital value tax are all based on this capital value.

System MNO. Interest deductions and capital gains are calculated on a nominal basis from market values, and depreciation allowances and capital value tax are based on the accounting capital at original cost.

System MNR. Interest deductions and capital gains are calculated on a nominal basis from market values, and depreciation allowances and capital value tax are based on the accounting capital at full replacement cost.

System MI. Interest deductions and capital gains are calculated from market values, depreciation allowances and capital value tax are based on the accounting capital, and a common indexation parameter ε is applied throughout.

Tables 5.1 and 5.2 give the formal definitions of these five tax systems. Two variants of the indexed system *MI* with which we shall also be concerned, denoted as *MI1* and *MI2*, are also included. They are obtained by modifying the definition of the inflation adjusted interest cost and/or capital gains.

5.5 A compact description. The present value of income deductions per unit of investment cost

Since the functions $\mu_A(s)$ and $\mu_M(s)$ summarize the effect of a one unit investment outlay on the income deductions in future periods, they are basic elements in the characterization of the effect of the tax system on the cost of using capital services. Consider now the present value of these deduction functions. Since they are defined in terms of the replacement value of the investment, we use a real interest rate in the discounting. Letting r denote the nominal rate of discount of the firm, so that its real interest rate, measured against the investment price, is $r - \gamma$ [confer section 4.3], these present values can be written as

$$(5.42) \qquad \lambda_A = \int_0^\infty e^{-(r-\gamma)s} \mu_A(s)\, ds \,,$$

$$(5.43) \qquad \lambda_M = \int_0^\infty e^{-(r-\gamma)s} \mu_M(s)\, ds \,,$$

Table 5.1: Survey of tax systems.

Tax system	Characteristics[a]			Parameter restrictions
	Depreciation allowances, capital value tax	Interest deductions	Capital gains	
AO	AO	AO	AO	(5.32) with $\varepsilon = 0$
AR	AR	AR	AR	(5.32) with $\varepsilon = \gamma$
MNO	AO	MN	MN	(5.34) with $\varepsilon_1 = \varepsilon_2 = 0$
MNR	AR	MN	MN	(5.34) with $\varepsilon_1 = \gamma, \varepsilon_2 = 0$
MI	A[b]	MI	MI	(5.34) with $\varepsilon_1 = \varepsilon_2 = \varepsilon$, $\alpha_I = \alpha_G = 1$
MI1	A[b]	MI	MI*	(5.34) with $\varepsilon_1 = \varepsilon_2 = \varepsilon$, $\alpha_I = 1, \alpha_G = 0$
MI2	A[b]	MI*	MI*	(5.34) with $\varepsilon_1 = \varepsilon_2 = \varepsilon$, $\alpha_I = \alpha_G = 0$

[a]See subsections 5.3.1–5.3.3.
[b]Eq. (5.26).

Table 5.2: The per unit income deduction function $\mu(s)$.

Eq. no.	System	
(5.35)	AO	$\mu_{AO}(s) = a(s)e^{-\gamma s} + (mi - \frac{v}{u})A(s)e^{-\gamma s}$
(5.36)	AR	$\mu_{AR}(s) = a(s) + (mi - n\gamma - \frac{v}{u})A(s)$
(5.37)	MNO	$\mu_{MNO}(s) = a(s)e^{-\gamma s} - \frac{v}{u}A(s)e^{-\gamma s} + (mi - n\gamma)G(s)$
(5.38)	MNR	$\mu_{MNR}(s) = a(s) - \frac{v}{u}A(s) + (mi - n\gamma)G(s)$
(5.39)	MI	$\mu_{MI}(s) = \{a(s) - \frac{v}{u}A(s)\}e^{(\varepsilon-\gamma)s}$ $+ \{m(i-\varepsilon) - n(\gamma-\varepsilon)\}G(s)$
(5.40)	$MI1$	$\mu_{MI1}(s) = \{a(s) + (n\varepsilon - \frac{v}{u})A(s)\}e^{(\varepsilon-\gamma)s}$ $+ \{m(i-\varepsilon) - n\gamma\}G(s)$
(5.41)	$MI2$	$\mu_{MI2}(s) = \{a(s) - [(m-n)\varepsilon + \frac{v}{u}]A(s)\}e^{(\varepsilon-\gamma)s}$ $+ (mi - n\gamma)G(s)$

for class A and class M, respectively. These parameters play a crucial role, as summary characteristics of the tax system, in the user cost formulae, as will be shown in chapter 6.

5.5.1 Definition

Let, for an arbitrary discounting rate ρ, Y_ρ be the present value of the weighting function used in defining the net capital $K_N(t)$, i.e.

$$(5.44) \qquad Y_\rho = \int_0^\infty e^{-\rho s} G(s)\, ds\,,$$

and let correspondingly Z_ρ be the present value of the weighting function used in defining the (volume component of the) accounting capital H,[12]

$$(5.45) \qquad\qquad Z_\rho = \int_0^\infty e^{-\rho s} A(s) \, ds \,,$$

and z_ρ be the present value of the rates of depreciation allowance, i.e.

$$(5.46) \qquad\qquad z_\rho = \int_0^\infty e^{-\rho s} a(s) \, ds \,.$$

Since it is easy to show from (5.5) and (5.45), by using integration by parts, that

$$(5.47) \qquad\qquad z_\mu - 1 - \rho Z_\mu \,.$$

we find, by inserting (5.32) in (5.42) and (5.34) in (5.43), that the present values of the per unit income deduction for class A and M of tax systems can be written as

$$(5.48) \qquad
\begin{aligned}
\lambda_A &= z_{r-\varepsilon} + \left(mi - n\varepsilon - \frac{v}{u} \right) Z_{r-\varepsilon} \\
&= 1 - \left[r - mi - (1-n)\varepsilon + \frac{v}{u} \right] Z_{r-\varepsilon} \,,
\end{aligned}$$

$$(5.49) \qquad
\begin{aligned}
\lambda_M &= z_{r-\varepsilon_1} - \frac{v}{u} Z_{r-\varepsilon_1} + [m(i - \alpha_I \varepsilon_2) - n(\gamma - \alpha_G \varepsilon_2)] Y_{r-\gamma} \\
&\quad - [m(1 - \alpha_I) - n(1 - \alpha_G)]\varepsilon_2 Z_{r-\varepsilon_2} \\
&= 1 - \left[r - \varepsilon_1 + \frac{v}{u} \right] Z_{r-\varepsilon_1} + [m(i - \alpha_I \varepsilon_2) \\
&\quad - n(\gamma - \alpha_G \varepsilon_2)] Y_{r-\gamma} - [m(1 - \alpha_I) - n(1 - \alpha_G)]\varepsilon_2 Z_{r-\varepsilon_2} \,.
\end{aligned}$$

The λ parameters are linear functions of the present values Z_ρ and Y_ρ, related to the accounting capital and to the net capital, respectively, *although based on different discounting rates*. Their values for the tax systems in table 5.1 are given in table 5.3.

---

[12] Note that Y_ρ and Z_ρ have the same formal relationship to net capital K_N and accounting capital H, respectively, as $\Phi_\rho(0)$ has to gross capital K.

Table 5.3: The present value of the per unit income deductions, discounted at the firm's real interest rate.

Tax system	
AO	$\lambda_{A0} = 1 - \{r - mi + \frac{v}{u}\}Z_r$
AR	$\lambda_{AR} = 1 - \{r - mi - (1-n)\gamma + \frac{v}{u}\}Z_{r-\gamma}$
MNO	$\lambda_{MNO} = 1 - \{r + \frac{v}{u}\}Z_r + \{mi - n\gamma\}Y_{r-\gamma}$
MNR	$\lambda_{MNR} = 1 - \{r - \gamma + \frac{v}{u}\}Z_{r-\gamma} + \{mi - n\gamma\}Y_{r-\gamma}$
MI	$\lambda_{MI} = 1 - \{r - \varepsilon + \frac{v}{u}\}Z_{r-\varepsilon} + \{m(i - \varepsilon) - n(\gamma - \varepsilon)\}Y_{r-\gamma}$
$MI1$	$\lambda_{MI1} = 1 - \{r - (1+n)\varepsilon + \frac{v}{u}\}Z_{r-\varepsilon} + \{m(i - \varepsilon) - n\gamma\}Y_{r-\gamma}$
$MI2$	$\lambda_{MI2} = 1 - \{r - (1+n-m)\varepsilon + \frac{v}{u}\}Z_{r-\varepsilon} + \{mi - n\gamma\}Y_{r-\gamma}$

5.5.2 *The effect of changes in the tax parameters*

We now examine the effect of changes in the tax parameters on the present values λ_A and λ_M for given values of r, i, and γ. Consider first changes in m, n, and v.[13]

From (5.48) we find, for *class A*,

$$(5.50) \qquad \frac{\partial \lambda_A}{\partial m} = iZ_{r-\varepsilon} > 0,$$

$$(5.51) \qquad \frac{\partial \lambda_A}{\partial n} = -\varepsilon Z_{r-\varepsilon} < 0,$$

---

[13] These parameter changes may also reflect changes in the financial position of the firm, to the extent that m, n, and v depend on this position [cf. subsections 5.3.2 and 5.3.3].

$$(5.52) \qquad \frac{\partial \lambda_A}{\partial v} = -\frac{1}{u} Z_{r-\varepsilon} < 0.$$

The corresponding derivatives for *class M*, obtained from (5.49), are

$$(5.53) \qquad \frac{\partial \lambda_M}{\partial m} = iY_{r-\gamma} - \varepsilon_2\{\alpha_I Y_{r-\gamma} + (1-\alpha_I)Z_{r-\varepsilon_2}\},$$

$$(5.54) \qquad \frac{\partial \lambda_M}{\partial n} = -[\gamma Y_{r-\gamma} - \varepsilon_2\{\alpha_G Y_{r-\gamma} + (1-\alpha_G)Z_{r-\varepsilon_2}\}],$$

$$(5.55) \qquad \frac{\partial \lambda_M}{\partial v} = -\frac{1}{u} Z_{r-\varepsilon_1} < 0.$$

An increase in the rate of capital value tax, v, will, for both classes of tax systems, lead to a lower value of λ. An increase in the interest deduction parameter m and a decrease in the capital gains taxation parameter n will always (when $\varepsilon > 0$) lead to a higher value of λ for a tax system in class A, and will normally give the same result for class M.[14]

Consider next the effect of changes in the inflation adjustment parameters. Now we do not, in general, get unique sign conclusions. Such changes do not only affect the depreciation allowances, but (in general) also the tax permitted interest deductions, the accounted capital gains, and the tax base for the capital value tax. These effects have opposite signs.

Consider first *class A*. From (5.45)–(5.47) we know that $Z'_\rho = \partial Z_\rho / \partial\rho < 0$ and $z'_\rho = \partial z_\rho / \partial\rho = -Z_\rho - \rho Z'_\rho < 0$. Eq. (5.48) then gives

$$(5.56) \qquad \begin{aligned} \frac{\partial \lambda_A}{\partial \varepsilon} &= -z'_{r-\varepsilon} - \left(mi - n\varepsilon - \frac{v}{u}\right) Z'_{r-\varepsilon} - nZ_{r-\varepsilon} \\ &= (1-n)Z_{r-\varepsilon} + \left(r - mi - (1-n)\varepsilon + \frac{v}{u}\right) Z'_{r-\varepsilon}. \end{aligned}$$

---

[14] Sufficient conditions for $\partial\lambda_M/\partial m > 0$ to hold are (provided that $\gamma < r$)

$$\varepsilon_2 < i, \quad \varepsilon_2 \le \gamma, \quad G(s) \ge A(s) \quad \text{for all } s[\Rightarrow Y_{r-\gamma} \ge Z_{r-\varepsilon_2}],$$

which follow from (5.53), (5.44), and (5.45). Similarly, from (5.54), (5.44), and (5.45) it follows that

$$\varepsilon_2 \le \gamma, \quad G(s) \ge A(s) \quad \text{for all } s[\Rightarrow Y_{r-\gamma} \ge Z_{r-\varepsilon_2}]$$

are sufficient conditions for $\partial\lambda_M/\partial n \le 0$. For $\partial\lambda_M/\partial n < 0$ to hold, either $\varepsilon_2 < \gamma$ or $G(s) > A(s)$ should be satisfied as strict inequalities. Otherwise, no capital gains would be recorded, and a change in n would have no effect.

This expression can be of either sign, but it is always positive if there is no taxation of capital gains, i.e. $n = 0$, and if the "net" interest rate exceeds the ratio between the capital value tax rate and the income tax rate; formally,

$$(5.57) \qquad n = 0, \quad mi > v/u \quad \Longrightarrow \quad \partial \lambda_A / \partial \varepsilon > 0 .$$

In this case, the positive effect on λ_A of an increase in ε via increased depreciation allowances and interest deductions (reflecting the increased value of the accounting capital) exceeds the negative effect via increased capital value tax. If, at the opposite extreme, all accounted capital gains are taxable, i.e. $n = 1$, and $v/u + r - mi > 0$, then an increase in the inflation adjustment parameter will always lead to a decrease in λ_A ; formally,

$$(5.58) \qquad n = 1, \quad v/u + r - mi > 0 \quad \Longrightarrow \quad \partial \lambda_A / \partial \varepsilon < 0 .$$

In the latter case, the negative effect of an increase in ε via increased taxable capital gains and increased capital value tax dominates over the positive effect via increased depreciation allowances and increased interest deductions.

For *class M*, the situation is more complex. From (5.49) we find

$$(5.59) \qquad \frac{\partial \lambda_M}{\partial \varepsilon_1} = -z'_{r-\varepsilon_1} + \frac{v}{u} Z'_{r-\varepsilon_1} = Z_{r-\varepsilon_1} + \left(r - \varepsilon_1 + \frac{v}{u} \right) Z'_{r-\varepsilon_1} .$$

The value of this expression can be of either sign; an increase in ε_1 tends to increasing λ_M via increasing depreciation allowances and tends to decreasing λ_M via increasing capital value tax. With a zero capital value tax ($v = 0$), the effect is unambiguously positive. The effect of a change in the common indexation parameter for the interest cost and the capital gain is given by

$$(5.60) \qquad \frac{\partial \lambda_M}{\partial \varepsilon_2} = -[m\alpha_I - n\alpha_G]Y_{r-\gamma}$$
$$- [m(1 - \alpha_I) - n(1 - \alpha_G)] \left(Z_{r-\varepsilon_2} - \varepsilon_2 Z'_{r-\varepsilon_2} \right),$$

which can also be of either sign. An increase in ε_2 tends to decreasing the real interest rate defining tax permitted interest deductions ($i - \varepsilon_2$), while at the same time decreasing the real rate of increase of capital prices used in defining capital gains ($\gamma - \varepsilon_2$). We see, however, that if the expressions in the two squares brackets of (5.60) have the same sign, then the sign of the effect will be unique; formally,

$$(5.61) \quad \begin{array}{ll} m\alpha_I \geq n\alpha_G, & m(1 - \alpha_I) \geq n(1 - \alpha_G) \implies \partial\lambda_M/\partial\varepsilon_2 \leq 0, \\ m\alpha_I \leq n\alpha_G, & m(1 - \alpha_I) \leq n(1 - \alpha_G) \implies \partial\lambda_M/\partial\varepsilon_2 \geq 0, \end{array}$$

If, in particular $\alpha_I = \alpha_G$, this condition can be simplified to

$$\frac{\partial\lambda_M}{\partial\varepsilon_2} \gtreqless 0 \quad \text{according as} \quad m \lesseqgtr n \quad \text{(when } \alpha_I = \alpha_G).$$

From this we can conclude that changes in the inflation adjustment parameter ε_2 will have no effect on λ_M unless either $\alpha_I \neq \alpha_G$ or $m \neq n$.

It follows from the above results that the effect of a uniform change in the degree of indexation, i.e. $\varepsilon_1 = \varepsilon_2 = \varepsilon$, is also ambiguous as to sign in general. Combining (5.59) and (5.60) we see, however, that $v = 0$, $\alpha_I = \alpha_G$ and $m < n$ are sufficient conditions for $\partial\lambda_M/\partial\varepsilon_1 + \partial\lambda_M/\partial\varepsilon_2$ to be positive. Then the positive effect on λ_M of the increased indexation via the increased depreciation allowances and the reduced accounted capital gains will dominate over the negative effect via the reduced interest deductions in the tax base.

This is about as far as a priori reasoning can bring us. In chapter 9, numerical illustrations related to specific survival functions will be given, from which we can obtain stronger conclusions.

CHAPTER 6

THE USER COST OF CAPITAL UNDER NEO-CLASSICAL TECHNOLOGY. PART 2. TAXES INCLUDED

6.1 Introduction

In chapter 4, we defined and interpreted the user cost of capital corresponding to a neo classical description of the technology, with no taxes specified in the cash-flow function of the firm. The purpose of this chapter is to extend this analysis to include the effect of the corporate tax system, as formalized in chapter 5. Throughout this study, we take a *partial* view on the modelling of the user cost of capital, in that we do not specify the effect of the personal sector and the personal tax system in our analysis. The focus is on the firm as the *user* of capital.

The chapter is organized as follows. By extending the definition of the cash-flow to include corporate taxes, we first, in section 6.2, derive the tax corrected investment price. It plays the same role to the firm's investment decisions in the presence of taxes as does the actual investment price when taxes are disregarded. On this base, we establish, in section 6.3, the tax corrected user cost of capital, giving it both a service price interpretation and a shadow price interpretation related to the conditions for optimal capital accumulation. A comment on the relationship between the rate of discount used in the cash-flow maximization and the market interest rate follows in section 6.4. The role of the debt-capital structure of the firm in this connection is also briefly considered. Finally, two examples with parametric survival functions are discussed, partly analytically and partly by means of numerical illustrations, in section 6.5. The analysis in this chapter, as the previous chapters, is based on the assumption of time invariant interest and inflation rates. A generalization allowing for time varying rates is outlined in appendix B.

6.2 The tax corrected cash-flow and investment price

When tax payments are accounted for, the firm's net cash-flow at time t will be equal to

(6.1) $$R_T(t) = R(t) - T(t),$$

where $R(t)$ is the cash-flow before taxes, defined in (4.7), and $T(t)$ is the tax payment.[1] The latter is expressed by (5.31)–(5.32) when the tax system belongs to class A and by (5.33)–(5.34) when it belongs to class M. We then have

(6.2)
$$R_T(t) = (1-u)X(t) - q(t)\left[J(t) - u\int_0^\infty \mu(s)J(t-s)\,ds\right]$$
$$= (1-u)R(t) - uq(t)\left[J(t) - \int_0^\infty \mu(s)J(t-s)\,ds\right],$$

where $\mu(s) = \mu_A(s)$ and $\mu(s) = \mu_M(s)$ for class A and class M, respectively. The last term after the second equality sign in eq. (6.2) may be interpreted as the adjustment which must be made in the firm's after tax cash-flow to account for the fact that it pays an *income tax*[2] at the rate u rather than a *cash-flow tax*, i.e. a tax on $R(t)$, at the same rate. This adjustment is negative, zero, or positive, according as

$$J(t) \gtreqless \int_0^\infty \mu(s)J(t-s)\,ds.$$

Eq. (6.2) shows that when the firm is subject to an income tax, the time path of the net after tax cash-flow may be widely different from the time path of the pre-tax cash-flow, the difference reflecting on the one hand the past fluctuations in investment and on the other hand the form of the income deduction function $\mu(s)$.

---

[1] As in chapter 4, we exclude cash-flow effects associated with the financing of the investment, i.e. the borrowing, the interest payment, and the debt repayment. The interpretation of this simplification and some of its implications will be discussed in section 6.4.

[2] Or, more correctly, a combined income/capital value tax, cf. section 5.3.

The present value of the net after tax cash-flow, discounted at the interest rate of the owners of the firm, r, is equal to

$$W_T = \int_0^\infty e^{-rt} R_T(t)\, dt$$

$$(6.3) \quad = \int_0^\infty e^{-rt}\left[(1-u)X(t) - q(t)\left\{J(t) - u\int_0^\infty \mu(s)J(t-s)ds\right\}\right] dt$$

$$= \int_0^\infty e^{-rt}\left[(1-u)R(t) - uq(t)\left\{J(t) - \int_0^\infty \mu(s)J(t-s)ds\right\}\right] dt.$$

This can be rewritten as

$$W_T = (1-u)W - u\int_0^\infty e^{-rt}q(t)J(t)\, dt$$

$$+ u\int_0^\infty e^{-rt}q(t)\int_0^t \mu(s)J(t-s)\, ds\, dt + W_{T0},$$

where W is the present value of the cash-flow before taxes, given by (4.8), and

$$(6.4) \qquad W_{T0} = u\int_0^\infty e^{-rt}q(t)\int_t^\infty \mu(s)J(t-s)\, ds\, dt$$

represents the part of the present value of the income deduction for capital expenditures in the tax base which is due to investment decisions made before $t = 0$, and hence is predetermined in relation to the investment plans. Using the transformation $\theta = t - s$, $\tau = s$, while recalling the price expectation process (5.24), we can write the double integral in the expression for W_T as

$$u\int_0^\infty e^{-rt}q(t)\int_0^t \mu(s)J(t-s)\, ds\, dt$$

$$= u\int_0^\infty\int_0^\infty e^{-r(\theta+\tau)}q(\theta)e^{\gamma\tau}\mu(\tau)J(\theta)\, d\tau\, d\theta = u\lambda\int_0^\infty e^{-r\theta}q(\theta)J(\theta)\, d\theta,$$

where

$$(6.5) \qquad\qquad \lambda = \int_0^\infty e^{-(r-\gamma)\tau}\mu(\tau)\, d\tau.$$

This shows that we can express the present value the net after tax cash-flow W_T in terms of the present value of the net before tax cash-flow W, the predetermined component W_{T0}, the parameter λ, and the time path of the investment value $q(t)J(t)$ as

$$(6.6) \qquad W_T = (1 - u)W - u(1 - \lambda) \int_0^\infty e^{-rt} q(t) J(t) \, dt + W_{T0}.$$

The parameter λ is equal to λ_A, as defined in (5.42), and equal to λ_M, as defined in (5.43), for class A and class M of tax systems, respectively. This parameter was discussed at some length in section 5.5, where we interpreted it as the present value of the flow of future deductions in the income tax base allowed per unit of investment outlay, when measuring investment outlay at its *replacement* value and discounting the deductions at the *real* interest rate $r - \gamma$. We could, however, equivalently have interpreted λ as the present value of the income deductions allowed per unit of investment outlay at *historic value*, discounted at the *nominal* interest rate r. This equivalence follows straightly from the identities

$$\mu(s)q(t)J(t - s) \equiv e^{\gamma s}\mu(s)q(t - s)J(t - s),$$

and

$$\lambda = \int_0^\infty e^{-(r-\gamma)s}\mu(s)\,ds \equiv \int_0^\infty e^{-rs}[e^{\gamma s}\mu(s)]\,ds,$$

with $\mu(s)$ and $e^{\gamma s}\mu(s)$ representing the deductions defined in terms of the replacement cost and in terms of the historic cost of the investment, respectively.

Eq. (6.6) implies that for any tax rate between zero and unity the following inequality holds between the present values of the before tax and the after tax cash-flows

$$W_T - W_{T0} \gtreqless (1 - u)W \qquad \text{according as } \lambda \gtreqless 1.$$

Define now the tax corrected investment price at time t as

$$(6.7) \qquad\qquad q^*(t) = q(t)\frac{1 - \lambda u}{1 - u}.$$

It is larger than, equal to, or smaller than the market price according as $\lambda \gtreqless 1$. The factor $(1 - \lambda u)/(1 - u)$ will be denoted as the *fiscal factor*, or the *tax factor*, in the following. Let $R^*(t)$ be the firm's net cash-flow before tax, if it, instead of calculating investment outlay at the market price, had used the tax corrected price, i.e. $R^*(t) = X(t) - q^*(t)J(t)$, and let W^* be the corresponding present value of the (pre-tax) cash-flow. From (6.6) and (6.7) we obtain the following equivalent ways of writing $W_T - W_{T0}$

$$W_T - W_{T0} = (1-u)W^*$$

(6.8)
$$= (1-u) \int_0^\infty e^{-rt} R^*(t)\, dt$$

$$= (1-u) \int_0^\infty e^{-rt} [X(t) - q^*(t)J(t)]\, dt\,.$$

A generalization of (6.7) is derived in appendix B. From eqs. (6.6) and (6.8) we can state

Proposition 6.A

1. For a given tax rate u, all tax systems which are characterized by the same value of λ are equivalent, in the sense that they imply the same present value of the net after tax cash-flow.
2. An income tax at the (constant) rate u is equivalent[3] to the following modified cash-flow tax: Impose a tax at the rate u on the present value of the firm's net cash-flow after replacing the market investment price $q(t)$ by the tax corrected price $q^*(t) = q(t)(1-\lambda u)/(1-u)$. Assuming perfect financial markets, this is again equivalent to imposing such a tax on all the components of the cash-flow.

We see that all information required, in addition to the tax rate, to describe the effect of the tax system on the present value of the net after tax cash-flow and on the effective investment price is summarized in the parameter λ.

6.3   The tax corrected user cost of capital. General expression

It is reasonable, in view of proposition 6.A and the user cost definition for the zero tax case, given in chapter 4, to interpret the ratio between the tax corrected investment price and the flow of services per capital unit over its service life, discounted at the real interest rate $\rho = r - \gamma$, as the firm's

---

[3] Strictly, equivalent in terms of the present value $W_T - W_{T0}$.

tax corrected user cost of capital. The tax corrected user cost of capital at time t, according to this *service price interpretation*, can be expressed as

$$(6.9) \qquad c(t) = \frac{q^*(t)}{\Phi_{r-\gamma}(0)} = \frac{q(t)}{\int_0^\infty e^{-(r-\gamma)s} B(s) \, ds} \cdot \frac{1 - \lambda u}{1 - u} .$$

This formula generalizes (4.1). Assuming, as before, a constant (expected) rate of increase of the investment price, γ [cf. (5.24)], so that $c(t)$ and $q^*(t)$ will also grow at this rate [cf. (4.2)], it is seen that (6.9) is equivalent to

$$(6.10) \qquad q(t) \frac{1 - \lambda u}{1 - u} = \int_0^\infty e^{-rs} c(t + s) B(s) \, ds .$$

This equation, which generalizes (4.3), says that the tax corrected purchase cost of a unit of capital invested is equal to the present value of its future user costs when allowance is made for retirement of capital and decline in its efficiency with age. An alternative interpretation of this relationship is that the cost of acquisition of a capital asset net of the present value of the future income tax deductions at time t, i.e. $q(t)(1 - \lambda u)$, is equal to the present value of the flow of future user costs, when allowing for retirement and decline in efficiency, net of the income tax, i.e. $c(t+s)(1-u)$ [cf. Jorgenson and Sullivan (1981, p. 176)].

The *shadow price interpretation* is based on the conditions for maximization of the tax corrected net cash-flow, W_T, subject to the restricted profit function (4.6).[4] Since, however, W_{T0} is predetermined in relation to the firm's investment plans and $q^*(t)$ can be treated as exogenous — because u and λ, by assumption, are unaffected by its investment decisions — this is equivalent to maximization of $W_T - W_{T0}$, as given in (6.8), subject to (3.3) and (4.6). But this maximization problem is similar to that considered in section 4.3 (when disregarding the constant $1 - u$) and we can write down its first order conditions directly by replacing $q(t)$ by $q^*(t)$ in (4.11). This gives

$$(6.11) \qquad \int_0^\infty e^{-rs} F'[K(t + s)] B(s) \, ds = \int_t^\infty e^{-r(\theta - t)} F'[K(\theta)] B(\theta - t) \, d\theta$$
$$= q(t) \frac{1 - \lambda u}{1 - u} .$$

---

[4] Since all costs of other inputs than capital are assumed to be completely and immediately deductible in the income tax base, the form of the restricted profit function F will be independent of the tax rate u and of the form of the tax system

This optimizing condition says that the total present value of a marginal pre-tax profit flow resulting from a one unit increase in the capital at time t shall be equal to the tax corrected investment price. Equivalently, the total present value of a marginal after tax profit flow induced by a one unit increase in capital at time t, i.e. $F'[K(\theta)]B(\theta - t)(1 - u)$, shall be equal to the investment price net of the income tax deductions, $q(t)(1 - \lambda u)$. Interpreting the user cost of capital as the shadow price of capital services, by setting $c(t + s) = F'[K(t + s)]$ for all $s \geq 0$, we see that (6.11) is equivalent to (6.10). They give the same implicit definition of the user cost, and it can be written in explicit form as (6.9).

Our conclusion, then, is that when the investment price is expected to grow at a constant rate, there is an equivalence between the service price interpretation of the user cost and the shadow price interpretation, regardless of the value of the tax rate and the form of the tax system. To go from the zero tax situation to a situation with taxes we only have to multiply the investment price, and the user cost, by the fiscal factor $f = (1 - \lambda u)/(1 - u)$.

6.4   A remark on the discounting rate. Financial constraints

In our analysis of the user cost of capital so far, two interest concepts have been involved: i, defined as the interest rate (cost of finance) relevant to the specification of the interest deduction component in the firm's income tax base [cf. subsection 5.3.2] and r, defined as the nominal interest rate used by the owners of the firm in discounting future net cash-flow W_T [cf. (6.3)]. Obviously, these two interest variables are related in some way, but how should this relationship be specified, and in particular, how does it depend on the tax system and on the financing of the investment?

Different answers to this question have been given in the literature. In their influential articles, Hall and Jorgenson (1967, 1971) set the discounting rate equal to the market interest rate *net of the corporate tax*, i.e. $r = i(1 - u)$ (with our symbols), while excluding the interest deduction component from the tax base and the cash-flow function.[5] In our framework, this would imply $\mu(s)$ and λ to be defined exclusive of the interest deduction component, while using the after tax real interest rate of the firm, i.e., with a nominal tax system $r = i(1 - u) - v - \gamma$, as the discounting rate in defining λ and Φ [cf. (6.5) and (6.9)].

---

[5] This formulation has also been adopted in later work by Jorgenson, see Jorgenson and Sullivan (1981), and by Bradford and Fullerton (1981).

This, however, would be an asymmetric specification of the tax function.

Boadway and Bruce (1979, pp. 98–103) have criticized this approach. They argue that the discounting rate should not be corrected for the corporate income tax. Possibly it should be corrected for the (marginal) tax rate in the personal sector. On the other hand, the tax function should be specified symmetrically with respect to depreciation allowances, interest deductions, and capital gains. Constraints must be imposed on borrowing to prevent the firm from issuing an infinite debt and exploiting the possibility of arbitrage which exists between the corporate and the personal sectors when they face different income tax rates.[6] In our framework, the need for borrowing constraints can be shown formally as follows: Let $M(t)$ be the debt outstanding at time t, and extend the definition of the net cash-flow to include the borrowing and the interest payment flow. Assuming that all debt interests are deductible, after indexation at the rate ε, the part of the cash-flow which is associated with borrowing, interest payment, and interest deduction in the tax base at time t is

$$\dot{M}(t) - [i - u(i - \varepsilon)]M(t),$$

whose present value over $(0, \infty)$, discounted at the owners' interest rate r is

$$[r - i + u(i - \varepsilon)] \int_0^\infty e^{-rt} M(t)\, dt - M(0),$$

provided $\lim_{t \to \infty} e^{-rt} M(t) = 0$. This present value may be made arbitrarily large by increasing $M(t)$ if $r > i - u(i - \varepsilon)$, or by decreasing $M(t)$ if $r < i - u(i - \varepsilon)$. If $r = i - u(i - \varepsilon)$, changes in $M(t)$, $t > 0$, will not affect this present value.

King and Fullerton, like Hall and Jorgenson, exclude debt interest deductions from the tax and cash-flow functions, and "compensate" for this by "tax correcting" the discounting rate. Since they consider different sources of finance of the investment, their tax corrected discounting rates are defined conditional on the source of finance under consideration. For

---

[6] Confer, in particular, the following statement: "Since the value of the firm should be maximized to its owners, and in view of the borrowing and lending at the firm's interest rate ... it is appropriate to discount receipts and outlays of the firm at the consumption rate of interest ..., net of personal tax rates (if any)". (Boadway and Bruce (1979, pp. 99).) See also Boadway (1978, 1980), Bergström and Södersten (1982), Boadway, Bruce, and Mintz (1983), King (1975), and Koskenkylä (1985, chapter II).

debt finance, the tax corrected discounting rate depends on the corporate income tax rate solely. In case of financing by new share issues or by retained earnings, their tax correction depends on the tax rates both in the corporate and the personal sector, as well as on the tax treatment of dividends paid and received and the taxation of capital gains on the part of the shareholders [cf. King and Fullerton (1984, pp. 21–22)].[7]

The present study takes a *partial* view on the modelling of the user cost of capital, and its focus is on the firm as the *user* of capital. For this reason we simplify our analysis in two ways. First, we do not represent the personal sector and the personal tax system in our model. Second, we follow Boadway and Bruce by (i) treating the financing as predetermined in relation to the investment decisions and (ii) setting the rate of discount equal to the pre-tax interest rate of the firm, i.e.

$$(6.12) \qquad\qquad r = i \, .$$

This equality is assumed to hold regardless of the value of u, m, and n, and the other tax parameters. Accordingly, we let the real interest rate used in defining the present values λ and Φ be

$$(6.13) \qquad\qquad \rho = i - \gamma \, .$$

An integrated analysis of the firm's financial decisions and its real investment decisions would in many ways have been more satisfactory. This would imply a simultaneous treatment of the user cost of capital and the financial decisions of the investor. We observe that most firms in practice choose a mixed debt and equity financing of their investment and that payment of debt interests and dividends occur simultaneously. Such a financial behaviour cannot be explained in a neo-classical model with linear budget constraints in the financial markets and full certainty. In this model, a rational firm would, because of the tax discrimination between different sources of finance, choose either a 100 per cent debt financing or a 100 per cent equity financing, depending on the relative tax rates, i.e. a corner solution. A mixed financing, as is assumed here, can, however, be explained if non-linearities in the budget constraints, e.g. absolute borrowing constraints or a positive relationship between the interest rate and the debt/equity ratio is allowed for [cf. Boadway and Bruce (1979), Boadway, Bruce and Mintz (1983), and Steigum (1983)]. Diversified financing

---

[7] See also Stiglitz (1973), Atkinson and Stiglitz (1980, section 5.3), and Auerbach (1983a, sections IV and V.B).

may also be a rational behaviour if uncertainty and risk aversion are taken into account or if differences in marginal tax rates among shareholders, reflecting the progressivity of the personal income taxation, are incorporated [cf. Feldstein and Green (1983)]. Asymmetric information between the firm and its creditors is an additional argument [cf. Stiglitz and Weiss (1981)]. Such extensions, however, would substantially complicate the analysis, in particular with regard to empirical tractability.

How will the inclusion of an exogenously imposed financial behaviour now affect the firm's net cash-flow and optimizing behaviour? Consider the same example as before, but assume that there is a constant ratio m between the firm's debt and the market value of its capital stock, i.e.

$$M(t) = mV(t), \qquad \text{for all } t,$$

where m may be fixed by the owners of the firm or by its creditors. The part of the cash-flow which is associated with the borrowing, interest payment, and interest deduction in the tax base at time t now is

$$m\dot{V}(t) - m[i - u(i - \varepsilon)]V(t),$$

whose present value, subject to (6.12), is

$$mu(i - \varepsilon) \int_0^\infty e^{-it}V(t)\, dt - mV(0),$$

provided $\lim_{t \to \infty} e^{-it}V(t) = 0$. The first term in this expression cannot be changed freely since it is restricted by [cf. section 3.5]

$$V(t) = q(t) \int_0^\infty G(s)J(t - s)\, ds.$$

Its effect will be represented by the interest deduction component in the tax function, i.e. it will be reflected in the form of $\mu(s)$. The only consequence of extending the cash-flow definition to include borrowing and interest payments under the financial constraint and the interest structure (6.12), would then be to deduct the initial debt, $M(0) = mV(0)$, from the present value of the cash-flow as previously defined. This, of course, does not alter the conditions for its maximization with respect to $J(t)$ and the implied user cost definition.

By inserting (6.12), (5.48), and (5.49) in (6.9), it follows that the user cost of capital corresponding to a tax system in class A and class M can be expressed as

$$(6.14) \qquad c_A(t) = \frac{q(t)}{\Phi_{i-\gamma}(0)} \cdot \frac{1 - \lambda_A u}{1 - u},$$

and

$$(6.15) \qquad c_M(t) = \frac{q(t)}{\Phi_{i-\gamma}(0)} \cdot \frac{1 - \lambda_M u}{1 - u},$$

respectively, where the income deduction parameters λ_A and λ_M are given by

$$(6.16) \qquad \lambda_A = 1 - \left[(1 - m)i - (1 - n)\varepsilon + \frac{v}{u}\right] Z_{i-\varepsilon},$$

$$(6.17) \qquad \lambda_M = 1 - \left[i - \varepsilon_1 + \frac{v}{u}\right] Z_{i-\varepsilon_1}$$

$$+ [m(i - \alpha_I \varepsilon_2) - n(\gamma - \alpha_G \varepsilon_2)]Y_{i-\gamma}$$

$$- [m(1 - \alpha_I) - n(1 - \alpha_G)]\varepsilon_2 Z_{i-\varepsilon_2}.$$

6.5 Examples and numerical illustrations

In this section, we illustrate the results above be means of two examples with parametric survival functions for the gross capital and corresponding weighting functions for the net capital and the accounting capital. The examples correspond to those considered in sections 3.6 and 4.4.

6.5.1 Exponentially declining survival function, depreciation allowances based on the declining balance schedule

Assume, as in subsections 3.6.1 and 4.4.1, that the survival function declines exponentially, i.e.

$$(6.18) \qquad B(s) = e^{-\delta s}, \qquad s \geq 0,$$

where δ is a positive constant. Since this parametrization implies $G(s) = e^{-\delta s}$ [cf. (3.67)], it follows from (3.65) and (5.44) that the common present value of the survival functions for gross and net capital equals

$$(6.19) \qquad \Phi_{i-\gamma}(0) = Y_{i-\gamma} = \frac{1}{i + \delta - \gamma} \, .$$

The declining balance depreciation allowance schedule, expressed in continuous time, implies a weighting function for the accounting capital of the form

$$(6.20) \qquad A(s) = e^{-\alpha s}, \qquad s \geq 0,$$

where α is a positive constant. From (5.5), (5.10), and (5.45) it follows that the relative depreciation function of the accounting capital and the age specific rates of depreciation allowances are, respectively

$$(6.21) \qquad a(s) = \alpha e^{-\alpha s}, \qquad s \geq 0,$$

$$(6.22) \qquad a^*(s) = \alpha, \qquad s \geq 0,$$

and that

$$(6.23) \qquad Z_{i-\varepsilon} = \frac{1}{i + \alpha - \varepsilon} \, .$$

By inserting (6.16), (6.19), and (6.23) in (6.14), we find that the user cost of capital for a tax system in *class A* can be written as

$$(6.24) \qquad c_A(t) = q(t)(i + \delta - \gamma)f_A \, ,$$

where the fiscal factor is given by

$$(6.25) \qquad \begin{aligned} f_A &= \frac{1 - \lambda_A u}{1 - u} \\ &= 1 + \frac{u[(1 - m)i - (1 - n)\varepsilon] + v}{(1 - u)(i + \alpha - \varepsilon)} \, . \end{aligned}$$

This factor is a decreasing function of the interest deduction parameter m and the depreciation allowance parameter α, and is an increasing function of the capital gains taxation parameter n and the capital value tax rate v, provided $i + \alpha - \varepsilon > 0$. If $(1 - m)i > (1 - n)\varepsilon$, it will always be an increasing function of the income tax rate u. Its direction of change when the inflation adjustment parameter ε is changed is ambiguous,[8] unless $m = n = 1$ and $v = 0$, in which case $f_A = 1$ holds regardless of the values of u, α, and ε.

The user cost for a tax system in *class M* with $\alpha_I = \alpha_G = 1$, obtained in a similar way by inserting (6.17), (6.19), and (6.23) in (6.15), is

$$(6.26) \qquad c_M(t) = q(t)(i + \delta - \gamma)f_M ,$$

where the fiscal factor is now given by

$$(6.27) \qquad \begin{aligned} f_M &= \frac{1 - \lambda_M u}{1 - u} \\ &= 1 + \frac{u}{1-u}\left[\frac{i - \varepsilon_1 + u/v}{i + \alpha - \varepsilon_1} - \frac{m(i - \varepsilon_2) - n(\gamma - \varepsilon_2)}{i + \delta - \gamma}\right]. \end{aligned}$$

This factor is monotonically decreasing in m (provided $i > \varepsilon_2$) and α, and is monotonically increasing in n (provided $\gamma > \varepsilon_2$) and v. The effect of changing the income tax rate u or the inflation adjustment parameters ε_1 and ε_2 will be ambiguous as to sign. If, however, $m = n = 1$, $\varepsilon_1 = \gamma$, $\alpha = \delta$, and $v = 0$, then $f_M = 1$ holds regardless of the values of u and ε_2. In this case, the income tax rate and the inflation adjustment parameter for interest deductions and capital gains will have no effect on the user cost. We shall elaborate this result further in chapter 9.

6.5.2 Simultaneous retirement. Linear depreciation allowances

Consider now the case where all capital units retain their full efficiency during N periods and then disappear completely, i.e.

$$(6.28) \qquad B(s) = \begin{cases} 1 & \text{for } 0 \le s \le N, \\ 0 & \text{for } s > N, \end{cases}$$

which we also considered in subsections 3.6.2 and 4.4.2. It follows from (3.73) and (3.75) that

$$(6.29) \qquad \Phi_{i-\gamma}(0) = H_{i-\gamma}(N)$$

and

---

[8] Confer (5.56) and (5.57).

$$(6.30) \qquad G(s) = \frac{H_{i-\gamma}(N-s)}{H_{i-\gamma}(N)} \xrightarrow[\gamma \to i]{} 1 - \frac{s}{N}, \qquad 0 \le s \le N,$$

where, as before, $H_a(M) = (1 - e^{-aM})/a$ denotes the present value of a constant annuity of 1 discounted over M years at the rate a. Inserting (6.30) in (5.44), we obtain

$$(6.31) \quad Y_{i-\gamma} = \int_0^N e^{-(i-\gamma)s} \frac{H_{i-\gamma}(N-s)}{H_{i-\gamma}(N)} \, ds = \frac{1}{i-\gamma} \left[1 - \frac{N e^{-(i-\gamma)N}}{H_{i-\gamma}(N)} \right].$$

This is the *exact* formula for the present value of the weighting function for net capital when gross capital follows a simultaneous retirement pattern. An *approximate* formula is obtained by replacing $H_{i-\gamma}(N-s)/H_{i-\gamma}(N)$ by its limiting value based on a zero real interest rate, given by (6.30). This gives[9]

$$(6.32) \qquad Y_{i-\gamma} = \int_0^N e^{-(i-\gamma)s} \left(1 - \frac{s}{N}\right) ds = \frac{1}{i-\gamma} \left[1 - \frac{H_{i-\gamma}(N)}{N} \right].$$

It is convenient in this case to use the approximate formula $G(s) = 1 - s/N$ (based on a zero discounting rate) since it is similar to the linear weighting function that we apply for the accounting capital, i.e.

$$(6.33) \qquad\qquad A(s) = 1 - \frac{s}{T}, \qquad 0 \le s \le T,$$

where T is the maximal life time of the capital as prescribed in the tax code. Using (5.5) and (5.10) we get

$$(6.34) \qquad\qquad a(s) = \frac{1}{T}, \qquad 0 \le s \le T,$$

$$(6.35) \qquad\qquad a^*(s) = \frac{1}{T-s}, \qquad 0 \le s < T.$$

Inserting (6.33) in (5.45), we obtain

$$(6.36) \qquad\qquad Z_{i-\varepsilon} = \frac{1}{i-\varepsilon} \left[1 - \frac{H_{i-\varepsilon}(T)}{T} \right],$$

----

[9] If, for instance, $i - \gamma = 0.01$ and $N = 20$, the value of $Y_{i-\gamma}$ calculated from the exact formula is 9.667 whereas that obtained from the approximate formula is 9.365. It is easy to show, by using l'Hôpital's rule, that (6.31) and (6.32) give the same limiting value for $Y_{i-\gamma}$, $N/2$, when $\gamma \to i$.

which is similar to (6.32).

From (6.14), (6.16), (6.29), and (6.36) it follows that the formula for the user cost of capital for a tax system belonging to *class A* becomes

$$(6.37) \qquad c_A(t) = \frac{q(t)}{H_{i-\gamma}(N)} f_A \,,$$

where the fiscal factor is given by

$$(6.38) \qquad f_A = 1 + \frac{u[(1-m)i - (1-n)\varepsilon] + v}{(1-u)(i-\varepsilon)} \left[1 - \frac{H_{i-\varepsilon}(T)}{T} \right].$$

This factor will be an increasing function of the tax-permitted life time T whenever $i > \varepsilon$ and $(1-m)i - (1-n)\varepsilon + v/u > 0$, i.e. an increase in T will lead to an increase in the user cost. If, however, $m = n = 1$ and $v = 0$, the values of u, T, and ε have no effect on the user cost, since then $f_A = 1$ always. On the whole, we get the same sign conclusions as in the declining balance case discussed in the first example. An *increase* in the tax permitted service life T has, by and large, the same *qualitative* implications as a *decrease* in the declining balance depreciation parameter α. But, as a comparison of (6.25) and (6.38) makes clear, there is no simple way of translating a given value of α into a corresponding value of T, and vice versa.

Similar results holds for *class M*. Inserting (6.17), (6.29), (6.32), and (6.36) in (6.15), while letting $\alpha_I = \alpha_G = 1$, yields

$$(6.39) \qquad c_M(t) = \frac{q(t)}{H_{i-\gamma}(N)} f_M \,,$$

where

$$(6.40) \qquad \begin{aligned} f_M = 1 &+ \frac{u(i-\varepsilon_1) + v}{(1-u)(i-\varepsilon_1)} \left[1 - \frac{H_{i-\varepsilon_1}(T)}{T} \right] \\ &- \frac{u[m(i-\varepsilon_2) - n(\gamma-\varepsilon_2)]}{(1-u)(i-\gamma)} \left[1 - \frac{H_{i-\gamma}(N)}{N} \right]. \end{aligned}$$

Again, we find that an increase in T will lead to an increase in the fiscal factor whenever $i > \varepsilon_1$. If $m = n = 1$, $\varepsilon_1 = \gamma$, $T = N$, and $v = 0$, then the second and third term of (6.40) cancel against each other, and we obtain $f_M = 1$ regardless of the values of u and ε_2.

In order to get a better understanding on the user cost formula for class M, (6.39), which is a highly nonlinear expression, numerical illustrations are given. Table 6.1 shows, for values of the technical life time N equal to 6, 20, and 50 years, the variation of the user cost of capital with the interest rate i, the interest deduction parameter m, and the capital gains taxation parameter n[10] for the nominal tax system with no indexation of the tax base (MNO: $\varepsilon_1 = \varepsilon_2 = 0$), and the system with indexation of the depreciation allowances (MNR: $\varepsilon_1 = \gamma, \varepsilon_2 = 0$). The rate of increase of the investment price is set to $\gamma = 10$ per cent p.a.,[11] the income tax rate is set to 50.8 per cent, which is the actual tax rate for joint stock companies in Norway, and the capital value tax rate is set to zero. Correspondingly, the variation of the user cost with the inflation rate for a given nominal interest rate, $i = 10$ per cent p.a., is shown in table 6.2.

Tables 6.3 and 6.4 give similar illustrations for a tax system with joint indexation of the depreciation allowances, interest deductions, and capital gains (specifically system $MI1$), with the indexation parameter ε set to 0, 50, 100, and 150 per cent of the rate of increase of the investment price.

We can make the following observations from the four tables:

1. On the whole, the user cost of capital for the nominal tax systems (tables 6.1 and 6.2) is quite sensitive to changes in the interest deduction parameter m and the capital gains taxation parameter n. The effect of changes in m is larger the higher is the interest rate i, and the effect of changes in n is larger the higher is the rate of inflation γ. The user cost is relatively more sensitive to such parameter changes for long-lived than for short-lived capital goods.

2. The reduction in the user cost obtained by allowing depreciation to be based on replacement cost (MNR) instead of on original cost (MNO) is independent of the value of the tax parameters m and n, but it depends essentially on the tax permitted life time T, the interest rate, and the rate of inflation. The relative reduction in the user cost is independent of the technical life time.[12]

3. A tax reform replacing a system with depreciation allowances based on original cost and no taxation of capital gains (i.e. MNO, $n = 0$) by

---

[10] Results are reported for $(m, n) = (0, 0)$, $(0, 1)$, $(1, 0)$, and $(1, 1)$ only. Since the user cost function is linear in these two parameters, linear interpolation will give its value for other constellations.

[11] The interest and inflation rates are given as annual rates. These rates are "translated" into the continuous rates assumed in (6.39) and (6.40) by replacing the continuous annuity factor $H_a(M) = (1 - e^{-aM})/a$ by its discrete time counterpart $[1 - (1 + a)^{-M}]/a$.

[12] This follows from the fact that $\partial f_M/\partial \varepsilon_1$ is independent of N (but it depends on T), cf. (6.40).

a system with indexation of depreciation allowances and full taxation of accrued capital gains (i.e. *MNR, n* = 1) will always, with positive inflation, lead to an increase in the user cost. This means that the advantage obtained by a lack of taxation of the capital gains will dominate over the disadvantage caused by a lack of indexation of the depreciation allowances.

4. There is also a trade-off between the tax permitted life time and the degree of indexation of the depreciation allowances. Consider a tax reform such that the tax permitted life time is made twice as long while allowing full instead of no indexation of the depreciation allowances. If the rate of inflation is more than 50 per cent of the interest rate, i.e. if $\gamma > i/2$ (so that the real interest rate is less than half of the nominal rate), then the firm will benefit from such a tax reform, since it implies that the present value of the depreciation allowances will increase. Mathematically, this follows from the fact that[13]

$$\int_0^T e^{-(i-\gamma)s} \frac{1}{T}\, ds > \int_0^{T/2} e^{-is} \frac{2}{T}\, ds \qquad \text{when } \gamma > i/2 .$$

This inequality is satisfied for all parameter combinations in table 6.1 and for those in table 6.2 with an inflation rate exceeding 5 per cent.[14]

5. If the rate of inflation exceeds the interest rate, a reduction in the tax permitted life time will bring an increase in the user cost for a system in which the depreciation allowances are based on replacement cost (*MNR*). The present value of the depreciation allowances will then be a decreasing function of the life time T.

6. Full or partial indexation of the tax base will not invariably give a reduction in the user cost when compared with a fully nominal system (tables 6.3 and 6.4). The impact of an increased degree of indexation is more pronounced for long-lived than for short-lived assets. A reduction in the tax permitted life time will not always be favourable to the firm.

---

[13] This is an example of the following general result: If T and ε_1 are changed from (T^*, ε_1^*) to $(T^{**}, \varepsilon_1^{**})$, the present value of the depreciation allowances will increase/remain constant/decrease according as

$$T^{**}(i - \varepsilon_1^{**}) \overset{<}{\underset{>}{=}} T^*(i - \varepsilon_1^*) .$$

[14] The break-even point for the inflation rate in the two tables is *approximately* 5 per cent, since γ and i are given as annual rates. Confer footnote 11.

Such an "adverse" effect of a decrease in T may occur even if the real interest rate is positive, since this decrease will imply a decrease in the value of the accounting capital and hence an increase in the accounted inflation adjusted capital gains [cf. (5.25) and (5.30)]. If this effect dominates over the increase in the depreciation allowances caused by the decrease in T, the net result will be an increase in the user cost.

Table 6.1: User cost of capital as a function of nominal interest rate, per cent of investment price.

A. No taxation of capital gains: $n = 0$

Interest rate, %	$N = 6,\ T = 6$				$N = 6,\ T = 3$			
	$m = 0$		$m = 1$		$m = 0$		$m = 1$	
	MNO	MNR	MNO	MNR	MNO	MNR	MNO	MNR
5	16.08	10.99	13.20	8.11	15.20	12.31	12.31	9.43
6	17.10	12.09	13.61	8.59	16.03	13.14	12.54	9.65
7	18.14	13.20	14.03	9.09	16.90	13.99	12.79	9.88
8	19.20	14.34	14.46	9.60	17.78	14.86	13.04	10.12
9	20.28	15.49	14.91	10.12	18.68	15.75	13.31	10.38
10	21.38	16.67	16.22	11.50	19.61	16.67	14.45	11.50
11	22.51	17.87	15.81	11.16	20.56	17.61	13.86	10.91
12	23.66	19.08	16.30	11.73	21.53	18.57	14.18	11.22
13	24.82	20.31	16.80	12.29	22.52	19.55	14.49	11.52
14	26.01	21.56	17.30	12.86	23.53	20.55	14.82	11.84
15	27.21	22.84	17.81	13.43	24.56	21.58	15.16	12.18

Interest rate, %	$N = 20,\ T = 20$				$N = 20,\ T = 10$			
	$m = 0$		$m = 1$		$m = 0$		$m = 1$	
	MNO	MNR	MNO	MNR	MNO	MNR	MNO	MNR
5	3.88	0.52	1.60	-1.76	3.45	1.81	1.17	-0.47
6	4.56	1.28	1.73	-1.56	4.03	2.32	1.20	-0.52
7	5.31	2.11	1.88	-1.33	4.67	2.89	1.24	-0.54
8	6.13	3.00	2.07	-1.06	5.38	3.52	1.32	-0.54
9	7.01	3.97	2.29	-0.76	6.15	4.23	1.43	-0.50
10	7.96	5.00	2.80	-0.16	6.99	5.00	1.83	-0.16
11	8.99	6.10	2.83	-0.06	7.89	5.85	1.74	-0.31
12	10.07	7.27	3.16	0.36	8.86	6.76	1.95	-0.15
13	11.22	8.50	3.52	0.80	9.90	7.74	2.19	0.04
14	12.44	9.79	3.92	1.27	10.99	8.79	2.47	0.27
15	13.72	11.15	4.35	1.78	12.15	9.91	2.78	0.54

Interest rate, %	$N = 50,\ T = 50$				$N = 50,\ T = 25$			
	$m = 0$		$m = 1$		$m = 0$		$m = 1$	
	MNO	MNR	MNO	MNR	MNO	MNR	MNO	MNR
5	0.69	-1.22	-0.94	-2.85	0.60	-0.05	-1.03	-1.68
6	1.02	-0.85	-1.15	-3.02	0.90	0.12	-1.27	-2.05
7	1.46	-0.36	-1.34	-3.17	1.30	0.39	-1.50	-2.42
8	2.04	0.26	-1.49	-3.27	1.82	0.77	-1.71	-2.76
9	2.77	1.05	-1.59	-3.30	2.49	1.31	-1.86	-3.05
10	3.66	2.00	-1.51	-3.16	3.32	2.00	-1.85	-3.16
11	4.71	3.12	-1.55	-3.14	4.30	2.87	-1.97	-3.40
12	5.92	4.40	-1.40	-2.92	5.44	3.90	-1.89	-3.42
13	7.28	5.83	-1.16	-2.61	6.72	5.10	-1.72	-3.34
14	8.78	7.40	-0.82	-2.20	8.14	6.46	-1.45	-3.14
15	10.38	9.07	-0.39	-1.70	9.67	7.95	-1.10	-2.83

Inflation rate: $\gamma = 10\%$ p.a. Tax system: Nominal: $MNO : \varepsilon_1 = \varepsilon_2 = 0$. $MNR : \varepsilon_1 = \gamma, \varepsilon_2 = 0$. Survival function: Simultaneous retirement after N years. Depreciation allowance schedule: Linear over T years. Income tax rate: $u = 0.508$. Capital value tax rate: $v = 0$.

Table 6.1: (cont.) User cost of capital as a function of nominal interest rate, per cent of investment price.

B. Full taxation of capital gains: $n = 1$.

Interest rate, %	$N = 6, T = 6$				$N = 6, T = 3$			
	$m = 0$		$m = 1$		$m = 0$		$m = 1$	
	MNO	MNR	MNO	MNR	MNO	MNR	MNO	MNR
5	21.85	16.76	18.96	13.87	20.96	18.08	18.08	15.20
6	22.92	17.90	19.43	14.41	21.85	18.96	18.36	15.47
7	24.01	19.07	19.90	14.96	22.77	19.86	18.66	15.75
8	25.12	20.26	20.38	15.52	23.70	20.78	18.96	16.04
9	26.25	21.46	20.88	16.09	24.65	21.72	19.28	16.35
10	26.55	21.83	21.38	16.67	24.77	21.83	19.61	16.67
11	28.61	23.96	21.90	17.26	26.66	23.70	19.95	17.00
12	29.78	25.20	22.43	17.85	27.65	24.69	20.30	17.34
13	30.99	26.48	22.97	18.46	28.69	25.72	20.67	17.70
14	32.23	27.78	23.52	19.08	29.75	26.77	21.04	18.07
15	33.48	29.10	24.08	19.70	30.83	27.85	21.43	18.44

Interest rate, %	$N = 20, T = 20$				$N = 20, T = 10$			
	$m = 0$		$m = 1$		$m = 0$		$m = 1$	
	MNO	MNR	MNO	MNR	MNO	MNR	MNO	MNR
5	8.44	5.07	6.16	2.79	8.01	6.37	5.73	4.09
6	9.29	6.01	6.45	3.17	8.76	7.04	5.92	4.21
7	10.21	7.01	6.78	3.58	9.58	7.79	6.15	4.36
8	11.20	8.08	7.14	4.02	10.46	8.60	6.40	4.54
9	12.26	9.22	7.54	4.49	11.40	9.47	6.68	4.75
10	13.13	10.16	7.96	5.00	12.15	10.16	6.99	5.00
11	14.58	11.70	8.43	5.54	13.49	11.44	7.33	5.29
12	15.83	13.03	8.92	6.12	14.62	12.52	7.71	5.61
13	17.15	14.43	9.45	6.72	15.82	13.67	8.12	5.96
14	18.53	15.88	10.00	7.36	17.08	14.88	8.56	6.36
15	19.96	17.39	10.59	8.02	18.40	16.16	9.03	6.79

Interest rate, %	$N = 50, T = 50$				$N = 50, T = 25$			
	$m = 0$		$m = 1$		$m = 0$		$m = 1$	
	MNO	MNR	MNO	MNR	MNO	MNR	MNO	MNR
5	3.96	2.05	2.32	0.42	3.87	3.22	2.24	1.58
6	4.64	2.77	2.47	0.60	4.52	3.74	2.35	1.57
7	5.47	3.64	2.66	0.84	5.30	4.39	2.50	1.59
8	6.45	4.67	2.92	1.15	6.23	5.19	2.71	1.66
9	7.60	5.88	3.25	1.53	7.33	6.14	2.98	1.79
10	8.82	7.16	3.66	2.00	8.48	7.16	3.32	2.00
11	10.40	8.82	4.14	2.55	9.99	8.56	3.73	2.30
12	12.03	10.51	4.70	3.18	11.54	10.01	4.22	2.68
13	13.78	12.33	5.34	3.89	13.22	11.60	4.78	3.16
14	15.63	14.25	6.03	4.66	14.99	13.31	5.40	3.72
15	17.56	16.25	6.79	5.48	16.85	15.13	6.08	4.35

Inflation rate: $\gamma = 10\%$ p.a. Tax system: Nominal: $MNO : \varepsilon_1 = \varepsilon_2 = 0$. $MNR :$ $\varepsilon_1 = \gamma, \varepsilon_2 = 0$. Survival function: Simultaneous retirement after N years. Depreciation allowance schedule: Linear over T years. Income tax rate: $u = 0.508$. Capital value tax rate: $v = 0$.

Table 6.2: User cost of capital as a function of inflation rate, per cent of investment price.

A. No taxation of capital gains: $n = 0$

Inflation rate, %	$N = 6, T = 6$				$N = 6, T = 3$			
	$m = 0$		$m = 1$		$m = 0$		$m = 1$	
	MNO	MNR	MNO	MNR	MNO	MNR	MNO	MNR
0	29.46	29.46	22.96	22.96	27.02	27.02	20.52	20.52
2	27.75	26.76	21.35	20.35	25.45	24.78	19.04	18.37
4	26.09	24.13	19.78	17.81	23.93	22.63	17.61	16.31
6	24.48	21.56	18.26	15.34	22.45	20.55	16.23	14.33
8	22.91	19.08	16.78	12.95	21.01	18.57	14.88	12.44
10	21.38	16.67	16.22	11.50	19.61	16.67	14.45	11.50
12	19.91	14.34	13.99	8.41	18.26	14.86	12.34	8.93
14	18.49	12.09	12.67	6.27	16.96	13.14	11.14	7.32
16	17.12	9.92	11.41	4.21	15.70	11.51	9.99	5.80
18	15.81	7.84	10.20	2.23	14.50	9.98	8.89	4.37
20	14.55	5.84	9.05	0.35	13.35	8.54	7.85	3.04

Inflation rate, %	$N = 20, T = 20$				$N = 20, T = 10$			
	$m = 0$		$m = 1$		$m = 0$		$m = 1$	
	MNO	MNR	MNO	MNR	MNO	MNR	MNO	MNR
0	18.71	18.71	11.75	11.75	16.42	16.42	9.46	9.46
2	16.23	15.54	9.53	8.85	14.24	13.65	7.55	6.95
4	13.89	12.56	7.49	6.16	12.19	11.10	5.79	4.70
6	11.72	9.79	5.63	3.71	10.29	8.79	4.20	2.71
8	9.74	7.27	3.98	1.51	8.55	6.76	2.79	1.00
10	7.96	5.00	2.80	-0.16	6.99	5.00	1.83	-0.16
12	6.40	3.00	1.32	-2.07	5.62	3.52	0.54	-1.55
14	5.05	1.28	0.32	-3.45	4.43	2.32	-0.30	-2.41
16	3.91	-0.18	-0.48	-4.56	3.43	1.37	-0.96	-3.02
18	2.96	-1.38	-1.09	-5.43	2.60	0.65	-1.45	-3.40
20	2.20	-2.35	-1.53	-6.08	1.93	0.14	-1.80	-3.59

Inflation rate, %	$N = 50, T = 50$				$N = 50, T = 25$			
	$m = 0$		$m = 1$		$m = 0$		$m = 1$	
	MNO	MNR	MNO	MNR	MNO	MNR	MNO	MNR
0	18.43	18.43	10.09	10.09	16.72	16.72	8.37	8.37
2	14.94	14.55	6.97	6.58	13.55	13.01	5.58	5.04
4	11.60	10.83	4.12	3.35	10.52	9.55	3.04	2.07
6	8.51	7.40	1.65	0.54	7.72	6.46	0.86	-0.40
8	5.82	4.40	-0.29	-1.70	5.28	3.90	-0.83	-2.20
10	3.66	2.00	-1.51	-3.16	3.32	2.00	-1.85	-3.16
12	2.09	0.26	-2.32	-4.15	1.90	0.77	-2.51	-3.64
14	1.09	-0.85	-2.53	-4.47	0.99	0.12	-2.63	-3.50
16	0.52	-1.49	-2.43	-4.44	0.47	-0.15	-2.48	-3.10
18	0.23	-1.81	-2.19	-4.23	0.21	-0.20	-2.21	-2.62
20	0.09	-1.96	-1.92	-3.97	0.09	-0.17	-1.93	-2.18

Interest rate: $i = 10\%$ p.a. Tax system: Nominal: $MNO : \varepsilon_1 = \varepsilon_2 = 0$. MNR : $\varepsilon_1 = \gamma, \varepsilon_2 = 0$. Survival function: Simultaneous retirement after N years. Depreciation allowance schedule: Linear over T years. Income tax rate: $u = 0.508$. Capital value tax rate: $v = 0$.

Table 6.2: (cont.)   User cost of capital as a function of inflation rate, per cent of investment price.

B. Full taxation of capital gains: $n = 1$

Inflation rate, %	$N = 6, T = 6$				$N = 6, T = 3$			
	$m = 0$		$m = 1$		$m = 0$		$m = 1$	
	MNO	MNR	MNO	MNR	MNO	MNR	MNO	MNR
0	29.46	29.46	22.96	22.96	27.02	27.02	20.52	20.52
2	29.04	28.04	22.63	21.63	26.73	26.06	20.33	19.65
4	28.62	26.65	22.30	20.34	26.45	25.15	20.14	18.84
6	28.21	25.30	21.99	19.08	26.18	24.29	19.96	18.07
8	27.81	23.98	21.68	17.85	25.91	23.47	19.78	17.34
10	26.55	21.83	21.38	16.67	24.77	21.83	19.61	16.67
12	27.02	21.44	21.10	15.52	25.37	21.96	19.45	16.04
14	26.64	20.23	20.82	14.41	25.10	21.28	19.29	15.47
16	26.27	19.06	20.55	13.35	24.85	20.65	19.13	14.94
18	25.90	17.93	20.30	12.32	24.59	20.07	18.98	14.46
20	25.55	16.84	20.05	11.34	24.34	19.54	18.84	14.04

Inflation rate, %	$N = 20, T = 20$				$N = 20, T = 10$			
	$m = 0$		$m = 1$		$m = 0$		$m = 1$	
	MNO	MNR	MNO	MNR	MNO	MNR	MNO	MNR
0	18.71	18.71	11.75	11.75	16.42	16.42	9.46	9.46
2	17.56	16.88	10.87	10.19	15.58	14.98	8.89	8.29
4	16.45	15.12	10.05	8.72	14.75	13.65	8.35	7.26
6	15.37	13.45	9.29	7.36	13.94	12.45	7.85	6.36
8	14.35	11.88	8.59	6.12	13.16	11.37	7.40	5.61
10	13.13	10.16	7.96	5.00	12.15	10.16	6.99	5.00
12	12.49	9.09	7.41	4.02	11.71	9.61	6.63	4.54
14	11.67	7.90	6.94	3.17	11.05	8.94	6.32	4.21
16	10.92	6.84	6.54	2.45	10.44	8.38	6.06	4.00
18	10.26	5.91	6.21	1.86	9.89	7.95	5.84	3.90
20	9.67	5.12	5.94	1.38	9.40	7.61	5.67	3.88

Inflation rate, %	$N = 50, T = 50$				$N = 50, T = 25$			
	$m = 0$		$m = 1$		$m = 0$		$m = 1$	
	MNO	MNR	MNO	MNR	MNO	MNR	MNO	MNR
0	18.43	18.43	10.09	10.09	16.72	16.72	8.37	8.37
2	16.53	16.14	8.57	8.17	15.14	14.60	7.17	6.64
4	14.59	13.82	7.11	6.34	13.51	12.54	6.03	5.06
6	12.62	11.51	5.77	4.66	11.83	10.57	4.97	3.72
8	10.70	9.29	4.60	3.18	10.16	8.79	4.05	2.68
10	8.82	7.16	3.66	2.00	8.48	7.16	3.32	2.00
12	7.39	5.56	2.98	1.15	7.19	6.07	2.78	1.66
14	6.16	4.22	2.54	0.60	6.06	5.19	2.44	1.57
16	5.24	3.24	2.29	0.28	5.19	4.58	2.24	1.62
18	4.58	2.54	2.16	0.13	4.56	4.15	2.14	1.73
20	4.12	2.06	2.11	0.05	4.11	3.85	2.10	1.84

Interest rate: $i = 10\%$ p.a. Tax system: Nominal: $MNO : \varepsilon_1 = \varepsilon_2 = 0$. $MNR : \varepsilon_1 = \gamma, \varepsilon_2 = 0$. Survival function: Simultaneous retirement after N years. Depreciation allowance schedule: Linear over T years. Income tax rate: $u = 0.508$. Capital value tax rate: $v = 0$.

Table 6.3: User cost of capital as a function of nominal interest rate, per cent of investment price.

A. No taxation of capital gains: $n = 0$
Full deductibility of (indexed) interest cost: $m = 1$

Interest rate, %	$N = 6, T = 6$ degree of indexation, % of inflation				$N = 6, T = 3$ degree of indexation, % of inflation			
	0%	50%	100%	150%	0%	50%	100%	150%
5	13.20	13.87	13.87	12.92	12.31	13.87	15.20	16.21
6	13.61	14.34	14.41	13.56	12.54	14.13	15.47	16.51
7	14.03	14.81	14.96	14.21	12.79	14.39	15.75	16.81
8	14.46	15.30	15.52	14.87	13.04	14.66	16.04	17.13
9	14.91	15.80	16.09	15.54	13.31	14.95	16.35	17.46
10	16.22	16.74	16.67	15.78	14.45	15.67	16.67	17.37
11	15.81	16.82	17.26	16.91	13.86	15.54	17.00	18.17
12	16.30	17.35	17.85	17.59	14.18	15.87	17.34	18.53
13	16.80	17.90	18.46	18.29	14.49	16.21	17.70	18.91
14	17.30	18.45	19.08	18.99	14.82	16.56	18.07	19.30
15	17.81	19.01	19.70	19.70	15.16	16.91	18.44	19.70

Interest rate, %	$N = 20, T = 20$ degree of indexation, % of inflation				$N = 20, T = 10$ degree of indexation, % of inflation			
	0%	50%	100%	150%	0%	50%	100%	150%
5	1.60	2.79	2.79	-0.19	1.17	2.79	4.09	4.85
6	1.73	3.02	3.17	0.53	1.20	2.87	4.21	5.00
7	1.88	3.27	3.58	1.27	1.24	2.97	4.36	5.18
8	2.07	3.56	4.02	2.03	1.32	3.10	4.54	5.40
9	2.29	3.88	4.49	2.82	1.43	3.27	4.75	5.66
10	2.80	4.36	5.00	3.51	1.83	3.59	5.00	5.82
11	2.83	4.62	5.54	4.47	1.74	3.69	5.29	6.29
12	3.16	5.05	6.12	5.33	1.95	3.96	5.61	6.66
13	3.52	5.51	6.72	6.21	2.19	4.26	5.96	7.08
14	3.92	6.01	7.36	7.11	2.47	4.60	6.36	7.53
15	4.35	6.54	8.02	8.02	2.78	4.97	6.79	8.02

Interest rate, %	$N = 50, T = 50$ degree of indexation, % of inflation				$N = 50, T = 25$ degree of indexation, % of inflation			
	0%	50%	100%	150%	0%	50%	100%	150%
5	-0.94	0.42	0.42	-12.50	-1.03	0.42	1.58	1.89
6	-1.15	0.37	0.60	-10.69	-1.27	0.31	1.57	1.85
7	-1.34	0.36	0.84	-8.84	-1.50	0.23	1.59	1.86
8	-1.49	0.40	1.15	-6.97	-1.71	0.18	1.66	1.94
9	-1.59	0.50	1.53	-5.09	-1.86	0.19	1.79	2.12
10	-1.51	0.73	2.00	-3.26	-1.85	0.32	2.00	2.34
11	-1.55	0.94	2.55	-1.36	-1.97	0.42	2.30	2.79
12	-1.40	1.29	3.18	0.44	-1.89	0.66	2.68	3.30
13	-1.16	1.72	3.89	2.19	-1.72	0.99	3.16	3.92
14	-0.82	2.24	4.66	3.87	-1.45	1.40	3.72	4.66
15	-0.39	2.83	5.48	5.48	-1.10	1.90	4.35	5.48

Inflation rate: $\gamma = 10\%$ p.a. Tax system: System with indexation: $MI1 : \varepsilon_1 = \varepsilon_2 = \varepsilon$. Survival function: Simultaneous retirement after N years. Depreciation allowance schedule: Linear over T years. Income tax rate: $u = 0.508$. Capital value tax rate: $v = 0$.

Table 6.3: (cont.) User cost of capital as a function of nominal interest rate, per cent of investment price.

B. Full taxation of (indexed) capital gains: $n = 1$
Full deductibility of (indexed) interest cost: $m = 1$

Interest rate, %	$N = 6, T = 6$ degree of indexation, % of inflation				$N = 6, T = 3$ degree of indexation, % of inflation			
	0%	50%	100%	150%	0%	50%	100%	150%
5	18.96	17.49	13.87	8.59	18.08	18.57	17.84	16.84
6	19.43	17.61	14.41	9.23	18.36	18.47	18.10	17.09
7	19.90	18.12	14.96	9.87	18.66	18.76	18.37	17.35
8	20.38	18.63	15.52	10.52	18.96	19.05	18.65	17.62
9	20.88	19.15	16.09	11.18	19.28	19.36	18.94	17.90
10	21.38	19.25	16.67	10.56	19.61	19.25	19.25	16.91
11	21.90	20.23	17.26	12.55	19.95	20.02	19.57	18.54
12	22.43	20.77	17.85	13.21	20.30	20.35	19.90	18.83
13	22.97	21.34	18.46	13.89	20.67	20.70	20.24	19.16
14	23.52	21.91	19.08	14.59	21.04	21.07	20.59	19.52
15	24.08	22.49	19.70	16.82	21.43	21.44	20.96	21.39

Interest rate, %	$N = 20, T = 20$ degree of indexation, % of inflation				$N = 20, T = 10$ degree of indexation, % of inflation			
	0%	50%	100%	150%	0%	50%	100%	150%
5	6.16	5.91	2.79	-6.94	5.73	6.63	6.68	5.64
6	6.45	6.14	3.17	-6.24	5.92	6.73	6.81	5.68
7	6.78	6.49	3.58	-5.51	6.15	6.93	6.96	5.74
8	7.14	6.86	4.02	-4.76	6.40	7.16	7.14	5.83
9	7.54	7.27	4.49	-3.98	6.68	7.42	7.34	5.95
10	7.96	7.58	5.00	-3.56	6.99	7.58	7.58	5.72
11	8.43	8.19	5.54	-2.33	7.33	8.03	7.85	6.30
12	8.92	8.69	6.12	-1.48	7.71	8.38	8.15	6.52
13	9.45	9.23	6.72	-0.60	8.12	8.76	8.49	6.79
14	10.00	9.80	7.36	0.30	8.56	9.18	8.86	7.09
15	10.59	10.40	8.02	1.84	9.03	9.62	9.26	8.06

Interest rate, %	$N = 50, T = 50$ degree of indexation, % of inflation				$N = 50, T = 25$ degree of indexation, % of inflation			
	0%	50%	100%	150%	0%	50%	100%	150%
5	2.32	3.15	0.42	-33.50	2.24	3.42	3.92	2.47
6	2.47	3.32	0.60	-31.31	2.35	3.56	4.00	2.13
7	2.66	3.56	0.84	-29.00	2.50	3.76	4.09	1.78
8	2.92	3.85	1.15	-26.57	2.71	3.99	4.21	1.45
9	3.25	4.21	1.53	-24.05	2.98	4.28	4.37	1.16
10	3.66	4.58	2.00	-21.63	3.32	4.58	4.58	0.79
11	4.14	5.13	2.55	-18.88	3.73	5.04	4.85	0.83
12	4.70	5.69	3.18	-16.30	4.22	5.51	5.19	0.83
13	5.34	6.32	3.89	-13.77	4.78	6.05	5.59	0.96
14	6.03	7.01	4.66	-11.32	5.40	6.64	6.06	1.23
15	6.79	7.74	5.48	-8.55	6.08	7.28	6.60	2.05

Inflation rate: $\gamma = 10\%$ p.a. Tax system: System with indexation: $MI1 : \varepsilon_1 = \varepsilon_2 = \varepsilon$. Survival function: Simultaneous retirement after N years. Depreciation allowance schedule: Linear over T years. Income tax rate: $u = 0.508$. Capital value tax rate: $v = 0$.

Table 6.4: User cost of capital as a function of inflation rate, per cent of investment price.

A. No taxation of capital gains: $n = 0$
Full deductibility of (indexed) interest cost: $m = 1$

Inflation rate, %	$N = 6, T = 6$ degree of indexation, % of inflation				$N = 6, T = 3$ degree of indexation, % of inflation			
	0%	50%	100%	150%	0%	50%	100%	150%
0	22.96	22.96	22.96	22.96	20.52	20.52	20.52	20.52
2	21.35	21.50	21.63	21.74	19.04	19.35	19.65	19.94
4	19.78	20.10	20.34	20.46	17.61	18.24	18.84	19.38
6	18.26	18.77	19.08	19.13	16.23	17.19	18.07	18.84
8	16.78	17.50	17.85	17.72	14.88	16.19	17.34	18.32
10	16.22	16.74	16.67	15.78	14.45	15.67	16.67	17.37
12	13.99	15.18	15.52	14.61	12.34	14.35	16.04	17.31
14	12.67	14.11	14.41	12.87	11.14	13.52	15.47	16.82
16	11.41	13.12	13.35	10.98	9.99	12.74	14.94	16.35
18	10.20	12.20	12.32	8.90	8.89	12.01	14.46	15.89
20	9.05	11.34	11.34	6.58	7.85	11.34	14.04	15.45

Inflation rate, %	$N = 20, T = 20$ degree of indexation, % of inflation				$N = 20, T = 10$ degree of indexation, % of inflation			
	0%	50%	100%	150%	0%	50%	100%	150%
0	11.75	11.75	11.75	11.75	9.46	9.46	9.46	9.46
2	9.53	9.88	10.19	10.45	7.55	7.93	8.29	8.63
4	7.49	8.18	8.72	9.04	5.79	6.56	7.26	7.86
6	5.63	6.67	7.36	7.49	4.20	5.36	6.36	7.15
8	3.98	5.35	6.12	5.72	2.79	4.33	5.61	6.51
10	2.80	4.36	5.00	3.51	1.83	3.59	5.00	5.82
12	1.32	3.32	4.02	1.08	0.54	2.77	4.54	5.47
14	0.32	2.59	3.17	-2.17	-0.30	2.23	4.21	5.08
16	-0.48	2.04	2.45	-6.44	-0.96	1.83	4.00	4.76
18	-1.09	1.64	1.86	-12.24	-1.45	1.56	3.90	4.52
20	-1.53	1.38	1.38	-20.35	-1.80	1.38	3.88	4.34

Inflation rate, %	$N = 50, T = 50$ degree of indexation, % of inflation				$N = 50, T = 25$ degree of indexation, % of inflation			
	0%	50%	100%	150%	0%	50%	100%	150%
0	10.09	10.09	10.09	10.09	8.37	8.37	8.37	8.37
2	6.97	7.59	8.17	8.71	5.58	6.13	6.64	7.10
4	4.12	5.31	6.34	7.09	3.04	4.12	5.06	5.81
6	1.65	3.34	4.66	5.01	0.86	2.42	3.72	4.54
8	-0.29	1.77	3.18	1.95	-0.83	1.13	2.68	3.37
10	-1.51	0.73	2.00	-3.26	-1.85	0.32	2.00	2.34
12	-2.32	0.06	1.15	-12.96	-2.51	-0.18	1.66	1.69
14	-2.53	-0.19	0.60	-32.72	-2.63	-0.30	1.57	1.29
16	-2.43	-0.20	0.28	-74.42	-2.48	-0.24	1.62	1.15
18	-2.19	-0.09	0.13	-165.37	-2.21	-0.10	1.73	1.18
20	-1.92	0.05	0.05	-370.64	-1.93	0.05	1.84	1.31

Interest rate: $i = 10\%$ p.a. Tax system: System with indexation: $MI1 : \varepsilon_1 = \varepsilon_2 = \varepsilon$. Survival function: Simultaneous retirement after N years. Depreciation allowance schedule: Linear over T years. Income tax rate: $u = 0.508$. Capital value tax rate: $v = 0$.

Table 6.4: (cont.) User cost of capital as a function of inflation rate, per cent of investment price.

B. Full taxation of (indexed) capital gains: $n = 0$
Full deductibility of (indexed) interest cost: $m = 1$

Inflation rate, %	$N = 6, T = 6$ degree of indexation, % of inflation				$N = 6, T = 3$ degree of indexation, % of inflation			
	0%	50%	100%	150%	0%	50%	100%	150%
0	22.96	22.96	22.96	22.96	20.52	20.52	20.52	20.52
2	22.63	22.16	21.63	21.05	20.33	20.25	20.15	20.03
4	22.30	21.43	20.34	19.01	20.14	20.03	19.84	19.55
6	21.99	20.77	19.08	16.80	19.96	19.86	19.58	19.07
8	21.68	20.19	17.85	14.44	19.78	19.75	19.39	18.64
10	21.38	19.25	16.67	10.56	19.61	19.25	19.25	16.91
12	21.10	19.24	15.52	9.01	19.45	19.66	19.17	17.77
14	20.82	18.89	14.41	5.86	19.29	19.68	19.15	17.35
16	20.55	18.60	13.35	2.35	19.13	19.74	19.19	16.93
18	20.30	18.37	12.32	-1.59	18.98	19.84	19.28	16.52
20	20.05	18.82	11.34	-6.06	18.84	20.58	19.43	16.10

Inflation rate, %	$N = 20, T = 20$ degree of indexation, % of inflation				$N = 20, T = 10$ degree of indexation, % of inflation			
	0%	50%	100%	150%	0%	50%	100%	150%
0	11.75	11.75	11.75	11.75	9.46	9.46	9.46	9.46
2	10.87	10.58	10.19	9.67	8.89	8.85	8.76	8.63
4	10.05	9.60	8.72	7.28	8.35	8.38	8.23	7.87
6	9.29	8.79	7.36	4.46	7.85	8.04	7.86	7.18
8	8.59	8.17	6.12	1.06	7.40	7.82	7.64	6.60
10	7.96	7.58	5.00	-3.56	6.99	7.58	7.58	5.72
12	7.41	7.41	4.02	-8.58	6.63	7.69	7.66	5.71
14	6.94	7.25	3.17	-15.66	6.32	7.73	7.85	5.41
16	6.54	7.20	2.45	-25.18	6.06	7.82	8.13	5.21
18	6.21	7.25	1.86	-38.27	5.84	7.93	8.48	5.09
20	5.94	7.42	1.38	-56.68	5.67	8.14	8.86	5.04

Inflation rate, %	$N = 50, T = 50$ degree of indexation, % of inflation				$N = 50, T = 25$ degree of indexation, % of inflation			
	0%	50%	100%	150%	0%	50%	100%	150%
0	10.09	10.09	10.09	10.09	8.37	8.37	8.37	8.37
2	8.57	8.45	8.17	7.68	7.17	7.15	7.02	6.76
4	7.11	7.06	6.34	4.48	6.03	6.17	5.92	5.12
6	5.77	5.96	4.66	-0.23	4.97	5.44	5.12	3.50
8	4.60	5.15	3.18	-7.87	4.05	4.94	4.69	2.06
10	3.66	4.58	2.00	-21.63	3.32	4.58	4.58	0.79
12	2.98	4.34	1.15	-47.36	2.78	4.45	4.72	0.28
14	2.54	4.18	0.60	-98.85	2.44	4.33	4.97	0.08
16	2.29	4.09	0.28	-204.84	2.24	4.22	5.20	0.26
18	2.16	4.01	0.13	-430.40	2.14	4.11	5.35	0.67
20	2.11	3.94	0.05	-928.68	2.10	4.01	5.42	1.18

Interest rate: $i = 10\%$ p.a. Tax system: System with indexation: $MI1 : \varepsilon_1 = \varepsilon_2 = \varepsilon$. Survival function: Simultaneous retirement after N years. Depreciation allowance schedule: Linear over T years. Income tax rate: $u = 0.508$. Capital value tax rate: $v = 0$.

CHAPTER 7

THE USER COST OF CAPITAL UNDER A PUTTY-CLAY TECHNOLOGY. PART 1: NO TAXES

7.1 Introduction

In chapters 4–6, we have been concerned with the user cost of capital in the context of a neo-classical production technology. The crucial assumption in this description of the technology from the point of view of measuring the user cost is the assumption that old and new capital units are equivalent inputs in the production process. Existing capital units can be substituted with other inputs to the same degree after they have been installed as they could before the equipment had got its specific form. This assumption of perfect substitutability manifests itself in the equalization of capital service prices across vintages. This is expressed mathematically in subsection 3.5.2 for the case with no discounting of capital services and in subsection 3.5.4 when a discounting of the services is performed, [cf. eqs. (3.26) and (3.48), respectively]. The neo-classical model has been the standard framework for defining and measuring the user cost of capital since Jorgenson and his collaborators introduced this concept and its dependence on the corporate tax system into the econometric analysis of investment behaviour in the 1960's [cf. Jorgenson (1967), Hall and Jorgenson (1967)]. Unfortunately, the strong reliance of the resulting user cost formulae on the neo-classical assumption of full substitutability between capital and other inputs has not always been recognized in the literature.

In this chapter, we reconsider and reinterpret the user cost when the neo-classical technology is replaced by a vintage production model of the *putty-clay* type. *Ex ante*, i.e. before an investment is made, the firm is assumed to face a neo-classical production technology. *Ex post*, i.e. after the investment has got its specific form, as machinery, transport equipment, buildings, structures, etc., the factor proportions are "frozen": some or all of the other inputs must be employed in fixed proportions to capital.[1]

---

[1] The model was originally presented in Johansen (1959) and further developed in

There is one specific technique attached to each vintage. Ex post, the net payment flow from the vintage, to be called its *quasi rent*, is fixed once the scale of the vintage and its technique has been chosen. This description of the technology is arguably more realistic than the neo-classical one, especially at the *micro* level, i.e. for an individual firm or a production plant within a firm [cf. Johansen (1959), Johansen (1972, chapter 2) and Førsund and Hjalmarsson (1987)]. For expository simplicity, we assume that only one other input, labour, is subject to an ex post fixity of factor proportions. This is no essential limitation, however, since the model may be extended to include more than one input with this property without materially affecting the conclusions. [See e.g. Biørn and Frenger (1986).] For simplicity, technical change, i.e. changes in the ex ante technology over time, is also disregarded.

Since the putty-clay technology implies a strong degree of *irreversibility* of the investment process,[2] *expectations* about future output and input prices play a more fundamental role here than they do in the case of a neo-classical technology. The endogeneity of the firm's *scrapping* decisions for capital goods and its revision of these plans as time passes, should also be taken into account. The latter property of the model has been utilized by Ando et al. (1974), Malcomson (1975,1979), and Malcomson and Prior (1979).

There is a similarity between the *vintage* concept as it will be used in this chapter and the concept of an investment *project* as used in chapter 2. The assumption made in chapter 2, that each project has a given cost, represented by an instantaneous outlay, and a given yield flow, finds its counterpart here in the assumption that any vintage has a given production technique *ex post*. There are, however, notable differences. First, in the present chapter, distinct factors of production, including capital, which are *substitutes ex ante*, are specified. The project, in the terminology of chapter 2, had both a fixed scale and a predetermined service life and payment flow, neither of which could be altered by the firm. The notion of an

---

Johansen (1972). See also Phelps (1963), who aptly denoted the technology as "putty-clay". A useful survey of vintage production models is Allen (1967, Ch. 15).

[2] Reversibility of the investment process is a basic implicit assumption of the neo-classical model: "... the decision as to the stock of capital to be held at any instant of time is myopic, being independent of future developments in technology, demand or anything else; forecasts for only the most immediate future are needed and then only as to capital goods prices. The argument for this rule is simple; when investment is reversible, then the firm can buy a unit of capital goods, use it and derive its marginal product for an arbitrarily short time span, and then sell the undepreciated portion, possibly at a different price."(Arrow (1968, p. 3)).

investment project as used in chapter 2 is closer to the technology often
denoted as *clay-clay* (i.e. one with the same fixed input coefficients ex ante
and ex post) than to a putty-clay technology. Second, in chapter 2, no distinction was made between ex ante and ex post variables and relationships
or between expected and realized values of the variables involved. In the
present chapter, this distinction will be highly important, as will also be
the distinction between inflation in terms of the output price and in terms
of the input prices.

In this chapter, for expository reasons, taxes will be disregarded. In
chapter 8, this description will be generalized to include a tax system similar to the one considered in chapter 5 and 6 for the neo-classical model.
The present chapter proceeds as follows. First, in section 7.2, we briefly
describe the two-factor version of the putty-clay model that will be used as
a reference, and in section 7.3, the associated quasi rent, service life, and
profit functions are defined. As in the neo-classical model, the problem of
defining the user cost of capital may be approached in two different ways,
which are discussed in the next two sections. Section 7.4 is concerned with
different service price definitions, obtained by reformulating the cash-flow
function in a suitable manner. Since there is one specific production technique attached to each vintage, there will also be one specific cash-flow
function for each vintage. As a consequence, the service prices will be
vintage specific variables, which distinguishes the putty-clay model from
the neo-classical model. In section 7.5, these vintage specific service prices
are reinterpreted as shadow values derived from the firm's conditions for
profit maximization and cost minimization, and they are compared with
the corresponding optimizing conditions in the neo-classical case. The final
section, section 7.6, presents examples for a Cobb-Douglas and a CES ex
ante technology.

7.2   Production technology

7.2.1 Ex ante technology

Consider a firm at time t and let the ex ante technology available when
investing in a new vintage, i.e. vintage t, be represented by a *neo-classical*
production function. We specify this menu of possible techniques, i.e. the
menu of potential relationships between the output from and inputs into

vintage t over its life cycle, as

(7.1) $X(t + s, s) = F[L(t + s, s), K(t + s, s)], \qquad s \geq 0,$

where s denotes the age of the equipment, $t + s$ is the time at which the capital reaches this age, and $X(t + s, s)$, $K(t + s, s)$, and $L(t + s, s)$ are respectively (potential) output from, flow of capital services from, and labour input allocated to vintage t at time $t + s$. We assume that F is *homothetic*, i.e. it can be written as

(7.2) $F(L, K) = f[\Phi(L, K)],$

where f is monotone increasing and Φ is linear homogeneous. For simplicity, technical change is disregarded, i.e. f and Φ are assumed to have the same form for all t.

Let, as in the neo-classical model, $J(t)$ denote the volume of capital invested at time t. In most expositions of the putty-clay vintage model, the capacity (efficiency) of each vintage is considered as constant ex post and equal to its ex ante value [cf. e.g. Johansen (1972, sections 2.2–2.3) and Førsund and Hjalmarsson (1987, section 2.2)]. The present exposition is based on less rigid assumptions since the efficiency of the capital units is allowed to be declining over time, as described by the function $B(s)$. This function corresponds formally to the survival function in the neo-classical model and has the same properties, namely [cf. (3.1)],

(7.3)
$$0 \leq B(s) \leq 1, \qquad B'(s) \leq 0, \qquad \text{for all } s \geq 0,$$
$$B(0) = 1, \qquad \lim_{s \to \infty} B(s) = 0.$$

The standard exposition of the putty-clay model assumes $B(s) = 1$ for all $s \geq 0$. As to economic interpretation, there is a basic difference between the two models. In the putty-clay model, $B(s)$ indicates the *potential* number of (efficiency) units at age s, rather than the actual number as in the neo-classical model, since the firm may choose to take a capital vintage which is technically useful out of operation if it has become economically obsolete. As in the neo-classical model, $B(s)$ is a technical concept, unaffected by economic decisions. *Scrapping*, on the other hand, is an economic decision. [Cf. section 7.5.] Then, assuming that one (efficiency) unit of capital produces one (potential) unit of capital services per unit of time,

(7.4) $K(t + s, s) = B(s)J(t)$

will represent the flow of capital services which can be obtained at maximum from vintage t at age s.

7.2.2 Ex post technology

The ex post technology is characterized by the assumption that labour and capital must be used in *fixed proportions* once the investment has been made. We formalize this, for vintage t, as

$$(7.5) \qquad \frac{L(t+s,s)}{K(t+s,s)} = h(s)\frac{L(t,0)}{J(t)} \qquad \text{for all } t \text{ and } s \geq 0,$$

where $h(s)$ is a positively valued function, $h(0) = 1$ by assumption, intended to represent the fact that the operation of each capital vintage, *for technical reasons* (maintenance, care, etc.), may become more (or, more unlikely, less) labour consuming as it grows older. The latter assumption also serves to make the model more flexible than the standard expositions of the putty-clay model. The function $h(s)$ is thus, like $F(L, K)$ and $B(s)$, to be regarded as a technical datum, completely known by the firm ex ante.[3] Labour input per remaining capital unit is increasing, constant, or decreasing with age at age s, according as $h'(s)$ is positive, zero or negative.

Together, (7.1), (7.4), and (7.5) describe the technology of the firm. For $s = 0$, these equations represent the ex ante technology (since (7.5) is no effective restriction in this case). For $s > 0$, they represent the ex post technology. Eqs. (7.4) and (7.5) imply that the time path of the labour input allocated to vintage t can be expressed in terms of the initial input, i.e. the labour input allocated to the vintage at the time of investment, $L(t,0)$, as

$$(7.6) \qquad L(t+s,s) = B(s)h(s)L(t,0), \qquad s \geq 0.$$

We find, by using (7.1), (7.2), (7.4), and (7.6), that the time path of the output from vintage t can be expressed as

$$(7.7) \qquad X(t+s,s) = f(B(s)\,\Phi[h(s)L(t,0), J(t)]), \qquad s \geq 0,$$

---

[3] In the standard version of the putty-clay model, both $B(s)$ and $h(s)$ are set equal to unity for all s. The case where $h'(s) > 0$ corresponds, with minor modifications, to 'input decay', in the terminology of Feldstein and Rothschild (1974, p.394). The formulation (7.4)–(7.5) is more interesting for the purpose of obtaining a user cost of capital concept which is comparable with the neo-classical one.

since the ex ante production function is assumed to be always satisfied as a strict equality ex post.[4] In general, this output path will not imply $X(t + s, s)$ to be proportional to $X(t, 0)$ for any s. But in the simplified case where $B(s) = h(s) = 1$ for all s and $f(\cdot) = 1$, we find that $K(t+s, s) = J(t), L(t + s, s) = L(t, 0)$, and $X(t + s, s) = X(t, 0)$ will hold for any s less than the scrapping age (see below).

Let us take a look at the formal difference between this specification of the technology and the neo-classical one in chapter 3. Aggregate capital $K(t)$, given by (3.3), in the neo-classical model corresponds to $\int_0^\infty K(t, s)\, ds$ in the putty-clay model. In the former, this aggregate is the only capital variable involved in the description of the technique, since capital units belonging to different vintages are perfect substitutes ex post. In the latter, all of its components are involved in the description of the ex post relationship between inputs and output, since there is one specific technique attached to each vintage: $K(t, s)$ and $K(t, s')$ are not substitutable inputs ex post at time t. Potential aggregate output at time t, with all vintages previously installed fully utilized, would now be given by

$$\int_0^\infty X(t, s)\, ds = \int_0^\infty F[L(t, s), K(t, s)]\, ds$$

$$= \int_0^\infty F[B(s)h(s)L(t - s, 0), B(s)J(t - s)]\, ds\,,$$

which depends on the entire paths of labour input and investment up to time t.

7.2.3 Specific assumptions

Assume now that the ex ante production function (7.1) has a constant degree of homogeneity, ε, and non-increasing returns to scale, i.e. its "outer" part has the form

$$(7.8) \qquad\qquad f[\Phi(L, K)] = [\Phi(L, K)]^\varepsilon\,, \qquad 0 < \varepsilon \leq 1\,.$$

We will consider the following two cases:

---

[4] I.e. we assume either a 100 per cent or a 0 per cent utilization of the capacity of each vintage. A generalization allowing for variable capacity utilization in a two-factor context is considered in Biørn (1986). See also Moene (1985) and Seierstad (1985).

(i) *Cobb-Douglas production function ex ante:*

$$\Phi(L, J) = AL^\beta J^{1-\beta}, \qquad A > 0, \qquad 0 < \beta < 1,$$

$h(s)$ is arbitrary.

(ii) *Constant labour input per capital unit ex post:*

$$h(s) = 1 \text{ for all } s,$$

$\Phi(L, J)$ is arbitrary.

It follows from (7.1), (7.2), (7.4)–(7.8) that the technology in case (i) satisfies

$$(7.9) \quad \begin{cases} X(t, 0) = [AL(t, 0)^\beta J(t)^{1-\beta}]^\varepsilon, \\[2mm] \dfrac{K(t+s, s)}{J(t)} = B(s), & s \geq 0, \\[3mm] \dfrac{L(t+s, s)}{L(t, 0)} = h(s)B(s), & s \geq 0, \\[3mm] \dfrac{X(t+s, s)}{X(t, 0)} = h(s)^{\beta\varepsilon} B(s)^\varepsilon, & s \geq 0. \end{cases}$$

In case (ii) it satisfies

$$(7.10) \quad \begin{cases} X(t, 0) = \Phi[L(t, 0), J(t)]^\varepsilon, \\[2mm] \dfrac{K(t+s, s)}{J(t)} = \dfrac{L(t+s, s)}{L(t, 0)} = B(s), & s \geq 0, \\[3mm] \dfrac{X(t+s, s)}{X(t, 0)} = B(s)^\varepsilon, & s \geq 0. \end{cases}$$

In both cases, the (potential) output flow from vintage t over its life cycle will be determined once the firm has made its decision about the initial scale of operation for this vintage, i.e. $X(t, 0)$.[5]

---

[5] Note that assuming decreasing returns to scale ($\varepsilon < 1$), implies that output will decrease with age at a slower speed than capital input in case (ii), since $B(s)^\varepsilon > B(s)$ when $0 < B(s) < 1$. In case (i), the same will hold true if $h(s)^{\beta\varepsilon} > B(s)^{1-\varepsilon}$.

7.3   The vintage specific quasi rent, profit and service life functions

Consider now the payment flows attached to each vintage. In the neo-classical model — because of the absence of ex post restrictions on the input proportions — we could aggregate all payment flows over vintages and consider the total net cash-flow, (4.7), only. In the putty-clay model, we follow the flows related to vintage t, i.e. the investment $J(t)$, the labour input $L(t+s,s)$, and the output $X(t+s,s)$ for $0 \leq s \leq N(t)$, where $N(t)$ denotes the *service life (scrapping age)* planned for vintage t. We assume that the firm at any time plans to use the entire (remaining) capacity of each vintage up to the scrapping age and then take it out of operation completely. The scrapping age will be *endogenously* determined as a part of the firm's optimization.

7.3.1 Price expectations. The ex ante quasi rent function

In any case where a firm faces a vintage specific technology characterized by ex post rigidities in the factor proportions, including the putty-clay case, it must form expectations about future prices of output and variable inputs in order to make decisions about output, investment, and factor proportions today.[6] Let $p^*(t+s,t)$ and $w^*(t+s,t)$ denote the output price and the wage rate, respectively, which at time t is expected by the firm to prevail at time $t+s$. Throughout asterisks are used to represent expected values. These price expectations are assumed to hold with certainty at time t, but may be subject to revision, as indicated by the double time subscript.

The *ex ante quasi rent* from vintage t at time $t+s$ is the difference between the output value and the cost of the *variable* inputs, in this case the labour cost, as expected by the firm when investing in the vintage.

---

[6] Or stated differently, its decision rules are *non-myopic*. Non-myopic decision rules are implied by all models involving costs of adjustment in some form. Convex adjustment costs are discussed in Lucas (1967), Gould (1968), and Treadway (1971). Confer also Arrow (1968). The putty-clay technology can be interpreted as a particular specification of the cost of adjustment function, the investment outlay being sunk cost.

Using (7.9)–(7.10), the quasi rent from vintage t can be written as

$$R^*(t+s,t) = p^*(t+s,t)X(t+s,s) - w^*(t+s,t)L(t+s,s)$$

(7.11)
$$= p^*(t+s,t)B_X(s)X(t,0) - w^*(t+s,t)B_L(s)L(t,0),$$

$$0 \le s \le N(t),$$

where $B_L(s)$ and $B_X(s)$ are *age profile functions* for labour input and output, respectively, defined as

(7.12)
$$B_L(s) = \begin{cases} h(s)B(s) & \text{in case (i),} \\ B(s) & \text{in case (ii),} \end{cases}$$

(7.13)
$$B_X(s) = \begin{cases} h(s)^{\beta_e}B(s)^c & \text{in case (i),} \\ B(s)^\varepsilon & \text{in case (ii).} \end{cases}$$

These functions have the same formal relationship to labour input and output as the survival function $B(s)$ has to capital, cf. (7.4). For an age $s > 0$, the quasi rent $R^*(t+s,t)$ represents the (expected) contribution to the firm's total cash-flow which comes from vintage t. From a formal point of view, it corresponds to the yield from the investment project at age $s, y(s)$, as defined in chapter 2 [cf. section 2.2]. The investment cost $q(t)J(t)$ here is the counterpart to the project cost A in chapter 2.

7.3.2 The vintage specific ex ante profit function

Consider the entire cash-flow from vintage t up to the scrapping age $N(t)$. Its present value can be expressed as

(7.14)
$$\Pi^*(t) = \int_0^{N(t)} e^{-r(t)s}R^*(t+s,t)\,ds - q(t)J(t),$$

where $r(t)$ denotes the rate of discount of the firm expected at time t for the relevant horizon. We shall denote it as the *ex ante profit function* of vintage t. This profit function is the counterpart to the project related profit function, Π, in chapter 2 [cf. eq. (2.2)].

7.4   Service price interpretations of the user cost

In section 4.2, we gave the following service price interpretation of the user cost of capital for a neo-classical model: the user cost of capital at an arbitrary time t is the current investment price divided by the present value of the service flow which one capital unit is expected to yield during its life time. The discounting of this service flow was based on the real interest rate ρ, which is the interest rate measured relative to the rate of increase of the investment price. The resulting service price formula, (4.1), stated an ex post relationship which is equally valid for and old capital unit as it is for a new one, regardless of its age. This followed from the (ex post) equalization of the vintage prices in the neo-classical model under perfect market conditions.

In this section, we give a similar service price interpretation for the putty-clay model. Now it will not be possible to establish a common service price for all vintages, neither ex ante nor ex post, because of the ex post rigidities in the factor proportions. In the putty-clay model, there will, apart from numerical coincidence, and under perfect foresight, be *one distinct service price for each vintage* at a given time t.

7.4.1 Annualization of the investment cost. Vintage specific service prices

One possible definition of a vintage specific user cost of capital for vintage t in a putty-clay would be simply *the investment price* at time t, $q(t)$. This price in fact represents, in the absence of taxes, the actual cost to the firm of using the services from one unit invested in vintage t, during its anticipated service period, i.e. $(t, t + N(t))$. At the time when the vintage is scrapped, it will also be an ex post life cycle capital service price. This definition, although perfectly possible, has one major drawback. The service price obtained has an order of magnitude which depends on $N(t)$, since the purchase price of a new capital good will usually be an increasing function of its anticipated service life. The price $q(t)$ is *not normalized to a suitable per unit base*. As a consequence, its "dimension" will not be comparable with that of the prices of the flow variables in the model, i.e. the output price $p(t)$ and the wage rate $w(t)$.

This problem of "dimensionality" can be "solved" by performing an *annualization* of the investment cost, $q(t)J(t)$. We can do this by rewriting the profit function for vintage t, (7.14), as

$$(7.15) \quad \Pi^*(t) = \int_0^{N(t)} e^{-r(t)s} \left[R^*(t+s,t) - c(t+s,t)K(t+s,s) \right] ds,$$

where $c(t+s,t)$, which is a so far unspecified function, represents the *ex ante price of capital services* from vintage t at time $t+s$, and $K(t+s,s)$ is the volume of these services. [Cf. section 2.4.] Here $R^*(t+s,t) - c(t+s,t)K(t+s,s)$, i.e. the quasi rent minus the cost of the capital services, can be interpreted as the anticipated profit from vintage t at time $t+s$. For this expression for the profit function to coincide with (7.14), when (7.4) is taken into account, the service prices must satisfy

$$(7.16) \quad q(t) = \int_0^{N(t)} e^{-r(t)s} c(t+s,t)B(s) ds.$$

This restriction says that the price of a new capital unit shall be equal to the present value of the flow of its future service price, when allowance is made for retirement and decline in efficiency of capital with age.

This relationship between the investment price and the service price has a *formal* similarity to (4.3), which, as noted in section 4.2, is implied by the service price definition of the user cost in the neo-classical model. As to economic interpretation there are, however, basic differences. First, the service prices in (7.16) have two time subscripts, current time, $t+s$, and vintage, t. In the neo-classical model, we could dispense with the latter, because of the model's equalization of service prices across vintages. From (7.16) solely, with a double subscript on c, we are unable to establish a relationship between (the time paths of) the service price and the investment price, even under perfect foresight with respect to the investment price. Second, (7.16), in contrast to (4.3), contains the anticipated service life $N(t)$, which is a time dependent variable.

We now consider three ways of proceeding.

7.4.2 Service price normalized against the capital price

First, let the time path of the vintage specific service price in (7.16) be restricted to grow in proportion to the corresponding price of a new capital good, i.e.

$$(7.17) \qquad \frac{c(t+s,t)}{q^*(t+s,t)} = \frac{c(t,t)}{q(t)} \qquad s \geq 0.$$

where $q^*(t+s,t)$ is the capital (investment) price which at time t is expected to prevail at time $t + s$. Assume furthermore that the capital price is expected to grow at a constant rate $\gamma(t)$ from the current time t, so that

$$(7.18) \qquad q^*(t+s,t) = q(t)e^{\gamma(t)s}, \qquad s \geq 0.$$

This is the same specification of the price expectations as applied in the neo-classical model, except that we now indicate that the rate of price increase is a vintage specific parameter. From (7.16)–(7.18) it follows that the time path of the (ex ante) vintage specific service price for vintage t is given by

$$(7.19) \qquad c(t+s,t) = c_K(t+s,t) = \frac{q(t)}{\Lambda_K(t)}e^{\gamma(t)s}, \qquad s \geq 0.$$

where $\Lambda_K(t)$ is an *annualization factor* given by

$$(7.20) \qquad \Lambda_K(t) = \int_0^{N(t)} e^{-\{r(t)-\gamma(t)\}s}B(s)\,ds.$$

The subscript K on c and Λ indicates that the service price is normalized against the capital purchase price. The real interest rate refers to the capital price.

In this case, the service price specific to vintage t will start at the value $c_K(t,t) = q(t)/\Lambda_K(t)$ and will grow at the same rate $\gamma(t)$ as the investment price. Only if $r(t)$, $\gamma(t)$, *and* $N(t)$ are constants, will the service price be independent of the vintage to which it belongs, i.e. $c(t + s, t)$ will be a function of $t + s$ only. But this is a particular situation which is unlikely to occur in practice.

7.4.3 Service price normalized against the labour cost

A second way of determining vintage specific service prices is to impose on (7.16) the restriction that the service price follows the anticipated growth path of the labour cost. This can be specified in two ways: (a) the service *price* follows the wage *rate*, or (b) the capital service *cost* follows the labour *cost*. Let us consider these two cases in turn.

Case (a): Constant price ratio

Replace (7.17) by

$$
(7.21) \qquad \frac{c(t+s,t)}{w^*(t+s,t)} = \frac{c(t,t)}{w(t)} \,, \qquad s \geq 0,
$$

where $w(t)$ is the current wage rate at time t. By assumption, we have $w^*(t,t) = w(t)$, i.e. the price expectation process does not show a discrete jump at time t.[7] Assuming that the wage rate is expected to grow at the rate $\gamma_L(t)$ from time t, i.e.

$$
(7.22) \qquad w^*(t+s,t) = w(t)e^{\gamma_L(t)s}, \qquad s \geq 0,
$$

it follows, by using (7.16) and (7.21), that the service prices can be expressed as

$$
(7.23) \qquad c(t+s,t) = \frac{q(t)e^{\gamma_L(t)s}}{\int_0^{N(t)} e^{-\{r(t)-\gamma_L(t)\}s} B(s)\,ds} \,.
$$

Case (b): Constant cost ratio

Alternatively, we can impose the relationship between the ex ante service price and the wage rate in terms of *cost shares*. We then restrict the ratio between the cost of capital services and the labour cost of vintage t to be equal to its initial value at all future points of time, i.e.

$$
(7.24) \qquad \frac{c(t+s,t)K(t+s,s)}{w^*(t+s,t)L(t+s,s)} = \frac{c(t,t)J(t)}{w(t)L(t,0)} \,, \qquad s \geq 0.
$$

Inserting this relationship, together with (7.9), (7.10), and (7.22), in (7.16), we find a service price equal to[8]

$$
(7.25) \qquad c(t+s,t) = c_L(t+s,t) = \frac{q(t)}{\Lambda_L(t)}h(s)e^{\gamma_L(t)s}, \qquad s \geq 0,
$$

---

[7] I.e., the price forecasts satisfy the Burmeister-Turnovsky weak consistency axiom (Burmeister and Turnovsky (1976, pp. 882–883), Burmeister (1980, p. 230)).

[8] Note that (7.21) and (7.24), and hence (7.23) and (7.25), are equivalent when $h(s) = 1$ for all s.

where $\Lambda_L(t)$ is an *annualization factor* given by

$$(7.26) \qquad \Lambda_L(t) = \int_0^{N(t)} e^{-\{r(t)-\gamma_L(t)\}s} B_L(s)\, ds\,.$$

The subscript L on c and Λ indicates that the service price is normalized against the labour cost. The real interest rate refers to the labour price. Now the service price starts at $c_L(t,t) = q(t)/\Lambda_L(t)$, and its growth factor is the product of the growth factor for the wage rate and the factor of relative labour/capital growth, $h(s) = B_L(s)/B(s)$.

7.4.4 Service price normalized against the output value

A third way of constructing the vintage specific service price from (7.16) is to relate the service price to the anticipated growth path of the output price. This can also be specified in two ways: (a) the service *price* follows the output *price*, or (b) the capital service *cost* follows the output *value*.

Case (a): Constant price ratio

Replace (7.17) by

$$(7.27) \qquad \frac{c(t+s,t)}{p^*(t+s,t)} = \frac{c(t,t)}{p(t)}\,,$$

where $p(t)$ is the current output price at time t, and where, by assumption, $p^*(t,t) = p(t)$. If we assume that the output price has an expected growth rate $\gamma_X(t)$ from time t, i.e.

$$(7.28) \qquad p^*(t+s,t) = p(t)e^{\gamma_X(t)s}\,, \qquad s \geq 0\,,$$

it follows, by using (7.16) and (7.27), that the service prices becomes

$$(7.29) \qquad c(t+s,t) = \frac{q(t)e^{\gamma_X(t)s}}{\int_0^{N(t)} e^{-\{r(t)-\gamma_X(t)\}s} B(s)\, ds}\,.$$

Case (b): Constant cost ratio

Alternatively, we can express the relationship in terms of *cost shares*. We then restrict the ratio between the cost of capital services and the output value of vintage t to be equal to the initial cost share at all future points of time, i.e.

$$(7.30) \qquad \frac{c(t+s,t)K(t+s,s)}{p^*(t+s,t)X(t+s,s)} = \frac{c(t,t)J(t)}{p(t)X(t,0)}, \qquad s \geq 0.$$

Combining this relationship with (7.9), (7.10), and (7.28), we find a service price equal to[9]

$$(7.31) \qquad c(t+s,t) = c_X(t+s,t) = \frac{q(t)}{\Lambda_X(t)} \frac{B_X(s)}{B(s)} e^{\gamma_X(t)s}, \qquad s \geq 0,$$

where $\Lambda_X(t)$ is an *annualization factor* given by

$$(7.32) \qquad \Lambda_X(t) = \int_0^{N(t)} e^{-\{r(t) - \gamma_X(t)\}s} B_X(s)\, ds.$$

The subscript X on c and Λ indicates normalization against the output value. The real interest rate refers to the output price. In this case, the initial service price is $c_X(t,t) = q(t)/\Lambda_X(t)$, and it grows with a factor equal to the product of the growth factor for the output price and the factor of relative output/capital growth, $B_X(s)/B(s)$.

The service prices $c(t+s,t)$ defined by (7.19), (7.23), (7.25), (7.29), and (7.31) will, in general, be different and will coincide only if $\gamma_L(t) = \gamma_X(t) = \gamma(t)$, $h(s) = 1$, and $\varepsilon = 1$, in which case the annualization factors $\Lambda_L(t)$, $\Lambda_X(t)$, and $\Lambda_K(t)$ are identical. This common value of the ex ante vintage service price will be different for different vintages. Only if the interest rate r, the common value of the inflation rate $\gamma_L = \gamma_X = \gamma$, and the service life N are all time invariant (which are, of course, very rigid assumptions) will this common service price be vintage invariant.

7.5   Shadow value interpretations based on optimizing conditions

The shadow value interpretations of the service price in the putty-clay model, like those in the neo-classical model, are derived from the first order conditions for an optimizing firm. In this section, we discuss the case

---

[9] Note that (7.27) and (7.30), and hence (7.29) and (7.31), are equivalent when $h(s) = 1$ for all s and the ex ante technology is characterized by constant returns to scale ($e = 1$).

with profit maximization in some detail and refer briefly the case with cost minimization.[10] We also compare these shadow value interpretations with the service price interpretations given in the previous section.

7.5.1 Profit maximization

The profit function (7.14), after inserting (7.11), (7.22), and (7.28), can be written as

$$(7.33) \qquad \Pi^*(t) = \Lambda_X(t)p(t)X(t,0) - \Lambda_L(t)w(t)L(t,0) - q(t)J(t).$$

The firm chooses, for each t, the initial labour input $L(t,0)$, the quantity invested, $J(t)$, *and the planned service life $N(t)$* in such a way that $\Pi^*(t)$ is maximized, subject to the ex ante production function (7.1) and the definition of the annualization factors (7.26) and (7.32). From a formal point of view, the difference between this optimization problem and that in the neo-classical model, is the presence of $\Lambda_X(t)$ and $\Lambda_L(t)$, which (i) are factors to the output price $p(t)$ and the wage rate $w(t)$ in the profit function, and (ii) depend on the endogenous variable $N(t)$.

The first-order conditions for this problem are

$$(7.34) \qquad \Lambda_X(t)p(t)\frac{\partial X(t,0)}{\partial L(t,0)} = \Lambda_L(t)w(t),$$

$$(7.35) \qquad \Lambda_X(t)p(t)\frac{\partial X(t,0)}{\partial J(t)} = q(t),$$

$$(7.36) \qquad \begin{cases} \dfrac{\partial \Lambda_X(t)}{\partial N(t)}p(t)X(t,0) = \dfrac{\partial \Lambda_L(t)}{\partial N(t)}w(t)L(t,0), \\[6pt] \text{which is equivalent to [cf. (7.26) and (7.32)]} \\[6pt] e^{\gamma_X(t)N(t)}B_X[N(t)]\,p(t)X(t,0) \\[4pt] \qquad = e^{\gamma_L(t)N(t)}B_L[N(t)]\,w(t)L(t,0). \end{cases}$$

---

[10] In the neo-classical model, it was sufficient to discuss the shadow value interpretation in relation to profit maximization (i.e. maximization of the present value of cash-flow). We could have followed the same line of reasoning for the cost minimization problem, but this would have resulted in the same expression for the shadow value of capital services.

These conditions have the following interpretation: (i) The present value of the output flow to be obtained from an initial marginal increase of one unit in the labour input allocated to vintage t shall be equal to the present value of the induced increase in the total labour cost over the planned life cycle of this vintage. (ii) The present value of the output flow resulting from an initial marginal investment of one unit in vintage t shall be equal to the investment price at time t. (iii) The planned service life shall be chosen in such a way that the quasi rent equals zero at the scrapping age, since (7.36) is equivalent to $R^*\big(t + N(t), t\big) = 0$.[11] The latter is often denoted as the *quasi-rent criterion* for determination of the (ex ante) service life. We shall also refer to it as the *scrapping condition*.[12]

The marginal conditions for labour and capital, (7.34) and (7.35), are stated in terms of three prices, $p(t)$, $w(t)$, and $q(t)$, and two annualization factors, $\Lambda_X(t)$ and $\Lambda_L(t)$, of which the first is related to output and the second to labour. The consequence of this is that the investment price $q(t)$ can be interpreted as a shadow value of capital only if used in combination with the *life cycle output price*, $\Lambda_X(t)p(t)$, and the *life cycle wage rate*, $\Lambda_L(t)w(t)$. The latter life cycle prices are, formally, weighted present values of the expected future prices, the weights reflecting the decline in the capital's efficiency and in its labour requirement with age. The investment price is the life cycle price of capital, according to this interpretation. For a discussion of life cycle prices and an elaboration of their properties in a more general context, see Biørn and Frenger (1986, sections 2 and 3). A rescaling from annual prices of output and labour input to life cycle prices is required to bring the three prices on a comparable base. With respect to practical interpretability this may, however, be inconvenient, since the

---

[11] We assume that a positive and finite solution value for $N(t)$ exists and is unique, and that the maximal profit at this value is positive. Sufficient conditions for this to hold are

$$R^*(t,t) > 0 \quad \Pi^*(t) > 0, \quad \frac{\partial R^*(t + s, t)}{\partial s} < 0, \quad \text{for all } s.$$

[12] A similar criterion is established in Malcomson and Prior (1979). The joint determination of X, L, J, and N distinguishes our application of the putty-clay framework to analyze optimal capital accumulation from that in several other studies, where the service life is treated as an exogenous, time invariant parameter. The profit maximization problem that we are considering here is a full profit maximization problem. It can conveniently be divided into two stages: (a) Profit maximization with respect to labour input and investment for a given service life, which gives a profit function conditional on the service life. (b) Maximization of the conditional profit function with respect to the service life. See Biørn and Frenger (1986, section 3) for a further elaboration of this two stage approach.

rescaled output price and wage rate will depend on the anticipated service life.

This suggests making a rescaling of the three life cycle prices so that they all get an "annual dimension". Since (7.34)–(7.35) are homogeneous of degree zero in the life cycle prices, there are numerous ways in which this can be done. The most relevant alternatives, which utilize the annualization factors for capital, labour, and output respectively, are given in table 7.1.

The capital service price normalized against the capital price, $c_K(t,t)$ [cf. subsection 7.4.2], is a shadow price of capital services only if combined with a shadow price of labour defined as a *corrected* wage rate equal to $\Lambda_L(t)/\Lambda_K(t)w(t)$. The correction factor is an increasing function of the rate of increase of the wage rate and a decreasing function of the rate of increase of the capital price. The relevant output price is then $\Lambda_X(t)/\Lambda_K(t)p(t)$ (second line of table 7.1). If the shadow price of labour in the first order condition is defined as the wage rate $w(t)$, then the relevant shadow price of capital services will be the service price normalized against the labour cost, $c_L(t,t)$ [cf. subsection 7.4.3]. This is a hybrid capital cost measure, since it depends on the rate of increase of the wage rate. The relevant output price is then $\Lambda_X(t)/\Lambda_L(t)p(t)$. Finally, if the output price is given "priority", then the shadow price of both the labour and the capital input will become hybrid measures. The price is $c_X(t,t)$ [cf. subsection 7.4.4] for capital services and $\Lambda_L(t)/\Lambda_X(t)w(t)$ for labour, which both depend on the rate of increase of the output price.[13]

7.5.2 Cost minimization

The cost function for vintage t — i.e. the present value of the total cost incurred by operating this vintage over its entire life time — can be written compactly as

$$(7.37)\qquad C^*(t) = \Lambda_L(t)w(t)L(t,0) + q(t)J(t).$$

As an alternative to full profit maximization, minimization of this life cycle cost, conditional on the initial production capacity of the vintage may be

---

[13] In the particular case where all prices grow at the same rate, i.e. $\gamma_X(t) = \gamma_L(t) = \gamma$, and $h(s) = 1$ and $\varepsilon = 1$, so that $B_X(s) = B_L(s) = B(s)$ for all s, we will have $\Lambda_X(t) = \Lambda_L(t) = \Lambda_K(t)$, regardless of the value of $N(t)$, and then the correction factors of the labour and output prices would disappear. But since no solution value for $N(t)$ then would exist — as in easily seen from (7.36) — this case is of little interest.

of some interest. The first order condition for minimization of $C^*(t)$ with respect to $L(t,0)$ and $J(t)$, subject to (7.9) or (7.10) for a given $X(t,0)$ *and a given value of the service life*, is that the marginal rate of substitution between the capital and the labour allocated to vintage t shall be equal to the ratio between their life cycle prices, i.e.[14]

$$(7.38) \qquad \frac{\dfrac{\partial X(t,0)}{\partial J(t)}}{\dfrac{\partial X(t,0)}{\partial L(t,0)}} = \frac{q(t)}{\Lambda_L(t)w(t)} = \frac{c_L(l,l)}{w(t)} ,$$

where $c_L(t,t)$ is defined as in (7.25). This equation shows that $c_L(t,t)$ is by far the most convenient shadow value interpretation of the user cost of capital under two-factor cost minimization, since it leaves the wage rate unaffected.

7.5.3 Comparison of the service price and shadow value interpretations

The four alternative shadow value interpretations of the user cost of capital in a putty-clay model given in table 7.1, are obtained by "allocating" in different ways the annualization factors Λ_K, Λ_L, and Λ_X between prices. They coincide with the service price interpretations derived in section 7.4. In particular, $c_L(t,t)$ and $c_X(t,t)$ coincide with the cost share interpretations given in subsections 7.4.3 and 7.4.4, respectively. Under profit maximization, $c_L(t,t)$ and $c_X(t,t)$ give simpler expressions for the shadow values than $c_K(t,t)$, since the labour price is unaffected in the first case and the output price is unaffected in the second. Under two-factor cost minimization $c_L(t,t)$ is by far the most convenient measure.[15]

"What is the proper representation of the user cost of capital in a putty-clay model?" is thus a question with no definite answer. The appropriate measure in a given context should (at least) *be in accordance with the measure of the wage rate and of the output price with which it is combined.*

---

[14] Cost minimization gives no answer to the problem of determining optimal service life. Although the quasi rent criterion could possibly have been applied in this case as well, it would not be well founded, since it cannot be deduced from the specified optimization problem.

[15] Cost minimization is particularly simple in this case since only two prices, and hence one marginal condition, is involved. If more than two inputs had been specified — say capital, labour, energy, and other materials — a similar ambiguity in defining user cost would have arisen as in the case with profit maximization.

Table 7.1: Alternative shadow value interpretations of the user cost of capital for a putty-clay technology based on first order conditions for maximization of the life cycle vintage profit.*

Capital service price	Corresponding labour price	Corresponding output price
Investment price $q(t)$	$\Lambda_L(t)w(t)$	$\Lambda_X(t)p(t)$
Capital normalized service price $c_K(t,t) = \dfrac{q(t)}{\Lambda_K(t)}$	$\dfrac{\Lambda_L(t)}{\Lambda_K(t)}w(t)$	$\dfrac{\Lambda_X(t)}{\Lambda_K(t)}p(t)$
Labour normalized service price $c_L(t,t) = \dfrac{q(t)}{\Lambda_L(t)}$	$w(t)$	$\dfrac{\Lambda_X(t)}{\Lambda_L(t)}p(t)$
Output normalized service price $c_X(t,t) = \dfrac{q(t)}{\Lambda_X(t)}$	$\dfrac{\Lambda_L(t)}{\Lambda_X(t)}w(t)$	$p(t)$

$$* \ \Lambda_K(t) = \int_0^{N(t)} e^{-[r(t)-\gamma(t)]s} B(s)\,ds\,,$$

$$\Lambda_L(t) = \int_0^{N(t)} e^{-[r(t)-\gamma_L(t)]s} B_L(s)\,ds\,,$$

$$\Lambda_X(t) = \int_0^{N(t)} e^{-[r(t)-\gamma_X(t)]s} B_X(s)\,ds\,.$$

Otherwise, the relative prices will not represent shadow values.[16] The situation is more complicated than it is under a neo-classical technology,

---

[16] Ando et al. (1974), establish an implicit user cost of capital measure which strongly resembles $c_X(t,t)$ above. From this they state that "the real rate of interest relevant to the investment decision is the 'own' rate measured in terms of output" (p. 390), without noticing the fact that the normalization of the life cycle prices involved (i) is arbitrary, and (ii) affects the other price variables in the model. See also Malinvaud (1971), and Artus et al. (1981, section 3.2).

despite the formal similarity of the two models.

Considered from an econometric point of view, this has one important consequence. Great care should be shown when applying user cost measures constructed within a neo-classical framework in a putty-clay context, or vice versa. Specifically, testing, by means of a neo-classical user cost measure, a neo-classical description of the technology against a putty-clay specification, may not be a well defined problem in classical statistical testing.[17] The reason for this is that the two specifications are non-nested models, and a comparison of such models may require a statistical model which contains the neo-classical and the putty-clay specifications — *including their different user cost representations* — as special cases. Both the formulation of such a general 'encompassing' model and the construction of an appropriate testing procedure raise as yet unsolved problems. [Confer e.g. Pesaran and Deaton (1978) and Davidson and MacKinnon (1981) on the testing of non-nested hypotheses in a non-linear regression context, which is a far simpler problem.] For an attempt to construct a model which combines the neo-classical and the putty-clay technology, although with exogenous service lives assumed, see Fuss (1977, 1978).

7.6   Examples. Numerical illustrations

We end this chapter by considering two examples, the first based on the Cobb-Douglas ex ante technology and the second based on the less restrictive CES technology.

7.6.1 Cobb-Douglas ex ante technology. Exponential efficiency function and labour requirement function

Assume that the ex ante production function is Cobb-Douglas, so that (7.9) can be applied. Consider the exponential decay specification of the (potential) efficiency function, i.e.

$$(7.39) \qquad\qquad B(s) = e^{-\delta s}, \qquad s \geq 0,$$

where δ is a non-negative constant, and let also the labour requirement function be exponential, i.e.

$$(7.40) \qquad\qquad h(s) = e^{\nu s}, \qquad s \geq 0,$$

---

[17] Such attempts are made by Artus and Muet (1980) and Anderson (1981).

where ν is a constant which can be of either sign, but is usually non-negative. If $\delta = 0$, the capital has a constant efficiency. This corresponds to the simultaneous retirement survival function for the neo-classical model [cf. subsections 3.6.2 and 4.4.2]. If $\nu = 0$, the labour input per capital unit is also constant over time for each vintage.

Inserting (7.39) and (7.40) in (7.12) and (7.13) it follows that the age profile functions for labour input and output have the form

$$(7.41) \qquad B_L(s) = e^{(\nu-\delta)s}, \qquad B_X(s) = e^{(\nu\beta-\delta)\varepsilon s}, \qquad s \geq 0,$$

where β is the elasticity of labour in the linear homogeneous kernel function of the Cobb-Douglas technology, i.e. $\Phi(L, K)$ [cf. (7.2)]. If $\nu = 0$ and $\varepsilon = 1$, we have $B_L(s) = B_X(s) = B(s) = e^{-\delta s}$. From (7.19)–(7.20), (7.25)–(7.26), and (7.31)–(7.32) it then follows that the three alternative service price definitions of the user cost of vintage t, or rather their initial values, become

$$c_K(t, t) = \frac{q(t)}{\Lambda_K(t)}, \qquad c_L(t, t) = \frac{q(t)}{\Lambda_L(t)}, \qquad c_X(t, t) = \frac{q(t)}{\Lambda_X(t)},$$

with annualization factors given by

$$(7.42) \qquad \Lambda_K(t) = \frac{1 - e^{-\{r(t)-\gamma(t)+\delta\}N(t)}}{r(t) - \gamma(t) + \delta},$$

$$(7.43) \qquad \Lambda_L(t) = \frac{1 - e^{-\{r(t)-\gamma_L(t)+\delta-\nu\}N(t)}}{r(t) - \gamma_L(t) + \delta - \nu},$$

$$(7.44) \qquad \Lambda_X(t) = \frac{1 - e^{-\{r(t)-\gamma_X(t)+(\delta-\nu\beta)\varepsilon\}N(t)}}{r(t) - \gamma_X(t) + (\delta - \nu\beta)\varepsilon}.$$

We note that these factors are formally the value of a constant annuity of one discounted over N years by "interest rates" equal to

$$r - \gamma + \delta,$$
$$r - \gamma_L + \delta - \nu,$$
$$r - \gamma_X + (\delta - \nu\beta)\varepsilon,$$

respectively.

Numerical illustrations are given in tables 7.2 and 7.3. Part A of table 7.2 shows the "labour cost normalized" service price for selected values of the rate of increase of the wage rate and of the rate of decline of capital efficiency, δ, when $r = 0.1$, $\nu = 0$, $\beta = 0.5$, $\varepsilon = 0.9$, with an exogenous service life a priori fixed at $N(t) = 20$. Corresponding values of the "output value normalized" service price are given in part A of table 7.3. Since $N(t)$ is fixed, these service prices, which are obtained directly from (7.43) and (7.44), do not reflect the endogeneity of the firm's scrapping plans which is part of its full optimizing behaviour [cf. section 7.5]. The corresponding shadow value interpretations of the user cost when the joint endogeneity of the output, the labour input, the investment, *and the service life* is taken into account — i.e. obtained by solving the full system of first-order conditions for profit maximization, (7.34)–(7.36) — are given in part B of the two tables. The implied service lives are given in part C.

The effect of treating the planned service life as an endogenous variable may be substantial. From tables 7.2 and 7.3 the following conclusions can be drawn.

1. The "labour cost normalized" user cost $c_L(t,t)$ and the "output value normalized" user cost $c_X(t,t)$ are both independent of the rate of increase of the capital price. (This holds regardless of the specification of the ex ante technology and is not confined to the Cobb-Douglas case.) When the service life is treated as endogenous, the resulting user cost measure, however defined, will depend both on the rate of increase of the wage rate and the rate of increase of the output price. This follows from the fact that the service life, via the scrapping condition (7.36), will be a function of these parameters.[18]

2. The "labour cost normalized" user cost $c_L(t,t)$ is, ceteris paribus, *less responsive* to changes in the rate of increase of the wage rate, $\gamma_L(t)$, when the endogeneity of the service life is taken into account than when it is neglected. This reflects the *negative response* of $N(t)$ to an increase in $\gamma_L(t)$ [cf. part C of table 7.2]: the planned service life is shorter the faster is the wage rate expected to increase. Thus, the direct effect of the decrease in the real interest component in the user cost which follows from an increase in $\gamma_L(t)$ will, to some extent, be compensated by the induced shortening of the planned service life.

3. The "output value normalized" user cost $c_X(t,t)$ is, ceteris paribus, *more responsive* to changes in the rate of increase of the output price, $\gamma_X(t)$, when the endogeneity of the service life is taken into account

---

[18] Similar numerical illustrations of the response of the scrapping age to the price expectations for a CES ex ante technology, for different values of the elasticity of substitution and with reference to the energy/capital substitution, are given in Biørn (1986, section III).

Table 7.2: Labour cost normalized ex ante user cost of capital, $c_L(t,t)$, in two-factor putty-clay model. Ex ante production function: Cobb-Douglas, $\beta = 0.5$, $\varepsilon = 0.9$, $r = 0.1$, $q(t) = 1$, $B(s) = e^{-\delta s}$, $h(s) = 1$.

A. With exogenous service life: $N(t) = 20$

$\gamma_L(t)$	$\delta = 0$	$\delta = 0.02$	$\delta = 0.05$
0.02	0.10024	0.11565	0.14043
0.04	0.08586	0.10024	0.12371
0.06	0.07264	0.08586	0.10782
0.08	0.06066	0.07264	0.09291

B. With endogenous service life.

$\gamma_L(t)$	$\gamma_X(t)$	$\delta = 0$	$\delta = 0.02$	$\delta = 0.05$
0.02	0.00	0.08143	0.10049	0.13005
0.04	0.00	0.07242	0.08839	0.11421
0.06	0.00	0.06942	0.08330	0.10582
0.08	0.00	0.06903	0.08154	0.10182
0.04	0.02	0.06262	0.08098	0.11012
0.06	0.02	0.05637	0.07129	0.09590
0.08	0.02	0.05518	0.06809	0.08937
0.06	0.04	0.04469	0.06194	0.09030
0.08	0.04	0.04146	0.05512	0.07820
0.08	0.06	0.02818	0.04372	0.07071

C. Ex ante service life, endogenously determined.

$\gamma_L(t)$	$\gamma_X(t)$	$\delta = 0$	$\delta = 0.02$	$\delta = 0.05$
0.02	0.00	50.52	53.39	60.50
0.04	0.00	29.39	29.45	30.01
0.06	0.00	21.46	21.24	21.12
0.08	0.00	17.11	16.86	16.62
0.04	0.02	52.90	55.21	61.71
0.06	0.02	30.92	30.72	30.99
0.08	0.02	22.51	22.14	21.84
0.06	0.04	56.39	57.79	63.37
0.08	0.04	32.84	32.36	32.22
0.08	0.06	61.84	61.65	65.76

than when it is neglected. This reflects the *positive response* of $N(t)$ to an increase in $\gamma_X(t)$ [cf. part C of table 7.3]: the planned service life is longer the faster is the output price expected to increase. Thus, an increase in $\gamma_X(t)$ will induce a decrease in the user cost both through its effect on the real interest component in the user cost and through its effect on the planned service life.

Table 7.3: Output value normalized ex ante user cost of capital, $c_X(t,t)$, in two-factor putty-clay model. Ex ante production function: Cobb-Douglas, $\beta = 0.5$, $\varepsilon = 0.9$, $r = 0.1$, $q(t) = 1$, $B(s) = e^{-\delta s}$, $h(s) = 1$.

A. With exogenous service life: $N(t) = 20$

$\gamma_X(t)$	$\delta = 0$	$\delta = 0.02$	$\delta = 0.05$
0.00	0.11565	0.13030	0.15344
0.02	0.10024	0.11407	0.13618
0.04	0.08586	0.09875	0.11965
0.06	0.07264	0.08448	0.10400

B. With endogenous service life.

$\gamma_X(t)$	$\gamma_L(t)$	$\delta = 0$	$\delta = 0.02$	$\delta = 0.05$
0.00	0.08	0.12207	0.13670	0.15932
0.02	0.08	0.09584	0.11064	0.13372
0.04	0.08	0.06966	0.08481	0.10869
0.06	0.08	0.04369	0.05968	0.08532
0.00	0.06	0.11325	0.12848	0.15212
0.02	0.06	0.08737	0.10309	0.12765
0.04	0.06	0.06212	0.07887	0.10514
0.00	0.04	0.10559	0.12178	0.14689
0.02	0.04	0.08119	0.09845	0.12506
0.00	0.02	0.10065	0.11823	0.14604

C. Ex ante service life, endogenously determined.

$\gamma_X(t)$	$\gamma_L(t)$	$\delta = 0$	$\delta = 0.02$	$\delta = 0.05$
0.00	0.08	17.41	16.86	16.62
0.02	0.08	22.51	22.14	21.84
0.04	0.08	32.84	32.36	32.22
0.06	0.08	61.84	61.65	65.76
0.00	0.06	21.46	21.24	21.12
0.02	0.06	30.92	30.72	30.99
0.04	0.06	56.39	57.79	63.37
0.00	0.04	29.39	29.45	30.01
0.02	0.04	52.90	55.21	61.71
0.00	0.02	50.52	53.39	60.50

The relationship between the ex ante service life and the anticipated rates of increase of the labour input and the output price may be better explained by considering the scrapping condition (7.36). Inserting (7.41) and solving for $N(t)$, we obtain

$$(7.45) \quad N(t) = \frac{1}{\gamma_L(t) - \gamma_X(t) + \nu(1 - \beta\varepsilon) - \delta(1 - \varepsilon)} \ln\left[\frac{p(t)X(t,0)}{w(t)L(t,0)}\right],$$

provided $\gamma_L(t) - \gamma_X(t) + \nu(1 - \beta\varepsilon) - \delta(1 - \varepsilon) > 0$.[19] This equation states that the ex ante service life is equal to minus the logarithm of the *initial* labour cost share in the output value (which is less than unity if vintage t is expected to earn a positive quasi-rent at age 0) divided by a corrected rate of increase of the relative wage rate/output price (which is positive if a regular solution value for $N(t)$ exists). The correction in this relative rate of increase adjusts for changes in the labour/capital ratio ex post [cf. (7.39)–(7.40)] and the decreasing returns to scale in production ($\varepsilon < 1$). An increase in γ_L, or a decrease in γ_X, will tend to decreasing $N(t)$ through their effect on the denominator of (7.45). But they will also affect $N(t)$ via the life cycle prices and hence via the choice of labour/output ratio. From (7.34) it follows for the Cobb-Douglas case that

$$\Lambda_X(t)p(t)\beta\varepsilon\frac{X(t,0)}{L(t,0)} = \Lambda_L(t)w(t),$$

which implies that the (ex ante) value of the *life cycle* labour cost ($\Lambda_L wL$) is a constant share, equal to $\beta\varepsilon$, of the *life cycle* output value ($\Lambda_X pX$) at any time t. This reflects the property of constant factor shares of the Cobb-Douglas function under profit maximization. Eliminating $X(t,0)/L(t,0)$ in (7.45) we get

$$(7.46) \qquad N(t) = \frac{\ln\left[\Lambda_L(t)/\Lambda_X(t)\right] - \ln(\beta\varepsilon)}{\gamma_L(t) - \gamma_X(t) + \nu(1 - \beta\varepsilon) - \delta(1 - \varepsilon)}.$$

This equation, with (7.43) and (7.44) inserted, implicitly determines N under profit maximization for a Cobb-Douglas ex ante technology. The optimal value of N, and hence the associated user cost of capital, depends on (i) the technology parameters β, ε, δ, and ν, (ii) the interest rate r, and (iii) the expected rates of price increase of labour input γ_L and output γ_X. Otherwise, it is independent of the price forecasts of the firm.

---

[19] If this inequality is not satisfied, a (finite and positive) value of the optimal service life does not exist.

7.6.2 CES ex ante technology. Exponential efficiency function. Constant labour requirement

Assume now that the labour requirement per capital unit is constant (i.e. $\nu = 0$) and that the ex ante production function is of the Constant Elasticity of Substitution (CES) form. Let $\Psi(\Lambda_L w, q)$ be the life cycle unit cost function (with the life cycle labour and capital prices as arguments) which is dual to the linear homogeneous part of the ex ante production function $\Phi(L, K)$. This dual unit cost function will also belong to the CES family [cf. e.g. Varian (1978, pp. 18–20)], and it can be written in the form (omitting, for simplicity, the time subscripts)

$$\Psi(\Lambda_L w, q) = a\big[\beta(\Lambda_L w)^{1-\sigma} + (1-\beta)q^{1-\sigma}\big]^{1/(1-\sigma)},$$

where a is positive constant, β is a constant between 0 and 1 (corresponding to the "distribution parameter" in the production function), and σ is the elasticity of substitution between capital and labour. In optimum, the labour cost as a share of the life cycle output value can be written as

$$\frac{\Lambda_L w L}{\Lambda_X p X} = \frac{\partial X}{\partial L}\frac{L}{X} = \left(\frac{\partial X}{\partial \Phi}\frac{\Phi}{X}\right)\left(\frac{\partial \Phi}{\partial L}\frac{L}{\phi}\right) = \varepsilon\frac{\partial \Phi}{\partial L}\frac{L}{\Phi},$$

where [cf. (7.43) and (7.44)]

$$\Lambda_L = \frac{1 - e^{-(r-\gamma_L+\delta)N}}{r - \gamma_L + \delta}, \qquad \Lambda_X = \frac{1 - e^{-(r-\gamma_X+\delta\varepsilon)N}}{r - \gamma_X + \delta\varepsilon},$$

when using the homogeneity property of the production function. The scrapping condition (7.36) now reads

$$N = \frac{1}{\gamma_L - \gamma_X - \delta(1-\varepsilon)} \ln\left[\frac{pX}{wL}\right],$$

provided $\gamma_L - \gamma_X - \delta(1-\varepsilon) > 0$. Inserting from the cost share equation, we obtain

$$(7.47) \qquad N = \frac{1}{\gamma_L - \gamma_X - \delta(1-\varepsilon)}\left[\ln\left(\frac{\Lambda_L}{\Lambda_X}\right) - \ln(\varepsilon) - \ln\left(\frac{\partial\Phi}{\partial L}\frac{L}{\Phi}\right)\right].$$

In the Cobb-Douglas case, $(\partial\Phi/\partial L)(L/\Phi)$ is constant and equal to β [cf. (7.46)]. Under a CES technology, it is price dependent and equal to

$$\frac{\partial\Phi}{\partial L}\frac{L}{\Phi} = \frac{\partial\Psi}{\partial(\Lambda_L w)}\frac{\Lambda_L w}{\Psi} = \frac{\beta(\Lambda_L w)^{1-\sigma}}{\beta(\Lambda_L w)^{1-\sigma} + (1-\beta)q^{1-\sigma}},$$

whose first equality follows from the duality between Φ and Ψ [cf. e.g. Jorgenson (1986, section 2.1)].

The optimal value of N, and hence the associated user cost of capital, depends on (i) the technology parameters β, ε, σ, and δ, (ii) the interest rate r, (iii) the rates of price increase increase γ_L and γ_X, and (iv) the initial wage rate/investment price ratio w/q. The latter variable had no effect on the user cost in the case of a Cobb-Douglas technology, because of the implied constancy of the life cycle factor shares under profit maximization.

THE USER COST OF CAPITAL UNDER A PUTTY-CLAY TECHNOLOGY. PART 2: TAXES INCLUDED

8.1 Introduction

The purpose of this chapter is to extend the definition of the user cost of capital under a putty-clay technology, given in chapter 7, to comprise the effect of taxes. The taxes considered include an income tax and a wealth tax imposed on the firm's assets. Although the description of the technology is different, our formalization of the tax system for the neo-classical model, given in chapter 5, can, to a substantial degree, be adapted to the putty-clay framework. There are, however, notable differences. They stem from the ex post rigidity of the input structure in the putty-clay model and the endogeneity of the scrapping decisions which it implies. Under the putty-clay technology, the tax system may, for instance, affect the scrapping plans. There is no counterpart to this in a neo-classical model assuming that capital can be transferred freely from one production activity to another, and treating retirement as an exogenous process which is unaffected by prices and tax rates. [Cf. chapter 4.] Neither did endogenous scrapping of capital occur for the kind of investment projects we considered in chapter 2. These projects were assumed to have a given service life and a payment flow which is unaffected by the firm's decisions [cf. sections 2.3 and 7.1].

Since, under a putty-clay technology, all input and output variables, as well as the expectational variables for prices, have a vintage dimension, a corresponding disaggregation of the tax function will be convenient. All components of the tax payment flow, like the cash-flow, will be identified by a double time subscript. The first subscript represents current time, and the second represents the vintage (or age) to which the income and wealth subject to taxation belongs.

The chapter now proceeds as follows. In section 8.2, the basic vintage specific functions related to the tax system are defined. These include the vintage specific tax function, the tax corrected quasi rent function, and the tax corrected profit functions. The description generalizes in several respects the description in section 2.6, which was related to a single investment project with a given service life and with no substitutable inputs specified. Again, as in section 7.1, there is a similarity between the concepts vintage and project. On this basis, we establish, in section 8.3, the tax corrected user cost. As in the neo-classical model, two interpretations of this cost are given, a service price interpretation and a shadow value interpretation derived from the firm's conditions for profit maximization. We pay particular attention to the relationship between the user cost and the service life of the capital as it is determined from the firm's optimizing behaviour. This is a problem that was not under discussion in chapter 2. Finally, section 8.4 is concerned, more specifically, with the effect of the tax system on the scrapping plans of the firm and with the role of the ex ante technology in this context.

8.2   The vintage specific tax function, quasi rent function, and profit function

Consider a firm at time t and let us follow all transactions related to the capital invested at this time, i.e. vintage t, including the tax payment flow generated by these transactions. This way of considering the tax system may seem somewhat artificial. In practice, the tax liability of a firm is usually based on its payment flows aggregated over vintages; the taxes in a given year are assessed on the basis of its *total* income and wealth, without regard to which vintages the "components" of the income and wealth refer. Often such a decomposition cannot be performed in practice. However, no objection can be raised against this procedure *in principle*. When the taxes are proportional and the tax rates remain constant over time, as is assumed here, a disaggregation of the tax function by vintages has no practical consequence. We can, without loss of realism, consider the tax function at a given time as an aggregate of vintage specific tax functions with identical tax rates, equal to the current rates.

The expected tax payment from vintage t which is due at time $t + s$ can then be written as

$$
(8.1) \quad \begin{aligned}
T^*(t+s,t) = u\,[\,p^*(t+s,t)X(t+s,s) - w^*(t+s,t)L(t+s,s) \\
- \mu(s)q^*(t+s,t)J(t)\,]\,, \qquad 0 \le s \le N(t),
\end{aligned}
$$

where u is the income tax rate, assumed to remain constant over the planning period, $p^*(t+s,t)$, $w^*(t+s,t)$, and $q^*(t+s,t)$ are the output price, the wage rate, and the investment price, respectively, which at time t is expected to prevail at time $t+s$, $X(t+s,s)$ and $L(t+s,s)$ are, respectively, output from and labour input allocated to vintage t at age s, $J(t)$ is the capital invested in vintage t, $\mu(s)$ is the share of the value of the investment in a specific vintage *at expected replacement cost* which is deductible against income expected s years later, and $N(t)$ is the planned service life of vintage t. This function will be denoted as the *ex ante tax function* for vintage t. As in the neo-classical model, $\mu(s)$ represents, in a compact way, the rules for interest deductions, depreciation allowances, taxation of capital gains, and capital value taxation.[1] Note that the weight $\mu(s)$ operates on an *ex ante* variable at time t: the *expected* investment price s *years ahead* times the *current* quantity invested. The corresponding weighting function in the neo-classical model operated on an *ex post* variable: the *current* investment price times the quantity invested s *years ago*. For a tax system belonging to class A [cf. subsection 5.4.1] we have specifically [cf. eq. (5.32)]

$$\mu(s) = \mu_A(s)$$

$$= a(s)e^{(\varepsilon-\gamma)s} \qquad \text{(depreciation allowances)}$$

$$+ miA(s)e^{(\varepsilon-\gamma)s} \qquad \text{(interest deductions)}$$

(8.2.a)
$$- n\varepsilon A(s)e^{(\varepsilon-\gamma)s} \qquad \text{(capital gains)}$$

$$- \frac{v}{u}A(s)e^{(\varepsilon-\gamma)s} \qquad \text{(capital value tax)}$$

$$= \left[a(s) + \left(mi + n\varepsilon - \frac{u}{v} \right) A(s) \right] e^{(\varepsilon-\gamma)s}\,.$$

---

[1] It is not, however, obvious that $\mu(s)$ will be a function only of s and not of t in this case. "Stationarity" of $\mu(s)$ is a more critical assumption here than it is in the neo-classical model. This complication and its possible consequences will be discussed in section 8.3 below.

A tax system in class M is characterized by [cf. eq. (5.34)]

$$\mu(s) = \mu_M(s)$$

$$= a(s)e^{(\varepsilon_1-\gamma)s} \qquad \text{(depreciation allowances)}$$

$$+ m\big[(i - \alpha_I\varepsilon_2)\,G(s)$$

$$- (1 - \alpha_I)\varepsilon_2 A(s)e^{(\varepsilon_2-\gamma)s}\big]\text{(interest deductions)}$$

$$- n\big[(\gamma - \alpha_G\varepsilon_2)\,G(s)$$

(8.2.b)
$$- (1 - \alpha_G)\varepsilon_2 A(s)e^{(\varepsilon_2-\gamma)s}\big] \qquad \text{(capital gains)}$$

$$- \frac{v}{u}A(s)e^{(\varepsilon_1-\gamma)s} \qquad \text{(capital value tax)}$$

$$= \Big[a(s) - \frac{v}{u}A(s)\Big]\,e^{(\varepsilon_1-\gamma)s}$$

$$+ \big[m(i - \alpha_I\varepsilon_2) - n(\gamma - \alpha_G\varepsilon_2)\big]\,G(s)$$

$$- \big[m(1 - \alpha_I) - n(1 - \alpha_G)\big]\,\varepsilon_2 A(s)\,e^{(\varepsilon_2-\gamma)s}\,.$$

The *ex ante quasi rent after taxes* from vintage t at time $t + s$ is

(8.3) $\qquad R_T^*(t + s, t) = R^*(t + s, t) - T^*(t + s, t)\,, \qquad 0 \le s \le N(t)\,.$

After inserting from (7.11) and (8.1), it can be written as

$$R_T^*(t + s, t) = (1 - u)\,[p^*(t + s, t)B_X(s)X(t, 0)$$

(8.4)
$$- w^*(t + s, t)B_L(s)L(t, 0)]$$

$$+ u\mu(s)q^*(t + s, t)J(t)\,, \qquad 0 \le s \le N(t)\,,$$

where $B_L(s)$ and $B_X(s)$ are the age profile functions for labour input and output, defined as in (7.12) and (7.13). This equation generalizes (7.11).

Note the conceptual difference between the net cash-flow function $R_T(t)$, given by (6.2), in the neo-classical model and the net cash-flow function $R_T^*(t + s, t)$ in the putty-clay model: The former is *time* specific and *backward* looking, since it represents the net payment flow at time t of *all previous* investment decisions. The latter is *vintage* specific and *forward* looking, it gives the expected net payment flow at time $t + s$ of all present and future production decisions which are related to the *current* investment decision at time t.

By discounting this flow of quasi rents to time t at the interest rate $r(t)$ and deducting the investment cost, we get the *after tax profit function* for vintage t:

$$(8.5) \qquad \Pi_T^*(t) = \int_0^{N(t)} e^{-r(t)s} R_T^*(t+s,t)\,ds - q(t)J(t)\,.$$

This expression generalizes (7.14). If we make the same assumptions about price expectations as in chapter 7, i.e. constant rates of increase equal to $\gamma(t)$, $\gamma_L(t)$, and $\gamma_X(t)$ for the investment price, the wage rate, and the output price, respectively [cf. (7.18), (7.22), and (7.28)], we can rewrite the profit function (8.5) with (8.4) inserted as

$$
\begin{aligned}
(8.6) \qquad \Pi_T^*(t) &= (1-u)\left[\Lambda_X(t)p(t)X(t,0) - \Lambda_L(t)w(t)L(t,0)\right] \\
&\quad - (1-\lambda u)\,q(t)\,J(t) \\
&= (1-u)\Pi^*(t) - u(1-\lambda)\,q(t)\,J(t)\,,
\end{aligned}
$$

where

$$(8.7) \qquad \lambda = \lambda(t) = \int_0^{N(t)} e^{-[r(t)-\gamma(t)]\tau}\mu(\tau)\,d\tau\,,$$

$\Pi^*(t)$ denotes the profit before taxes, defined in (7.14), and $\Lambda_X(t)$ and $\Lambda_L(t)$ are the annualization factors for output and labour input, given in (7.32) and (7.26), respectively. Eq. (8.6) generalizes (7.33).

Formally, λ has the same interpretation as in the neo-classical model [cf. (6.5)]. It represents the present value of the per unit net deduction in the income tax base. There is, however, one important difference: While in the neo-classical model the discounting of $\mu(s)$ goes to infinity (in principle), in the putty-clay model, it goes up to the planned service life of the vintage only.[2] This means that now λ will be *endogenous* since it depends on a variable, $N(t)$, which is a decision variable for the firm. Even if r and γ are time invariant parameters, λ will be time dependent to the extent that the planned service life $N(t)$ changes over time. This property also

---

[2] Or, equivalently, we may assume that the discounting goes to infinity while $\mu(s)$ is equal to zero when s exceeds the planned scrapping age $N(t)$. Then $\mu(s)$ will implicitly be a function of t. Another way of stating this assumption is that no capital good is planned to occur in the firm's tax account when it has become economically obsolete. This will be elaborated in section 8.3.

distinguishes the putty-clay model with taxes from the corresponding neo-classical model.

From eq. (8.6) we can state:

Proposition 8.A

1. For a given time invariant tax rate u, all tax systems which give the same value of λ are equivalent, in the sense that they give the same vintage specific profit function.

2. An income tax at the rate u is equivalent (in the present value sense) to a tax at the rate u on the present value of the firm's vintage specific cash-flow, defined by replacing the market investment price $q(t)$ by the tax corrected price $q(t)(1 - \lambda u)/(1 - u)$. Assuming perfect financial markets, this is equivalent to the following vintage specific cash-flow tax: At the initial time, i.e. for age $s = 0$, impose a tax at the rate u on the quasi rent minus the full tax corrected investment cost, i.e. $R^*(t,t) - q(t)J(t)(1 - \lambda u)/(1 - u)$. (If this difference is negative, give a subsidy to the firm.) At ages $s > 0$, impose a tax at the rate u on the quasi rent $R^*(t + s, t)$.

This is the counterpart to proposition 6.A, derived in chapter 6 for the neo-classical model. All information needed in addition to the tax rate, to describe the effect of the tax system on the after tax life cycle profit, is the value of λ.

The term $-u(1 - \lambda)q(t)J(t)$ after the second equality sign in (8.6) represents the adjustment which must be made in the firm's after tax ex ante profit from vintage t to account for the fact that its tax base differs from its true ex ante profit, $\Pi^*(t)$. This adjustment is positive, zero, and negative according as $\lambda \mathrel{\overset{>}{\underset{<}{=}}} 1$, i.e. according as the present value of the per unit net deductions in the income tax base is greater than, equal to, or less than one.

Despite the differences with respect to technology, there is an arresting formal analogy between the expression for the vintage specific net profit in the putty-clay model, (8.6), and the present value of the total net cash-flow in the neo-classical model, (6.6). The correspondence between the different variables is summarized in table 8.1. In both models, the tax system comes in through two parameters, the income tax rate u and the composite per unit income deduction parameter, λ, only.

Table 8.1: Formal correspondence between the vintage specific profit function in the putty-clay model, (8.6), and the overall profit function in the neo-classical model, (6.6).

Putty-clay	Neo-classical
$\Pi^*(t)$	W
$\Pi_T^*(t)$	$W_T - W_{T0}$
$\int_0^{N(t)} c^{-r(t)s} R^*(t+s,t)\,ds =$	
$\Lambda_X(t)\,p(t)X(t,0) - \Lambda_L(t)\,w(t)\,L(t,0)$	$\int_0^\infty e^{-rt} X(t)\,dt$
$q(t)\,J(t)$	$\int_0^\infty e^{-rt} q(t)J(t)\,dt$

8.3 The tax corrected service price. The shadow value interpretation

From (8.6) we observe that if the market investment price $q(t)$ is replaced by the tax corrected price, defined as $q(t)(1 - \lambda(t)u)/(1 - u)$, and the pre-tax profit is redefined accordingly, then we will get the after tax profit from vintage t simply by multiplying this redefined pre-tax profit by $1 - u$. This is, formally, the same definition of the tax corrected investment price as in the neo-classical model [cf. eq. (6.7)]. Let us now insert the tax corrected investment price into the three alternative service price formulae for the zero-tax case which we derived in section 7.4, i.e. (7.19), (7.25), and (7.31). This gives the following values of the service prices for vintage t at age $s = 0$:

Tax corrected service price normalized against capital value:

$$(8.8) \qquad c_K(t,t) = \frac{q(t)}{\Lambda_K(t)} \cdot \frac{1 - \lambda(t)u}{1 - u}.$$

Tax corrected service price normalized against labour cost:

$$(8.9) \qquad c_L(t,t) = \frac{q(t)}{\Lambda_L(t)} \cdot \frac{1 - \lambda(t)u}{1 - u}.$$

Tax corrected service price normalized against output value:

$$(8.10) \qquad c_X(t,t) = \frac{q(t)}{\Lambda_X(t)} \cdot \frac{1 - \lambda(t)u}{1 - u}.$$

In the corresponding putty-clay model without taxes, three *different* real interest rates were involved in the expressions for c_K, c_L, and c_X, namely, $r - \gamma$, $r - \gamma_L$, and $r - \gamma_X$, respectively. When taxes are included, this will no longer hold. Since the tax deduction parameter λ, by virtue of (8.7), will contain the real interest rate relating to the capital price, $r - \gamma$, all the three versions of the service price will be functions of this real interest rate. There is thus an asymmetry between the service prices corresponding to the putty-clay models in the presence and in the absence of taxes.

Substituting these three alternative service price expressions into the profit function (8.6), it is easy to show that they can also be given shadow value interpretations. We find

$$\text{(a)} \qquad \Pi_T^*(t) = (1 - u)\left[\Lambda_X(t)p(t)X(t,0) - \Lambda_L(t)w(t)L(t,0)\right.$$
$$\left. - \Lambda_K(t)c_K(t,t)J(t)\right],$$

$$(8.11) \quad \text{(b)} \qquad \Pi_T^*(t) = (1 - u)\left[\Lambda_X(t)p(t)X(t,0)\right.$$
$$\left. - \Lambda_L(t)\{w(t)L(t,0) + c_L(t,t)J(t)\}\right],$$

$$\text{(c)} \qquad \Pi_T^*(t) = (1 - u)\left[\Lambda_X(t)\{p(t)X(t,0) - c_X(t,t)J(t)\}\right.$$
$$\left. - \Lambda_L(t)w(t)L(t,0)\right].$$

From this it follows that the first order condition for profit maximization with respect to investment can be stated in three alternative ways,[3]

$$\text{(a)} \qquad \frac{\Lambda_X(t)}{\Lambda_K(t)}p(t)\frac{\partial X(t,0)}{\partial J(t)} = c_K(t,t),$$

$$(8.12) \quad \text{(b)} \qquad \frac{\Lambda_X(t)}{\Lambda_L(t)}p(t)\frac{\partial X(t,0)}{\partial J(t)} = c_L(t,t),$$

$$\text{(c)} \qquad p(t)\frac{\partial X(t,0)}{\partial J(t)} = c_X(t,t).$$

---

[3] The marginal condition for labour is expressed conformably; confer (7.34).

Thus, the equivalence between the service price and the shadow value interpretations of the user cost, noted in section 7.5 for the model without taxes, carries over to the case where taxes are included.

One problem, however, remains. It relates to the endogeneity of the service life. The first order condition for maximization of the life cycle profit of vintage t, (8.6), with respect to the service life $N(t)$ is

$$(1-u)\frac{\partial \Lambda_X(t)}{\partial N(t)}p(t)X(t,0) = (1-u)\frac{\partial \Lambda_L(t)}{\partial N(t)}w(t)L(t,0) - u\frac{\partial \lambda(t)}{\partial N(t)}q(t)J(t,0).$$

Using (7.26), (7.32), and (8.7), this condition can be rewritten as

$$
\begin{aligned}
(8.13) \qquad & e^{\gamma_X(t)N(t)}B_X[N(t)]p(t)X(t,0) \\
& - e^{\gamma_L(t)N(t)}R_L[N(t)]w(t)L(t,0) \\
& - \frac{u}{1-u}e^{\gamma(t)N(t)}\mu[N(t)]q(t)J(t,0).
\end{aligned}
$$

This expression generalizes the quasi-rent criterion for the zero tax case, (7.36), and coincides with it *if and only if* $\mu[N(t)] = 0$. The latter condition has the interpretation that the net deduction in the income tax base allowed per unit of the initial investment outlay shall be zero at the expected scrapping age. This condition will be satisfied if no interest deductions or depreciation allowances and no capital gains are recorded in the tax base at the (expected) scrapping age or after. Stated more simply, the condition $\mu[N(t)] = 0$ says that *no capital vintage occurs in the firm's tax account at the time when it has become economically obsolete.*

This is a reasonable condition as far as the accounting capital is concerned. A firm will usually be allowed to write off a capital good completely — possibly by means of extraordinary depreciation allowances — if it can convince the tax authorities that the capital good has become economically obsolete. Formally, this implies that the weighting functions $A(s)$ and $a(s)$ [cf. (5.1) and (5.5)] are defined to be zero for $s \geq N(t)$, or if this condition is not satisfied, that the functions are *truncated* at the scrapping age in the following way

$$
(8.14) \qquad A(s;t) = \begin{cases} A(s), & \text{for } 0 \leq s < N(t), \\ 0, & \text{for } s \geq N(t), \end{cases}
$$

$$
(8.15) \qquad a(s;t) = \begin{cases} a(s) = A'(s), & \text{for } 0 \leq s < N(t), \\ 0, & \text{for } s \geq N(t). \end{cases}
$$

By inserting these truncated weighting functions in (8.2.a), we see that $\mu[N(t)] = 0$ is ensured for any tax system in *class A*. Then the scrapping condition will be the same as in the no-tax case, i.e. $R^*(t + N(t), t) = 0$.[4]

The situation is not so simple if the tax system belongs to *class M*, i.e. if the interest cost and the capital gains recorded for tax purposes are based on the *market* value of the capital stock, not on its accounting value [cf. subsection 5.4.1]. The firm may, for instance, pay interests on a loan used to finance a capital good after it has been scrapped. In the neo-classical model, the market value of an old capital vintage affects $\mu(s)$ through the weighting function for the net capital, $G(s)$ [cf. (5.34)], which is derived from the survival function $B(s)$ by assuming a perfect capital market characterized by an equalization of capital prices across vintages [cf. subsections 3.5.2 and 3.5.4]. When there is a specific technique attached to each vintage ex post, and $B(s)$ represents the maximal (potential), rather than the actual, flow of capital services from a vintage at age s [cf. subsection 7.2.1], however, this indifference between vintages will not hold any longer. The interpretation of $G(s)$ in (8.2.b) is then less obvious. Let us, without going into details, outline two ways of proceeding.

First, we could truncate the weighting function for net capital as defined for a corresponding neo-classical technology, $G(s)$, at the scrapping age, and otherwise represent the tax system as in the neo-classical case. We would then change the definition of $G(s)$, (3.51), into

$$(8.16) \qquad G(s;t) = \frac{\int_s^{N(t)} e^{-\rho(z-s)} B(z) \, dz}{\int_0^{N(t)} e^{-\rho z} B(z) \, dz}, \qquad 0 \le s \le N(t),$$

and let this weighting function replace $G(s)$ in (8.2.b) when defining the tax deductible interest cost and the capital gains. This modification would for instance imply that all loans are (planned to be) fully repaid at the scrapping age.

The second way of calculating capital values when defining interest deductions and capital gains in the tax base would be to replace $G(s)$ by an assumption that the value of any vintage ex post equals (or at least reflects) the present value of the flow of (expected) *quasi rents* during its remaining

---

[4] Since the vintage specific tax function for vintage t at age s can be written as

$$T^*(t + s, t) = u \left[R^*(t + s, t) - \mu(s) q^*(t + s, t) J(t) \right],$$

it follows from (8.3) that $R_T^*(t + N(t), t) = 0$ and $\mu(N(t)) = 0$ implies $R^*(t + N(t), t) = 0$.

service life.[5] This is a theoretically more satisfactory, although mathematically substantially more complicated, approach. The reason for this is that the decline in the capital value over time could not be represented by the weighting function $G(s;t)$, but would depend on the tax system and the market parameters r, γ_X, and γ_L in a complex way. Such a modification would, of course, alter the definition of $\mu(s)$. Formally, we would have to replace the "exogenous" function $\mu(s)$, given by (8.2.b), in (8.1) and (8.4) by a function depending on the present value of the expected flow of net quasi rents $R^*(\theta, t)$ from time $\theta = t + s$ to time $\theta = t + N(t)$. This approach is better integrated with the putty-clay assumption than the first, which is, strictly, an ad hoc modification of the neo-classical specification.

Regardless of which approach we take to the incorporation of tax systems belonging to class M in our putty-clay framework, it seems reasonable to conclude — as we did for class A — that the weighting function for defining capital expenditures deductible in the tax base, $\mu(s)$, is zero for ages larger than the expected scrapping age, i.e. for $s \geq N(t)$. As a consequence, the quasi-rent criterion for determination of the optimal scrapping age, (8.13), will remain the same as in the zero tax case, i.e. (7.36). This does not mean, however, that the tax system has no impact on the service life. Since the tax parameters will, in general, affect the effective capital service price through the parameter λ [cf. (8.8)–(8.10)], and hence affect the optimal output and labour input, it will also, through (8.13), affect the optimal service life. In the final section, this relationship is discussed.

8.4   The effect of the tax system on the scrapping plans and on the user cost of capital

Let us make the same assumptions as in the CES function example in section 7.6, except that taxes are now included. The life cycle unit cost function which is dual to the linear homogeneous part of the ex ante production function then is

$$\Psi\left[\Lambda_L w, q(1 - \lambda u)/(1 - u)\right]$$
$$= a\left[\beta(\Lambda_L w)^{1-\sigma} + (1 - \beta)\{q(1 - \lambda u)/(1 - u)\}^{1-\sigma}\right]^{1/(1-\sigma)},$$

---

[5] This way of treating capital evaluation within a putty-clay context is discussed, for the zero tax case and with reference to the energy/capital substitution, in Biørn (1986, section IV).

where the market price of capital q is replaced by the tax corrected price $q(1 - \lambda u)/(1 - u)$.

Assuming that the scrapping condition (8.13) is not affected by the tax system, so that $\mu(N) = 0$, N being the optimal scrapping age [cf. section 8.3], this scrapping age satisfies [cf. (7.47)]

$$N = \frac{1}{\gamma_L - \gamma_X - \delta(1 - \varepsilon)} \left[\ln\left(\frac{\Lambda_L}{\Lambda_X}\right) - \ln(\varepsilon) - \ln\left(\frac{\partial \Phi}{\partial L} \frac{L}{\Phi}\right) \right],$$

where $(\partial \Phi / \partial L)(L/\Phi)$ is now given by

$$\frac{\partial \Phi}{\partial L} \cdot \frac{L}{\Phi} = \frac{\partial \Psi}{\partial (\Lambda_L w)} \cdot \frac{\Lambda_L w}{\Psi} = \frac{\beta(\Lambda_L w)^{1-\sigma}}{\beta(\Lambda_L w)^{1-\sigma} + (1 - \beta)\{q(1 - \lambda u)/(1 - u)\}^{1-\sigma}} \cdot$$

Again, the first equality in this expression follows from the duality between Φ and Ψ. We see that changes in the tax system, as represented by the tax rate u and the income deduction parameter λ, will affect the labour elasticity $(\partial \Phi / \partial L)(L/\Phi)$. Hence, such changes will affect the planned service life under a CES technology in the general case. Only if $\sigma = 1$, i.e. only if the ex ante technology is Cobb-Douglas, will changes in the tax system — as long as they are not shifted into γ_L and γ_X — have no effect on N, since $(\partial \Phi / \partial L)(L/\Phi)$ is then constant and equal to β.

Our conclusion, then, is that the degree of ex ante substitution between labour and capital may substantially affect the impact of the corporate tax system on the ex ante service life. The user cost of capital will usually respond to changes in the tax system not only via the tax factor $(1 - \lambda u)/(1 - u)$, but also via the service life $N(t)$. To get a closer understanding of these effects, they will have to be calculated numerically.

CHAPTER 9

NEUTRALITY AND DEPARTURE FROM NEUTRALITY IN CORPORATE TAXATION

9.1 Introduction. The concept of neutrality

"There are few problems in tax analysis which have generated as much study and discussion among economists as the question of how to formulate 'neutral' tax incentives for investment" (Auerbach (1983b, p. 33)). In this study, a corporate tax system will be defined to be neutral if its imposition does not interfere with the firm's marginal conditions for optimal production and factor allocation. This concept of neutrality is a *partial* one, since it involves the optimization performed within the corporate sector and the taxes imposed on this sector only. Neutrality in this sense is a *necessary*, but not sufficient condition for neutrality of the tax system as a whole.[1] We do not, for instance, consider the effect of personal taxes on the firm's factor allocation in general, and on its capital accumulation in particular, *inter alia* via the financing of the investment. It should be recalled that neutrality confined to corporate taxation is not necessarily an attractive property of a tax system when its overall effect on capital allocation is in focus, if the personal tax system does not satisfy the conditions for optimal factor allocation. An investigation of our partial concept of neutrality from a "second best" point of view is, however, beyond the scope of this study.

---

[1] To characterize completely the neutrality of the tax system, we should also include the effect of the personal income and wealth tax, the value added tax, and the system of excises and subsidies on the allocation of consumption (including the purchase of durables), saving, and labour supply in the household sector. From general welfare economics it is well known that full neutrality, in the sense of Pareto efficiency, in a neo-classical model of intertemporal production, consumption, and saving, implies, *inter alia*, equality between the rate of time preference in consumption and the marginal rate of return to capital in production. [See for instance Malinvaud (1972, Ch. 10).] If the tax system distorts this Pareto efficiency condition, it will be non-neutral in a general equilibrium context.

The purpose of this chapter is twofold. First, we demonstrate how the user cost of capital, as defined in the previous chapters, can be applied to establish conditions for neutrality of the corporate taxation in the above mentioned sense. The second purpose is to define ways of measuring the departure from neutrality. In several respects, the chapter generalizes results in the literature. This reflects, *inter alia,* our more general way of treating retirement of capital and our more flexible parametrization of tax indexation. The material is organized as follows. In section 9.2, the formal conditions for neutrality are derived, with reference both to the neo-classical technology and to the putty-clay technology. In section 9.3, the concept of a neutrality locus is introduced, by means of which we can characterize more precisely the class of corporate tax systems which ensure neutrality. Finally, section 9.4 deals with alternative ways of measuring the departure from neutrality of a given tax system, and presents numerical illustrations for a wide selection of tax codes.

9.2   General conditions for neutrality

9.2.1 *The neo-classical model*

The user cost of capital corresponding to a neo-classical model without taxes is equal to

$$(9.1) \qquad \bar{c}(t) = \frac{q(t)}{\Phi_{i-\gamma}(0)} = \frac{q(t)}{\int_0^\infty e^{-(i-\gamma)s} B(s)ds},$$

when the rate of discount for future cash-flow is set equal to the market interest rate [cf. (4.1) and (6.13)]. A tax system which has the property that $c(t) = \bar{c}(t)$ for all t, regardless of the economic situation, is *uniformly neutral*[2] in the sense that its imposition will not distort the marginal conditions for a neo-classical firm maximizing the present value of its net after tax cash-flow. Equivalently, the tax system is uniformly neutral if the tax corrected investment price $q^*(t)$ coincides with the market price $q(t)$ at any time t, regardless of the interest rate, the rate of inflation, and the retirement structure of the capital.[3] We see from (6.7) that the latter condition

---

[2] Strictly, uniformly neutral with respect to the class of corporate tax systems.

[3] This follows from the fact that only the marginal condition for capital, (6.11), is affected by the tax system, since costs of other inputs are assumed always to be completely deductible in the income tax base. Confer section 5.3.

will be satisfied — for any value of the income tax rate u — if and only if $\lambda = 1$. Summarizing, we have

Proposition 9.A When the rate of discount used in maximizing the present value of net cash-flow is equal to the nominal market interest rate $(r = i)$, a necessary and sufficient condition for neutrality under a neo-classical technology is that the present value of the future deductions in the income base allowed per unit of investment outlay,

$$\lambda = \int_0^\infty e^{-(i-\gamma)s} \mu(s)\, ds\,,$$

is equal to one regardless of the value of the income tax rate u. If this property holds regardless of the value of the interest rate i, the inflation rate γ, and the form of the survival function $B(s)$, the tax system is uniformly neutral.

The latter part of this proportion is important since a tax system may imply $\lambda = 1$ for certain constellations of i, γ, and $B(s)$, while it gives $\lambda \neq 1$ for others. Uniform neutrality refers to a tax system whose constellation of the parameters m, n, u, v, ε, ε_1, ε_2, and $A(s)$ ensures $\lambda = 1$ regardless of the values of i and γ, and of the form of $B(s)$.

This condition is intuitively appealing: A tax system does not distort the capital allocation if the firm is allowed, *in the present value sense*, to deduct from taxable income exactly the replacement value of its investment cost. It is not a claim for neutrality that the firm's true net profit *at any point of time* be the basis of the income taxation.

To explain this difference we refer back to section 3.5 and consider the firm's net profit (true income), defined by

Net profit = Gross operating surplus

       − Imputed interest on value of capital stock

       − Net value of depreciation of capital stock,

or with symbols,

$$I(t) = X(t) - iV(t) - E(t) = X(t) - \int_0^\infty [iV(t,s) + E(t,s)]\, ds\,.$$

Inserting from (3.49) and (3.61), while using (5.24) and (6.13), this can be written as

$$(9.2) \qquad I(t) = X(t) - q(t) \int_0^\infty [(i - \gamma)G_{i-\gamma}(s) + g_{i-\gamma}(s)]J(t - s)\, ds\,.$$

The taxable income is, on the other hand, [cf. (5.31) and (5.33)]

$$(9.3) \qquad\qquad I_T(t) = X(t) - q(t) \int_0^\infty \mu(s)J(t - s)\, ds\,.$$

For $I_T(t)$ to coincide with $I(t)$ regardless of the time paths of the investment quantity $J(t)$ and the investment price $q(t)$, we should have

$$\mu(s) = (i - \gamma)G_{i-\gamma}(s) + g_{i-\gamma}(s) \qquad \text{for all } s.$$

Neutrality does not presume this equality to hold for all values of s, however, it only requires equality in terms of present values, i.e.

$$\int_0^\infty e^{-(i-\gamma)s} \mu(s)\, ds = \int_0^\infty e^{-(i-\gamma)s}[(i - \gamma)G_{i-\gamma}(s) + g_{i-\gamma}(s)]\, ds\,.$$

Since the latter integral is equal to 1 for all values of $i - \gamma$[4] this condition is equivalent to $\lambda = 1$.

9.2.2 The putty-clay model

When considering the neutrality conditions for the putty-clay model, things become more complicated for two reasons. First, as we noted in section 7.5 [cf. table 7.1], there is no unique way of defining a user cost of capital concept for this sort of model. A change in the interest rate will affect not only the marginal condition for capital, as in the neo-classical model, but also — via the annualization factors — the marginal condition for labour. Second, as shown in section 8.4, a change in the tax parameters will normally affect the optimal service life, and hence it will have one direct and one indirect link to the user cost. How should then neutrality be defined?

We can give the following answer to this question: Let $\bar{N}(t)$ be the service life that would be planned for vintage t if no taxes were imposed on the

---

[4] This follows straightly from (3.54) by using integration by parts.

firm. If $\lambda(t) = 1$ for $N(t) = \bar{N}(t)$ and $\mu(s) = 0$ for $s \geq \bar{N}(t)$ regardless of the value of the tax rate u, then the optimizing conditions for capital, labour, and the ex ante service life would not be affected by the tax system. This follows from (8.7)–(8.13). Such a tax system can be said to be neutral for a putty-clay model and uniformly neutral if it satisfies these conditions for all t. Summarizing, we have

Proposition 9.B When the rate of discount is equal to the nominal market interest rate $(r = i)$, necessary and sufficient conditions for neutrality under a putty-clay technology are

(a) the ex ante service life is not affected by the tax system, i.e. $N(t) = N(t)$,
(b) the present value of the future deductions in the income base allowed per unit of investment outlay over the (ex ante) service life,

$$\lambda(t) = \int_0^{\bar{N}(t)} e^{-(i-\gamma)s} \mu(s) \, ds \,,$$

is equal to one regardless of the value of the income tax rate u, and
(c) no deductions in the income tax base are performed after the scrapping age, i.e. $\mu(s) = 0$ for $s \geq \bar{N}(t)$.
If (a)–(c) hold regardless of the value of the interest rate i, the inflation rate γ, and the form of the survival function $B(s)$, the tax system is uniformly neutral.

9.2.3 Uniformly neutral tax systems

Consider first the tax systems which ensure uniform neutrality. For simplicity, we limit attention to the neo-classical case, but the results can, with minor modifications, be made applicable to the putty-clay case as well.
From (6.16) and (6.17) it follows directly that

$\lambda_A = 1$ when $Z_{i-\epsilon} = 0$, irrespective of the values of

     $m \,, n \,, u \,, v \,,$ and $\varepsilon \,.$

$\lambda_M = 1$ when $Z_{i-\epsilon_1} = 0$ and $m = n = 0$, irrespective of the values of

     $u \,, v \,, \varepsilon_1 \,,$ and $\varepsilon_2 \,.$

These conditions can be given simple interpretations.

For $Z_{i-\varepsilon} = 0$ — or equivalently $z_{i-\varepsilon} = 1$ [cf. (5.47)] — to be satisfied regardless of the value of $i - \varepsilon$, instantaneous depreciation must be permitted, i.e. the firm should be allowed to write off its investment expenditures immediately at the time of purchase.[5] This condition is sufficient for neutrality of a tax system in class A. The additional conditions for class M are that no interest cost shall be deductible $(m = 0)$ and no capital gains shall be included in the income tax base $(n = 0)$. We summarize these conclusions in

Proposition 9.C Provided that the rate of discount is equal to the market interest rate $(r = i)$, neutrality is ensured uniformly if

(i) instantaneous depreciation is permitted: $A(s) = 0$ for $s > 0 \Rightarrow Z_\rho = 0$, or $z_\rho = 1$, and

(ii) no deduction of imputed interests in income tax base is permitted: $m = 0$, and no capital gain is accounted: $n = 0$.[6]

A tax system permitting immediate deduction of the investment cost, no deduction of interests, and no taxation of capital gains — often called a cash-flow tax — has been discussed *inter alia* by Musgrave (1959, p. 343), Smith (1963), King (1974, p. 31), (1975, p. 275), and Boadway (1980, p. 254). Musgrave in fact characterizes it as "a perfectly neutral solution".[7]

---

[5] To show this formally, we consider the case where the capital is written off linearly during a short interval of length Δ immediately after investment, i.e.

$$A(s) = \begin{cases} 1 - s/\Delta & \text{for } 0 \le s \le \Delta, \\ 0 & \text{for } s > \Delta. \end{cases}$$

Hence,

$$a(s) = \begin{cases} 1/\Delta & \text{for } 0 \le s < \Delta, \\ 0 & \text{for } s > \Delta. \end{cases}$$

Inserting this into (5.46) and letting $\Delta \to 0$ while using l'Hôpital's rule, we obtain

$$z_\rho = \int_0^\Delta \frac{1}{\Delta} e^{-\rho s}\, ds = \frac{1}{\rho\Delta}(1 - e^{-\rho\Delta}) \underset{\Delta \to 0}{\to} 1 \Longrightarrow Z_\rho \underset{\Delta \to 0}{\to} 0 \quad \text{for all } \rho.$$

[6] Note that interest deductions or capital gains will never be accounted for in a tax system belonging to class A in this case; condition (ii) is effective for class M only. The value of the capital value tax rate v is irrelevant since instantaneous depreciation of the accounting capital implies that the taxable capital value will be zero by definition, cf. (5.52) and (5.55).

[7] The neutrality of the cash-flow tax, however, relies strongly on the assumption that the income tax rate is a time invariant parameter. The more general case allowing for changes in expectations about u is discussed in Muzondo (1979) and Sandmo (1979).

The general condition for neutrality in Proposition 9.A, i.e. $\lambda = 1$, can be satisfied uniformly also in other ways. From (6.16) and (6.17) it follows that

$\lambda_A = 1$ when $m = n = 1$, and $v = 0$, irrespective of the values of

$\varepsilon, Z_{i-\varepsilon}$, and u.

$\lambda_M = 1$ when $m = n = 1$, $\varepsilon_1 = \gamma$, $v = 0$, $Z_{i-\gamma} = Y_{i-\gamma}$, and $\alpha_I = \alpha_G$,

irrespective of the values of ε_2 and u.

The implications of these conditions can be stated as follows:

Proposition 9.D Assume that the rate of discount is equal to the market interest rate $(r = i)$, that non-instantaneous depreciation is permitted $(Z_p > 0, z_p < 1)$, and that no tax is imposed on the value of the capital stock $(v = 0)$. Uniform neutrality will then be satisfied

(i) for any tax system in *class A*, permitting full deduction of imputed interests $(m = 1)$ and full inclusion of accrued capital gains $(n = 1)$, regardless of the degree of indexation ε and of the form of the weighting function for the accounting capital $A(s)$, and

(ii) for any tax system in *class M*, with $\alpha_I = \alpha_G$, permitting full deduction of imputed (possibly inflation adjusted) interests $(m = 1)$, full inclusion of accrued (possibly inflation adjusted) capital gains $(n = 1)$, with an indexation parameter for depreciation allowances equal to the true inflation rate $(\varepsilon_1 = \gamma)$, and with a depreciation profile for the accounting capital which agrees with true economic depreciation $[A(s) = G(s)$ for all $s \Rightarrow Z_{i-\gamma} = Y_{i-\gamma}$ for all i and $\gamma]$.

The conditions for neutrality in Proposition 9.D are stronger for class M than for class A. *For class A, neutrality does not imply that the definition of the accounting capital agrees with true economic depreciation.* The reason is that $m = n = 1$ ensures that "erroneous" depreciation allowances will always be fully compensated by "erroneous" accounted interest deductions and capital gains in this case, in such a way that the sum of their present values is independent of the form of $A(s)$. For class M, on the other hand, the only parameter in the tax system which can be changed freely without disturbing neutrality is the indexation parameter for interest deductions and capital gains, ε_2. This follows from the fact that λ_M is independent of ε_2 when $m = n$ and $\alpha_I = \alpha_G$ [cf. (5.60) and (5.61)].

Proposition 9.D generalizes and modifies the conclusions of Sandmo (1974, sections 4, 6, and 7), King (1975, p. 275), Hartman (1978), and

Boadway (1980, pp. 254–255), which (i) are confined to exponential depreciation allowances, (ii) do not include situations with indexation of the interest deductions and capital gains, and (iii) make no distinction between tax systems in class A and in class M. See also Samuelson (1964).

So far, we have been concerned with the neutrality properties of the two general classes of tax systems, class A and M, only. Consider now the specific tax systems defined in subsection 5.4.2 [cf. table 5.1]. Propositions 9.C and 9.D imply that

> *System AO is neutral if either $A(s) = 0$ for $s > 0$ or $m = 1$, $v = 0$.*

> *System AR is neutral if either $A(s) = 0$ for $s > 0$ or $m = n = 1$, $v = 0$.*

> *System MNO is neutral if $A(s) = 0$ for $s > 0$ and $m = n = 0$.*

> *System MNR is neutral if either (i) $A(s) = 0$ for $s > 0$ and $m = n = 0$ or (ii) $A(s) = G(s)$ for all s and $m = n = 1$, $v = 0$.*

> *Systems MI, $MI1$, and $MI2$ are neutral if either (i) $A(s) = 0$ for $s > 0$ and $m = n = 0$ or (ii) $A(s) = G(s)$ for all s and $\varepsilon = \gamma$, $m = n = 1$, $v = 0$.*

These are conditions for uniform neutrality since they do not restrict the interest rate i, the inflation rate γ, and the survival function $B(s)$. For all tax systems except the fully nominal system MNO, neutrality will be satisfied under two alternative sets of restrictions, one leading to a cash-flow tax, and one involving full deductibility of interest costs and (except for system AO) full taxation of capital gains. System MNO can be neutral under a cash-flow tax only.

9.3   The neutrality locus

9.3.1 Definition

The conditions for neutrality stated in Propositions 9.A–9.D are valid regardless of the specific retirement structure, as represented by the form of the survival function in the firm's technology, and regardless of the weighting function for the accounting capital, as prescribed in the tax system. Their primary interest lies in their generality. We define the set of tax parameters which satisfy neutrality as the *neutrality locus*. From (6.16) and (6.17) it follows that its analytical representation is

$$(9.4) \qquad \left[(1-m)i - (1-n)\varepsilon + \frac{v}{u}\right] Z_{i-\varepsilon} = 0, \qquad \text{for class } A,$$

and

$$
\left[i - \varepsilon_1 + \frac{v}{u}\right] Z_{i-\varepsilon_1} = \left[m(i - \alpha_I \varepsilon_2) - n(\gamma - \alpha_G \varepsilon_2)\right] Y_{i-\gamma}
$$

$$(9.5)$$

$$
- \left[m(1 - \alpha_I) - n(1 - \alpha_G)\right] \varepsilon_2 Z_{i-\varepsilon_2},
$$

$$\text{for class } M.$$

These equations define — for any interest rate i, any inflation rate γ, and any survival function $B(s)$ — a relationship between the tax parameters ε (or ε_1, ε_2, α_I, α_G), m, n, u, and v and the parameters of the weighting function for the accounting capital, $A(s)$. In this section, we take a closer look at this relationship.

9.3.2 General properties

The neutrality locus for the two classes of tax systems has the following general properties.

Class A The neutrality locus is
(i) independent of m, n, ε, and v when $Z_{i-\varepsilon} = 0$, i.e. when $A(s) = 0$ for $s > 0$, and
(ii) independent of $Z_{i-\varepsilon}$, i.e. independent of $A(s)$, when $m = n = 1$, and $v = 0$,
(iii) independent of $Y_{i-\gamma}$, i.e. independent of $B(s)$, always.

Class M The neutrality locus is
(i) independent of ε_1 and v when $Z_{i-\varepsilon_1} = 0$, i.e. when $A(s) = 0$ for $s > 0$,
(ii) independent of ε_2 when $m = n$ and $\alpha_I = \alpha_G$, and
(iii) independent of $Y_{i-\gamma}$, i.e. independent of $B(s)$, when $m = n = 0$.

The equations for the neutrality locus of the tax systems defined in subsection 5.4.2 are given in table 9.1. Note in particular that when $m = n$, the neutrality locus of system MNR depends on i and γ through their effect on the real interest rate $i - \gamma$ only.

Table 9.1: Neutrality locus of specific tax systems.*

Tax system**	Neutrality locus
AO	$\{(1-m)i + v/u\}Z_i = 0$
AR	$\{(1-m)i - (1-n)\gamma + v/u\}Z_{i-\gamma} = 0$
MNO	$(i + v/u)Z_i = (mi - n\gamma)Y_{i-\gamma}$
MNR	$(i - \gamma + v/u)Z_{i-\gamma} = (mi - n\gamma)Y_{i-\gamma}$
MI	$(i - \varepsilon + v/u)Z_{i-\varepsilon} = \{m(i-\varepsilon) - n(\gamma-\varepsilon)\}Y_{i-\gamma}$
MI1	$\{i - (1+n)\varepsilon + v/u\}Z_{i-\varepsilon} = \{m(i-\varepsilon) - n\gamma\}Y_{i-\gamma}$
MI2	$\{i - (1+n-m)\varepsilon + v/u\}Z_{i-\varepsilon} = (mi - n\gamma)Y_{i-\gamma}$

$*\ Z_\rho = \int_0^\infty e^{-\rho s}A(s)\,ds \qquad (\rho = i\,, i-\gamma\,, i-\varepsilon)\,, \qquad Y_{i-\gamma} = \int_0^\infty e^{-(i-\gamma)s}G(s)\,ds\,.$
$**$ See table 5.1 for detailed definitions.

9.3.3 Examples

Two examples serve to illustrate the results above.

Exponential survival function and declining balance depreciation

We first assume exponentially declining survival function and depreciation allowances based on the declining balance schedule, i.e.

$$B(s) = e^{-\delta s} \implies Y_{i-\gamma} = 1/(i + \delta - \gamma)\,,$$
$$A(s) = e^{-\alpha s} \implies Z_\rho = 1/(\rho + \alpha)\,, \qquad \rho = i\,, i - \gamma\,, i - \varepsilon\,,$$

where δ and α are non-negative constants [cf. subsection 6.5.1]. Inserting these expressions in the general equations for the neutrality locus in table 9.1, we obtain the relationships collected in table 9.2. Six constellations of tax parameters belonging to the neutrality locus for tax systems *MNO* and *MNR* are considered specifically in table 9.3. Case 5 corresponds to the uniformly neutral system with taxation of the firm's true income. If the depreciation allowances are based on the original investment cost instead of on its replacement cost, with α equal to the true depreciation

rate and with the interest cost completely deductible, then only a proportion $i/(i + \delta)$ of the capital gains should be included in the tax base to
preserve neutrality (case 2). This means that the tax rate for capital gains
should be differentiated according to the durability of the capital used —
the gains of firms with long-lived assets (low δ) should be taxed more heav-
ily than those of firms with short-lived assets (high δ). On the other hand,
if capital gains are tax-free, then neutrality implies that only a proportion
$1 - \gamma/(i + \delta)$ of the interest cost should be deductible (case 4); i.e. increasing inflation should be accompanied by decreasing interest deductibility,
and firms with short-lived assets should be allowed larger interest deductions than firms with long-lived assets. If, for a fully nominal tax system,
full interest deductibility is permitted while accrued capital gains are tax
free, then the tax-permitted depreciation rate should be set equal to the
true depreciation rate minus the inflation rate $(\delta - \gamma)$ for neutrality to be
preserved (case 3).[8]

For the tax systems with indexation of the tax base and with equal
treatment of interest deductions and capital gains (i.e. *MI* and *MI2*) , it
follows from table 9.2 that all parameter constellations such that $m = n =
1$, $v = 0$, and $\alpha/(i - \varepsilon) = \delta/(i - \gamma)$ belong to the neutrality locus. The
latter condition can be given the following interesting interpretation: the
ratio between the *tax permitted* depreciation rate, α, and the tax permitted
real interest rate, $i - \varepsilon$, shall be equal to the ratio between the true (gross)
depreciation rate and the true real interest rate. For the indexed tax system
with different treatment of the indexation of interest deductions and capital
gains (i.e. *MI1*), the parameter constellations satisfying

$$m = n = 1, \quad v = 0, \text{ and}$$

$$\alpha(i - \gamma) + \varepsilon(\delta - \gamma) = \delta(i - \varepsilon) + \varepsilon(\alpha - \varepsilon)$$

belong to the neutrality locus. In particular, we have that $m = n = 1$, $v =
0$, $\alpha = \delta$, and $\varepsilon = \gamma$ ensure neutrality for all tax systems with indexation
of the tax base.

The form of the neutrality locus based on an exponential survival function and declining balance depreciation depends, in general, not only on
the rate of retirement (depreciation) δ, but also on the rate of inflation
γ and the interest rate i. For class A, however, the neutrality locus is

---

[8] Or stated otherwise, the tax permitted rate of depreciation should be equal to the
firm's net rate of depreciation in value terms; cf. (3.61) and (3.70). The latter result
is also stated in Boadway (1980, p. 257).

Table 9.2: Neutrality locus of specific tax systems. Exponential survival functions: $B(s) = e^{-\delta s}, A(s) = e^{-\alpha s}$.*

Tax system**	Neutrality locus defined by
AO	$\{(1 - m)i + v/u\}/(i + \alpha) = 0$
AR	$\{(1 - m)i - (1 - n)\gamma + v/u\}/(i + \alpha - \gamma) = 0$
MNO	$\alpha(mi - n\gamma) = i\{(1 - m)i + \delta - (1 - n)\gamma\} + (i + \delta - \gamma)v/u$
MNR	$\alpha(mi - n\gamma) = (i - \gamma)\{(1 - m)i + \delta - (1 - n)\gamma\} + (i + \delta - \gamma)v/u$
MI	$\alpha(mi - n\gamma) = (i - \varepsilon)\{(1 - m)i + \delta - (1 - n)\gamma\}$ $+(m - n)\varepsilon(i + \alpha - \varepsilon) + (i + \delta - \gamma)v/u$
MI1	$\alpha(mi - n\gamma) = (i - \varepsilon)\{(1 - m)i + \delta - (1 - n)\gamma\}$ $+\{m(i + \alpha - \varepsilon) - n(i + \delta - \gamma)\}\varepsilon + (i + \delta - \gamma)v/u$
MI2	$\alpha(mi - n\gamma) = (i - \varepsilon)\{(1 - m)i + \delta - (1 - n)\gamma\}$ $+\{(m - n)\varepsilon + v/u\}(i + \delta - \gamma)$

  * We assume that $i + \alpha - \varepsilon > 0$ and $i + \delta - \gamma > 0$, where $\varepsilon = 0$ for tax systems AO and MNO, $\varepsilon = \gamma$ for AR and MNR, and ε is arbitrary for MI, $MI1$, and $MI2$.
** See table 5.1 for detailed definitions.

independent of δ. This is due to the fact that eq. (9.4) does not contain $Y_{i-\gamma} = 1/(i + \delta - \gamma)$. Tax systems *MNR*, *MI*, and *MI2*, with $m = n$, have the interesting property that the neutrality locus can be defined in terms of the market values of the depreciation rate and the real interest rate, δ and $i - \gamma$, and the corresponding tax permitted rates, α and $i - \varepsilon$, only.

Simultaneous retirement and linear depreciation

Our second example assumes simultaneous retirement of all capital units at age N years and linear depreciation allowances over T years. In subsection 6.5.2 this was shown to imply

$$Y_{i-\gamma} = \frac{1}{i - \gamma}[1 - H_{i-\gamma}(N)/N], \quad Z_\rho = \frac{1}{\rho}[1 - H_\rho(T)/T],$$

where $H_a(M) = (1 - e^{-aM})/a$ in general. Inserting these expressions in the general equations in table 9.1, we find that the neutrality locus will be

Table 9.3: Combinations of tax parameters which ensure neutrality. Exponential survival functions. Tax systems *MNO* and *MNR*.

Fully nominal tax system based on market values (MNO)

case	m	n	α	v
1	1	1	$\delta i/(i-\gamma)$	0
2	1	$i/(i+\delta)$	δ	0
3	1	0	$\delta-\gamma$	0
4	$1-\gamma/(i+\delta)$	0	δ	0

Nominal tax system based on market values, depreciation according to replacement cost (MNR)

case	m	n	α	v
5	1	1	δ	0
6	1	0	$(\delta-\gamma)(i-\gamma)/i$	0

represented as a non-linear relationship between the tax parameters m, n, ε, u, v, and T on the one hand, and the market variables i and γ and the technical parameter N on the other. To describe the "trade-off" between the different tax parameters, this equation has to be solved numerically. An illustration for tax system *MNO* (taken from Biørn (1984, p. 224)) is given in table 9.4. The critical value of the tax permitted life time T which ensures neutrality is quite sensitive to variations in the interest and inflation rates.

Table 9.4: Critical value of tax permitted life time T which ensures neutrality under a fully nominal tax system (MNO).* Survival function: Simultaneous retirement after N years. Depreciation allowances: Linear over T years. $v = 0, m = 1, n = 0.5$

i	γ	$N = 6$	$N = 20$
0.05	0.00	6.00	20.00
0.05	0.04	3.75	14.01
0.10	0.05	4.75	18.96
0.10	0.09	3.64	16.77
0.15	0.05	5.30	22.12
0.15	0.10	4.49	24.60
0.15	0.14	3.75	26.05

* Calculated from the equation $(i + v/u)\frac{1}{i}[1 - H_i(T)/T] = \frac{mi - n\gamma}{i - \gamma}[1 - H_{i-\gamma}(N)/N]$, where $H_a(M) = (1 - e^{-aM})a$.

9.4 Measures of the departure from neutrality

We have established formal conditions for neutrality of a tax system and discussed alternative ways of indicating whether or not neutrality is satisfied in a given situation. Now we turn to the related problem of measuring the departure from neutrality, i.e. defining a "metric" giving the "distance" between a given tax system and a corresponding neutral one. Three such indicators will be discussed, all of which can be expressed as functions of the income distribution parameter, i.e. the present value of the tax deductions per unit of investment outlay, λ, and the income tax rate u, and possibly other parameters. The discussion will be confined to the neo-classical case.

9.4.1 The relative distortion of the user cost

Since the user cost of capital under neutrality is $\bar{c} = q/\Phi_{i-\gamma}(0)$ [cf. (9.1)], we can take

$$(9.6) \qquad \beta = \beta(t) = \frac{c(t) - \bar{c}(t)}{\bar{c}(t)} = \frac{c(t)}{q(t)\Phi_{i-\gamma}(0)} - 1$$

as an indicator of the relative departure from neutrality of a tax system characterized by a user cost of capital equal to $c(t)$. If $\beta > 0$, the system is less favourable to the firm than a corresponding neutral system would have been, β indicating the relative distortion of the user cost. Conversely, $\beta < 0$ characterizes a tax system which is more favourable than a neutral system, whereas $\beta = 0$ indicates neutrality. By inserting from (6.14)–(6.15), we find that β can be expressed in terms of λ and u as follows

$$\text{(9.7)} \qquad \beta = \frac{u(1-\lambda)}{1-u},$$

where $\lambda = \lambda_A$ or λ_M depending on whether the tax system belongs to class A or class M. Since (6.7) and (9.7) imply

$$q^* = q(1+\beta), \quad \text{i.e.} \quad q = q^* \left(1 - \frac{\beta}{1+\beta}\right),$$

where q and q^* are the actual and the tax corrected investment prices, respectively, β can be given two alternative interpretations: (a) the actual tax system is equivalent to taxing the investment cost at the rate β, or (b) an investment subsidy at the rate $\beta/(1+\beta)$ would bring the tax system back to neutrality.

From (9.7) it follows that β is linearly decreasing in λ, with a rate of decline equal to

$$\frac{\partial \beta}{\partial \lambda} = -\frac{u}{1-u}.$$

It is more sensitive to changes in λ the larger is the income tax rate u. Since

$$\frac{\partial \beta}{\partial u} = \frac{1-\lambda}{(1-u)^2} = \frac{\beta}{u(1-u)},$$

an increase in u will lead to an increase in β when $\beta > 0$ and to a decrease when $\beta < 0$. This means that an increase in the income tax rate will always increase the relative distortion of the user cost.

9.4.2 The internal rate of return

It was shown in chapter 6 that the following relationship holds between the investment price at time t and the future tax corrected user cost:

$$(9.8) \qquad q^*(t) = q(t)\frac{1 - \lambda u}{1 - u} = \int_0^\infty e^{-(\rho+\gamma)s} c(t+s)B(s)\,ds\,,$$

where $q^*(t)$ is the tax corrected investment price, $\rho = i - \gamma$ is the (pretax) real interest rate, and γ is the rate of increase of the investment price [cf. (6.7), (6.10), (6.12), and (6.13)]. This equation says that the firm can "simulate" the effect of the tax system on its user cost by setting the tax corrected investment price equal to the present value of the future user cost discounted at the nominal market interest rate.

Let us now pose the related question: Which value of the real interest rate should the firm use to "simulate" the effect of the tax system on its user cost when performing a similar present value calculation based on the *actual* investment price? Or stated more simply, how could the effect of the fiscal factor $(1 - \lambda u)/(1 - u)$ be "translated" from q^* into ρ? The solution value, ρ^*, which we denote as the tax equivalent internal rate of return (on a marginal investment),[9] is implicitly defined by

$$(9.9) \qquad q(t) = \int_0^\infty e^{-(\rho^*+\gamma)s} c(t+s)B(s)\,ds\,.$$

Since the user cost of capital will always, with our assumptions, (be expected to) grow at the same rate, γ, as the investment price [cf. section 4.2], it follows from (9.8) and (9.9) that

$$(9.10) \qquad \varphi(\rho^*) = \varphi(\rho)\frac{1 - u}{1 - \lambda u} = \frac{q(t)}{c(t)}\,,$$

where we use the simplified notation

$$(9.11) \qquad \varphi(\rho) = \Phi_\rho(0) = \int_0^\infty e^{-\rho s} B(s)\,ds\,.$$

---

[9] Note that this rate of return is related to a marginal increase in the capital stock under a neo-classical technology with malleable capital (confer the shadow value interpretation of the user cost), while the rate of return discussed in section 2.2 is related to an investment project characterized by a given cost and a given yield flow. There is, however, a strong formal similarity between the two concepts.

Eqs. (9.7) and (9.10) imply the following relationship between the tax equivalent internal rate of return, the market real rate of interest, and the relative distortion of the user cost:

$$(9.12) \qquad \varphi(\rho^*)(1+\beta) = \varphi(\rho).$$

An explicit solution value for ρ^* will not exist in general.

Since $\varphi(\rho)$ is always positive and monotonically decreasing in ρ, the internal rate of return ρ^* is only defined for $\beta > -1$, i.e. for $\lambda < 1/u$, or $c > 0$. It is a monotonically increasing function of ρ and β; in particular, the following three inequalities are equivalent

$$(9.13) \qquad \rho^* \gtreqless \rho \quad \Longleftrightarrow \quad \beta \gtreqless 0 \quad \Longleftrightarrow \quad \lambda \lesseqgtr 1.$$

Differentiating (9.10) implicitly with respect to λ, u, and ρ, we obtain, in the general case,

$$\frac{\partial \rho^*}{\partial \lambda} = \frac{u\varphi(\rho^*)}{(1-u)(1+\beta)\varphi'(\rho^*)} = \frac{u\varphi(\rho^*)}{(1-\lambda u)\varphi'(\rho^*)},$$

$$\frac{\partial \rho^*}{\partial u} = -\frac{\beta\varphi(\rho^*)}{u(1-u)(1+\beta)\varphi'(\rho^*)} = -\frac{(1-\lambda)\varphi(\rho^*)}{(1-u)(1-\lambda u)\varphi'(\rho^*)},$$

$$\frac{\partial \rho^*}{\partial \rho} = \frac{\varphi'(\rho)}{(1+\beta)\varphi'(\rho^*)} = \frac{(1-u)\varphi'(\rho)}{(1-\lambda u)\varphi'(\rho^*)}.$$

We see that the tax equivalent internal rate of return is a decreasing function of λ. It is increasing, is independent of, or is decreasing in the tax rate u according as $\lambda \lesseqgtr 1$, i.e. according as $\beta \gtreqless 0$. Again, we find that an increase in the tax rate will, *ceteris paribus*, increase the departure from neutrality.

Consider again the two examples.

Exponential survival function and declining balance depreciation

When the survival function is exponentially declining, i.e. $B(s) = e^{-\delta s}$, which implies $\varphi(\rho) = 1/(\rho+\delta)$, we can find an *explicit solution* for the tax equivalent internal rate of return from (9.12). It is

$$(9.14) \qquad \rho^* = \rho + \beta(\rho+\delta) = \frac{(1-\lambda u)\rho + u(1-\lambda)\delta}{1-u} = \frac{c}{q} - \delta.$$

Similar expressions are found in Jorgenson and Sullivan (1981, p. 177) and King and Fullerton (1984, eqs. (2.14) and (2.17)).[10] In this case, the derivatives can be simplified to

$$\frac{\partial \rho^*}{\partial \lambda} = -\frac{u(\rho + \delta)}{1 - u},$$

$$\frac{\partial \rho^*}{\partial u} = \frac{\beta(\rho + \delta)}{u(1 - u)} = \frac{(1 - \lambda)(\rho + \delta)}{(1 - u)^2},$$

$$\frac{\partial \rho^*}{\partial \rho} = 1 + \beta = \frac{1 - \lambda u}{1 - u}.$$

The impact on the tax corrected internal rate of return ρ^* of changes in the pre-tax real rate of interest ρ still depends on λ and u, but it is independent of ρ and δ. (It should, however, be recalled that *indirectly* $\partial \rho^*/\partial \rho$ may be a function of ρ and δ, to the extent that λ and β depend on these parameters.) Independence of $\partial \rho^*/\partial \rho$ on the parameter which characterize the retirement process (i.e. δ) is a particular property of the exponential survival function and is due to the fact that it admits an additive decomposition of the user cost of capital into a (real) interest component and a retirement component [cf. subsection 4.4.1]. For this reason, we can give meaning to ρ^*, given by (9.14), as a rate of return *net of depreciation*, which is a term often used in the literature. But this interpretation does not carry over to the non-exponential case since ρ^* will then be a non-linear function not only of the parameters which characterize the retirement process but also of the pre-tax real interest rate [cf. (9.12)]. The next example illustrates this.

Simultaneous retirement and linear depreciation

When the survival function is of the simultaneous retirement type, i.e. $B(s) = 1$ for $s \leq N$, 0 for $s > N$, which implies $\varphi(\rho) = (1 - e^{-\rho N})/\rho$, (9.12) gives

$$(9.15) \qquad \frac{\rho^*}{\rho} = (1 + \beta)\frac{1 - e^{-\rho^* N}}{1 - e^{-\rho N}}.$$

In general, this equation has to be solved by numerical procedures. Only in the particular case where the capital has an infinite service life, i.e.

$N \rightarrow \infty$, an explicit solution exists, $\rho^* = \rho(1 + \beta)$.[11] Using the first order Taylor expansion $\rho/(1 - e^{-\rho N}) \approx \rho + 1/N$, it can be shown that (9.15), to a first order of approximation, has the solution

$$\rho^* = \rho + \beta \left(\rho + \frac{1}{N} \right).$$

This shows a formal similarity to (9.14), δ corresponding to $1/N$, but like the similar approximation formula for the user cost in the zero-tax case [confer subsection 4.4.2], it may be numerically very inaccurate.

9.4.3 The effective tax rule

A third way of characterizing the departure from neutrality of the corporate tax system is to transform the internal rate of return into an effective tax rate. There are several ways in which this can be done; see e.g. Bradford and Fullerton (1981, pp. 257–261), Jorgenson and Sullivan (1981, p. 177), and King and Fullerton (1984, section 2.1).

Consider a "marginal project", i.e. one for which the internal rate of return is exactly equal to ρ^*, and a saver investing in this project by means of nominal funds at the interest rate i. The saver's pre-tax real rate of return is equal to $\rho = i - \gamma$. Assume that the saver is a firm. Its after tax real rate of return will then be given by

(9.16) $\qquad \rho_T = i - \gamma - u(i - \varepsilon) = \rho(1 - u) - u(\gamma - \varepsilon),$

where $\varepsilon = 0$ if interest incomes are taxed on a nominal basis and $\varepsilon = \gamma$ when they are taxed on a fully indexed basis. [Confer subsection 5.3.2.] We define the *tax wedge* as the difference between the internal rate of return of the "marginal project" and the saver's after tax real rate of return, i.e.

$$\rho^* - \rho_T = \rho^* - \rho(1 - u) + u(\gamma - \varepsilon),$$

---

[11] This equation coincides with that obtained from (9.14) when $\delta = 0$.

and the effective tax rate as the ratio between the tax wedge and the *pre-tax* rate of return to the saver,[12] i.e.

$$(9.17) \qquad u^* = \frac{\rho^* - \rho_T}{\rho} = u + u\frac{\gamma - \varepsilon}{\rho} + \frac{\rho^* - \rho}{\rho}.$$

The *effective tax rate* thus defined has three additive components. The first is the statutory corporate income tax rate, the second represents the tax on the inflation component of the interest income on the part of the saver, and the third reflects the distortion of the rate of return which is caused by the system of corporate income taxation on the part of the investing firm. Neutrality is characterized by equality of the effective and the statutory tax rates, i.e. $u^* = u$, and is obtained when the taxation of the saver is subject to full indexation, i.e. $\varepsilon = \gamma$, and the taxation of the investing firm does not distort its real rate of return on a marginal investment, i.e. $\rho^* = \rho$. Since ρ^* is implicitly defined [cf. (9.12)], an explicit solution value for u^* will not exist in general.

In the case with an *exponentially declining survival function*, we find from (9.14) and (9.17) the following simple relationship between the effective tax rate, the statutory tax rate, and the relative distortion of the user cost of capital

$$(9.18) \qquad u^* = u\left(1 + \frac{\gamma - \varepsilon}{\rho}\right) + \beta\left(1 + \frac{\delta}{\rho}\right).$$

For given values of u, β, and ρ, the effective tax rate will be an increasing function both of $\gamma - \varepsilon$, the incompleteness of the inflation adjustment of the interest income and of δ, the rate of retirement. For given values of γ, ε, δ, and ρ, the effective tax rate is a linearly increasing function of the statutory income tax rate u and of the relative distortion of the user cost of capital β.

9.4.4 Overview. Numerical illustrations

An overview of the three neutrality indicators presented above and their main properties is given in table 9.5. Note that ρ^* and u^* exist only when

---

[12] This definition coincides with the effective corporate net tax rate as defined by Bradford and Fullerton (1981, p. 259) except that they relate the tax wedge to the saver's after tax rate of return rather than to the pre-tax one. We find the latter definition more convenient.

Table 9.5: Indicators of departure from neutrality. Overview.

Indicator	Neutrality characterized by	Better than neutrality	Worse than neutrality	Neutrality obtained for
Relative distortion of user cost: $\beta = \frac{u(1-\lambda)}{1-u}$	$\beta = 0$	$\beta < 0$	$\beta > 0$	$\lambda = 1$
Internal rate of return:† $\rho^* = \varphi^{-1}(\frac{\varphi(\rho)}{1+\beta})$	$\rho^* = \rho$	$\rho^* < \rho$	$\rho^* > \rho$	$\lambda = 1$
Effective tax rate:† $u^* = u(1 + \frac{\gamma-\varepsilon}{\rho}) + \frac{\rho^*-\rho}{\rho}$	$u^* = u$	$u^* < u$	$u^* > u$	$\lambda = 1$ and $\varepsilon = \gamma$

† ρ^* and u^* are only defined for $\beta > -1$, i.e. $\lambda < 1/u$.

the user cost of capital is positive, i.e. when $\lambda < 1/u$, whereas β can be defined for negative values of the user cost as well.

Values of the relative distortion of the user cost β corresponding to the values of the user cost in tables 6.1–6.4 are given in tables 9.6–9.9. Simultaneous retirement of the capital at age N and linear depreciation allowances over T years are assumed. In tables 9.10–9.13, the departure from neutrality is characterized by the corresponding values of the internal rate of return ρ^*. The cases where ρ^* does not exist are indicated by NA (not available). In tables 9.6 and 9.7 for β and tables 9.10 and 9.11 for ρ^*, we consider the system with no indexation of the tax base ($MNO : \varepsilon_1 = \varepsilon_2 = 0$) and the system with indexation of the depreciation allowances, but nominal taxation otherwise ($MNR : \varepsilon_1 = \gamma, \varepsilon_2 = 0$). Tables 9.8 and 9.9 for β and tables 9.12 and 9.13 for ρ^* relate to a tax system with indexation of the tax base ($MI1 : \varepsilon_1 = \varepsilon_2 = \varepsilon, \alpha_I = 1, \alpha_G = 0$).

From this set of tables, we can make the following observations:

1. A nominal tax system MNR with full deduction of (nominal) interests and full inclusion of (nominal) capital gains ($m = n = 1$) and a tax

permitted life time coinciding with the technical life time ($T = N$) is uniformly neutral, since $\beta = 0$ regardless of the interest rate i, the inflation rate γ, and the life time N. Equivalently, the tax equivalent net real rate of return is equal to the pre-tax real rate of interest ($\rho^* = \rho = i - \gamma$) regardless of the values of i, γ, and N. For other constellations of m and n, the relative distortion of the user cost is, on the whole, larger the longer is the life time. This means that the implicit rate of taxation of the investment price (if $\beta > 0$) or the implicit rate of subsidy (if $\beta < 0$) is larger for long-lived than for short-lived capital goods. The tax equivalent net real rate of return, however, is not related in a simple way to the life time of the capital.[13]

2. When the real rate of interest is zero and the depreciation allowances are based on replacement cost, i.e. $i = \gamma = \varepsilon_1$, $\varepsilon_2 = 0$, then neutrality is obtained regardless of the tax permitted life time if interests are completely deductible and all capital gains are included in the tax base ($m = n = 1$). The same will hold true if no interest cost is deductible and no capital gain is included ($m = n = 0$). (This neutrality is not uniform, of course, since equality of the interest and inflation rates is assumed.) The reason for this is simple. When $m = n$ and $i = \gamma$, then the interest deductions based on market values will, by definition, be equal to the accounted gains (i.e. their net effect is zero) and the present value of the depreciation allowances will be unity regardless of the tax permitted life time. Such parameter combinations thus belong to the neutrality locus, as can be confirmed from table 9.1.

3. Consider the neutral tax system $T = N$, $\varepsilon_1 = \gamma$, $\varepsilon_2 = 0$, $m = n = 1$. Assume that the depreciation allowances are based on original cost ($\varepsilon_1 = 0$) instead of on replacement cost, while a compensation is given by reducing the tax permitted life time to 50 per cent ($T = N/2$) and reducing the capital gains taxation to zero ($n = 0$). Then the new tax system will be more favourable than the neutral one ($\beta < 0$).

4. Consider a nominal tax system with depreciation allowances based on replacement cost and a tax permitted life time coinciding with the technical one ($\varepsilon_1 = \gamma$, $\varepsilon_2 = 0$, $T = N$). Assume that the tax permitted life time is reduced by 50 per cent ($T = N/2$). Then the value of β will decrease if the interest rate exceeds the inflation rate ($i > \gamma$) and increase in the opposite case.

---

[13] Since we have $\rho^* - \rho = \beta(1 + 1/N)$, to a first order of approximation, it follows that $\partial(\rho^* - \rho)/\partial N = (\rho + 1/N)\partial\beta/\partial N - \beta/N^2$, which can be of either sign.

5. Consider a nominal tax system with depreciation allowances based on original cost and a tax permitted life time which is equal to the technical life time ($\varepsilon_1 = \varepsilon_2 = 0$, $T = N$). An increase in the nominal interest rate by one per cent unit will then lead to an increase in the tax equivalent net real rate of return which is less than one per cent unit ($\partial \rho^* / \partial i < 1$) if interests are completely deductible in the income tax base ($m = 1$). If no interest deduction is permitted ($m = 0$), the tax equivalent net real rate of return will show a larger increase than the nominal interest rate ($\partial \rho^* / \partial i > 1$). A one per cent unit increase in the inflation rate will lead to a decrease in the tax equivalent net real rate of return which is less than one per cent unit ($-\partial \rho^* / \partial \gamma < 1$) if capital gains are subject to full taxation ($n = 1$) and to a decrease which is more than one per cent unit ($-\partial \rho^* / \partial \gamma > 1$) if capital gains are tax free ($n = 0$).[14]

6. For a tax system with indexation of the tax base, there is, in general, no monotone relationship between the degree of indexation and the relative distortion of the user cost. This holds true even if the other tax parameters are "correct". If, for instance, $T = N$, and $m = n = 1$, $i = 12$ per cent, and $\gamma = 10$ per cent, an increase in $\varepsilon_1 = \varepsilon_2$ from 0 to 50 per cent of γ (i.e. from 0 to 5 per cent) will lead to a decrease in β from 0.26 to 0.16 for $N = 6$, a decrease from 0.46 to 0.42 for $N = 20$, and an increase from 0.48 to 0.79 for $N = 50$. (Equivalently, the value of ρ^* shows a decrease from 9.2 to 6.7 per cent for $N = 6$, a decrease from 6.3 to 6.0 per cent for $N = 20$, and an increase from 4.1 to 5.3 per cent for $N = 50$.) An indexation by 100 per cent of the actual inflation will, as already declared, ensure uniform neutrality in this case, whereas an "over-indexation" ($\varepsilon > \gamma$) may give dramatic distortions for long-lived capital goods, in particular if the rate of inflation exceeds the interest rate.

---

[14] If the capital has an infinite service life and no depreciation allowances are made, we can give stronger conclusions. Since then

$$\rho^* = \rho(1 + \beta) = \frac{i(1 - mu) - \gamma(1 - nu)}{1 - u},$$

we have $\partial \rho^* / \partial i = (1 - mu)/(1 - u)$, which is equal to or greater than unity according as m is equal to or less than unity. Similarly, $-\partial \rho^* / \partial \gamma = (1 - nu)/(1 - u)$, which is equal to or greater than unity according as n is equal to or less than unity.

Taxation, technology and the user cost of capital

Table 9.6: Relative distortion of user cost as a function of nominal interest rate.

A. No taxation of capital gains: $n = 0$

Interest	N = 6, T = 6				N = 6, T = 3			
rate,	m = 0		m = 1		m = 0		m = 1	
%	MNO	MNR	MNO	MNR	MNO	MNR	MNO	MNR
5	0.1591	-0.2078	-0.0487	-0.4156	0.0953	-0.1125	-0.1125	-0.3203
6	0.1863	-0.1615	-0.0559	-0.4037	0.1126	-0.0885	-0.1297	-0.3307
7	0.2123	-0.1177	-0.0624	-0.3924	0.1293	-0.0652	-0.1453	-0.3398
8	0.2370	-0.0763	-0.0683	-0.3816	0.1456	-0.0427	-0.1597	-0.3480
9	0.2606	-0.0371	-0.0735	-0.3711	0.1613	-0.0210	-0.1727	-0.3550
10	0.2830	0.0000	-0.0267	-0.3098	0.1766	0.0000	-0.1331	-0.3098
11	0.3045	0.0353	-0.0840	-0.3532	0.1915	0.0204	-0.1970	-0.3681
12	0.3250	0.0686	-0.0867	-0.3431	0.2059	0.0400	-0.2059	-0.3718
13	0.3446	0.1003	-0.0901	-0.3344	0.2199	0.0590	-0.2148	-0.3757
14	0.3633	0.1304	-0.0932	-0.3261	0.2335	0.0774	-0.2230	-0.3791
15	0.3813	0.1591	-0.0960	-0.3182	0.2467	0.0953	-0.2305	-0.3820

Interest	N = 20, T = 20				N = 20, T = 10			
rate,	m = 0		m = 1		m = 0		m = 1	
%	MNO	MNR	MNO	MNR	MNO	MNR	MNO	MNR
5	0.3892	-0.8152	-0.4260	-1.6304	0.2352	-0.3514	-0.5799	-1.1666
6	0.4404	-0.5968	-0.4549	-1.4921	0.2726	-0.2688	-0.6227	-1.1641
7	0.4856	-0.4112	-0.4738	-1.3706	0.3073	-0.1930	-0.6521	-1.1524
8	0.5256	-0.2527	-0.4850	-1.2634	0.3397	-0.1233	-0.6710	-1.1340
9	0.5613	-0.1168	-0.4904	-1.1685	0.3699	-0.0591	-0.6817	-1.1108
10	0.5930	0.0000	-0.4395	-1.0325	0.3981	0.0000	-0.6344	-1.0325
11	0.6214	0.1010	-0.4897	-1.0101	0.4244	0.0547	-0.6867	-1.0564
12	0.6469	0.1884	-0.4834	-0.9419	0.4491	0.1051	-0.6812	-1.0252
13	0.6699	0.2645	-0.4762	-0.8816	0.4723	0.1518	-0.6738	-0.9943
14	0.6906	0.3309	-0.4676	-0.8273	0.4939	0.1951	-0.6642	-0.9631
15	0.7094	0.3892	-0.4581	-0.7783	0.5143	0.2352	-0.6531	-0.9322

Interest	N = 50, T = 50				N = 50, T = 25			
rate,	m = 0		m = 1		m = 0		m = 1	
%	MNO	MNR	MNO	MNR	MNO	MNR	MNO	MNR
5	0.6555	-3.9221	-3.2665	-7.8441	0.4504	-1.1193	-3.4716	-5.0413
6	0.7070	-2.4259	-2.9319	-6.0649	0.5046	-0.7999	-3.1344	-4.4388
7	0.7475	-1.4357	-2.6025	-4.7858	0.5512	-0.5389	-2.7988	-3.8890
8	0.7799	-0.7702	-2.3010	-3.8512	0.5916	-0.3244	-2.4893	-3.4054
9	0.8062	-0.3157	-2.0352	-3.1570	0.6268	-0.1472	-2.2145	-2.9885
10	0.8278	0.0000	-1.7535	-2.5813	0.6576	0.0000	-1.9237	-2.5813
11	0.8458	0.2232	-1.6092	-2.2319	0.6847	0.1231	-1.7704	-2.3320
12	0.8610	0.3836	-1.4407	-1.9181	0.7086	0.2262	-1.5932	-2.0755
13	0.8740	0.5012	-1.2978	-1.6707	0.7298	0.3134	-1.4421	-1.8585
14	0.8852	0.5889	-1.1759	-1.4723	0.7487	0.3873	-1.3125	-1.6739
15	0.8950	0.6555	-1.0716	-1.3111	0.7655	0.4504	-1.2010	-1.5162

Inflation rate: $\gamma = 10\%$ p.a. Tax system: Nominal: $MNO : \varepsilon_1 = \varepsilon_2 = 0$. $MNR :$ $\varepsilon_1 = \gamma, \varepsilon_2 = 0$. Survival function: Simultaneous retirement after N years. Depreciation allowance schedule: Linear over T years. Income tax rate: $u = 0.508$. Capital value tax rate: $v = 0$.

Table 9.6: (cont.) Relative distortion of user cost as a function of nominal interest rate.

B. Full taxation of capital gains: $n = 1$.

Interest rate, %	N = 6, T = 6				N = 6, T = 3			
	m = 0		m = 1		m = 0		m = 1	
	MNO	MNR	MNO	MNR	MNO	MNR	MNO	MNR
5	0.5747	0.2078	0.3669	0.0000	0.5108	0.3030	0.3031	0.0952
6	0.5900	0.2422	0.3478	0.0000	0.5162	0.3152	0.2740	0.0730
7	0.6046	0.2747	0.3300	0.0000	0.5217	0.3272	0.2470	0.0525
8	0.6186	0.3053	0.3133	0.0000	0.5271	0.3389	0.2219	0.0336
9	0.6317	0.3340	0.2977	0.0000	0.5325	0.3501	0.1984	0.0161
10	0.5928	0.3098	0.2830	0.0000	0.4864	0.3098	0.1766	0.0000
11	0.6577	0.3885	0.2692	0.0000	0.5446	0.3736	0.1561	-0.0149
12	0.6681	0.4118	0.2564	0.0000	0.5490	0.3831	0.1373	-0.0286
13	0.6790	0.4347	0.2443	0.0000	0.5543	0.3934	0.1196	-0.0413
14	0.6894	0.4565	0.2329	0.0000	0.5596	0.4035	0.1031	-0.0530
15	0.6994	0.4772	0.2222	0.0000	0.5648	0.4134	0.0876	-0.0638

Interest rate, %	N = 20, T = 20				N = 20, T = 10			
	m = 0		m = 1		m = 0		m = 1	
	MNO	MNR	MNO	MNR	MNO	MNR	MNO	MNR
5	2.0195	0.8152	1.2043	0.0000	1.8656	1.2789	1.0504	0.4638
6	1.9325	0.8953	1.0372	0.0000	1.7647	1.2233	0.8694	0.3280
7	1.8562	0.9594	0.8968	0.0000	1.6779	1.1776	0.7185	0.2182
8	1.7890	1.0107	0.7783	0.0000	1.6030	1.1401	0.5924	0.1294
9	1.7297	1.0516	0.6781	0.0000	1.5384	1.1093	0.4867	0.0577
10	1.6255	1.0325	0.5930	0.0000	1.4306	1.0325	0.3981	0.0000
11	1.6315	1.1111	0.5204	0.0000	1.4346	1.0648	0.3234	-0.0463
12	1.5888	1.1303	0.4585	0.0000	1.3911	1.0470	0.2607	-0.0833
13	1.5514	1.1460	0.4054	0.0000	1.3538	1.0334	0.2078	-0.1127
14	1.5179	1.1582	0.3597	0.0000	1.3212	1.0223	0.1630	-0.1358
15	1.4877	1.1675	0.3202	0.0000	1.2926	1.0136	0.1252	-0.1539

Interest rate, %	N = 50, T = 50				N = 50, T = 25			
	m = 0		m = 1		m = 0		m = 1	
	MNO	MNR	MNO	MNR	MNO	MNR	MNO	MNR
5	8.4996	3.9221	4.5776	0.0000	8.2945	6.7248	4.3725	2.8028
6	6.7719	3.6389	3.1330	0.0000	6.5694	5.2649	2.9305	1.6260
7	5.5333	3.3501	2.1833	0.0000	5.3370	4.2469	1.9870	0.8968
8	4.6311	3.0809	1.5501	0.0000	4.4428	3.5268	1.3619	0.4458
9	3.9632	2.8413	1.1219	0.0000	3.7839	3.0098	0.9425	0.1685
10	3.4091	2.5813	0.8278	0.0000	3.2389	2.5813	0.6576	0.0000
11	3.0777	2.4550	0.6226	0.0000	2.9166	2.3549	0.4615	-0.1001
12	2.7792	2.3018	0.4774	0.0000	2.6267	2.1443	0.3250	-0.1574
13	2.5447	2.1718	0.3728	0.0000	2.4004	1.9840	0.2286	-0.1878
14	2.3575	2.0612	0.2963	0.0000	2.2209	1.8596	0.1598	-0.2016
15	2.2060	1.9666	0.2394	0.0000	2.0766	1.7615	0.1100	-0.2051

Inflation rate: $\gamma = 10\%$ p.a. Tax system: Nominal: $MNO : \varepsilon_1 = \varepsilon_2 = 0$. $MNR : \varepsilon_1 = \gamma, \varepsilon_2 = 0$. Survival function: Simultaneous retirement after N years. Depreciation allowance schedule: Linear over T years. Income tax rate: $u = 0.508$. Capital value tax rate: $v = 0$.

Table 9.7: Relative distortion of user cost as a function of inflation rate.

A. No taxation of capital gains: $n = 0$

Inflation rate, %	N = 6, T = 6				N = 6, T = 3			
	m = 0		m = 1		m = 0		m = 1	
	MNO	MNR	MNO	MNR	MNO	MNR	MNO	MNR
0	0.2830	0.2830	0.0000	0.0000	0.1766	0.1766	-0.1064	-0.1064
2	0.2830	0.2370	-0.0132	-0.0592	0.1766	0.1456	-0.1196	-0.1507
4	0.2830	0.1863	-0.0275	-0.1242	0.1766	0.1126	-0.1339	-0.1980
6	0.2830	0.1304	-0.0430	-0.1956	0.1766	0.0774	-0.1495	-0.2487
8	0.2830	0.0686	-0.0601	-0.2745	0.1766	0.0400	-0.1665	-0.3031
10	0.2830	0.0000	-0.0267	-0.3098	0.1766	0.0000	-0.1331	-0.3098
12	0.2830	-0.0763	-0.0985	-0.4579	0.1766	-0.0427	-0.2049	-0.4243
14	0.2830	-0.1615	-0.1207	-0.5652	0.1766	-0.0885	-0.2271	-0.4922
16	0.2830	-0.2568	-0.1450	-0.6849	0.1766	-0.1375	-0.2514	-0.5656
18	0.2830	-0.3640	-0.1719	-0.8189	0.1766	-0.1902	-0.2783	-0.6452
20	0.2830	-0.4847	-0.2017	-0.9695	0.1766	-0.2469	-0.3081	-0.7316

Inflation rate, %	N = 20, T = 20				N = 20, T = 10			
	m = 0		m = 1		m = 0		m = 1	
	MNO	MNR	MNO	MNR	MNO	MNR	MNO	MNR
0	0.5930	0.5930	0.0000	0.0000	0.3981	0.3981	-0.1949	-0.1949
2	0.5930	0.5256	-0.0641	-0.1314	0.3981	0.3397	-0.2590	-0.3174
4	0.5930	0.4404	-0.1410	-0.2936	0.3981	0.2726	-0.3359	-0.4614
6	0.5930	0.3309	-0.2343	-0.4964	0.3981	0.1951	-0.4292	-0.6322
8	0.5930	0.1884	-0.3489	-0.7536	0.3981	0.1051	-0.5439	-0.8369
10	0.5930	0.0000	-0.4395	-1.0325	0.3981	0.0000	-0.6344	-1.0325
12	0.5930	-0.2527	-0.6704	-1.5160	0.3981	-0.1233	-0.8653	-1.3866
14	0.5930	-0.5968	-0.8991	-2.0889	0.3981	-0.2688	-1.0940	-1.7609
16	0.5930	-1.0730	-1.1953	-2.8613	0.3981	-0.4416	-1.3902	-2.2299
18	0.5930	-1.7421	-1.5847	-3.9198	0.3981	-0.6480	-1.7796	-2.8257
20	0.5930	-2.6976	-2.1046	-5.3952	0.3981	-0.8962	-2.2995	-3.5938

Inflation rate, %	N = 50, T = 50				N = 50, T = 25			
	m = 0		m = 1		m = 0		m = 1	
	MNO	MNR	MNO	MNR	MNO	MNR	MNO	MNR
0	0.8278	0.8278	0.0000	0.0000	0.6576	0.6576	-0.1701	-0.1701
2	0.8278	0.7799	-0.1471	-0.1950	0.6576	0.5916	-0.3172	-0.3832
4	0.8278	0.7070	-0.3506	-0.4714	0.6576	0.5046	-0.5208	-0.6738
6	0.8278	0.5889	-0.6445	-0.8834	0.6576	0.3873	-0.8146	-1.0849
8	0.8278	0.3836	-1.0904	-1.5345	0.6576	0.2262	-1.2605	-1.6919
10	0.8278	0.0000	-1.7535	-2.5813	0.6576	0.0000	-1.9237	-2.5813
12	0.8278	-0.7702	-3.0234	-4.6214	0.6576	-0.3244	-3.1935	-4.1756
14	0.8278	-2.4259	-5.2371	-8.4908	0.6576	-0.7999	-5.4072	-6.8648
16	0.8278	-6.2158	-9.5319	-16.5755	0.6576	-1.5122	-9.7021	-11.8719
18	0.8278	-15.3990	-18.4210	-34.6477	0.6576	-2.6024	-18.5911	-21.8512
20	0.8278	-38.8294	-38.0018	-77.6590	0.6576	-4.3075	-38.1719	-43.1370

Interest rate: $i = 10\%$ p.a. Tax system: Nominal: $MNO : \varepsilon_1 = \varepsilon_2 = 0$. $MNR :$ $\varepsilon_1 = \gamma$, $\varepsilon_2 = 0$. Survival function: Simultaneous retirement after N years. Depreciation allowance schedule: Linear over T years. Income tax rate: $u = 0.508$. Capital value tax rate: $v = 0$.

Table 9.7: (cont.) Relative distortion of user as a function of inflation rate.

B. Full taxation of capital gains: $n = 1$

Inflation rate, %	N = 6, T = 6				N = 6, T = 3			
	m = 0		m = 1		m = 0		m = 1	
	MNO	MNR	MNO	MNR	MNO	MNR	MNO	MNR
0	0.2830	0.2830	0.0000	0.0000	0.1766	0.1766	-0.1064	-0.1064
2	0.3423	0.2962	0.0461	0.0000	0.2359	0.2048	-0.0604	-0.0914
4	0.4073	0.3105	0.0967	0.0000	0.3008	0.2368	-0.0097	-0.0738
6	0.4787	0.3261	0.1526	0.0000	0.3723	0.2731	0.0462	-0.0530
8	0.5575	0.3431	0.2144	0.0000	0.4511	0.3145	0.1080	-0.0286
10	0.5928	0.3098	0.2830	0.0000	0.4864	0.3098	0.1766	0.0000
12	0.7409	0.3816	0.3594	0.0000	0.6345	0.4152	0.2529	0.0336
14	0.8482	0.4037	0.4445	0.0000	0.7418	0.4767	0.3381	0.0730
16	0.9679	0.4281	0.5399	0.0000	0.8615	0.5474	0.4335	0.1193
18	1.1020	0.4550	0.6470	0.0000	0.9955	0.6287	0.5406	0.1738
20	1.2525	0.4847	0.7678	0.0000	1.1461	0.7225	0.6613	0.2378

Inflation rate, %	N = 20, T = 20				N = 20, T = 10			
	m = 0		m = 1		m = 0		m = 1	
	MNO	MNR	MNO	MNR	MNO	MNR	MNO	MNR
0	0.5930	0.5930	0.0000	0.0000	0.3981	0.3981	-0.1949	-0.1949
2	0.7244	0.6571	0.0674	0.0000	0.5295	0.4711	-0.1276	-0.1860
4	0.8866	0.7340	0.1526	0.0000	0.6917	0.5662	-0.0423	-0.1678
6	1.0894	0.8273	0.2621	0.0000	0.8945	0.6914	0.0672	-0.1358
8	1.3466	0.9419	0.4046	0.0000	1.1516	0.8586	0.2097	-0.0833
10	1.6255	1.0325	0.5930	0.0000	1.4306	1.0325	0.3981	0.0000
12	2.1090	1.2634	0.8457	0.0000	1.9141	1.3927	0.6508	0.1294
14	2.6819	1.4921	1.1898	0.0000	2.4870	1.8201	0.9949	0.3280
16	3.4543	1.7883	1.6660	0.0000	3.2593	2.4197	1.4711	0.6314
18	4.5128	2.1777	2.3351	0.0000	4.3179	3.2718	2.1402	1.0941
20	5.9882	2.6976	3.2906	0.0000	5.7933	4.4990	3.0957	1.8014

Inflation rate, %	N = 50, T = 50				N = 50, T = 25			
	m = 0		m = 1		m = 0		m = 1	
	MNO	MNR	MNO	MNR	MNO	MNR	MNO	MNR
0	0.8278	0.8278	0.0000	0.0000	0.6576	0.6576	-0.1701	-0.1701
2	1.0227	0.9749	0.0479	0.0000	0.8526	0.7866	-0.1223	-0.1882
4	1.2991	1.1784	0.1207	0.0000	1.1290	0.9759	-0.0494	-0.2025
6	1.7111	1.4723	0.2389	0.0000	1.5410	1.2707	0.0687	-0.2016
8	2.3623	1.9181	0.4442	0.0000	2.1921	1.7607	0.2740	-0.1574
10	3.4091	2.5813	0.8278	0.0000	3.2389	2.5813	0.6576	0.0000
12	5.4492	3.8512	1.5980	0.0000	5.2790	4.2970	1.4279	0.4458
14	9.3186	6.0649	3.2537	0.0000	9.1485	7.6909	3.0836	1.6260
16	17.4033	10.3597	7.0436	0.0000	17.2331	15.0633	6.8734	4.7036
18	35.4755	19.2487	16.2268	0.0000	35.3054	32.0453	16.0567	12.7966
20	78.4869	38.8297	39.6574	0.0000	78.3168	73.3517	39.4872	34.5221

Interest rate: $i = 10\%$ p.a. Tax system: Nominal: $MNO : \varepsilon_1 = \varepsilon_2 = 0$. $MNR : \varepsilon_1 = \gamma, \varepsilon_2 = 0$. Survival function: Simultaneous retirement after N years. Depreciation allowance schedule: Linear over T years. Income tax rate: $u = 0.508$. Capital value tax rate: $v = 0$.

Table 9.8: Relative distortion of user cost as a function of nominal interest rate.

A. No taxation of capital gains: $n = 0$
Full deductibility of (indexed) interest cost: $m = 1$

Interest rate, %	N = 6, T = 6 degree of indexation, % of inflation				N = 6, T = 3 degree of indexation, % of inflation			
	0%	50%	100%	150%	0%	50%	100%	150%
5	-0.0487	0.0000	0.0000	-0.0691	-0.1125	0.0000	0.0952	0.1687
6	-0.0559	-0.0050	0.0000	-0.0592	-0.1297	-0.0199	0.0730	0.1453
7	-0.0624	-0.0098	0.0000	-0.0501	-0.1453	-0.0385	0.0525	0.1237
8	-0.0683	-0.0142	0.0000	-0.0417	-0.1597	-0.0555	0.0336	0.1037
9	-0.0735	-0.0180	0.0000	-0.0342	-0.1727	-0.0710	0.0161	0.0852
10	-0.0267	0.0042	0.0000	-0.0529	-0.1331	-0.0596	0.0000	0.0423
11	-0.0840	-0.0256	0.0000	-0.0202	-0.1970	-0.0994	-0.0149	0.0528
12	-0.0867	-0.0279	0.0000	-0.0148	-0.2059	-0.1109	-0.0286	0.0377
13	-0.0901	-0.0305	0.0000	-0.0094	-0.2148	-0.1220	-0.0413	0.0242
14	-0.0932	-0.0329	0.0000	-0.0045	-0.2230	-0.1321	-0.0530	0.0116
15	-0.0960	-0.0351	0.0000	0.0000	-0.2305	-0.1415	-0.0638	0.0000

Interest rate, %	N = 20, T = 20 degree of indexation, % of inflation				N = 20, T = 10 degree of indexation, % of inflation			
	0%	50%	100%	150%	0%	50%	100%	150%
5	-0.4260	0.0000	0.0000	-1.0672	-0.5799	0.0000	0.4638	0.7342
6	-0.4549	-0.0482	0.0000	-0.8336	-0.6227	-0.0945	0.3280	0.5766
7	-0.4738	-0.0857	0.0000	-0.6457	-0.6521	-0.1690	0.2182	0.4484
8	-0.4850	-0.1145	0.0000	-0.4942	-0.6710	-0.2272	0.1294	0.3442
9	-0.4904	-0.1365	0.0000	-0.3719	-0.6817	-0.2723	0.0577	0.2595
10	-0.4395	-0.1271	0.0000	-0.2989	-0.6344	-0.2810	0.0000	0.1648
11	-0.4897	-0.1657	0.0000	-0.1928	-0.6867	-0.3335	-0.0463	0.1352
12	-0.4834	-0.1738	0.0000	-0.1286	-0.6812	-0.3520	-0.0833	0.0896
13	-0.4762	-0.1796	0.0000	-0.0764	-0.6738	-0.3656	-0.1127	0.0530
14	-0.4676	-0.1833	0.0000	-0.0341	-0.6642	-0.3747	-0.1358	0.0236
15	-0.4581	-0.1853	0.0000	0.0000	-0.6531	-0.3802	-0.1539	0.0000

Interest rate, %	N = 50, T = 50 degree of indexation, % of inflation				N = 50, T = 25 degree of indexation, % of inflation			
	0%	50%	100%	150%	0%	50%	100%	150%
5	-3.2665	0.0000	0.0000	-30.9852	-3.4716	0.0000	2.8028	3.5366
6	-2.9319	-0.3833	0.0000	-18.9017	-3.1344	-0.4834	1.6260	2.1005
7	-2.6025	-0.5735	0.0000	-11.5703	-2.7988	-0.7309	0.8968	1.2262
8	-2.3010	-0.6542	0.0000	-7.0858	-2.4893	-0.8420	0.4458	0.6977
9	-2.0352	-0.6739	0.0000	-4.3216	-2.2145	-0.8755	0.1685	0.3820
10	-1.7535	-0.6351	0.0000	-2.6314	-1.9237	-0.8402	0.0000	0.1714
11	-1.6092	-0.6321	0.0000	-1.5332	-1.7704	-0.8346	-0.1001	0.0928
12	-1.4407	-0.5952	0.0000	-0.8603	-1.5932	-0.7915	-0.1574	0.0365
13	-1.2978	-0.5566	0.0000	-0.4361	-1.4421	-0.7449	-0.1878	0.0097
14	-1.1759	-0.5189	0.0000	-0.1685	-1.3125	-0.6982	-0.2016	0.0000
15	-1.0716	-0.4833	0.0000	0.0000	-1.2010	-0.6534	-0.2051	0.0000

Inflation rate: $\gamma = 10\%$ p.a. Tax system: System with indexation: $MI1 : \varepsilon_1 = \varepsilon_2 = \varepsilon$. Survival function: Simultaneous retirement after N years. Depreciation allowance schedule: Linear over T years. Income tax rate: $u = 0.508$. Capital value tax rate: $v = 0$.

Table 9.8: (cont.) Relative distortion of user cost as a function of nominal interest rate.

B. Full taxation of (indexed) capital gains: $n = 1$
Full deductibility of (indexed) interest cost: $m = 1$

Interest rate, %	N = 6, T = 6 degree of indexation, % of inflation				N = 6, T = 3 degree of indexation, % of inflation			
	0%	50%	100%	150%	0%	50%	100%	150%
5	0.3669	0.2607	0.0000	-0.3807	0.3031	0.3381	0.2857	0.2139
6	0.3478	0.2220	0.0000	-0.3597	0.2740	0.2816	0.2556	0.1856
7	0.3300	0.2110	0.0000	-0.3401	0.2470	0.2539	0.2276	0.1594
8	0.3133	0.2002	0.0000	-0.3219	0.2219	0.2278	0.2016	0.1352
9	0.2977	0.1901	0.0000	-0.3051	0.1984	0.2033	0.1773	0.1126
10	0.2830	0.1549	0.0000	-0.3665	0.1766	0.1549	0.1549	0.0144
11	0.2692	0.1723	0.0000	-0.2726	0.1561	0.1600	0.1340	0.0743
12	0.2564	0.1636	0.0000	-0.2602	0.1373	0.1399	0.1145	0.0549
13	0.2443	0.1557	0.0000	-0.2474	0.1196	0.1215	0.0964	0.0382
14	0.2329	0.1484	0.0000	-0.2351	0.1031	0.1043	0.0795	0.0230
15	0.2222	0.1415	0.0000	-0.1465	0.0876	0.0883	0.0638	0.0858

Interest rate, %	N = 20, T = 20 degree of indexation, % of inflation				N = 20, T = 10 degree of indexation, % of inflation			
	0%	50%	100%	150%	0%	50%	100%	150%
5	1.2043	1.1141	0.0000	-3.4832	1.0504	1.3722	1.3913	1.0202
6	1.0372	0.9388	0.0000	-2.9691	0.8694	1.1240	1.1481	0.7915
7	0.8968	0.8139	0.0000	-2.5416	0.7185	0.9388	0.9455	0.6040
8	0.7783	0.7080	0.0000	-2.1848	0.5924	0.7832	0.7763	0.4501
9	0.6781	0.6184	0.0000	-1.8858	0.4867	0.6523	0.6348	0.3240
10	0.5930	0.5163	0.0000	-1.7120	0.3981	0.5163	0.5163	0.1430
11	0.5204	0.4774	0.0000	-1.4208	0.3234	0.4495	0.4167	0.1373
12	0.4585	0.4213	0.0000	-1.2425	0.2607	0.3704	0.3332	0.0666
13	0.4054	0.3734	0.0000	-1.0898	0.2078	0.3037	0.2629	0.0100
14	0.3597	0.3322	0.0000	-0.9596	0.1630	0.2471	0.2038	-0.0362
15	0.3202	0.2965	0.0000	-0.7705	0.1252	0.1990	0.1539	0.0039

Interest rate, %	N = 50, T = 50 degree of indexation, % of inflation				N = 50, T = 25 degree of indexation, % of inflation			
	0%	50%	100%	150%	0%	50%	100%	150%
5	4.5776	6.5535	0.0000	-81.3851	4.3725	7.1988	8.4083	4.9195
6	3.1330	4.5656	0.0000	-53.4370	2.9305	4.9662	5.6911	2.5688
7	2.1833	3.2532	0.0000	-35.6575	1.9870	3.4893	3.8863	1.1325
8	1.5501	2.3617	0.0000	-24.1953	1.3619	2.4869	2.6749	0.2672
9	1.1219	1.7470	0.0000	-16.7040	0.9425	1.7974	1.8534	-0.2414
10	0.8278	1.2907	0.0000	-11.8163	0.6576	1.2907	1.2907	-0.6052
11	0.6226	1.0106	0.0000	-8.3986	0.4615	0.9768	0.9012	-0.6750
12	0.4774	0.7890	0.0000	-6.1209	0.3250	0.7329	0.6297	-0.7398
13	0.3728	0.6266	0.0000	-4.5422	0.2286	0.5560	0.4383	-0.7527
14	0.2963	0.5055	0.0000	-3.4317	0.1598	0.4258	0.3024	-0.7358
15	0.2394	0.4139	0.0000	-2.5609	0.1100	0.3288	0.2051	-0.6249

Inflation rate: $\gamma = 10\%$ p.a. Tax system: System with indexation: $MI1 : \varepsilon_1 = \varepsilon_2 = \varepsilon$. Survival function: Simultaneous retirement after N years. Depreciation allowance schedule: Linear over T years. Income tax rate: $u = 0.508$. Capital value tax rate: $v = 0$.

Table 9.9: Relative distortion of user cost as a function of inflation rate.

A. No taxation of capital gains: $n = 0$
Full deductibility of (indexed) interest cost: $m = 1$

Inflation rate, %	N = 6, T = 6 degree of indexation, % of inflation				N = 6, T = 3 degree of indexation, % of inflation			
	0%	50%	100%	150%	0%	50%	100%	150%
0	0.0000	0.0000	0.0000	0.0000	-0.1064	-0.1064	-0.1064	-0.1064
2	-0.0132	-0.0061	0.0000	0.0049	-0.1196	-0.1053	-0.0914	-0.0781
4	-0.0275	-0.0114	0.0000	0.0062	-0.1339	-0.1029	-0.0738	-0.0468
6	-0.0430	-0.0160	0.0000	0.0027	-0.1495	-0.0989	-0.0530	-0.0122
8	-0.0601	-0.0195	0.0000	-0.0077	-0.1665	-0.0933	-0.0286	0.0259
10	-0.0267	0.0042	0.0000	-0.0529	-0.1331	-0.0596	0.0000	0.0423
12	-0.0985	-0.0222	0.0000	-0.0587	-0.2049	-0.0752	0.0336	0.1151
14	-0.1207	-0.0208	0.0000	-0.1068	-0.2271	-0.0621	0.0730	0.1672
16	-0.1450	-0.0170	0.0000	-0.1773	-0.2514	-0.0456	0.1193	0.2251
18	-0.1719	-0.0102	0.0000	-0.2780	-0.2783	-0.0251	0.1738	0.2897
20	-0.2017	0.0000	0.0000	-0.4199	-0.3081	0.0000	0.2378	0.3618

Inflation rate, %	N = 20, T = 20 degree of indexation, % of inflation				N = 20, T = 10 degree of indexation, % of inflation			
	0%	50%	100%	150%	0%	50%	100%	150%
0	0.0000	0.0000	0.0000	0.0000	-0.1949	-0.1949	-0.1949	-0.1949
2	-0.0641	-0.0301	0.0000	0.0257	-0.2590	-0.2215	-0.1860	-0.1526
4	-0.1410	-0.0615	0.0000	0.0373	-0.3359	-0.2475	-0.1678	-0.0985
6	-0.2343	-0.0935	0.0000	0.0183	-0.4292	-0.2718	-0.1358	-0.0280
8	-0.3489	-0.1248	0.0000	-0.0643	-0.5439	-0.2926	-0.0833	0.0651
10	-0.4395	-0.1271	0.0000	-0.2989	-0.6344	-0.2810	0.0000	0.1648
12	-0.6704	-0.1744	0.0000	-0.7314	-0.8653	-0.3103	0.1294	0.3627
14	-0.8991	-0.1832	0.0000	-1.6838	-1.0940	-0.2958	0.3280	0.6022
16	-1.1953	-0.1693	0.0000	-3.6247	-1.3902	-0.2526	0.6314	0.9410
18	-1.5847	-0.1168	0.0000	-7.5759	-1.7796	-0.1631	1.0941	1.4275
20	-2.1046	0.0000	0.0000	-15.7033	-2.2995	0.0000	1.8014	2.1359

Inflation rate, %	N = 50, T = 50 degree of indexation, % of inflation				N = 50, T = 25 degree of indexation, % of inflation			
	0%	50%	100%	150%	0%	50%	100%	150%
0	0.0000	0.0000	0.0000	0.0000	-0.1701	-0.1701	-0.1701	-0.1701
2	-0.1471	-0.0712	0.0000	0.0651	-0.3172	-0.2505	-0.1882	-0.1312
4	-0.3506	-0.1628	0.0000	0.1176	-0.5208	-0.3511	-0.2025	-0.0840
6	-0.6445	-0.2831	0.0000	0.0760	-0.8146	-0.4794	-0.2016	-0.0242
8	-1.0904	-0.4438	0.0000	-0.3866	-1.2605	-0.6463	-0.1574	0.0592
10	-1.7535	-0.6351	0.0000	-2.6314	-1.9237	-0.8402	0.0000	0.1714
12	-3.0234	-0.9516	0.0000	-12.3180	-3.1935	-1.1531	0.4458	0.4785
14	-5.2371	-1.3183	0.0000	-55.7931	-5.4072	-1.5061	1.6260	1.1640
16	-9.5319	-1.6883	0.0000	-262.2080	-9.7021	-1.8457	4.7036	3.0264
18	-18.4210	-1.7017	0.0000	-1317	-18.5911	-1.8018	12.7966	8.3796
20	-38.0018	0.0000	0.0000	-7156	-38.1719	0.0000	34.5220	24.2370

Interest rate: $i = 10\%$ p.a. Tax system: System with indexation: $MI1 : \varepsilon_1 = \varepsilon_2 = \varepsilon$. Survival function: Simultaneous retirement after N years. Depreciation allowance schedule: Linear over T years. Income tax rate: $u = 0.508$. Capital value tax rate: $v = 0$.

Table 9.9: (cont.) Relative distortion of user cost as a function of inflation rate.

B. Full taxation of (indexed) capital gains: $n = 1$
Full deductibility of (indexed) interest cost: $m = 1$

Inflation rate, %	N = 6, T = 6 degree of indexation, % of inflation				N = 6, T = 3 degree of indexation, % of inflation			
	0%	50%	100%	150%	0%	50%	100%	150%
0	0.0000	0.0000	0.0000	0.0000	-0.1064	-0.1064	-0.1064	-0.1064
2	0.0461	0.0242	0.0000	-0.0268	-0.0604	-0.0640	-0.0686	-0.0742
4	0.0967	0.0535	0.0000	-0.0652	-0.0097	-0.0150	-0.0246	-0.0387
6	0.1526	0.0887	0.0000	-0.1195	0.0462	0.0413	0.0265	-0.0004
8	0.2144	0.1307	0.0000	-0.1910	0.1080	0.1061	0.0859	0.0441
10	0.2830	0.1549	0.0000	-0.3665	0.1766	0.1549	0.1549	0.0144
12	0.3594	0.2400	0.0000	-0.4197	0.2529	0.2665	0.2352	0.1450
14	0.4445	0.3103	0.0000	-0.5934	0.3381	0.3654	0.3286	0.2037
16	0.5399	0.3934	0.0000	-0.8237	0.4335	0.4793	0.4375	0.2687
18	0.6470	0.4909	0.0000	-1.1290	0.5406	0.6100	0.5647	0.3405
20	0.7678	0.6597	0.0000	-1.5344	0.6613	0.8146	0.7134	0.4197

Inflation rate, %	N = 20, T = 20 degree of indexation, % of inflation				N = 20, T = 10 degree of indexation, % of inflation			
	0%	50%	100%	150%	0%	50%	100%	150%
0	0.0000	0.0000	0.0000	0.0000	-0.1949	-0.1949	-0.1949	-0.1949
2	0.0674	0.0389	0.0000	-0.0510	-0.1276	-0.1312	-0.1395	-0.1529
4	0.1526	0.1007	0.0000	-0.1655	-0.0423	-0.0388	-0.0559	-0.0975
6	0.2621	0.1948	0.0000	-0.3945	0.0672	0.0929	0.0679	-0.0240
8	0.4046	0.3352	0.0000	-0.8267	0.2097	0.2793	0.2499	0.0789
10	0.5930	0.5163	0.0000	-1.7120	0.3981	0.5163	0.5163	0.1430
12	0.8457	0.8452	0.0000	-3.1352	0.6508	0.9132	0.9057	0.4207
14	1.1898	1.2887	0.0000	-5.9429	0.9949	1.4389	1.4761	0.7074
16	1.6660	1.9384	0.0000	-11.2691	1.4711	2.1884	2.3150	1.1236
18	2.3351	2.8939	0.0000	-21.5681	2.1402	3.2643	3.5558	1.7347
20	3.2906	4.3627	0.0000	-41.9559	3.0957	4.8789	5.4042	2.6422

Inflation rate, %	N = 50, T = 50 degree of indexation, % of inflation				N = 50, T = 25 degree of indexation, % of inflation			
	0%	50%	100%	150%	0%	50%	100%	150%
0	0.0000	0.0000	0.0000	0.0000	-0.1701	-0.1701	-0.1701	-0.1701
2	0.0479	0.0342	0.0000	-0.0603	-0.1223	-0.1252	-0.1412	-0.1725
4	0.1207	0.1136	0.0000	-0.2945	-0.0494	-0.0276	-0.0675	-0.1937
6	0.2389	0.2799	0.0000	-1.0494	0.0687	0.1678	0.1008	-0.2483
8	0.4442	0.6193	0.0000	-3.4735	0.2740	0.5518	0.4722	-0.3528
10	0.8278	1.2907	0.0000	-11.8163	0.6576	1.2907	1.2907	-0.6052
12	1.5980	2.7865	0.0000	-42.3443	1.4279	2.8873	3.1208	-0.7555
14	3.2537	6.0031	0.0000	-166.5530	3.0836	6.2536	7.3172	-0.8593
16	7.0436	13.3527	0.0000	-719.9970	6.8734	13.8249	17.2467	-0.0732
18	16.2268	30.9374	0.0000	-3426	16.0567	31.7385	41.5889	4.3646
20	39.6574	75.0779	0.0000	-17928	39.4872	76.3685	103.5660	21.7631

Interest rate: $i = 10\%$ p.a. Tax system: System with indexation: $MI1 : \varepsilon_1 = \varepsilon_2 = \varepsilon$. Survival function: Simultaneous retirement after N years. Depreciation allowance schedule: Linear over T years. Income tax rate: $u = 0.508$. Capital value tax rate: $v = 0$.

Table 9.10: Tax equivalent real rate of return as a function of nominal interest rate.

A. No taxation of capital gains: $n = 0$

Interest rate, %	N = 6, T = 6				N = 6, T = 3			
	m = 0		m = 1		m = 0		m = 1	
	MNO	MNR	MNO	MNR	MNO	MNR	MNO	MNR
5	-1.01	-10.74	-6.28	-17.37	-2.58	-8.02	-8.02	-14.19
6	0.74	-8.48	-5.50	-16.17	-1.09	-6.40	-7.56	-13.69
7	2.47	-6.28	-4.71	-14.98	0.39	-4.79	-7.08	-13.17
8	4.20	-4.14	-3.91	-13.80	1.88	-3.19	-6.59	-12.63
9	5.91	-2.05	-3.10	-12.63	3.37	-1.59	-6.07	-12.06
10	7.62	0.00	-0.77	-9.66	4.85	0.00	-3.94	-9.66
11	9.33	2.02	-1.49	-10.38	6.35	1.60	-5.03	-10.92
12	11.03	4.00	-0.62	-9.20	7.84	3.18	-4.43	-10.26
13	12.72	5.96	0.22	-8.07	9.34	4.76	-3.85	-9.62
14	14.41	7.90	1.07	-6.95	10.84	6.34	-3.25	-8.96
15	16.10	9.81	1.93	-5.83	12.35	7.92	-2.64	-8.29

Interest rate, %	N = 20, T = 20				N = 20, T = 10			
	m = 0		m = 1		m = 0		m = 1	
	MNO	MNR	MNO	MNR	MNO	MNR	MNO	MNR
5	-2.30	-15.88	-9.02	NA	-3.30	-8.18	-11.06	NA
6	-0.85	-10.52	-8.52	NA	-1.97	-6.42	-10.94	NA
7	0.58	-7.12	-7.92	NA	-0.63	-4.75	-10.69	NA
8	2.02	-4.43	-7.25	NA	0.71	-3.13	-10.30	NA
9	3.46	-2.11	-6.51	NA	2.06	-1.55	-9.79	NA
10	4.91	0.00	-4.98	NA	3.43	0.00	-8.12	NA
11	6.38	1.98	-4.91	NA	4.81	1.54	-8.48	NA
12	7.85	3.86	-4.02	-17.87	6.20	3.06	-7.67	NA
13	9.34	5.69	-3.13	-13.42	7.62	4.58	-6.83	-28.08
14	10.86	7.48	-2.22	-10.55	9.05	6.11	-5.94	-19.25
15	12.39	9.25	-1.29	-8.31	10.50	7.64	-5.03	-15.59

Interest rate, %	N = 50, T = 50				N = 50, T = 25			
	m = 0		m = 1		m = 0		m = 1	
	MNO	MNR	MNO	MNR	MNO	MNR	MNO	MNR
5	-3.58	NA	NA	NA	-3.96	NA	NA	NA
6	-2.38	NA	NA	NA	-2.78	-8.12	NA	NA
7	-1.17	NA	NA	NA	-1.58	-5.21	NA	NA
8	0.08	-6.20	NA	NA	-0.36	-3.24	NA	NA
9	1.36	-2.29	NA	NA	0.90	-1.56	NA	NA
10	2.68	0.00	NA	NA	2.20	0.00	NA	NA
11	4.07	1.91	NA	NA	3.55	1.51	NA	NA
12	5.52	3.68	NA	NA	4.95	3.02	NA	NA
13	7.04	5.42	NA	NA	6.42	4.55	NA	NA
14	8.64	7.16	NA	NA	7.96	6.13	NA	NA
15	10.30	8.94	NA	NA	9.57	7.76	NA	NA

Inflation rate: $\gamma = 10\%$ p.a. Tax system: Nominal: $MNO : \varepsilon_1 = \varepsilon_2 = 0$. $MNR : \varepsilon_1 = \gamma, \varepsilon_2 = 0$. Survival function: Simultaneous retirement after N years. Depreciation allowance schedule: Linear over T years. Income tax rate: $u = 0.508$. Capital value tax rate: $v = 0$.

Table 9.10: (cont.) Tax equivalent real rate of return as a function of nominal interest rate.

B. Full taxation of capital gains: $n = 1$.

Interest rate, %	N = 6, T = 6				N = 6, T = 3			
	m = 0		m = 1		m = 0		m = 1	
	MNO	MNR	MNO	MNR	MNO	MNR	MNO	MNR
5	8.33	0.16	3.82	-5.00	6.97	2.37	2.38	-2.58
6	9.93	2.08	4.56	-4.00	8.34	3.81	2.84	-2.10
7	11.54	3.99	5.31	-3.00	9.71	5.24	3.32	-1.60
8	13.15	5.88	6.07	-2.00	11.09	6.69	3.82	-1.08
9	14.76	7.74	6.84	-1.00	12.48	8.14	4.33	-0.55
10	15.17	8.30	7.62	0.00	12.65	8.30	4.85	0.00
11	18.02	11.47	8.41	1.00	15.33	11.10	5.40	0.57
12	19.61	13.27	9.21	2.00	16.71	12.54	5.95	1.15
13	21.23	15.09	10.01	3.00	18.14	14.01	6.52	1.74
14	22.85	16.89	10.83	4.00	19.57	15.49	7.10	2.35
15	24.48	18.70	11.65	5.00	21.01	16.98	7.69	2.98

Interest rate, %	N = 20, T = 20				N = 20, T = 10			
	m = 0		m = 1		m = 0		m = 1	
	MNO	MNR	MNO	MNR	MNO	MNR	MNO	MNR
5	5.60	0.14	2.07	-5.00	4.97	2.42	1.33	-1.84
6	6.80	1.81	2.57	-4.00	6.06	3.51	1.67	-1.59
7	8.04	3.45	3.10	-3.00	7.19	4.65	2.05	-1.28
8	9.32	5.08	3.67	-2.00	8.36	5.83	2.47	-0.91
9	10.64	6.69	4.27	-1.00	9.57	7.05	2.93	-0.48
10	11.69	7.97	4.91	0.00	10.50	7.97	3.43	0.00
11	13.41	9.94	5.58	1.00	12.12	9.62	3.96	0.53
12	14.84	11.57	6.28	2.00	13.45	10.95	4.53	1.12
13	16.32	13.22	7.01	3.00	14.83	12.33	5.14	1.74
14	17.83	14.89	7.76	4.00	16.24	13.75	5.77	2.41
15	19.38	16.58	8.53	5.00	17.69	15.20	6.43	3.11

Interest rate, %	N = 50, T = 50				N = 50, T = 25			
	m = 0		m = 1		m = 0		m = 1	
	MNO	MNR	MNO	MNR	MNO	MNR	MNO	MNR
5	3.10	0.10	0.61	-5.00	2.98	2.06	0.45	-0.88
6	3.98	1.36	0.86	-4.00	3.83	2.80	0.65	-0.92
7	4.99	2.66	1.19	-3.00	4.79	3.66	0.91	-0.87
8	6.12	4.02	1.60	-2.00	5.88	4.65	1.26	-0.72
9	7.39	5.47	2.10	-1.00	7.09	5.77	1.69	-0.43
10	8.68	6.91	2.68	-0.00	8.32	6.91	2.20	0.00
11	10.33	8.68	3.34	1.00	9.90	8.41	2.78	0.56
12	11.98	10.43	4.06	2.00	11.49	9.92	3.44	1.22
13	13.75	12.29	4.83	3.00	13.19	11.55	4.15	1.96
14	15.62	14.23	5.65	4.00	14.98	13.29	4.91	2.77
15	17.56	16.24	6.50	5.00	16.85	15.11	5.70	3.62

Inflation rate: $\gamma = 10\%$ p.a. Tax system: Nominal: $MNO : \varepsilon_1 = \varepsilon_2 = 0$. $MNR : \varepsilon_1 = \gamma, \varepsilon_2 = 0$. Survival function: Simultaneous retirement after N years. Depreciation allowance schedule: Linear over T years. Income tax rate: $u = 0.508$. Capital value tax rate: $v = 0$.

Table 9.11: Tax equivalent real rate of return as a function of inflation rate.

A. No taxation of capital gains: $n = 0$

Inflation rate, %	N = 6, T = 6				N = 6, T = 3			
	m = 0		m = 1		m = 0		m = 1	
	MNO	MNR	MNO	MNR	MNO	MNR	MNO	MNR
0	19.18	19.18	10.00	10.00	15.83	15.83	6.28	6.28
2	16.85	15.47	7.56	6.02	13.62	12.66	3.95	2.86
4	14.53	11.71	5.12	1.93	11.43	9.50	1.60	-0.61
6	12.22	7.90	2.67	-2.31	9.23	6.34	-0.76	-4.15
8	9.92	4.00	0.19	-6.76	7.04	3.18	-3.15	-7.76
10	7.62	0.00	-0.77	-9.66	4.85	0.00	-3.94	-9.66
12	5.33	-4.14	-4.78	-16.61	2.67	-3.19	-7.97	-15.35
14	3.05	-8.48	-7.31	-22.37	0.50	-6.40	-10.42	-19.42
16	0.78	-13.08	-9.86	-29.21	-1.67	-9.65	-12.92	-23.78
18	-1.49	-18.06	-12.44	-38.33	-3.84	-12.94	-15.45	-28.58
20	-3.74	-23.64	-15.07	-57.37	-6.00	-16.30	-18.04	-34.09

Inflation rate, %	N = 20, T = 20				N = 20, T = 10			
	m = 0		m = 1		m = 0		m = 1	
	MNO	MNR	MNO	MNR	MNO	MNR	MNO	MNR
0	18.03	18.03	10.00	10.00	15.50	15.50	7.02	7.02
2	15.28	14.50	7.13	6.18	13.01	12.31	4.29	3.37
4	12.59	11.00	4.20	2.07	10.55	9.18	1.44	-0.59
6	9.97	7.48	1.17	-2.70	8.13	6.11	-1.61	-5.25
8	7.41	3.86	-2.08	-9.44	5.76	3.06	-5.01	-12.07
10	4.91	0.00	-4.98	NA	3.43	0.00	-8.12	NA
12	2.47	-4.43	-10.29	NA	1.13	-3.13	-15.62	NA
14	0.09	-10.52	-18.42	NA	-1.13	-6.42	NA	NA
16	-2.24	NA	NA	NA	-3.35	-10.07	NA	NA
18	-4.54	NA	NA	NA	-5.55	-14.55	NA	NA
20	-6.79	NA	NA	NA	-7.72	-22.32	NA	NA

Inflation rate, %	N = 50, T = 50				N = 50, T = 25			
	m = 0		m = 1		m = 0		m = 1	
	MNO	MNR	MNO	MNR	MNO	MNR	MNO	MNR
0	18.43	18.43	10.00	10.00	16.71	16.71	8.21	8.21
2	14.93	14.53	6.70	6.27	13.53	12.98	5.12	4.48
4	11.55	10.76	3.31	2.25	10.44	9.44	1.79	0.13
6	8.35	7.16	-0.72	-4.27	7.51	6.13	-2.90	NA
8	5.40	3.68	NA	NA	4.76	3.02	NA	NA
10	2.68	0.00	NA	NA	2.20	0.00	NA	NA
12	0.18	-6.20	NA	NA	-0.20	-3.24	NA	NA
14	-2.16	NA	NA	NA	-2.47	-8.12	NA	NA
16	-4.39	NA	NA	NA	-4.66	NA	NA	NA
18	-6.54	NA	NA	NA	-6.79	NA	NA	NA
20	-8.65	NA	NA	NA	-8.88	NA	NA	NA

Interest rate: $i = 10\%$ p.a. Tax system: Nominal: $MNO : \varepsilon_1 = \varepsilon_2 = 0$. $MNR :$ $\varepsilon_1 = \gamma$, $\varepsilon_2 = 0$. Survival function: Simultaneous retirement after N years. Depreciation allowance schedule: Linear over T years. Income tax rate: $u = 0.508$. Capital value tax rate: $v = 0$.

Table 9.11: (cont.) Tax equivalent real rate of return as a function of inflation rate.

B. Full taxation of capital gains: $n = 1$

Inflation rate, %	N = 6, T = 6				N = 6, T = 3			
	m = 0		m = 1		m = 0		m = 1	
	MNO	MNR	MNO	MNR	MNO	MNR	MNO	MNR
0	19.18	19.18	10.00	10.00	15.83	15.83	6.28	6.28
2	18.61	17.25	9.50	8.00	15.43	14.49	5.98	4.92
4	18.04	15.32	9.02	6.00	15.04	13.20	5.69	3.61
6	17.48	13.40	8.54	4.00	14.65	11.95	5.40	2.35
8	16.93	11.50	8.08	2.00	14.27	10.75	5.13	1.15
10	15.17	8.30	7.62	0.00	12.65	8.30	4.85	0.00
12	15.83	7.71	7.18	-2.00	13.50	8.50	4.59	-1.08
14	15.30	5.84	6.75	-4.00	13.13	7.47	4.34	-2.10
16	14.78	3.97	6.34	-6.00	12.76	6.49	4.09	-3.04
18	14.26	2.13	5.94	-8.00	12.39	5.58	3.85	-3.91
20	13.76	0.30	5.55	-10.00	12.03	4.74	3.62	-4.69

Inflation rate, %	N = 20, T = 20				N = 20, T = 10			
	m = 0		m = 1		m = 0		m = 1	
	MNO	MNR	MNO	MNR	MNO	MNR	MNO	MNR
0	18.03	18.03	10.00	10.00	15.50	15.50	7.02	7.02
2	16.77	16.01	8.89	8.00	14.55	13.87	6.24	5.39
4	15.53	14.02	7.82	6.00	13.60	12.32	5.47	3.84
6	14.32	12.07	6.79	4.00	12.65	10.86	4.75	2.41
8	13.14	10.16	5.82	2.00	11.73	9.52	4.06	1.12
10	11.69	7.97	4.91	0.00	10.50	7.97	3.43	0.00
12	10.92	6.52	4.09	-2.00	9.95	7.23	2.85	-0.91
14	9.90	4.81	3.35	-4.00	9.12	6.30	2.34	-1.59
16	8.96	3.18	2.70	-6.00	8.34	5.52	1.90	-2.04
18	8.09	1.65	2.15	-8.00	7.61	4.89	1.53	-2.27
20	7.32	0.22	1.70	-10.00	6.95	4.38	1.23	-2.31

Inflation rate, %	N = 50, T = 50				N = 50, T = 25			
	m = 0		m = 1		m = 0		m = 1	
	MNO	MNR	MNO	MNR	MNO	MNR	MNO	MNR
0	18.43	18.43	10.00	10.00	16.71	16.71	8.21	8.21
2	16.53	16.13	8.41	8.00	15.13	14.59	6.92	6.33
4	14.57	13.80	6.85	6.00	13.48	12.50	5.64	4.50
6	12.59	11.46	5.34	4.00	11.78	10.50	4.40	2.77
8	10.63	9.17	3.93	2.00	10.07	8.65	3.23	1.22
10	8.68	6.91	2.68	-0.00	8.32	6.91	2.20	-0.00
12	7.15	5.09	1.69	-2.00	6.94	5.69	1.38	-0.72
14	5.79	3.44	0.98	-4.00	5.68	4.66	0.81	-0.92
16	4.72	2.08	0.55	-6.00	4.66	3.90	0.46	-0.79
18	3.91	0.99	0.32	-8.00	3.88	3.36	0.28	-0.55
20	3.31	0.12	0.20	-10.00	3.30	2.95	0.19	-0.32

Interest rate: $i = 10\%$ p.a. Tax system: Nominal: $MNO : \varepsilon_1 = \varepsilon_2 = 0$. $MNR : \varepsilon_1 = \gamma, \varepsilon_2 = 0$. Survival function: Simultaneous retirement after N years. Depreciation allowance schedule: Linear over T years. Income tax rate: $u = 0.508$. Capital value tax rate: $v = 0$.

Table 9.12: Tax equivalent real rate of return as a function of nominal interest rate.

A. No taxation of capital gains: $n = 0$
Full deductibility of (indexed) interest cost: $m = 1$

Interest rate, %	N = 6, T = 6 degree of indexation, % of inflation				N = 6, T = 3 degree of indexation, % of inflation			
	0%	50%	100%	150%	0%	50%	100%	150%
5	-6.28	-5.00	-5.00	-6.83	-8.02	-5.00	-2.58	-0.78
6	-5.50	-4.13	-4.00	-5.59	-7.56	-4.53	-2.10	-0.27
7	-4.71	-3.27	-3.00	-4.37	-7.08	-4.05	-1.60	0.25
8	-3.91	-2.39	-2.00	-3.16	-6.59	-3.55	-1.08	0.79
9	-3.10	-1.51	-1.00	-1.97	-6.07	-3.03	-0.55	1.34
10	-0.77	0.12	0.00	-1.53	-3.94	-1.73	0.00	1.20
11	-1.49	0.25	1.00	0.41	-5.03	-1.96	0.57	2.52
12	-0.62	1.17	2.00	1.56	-4.43	-1.38	1.15	3.11
13	0.22	2.07	3.00	2.72	-3.85	-0.79	1.74	3.73
14	1.07	2.98	4.00	3.86	-3.25	-0.19	2.35	4.36
15	1.93	3.89	5.00	5.00	-2.64	0.42	2.98	5.00

Interest rate, %	N = 20, T = 20 degree of indexation, % of inflation				N = 20, T = 10 degree of indexation, % of inflation			
	0%	50%	100%	150%	0%	50%	100%	150%
5	-9.02	-5.00	-5.00	NA	-11.06	-5.00	-1.84	-0.30
6	-8.52	-4.40	-4.00	-15.76	-10.94	-4.79	-1.59	-0.01
7	-7.92	-3.74	-3.00	-10.57	-10.69	-4.52	-1.28	0.34
8	-7.25	-3.05	-2.00	-7.38	-10.30	-4.17	-0.91	0.74
9	-6.51	-2.31	-1.00	-4.92	-9.79	-3.75	-0.48	1.21
10	-4.98	-1.26	0.00	-3.17	-8.12	-2.96	0.00	1.50
11	-4.91	-0.73	1.00	-1.04	-8.48	-2.72	0.53	2.30
12	-4.02	0.10	2.00	0.62	-7.67	-2.12	1.12	2.91
13	-3.13	0.95	3.00	2.16	-6.83	-1.47	1.74	3.57
14	-2.22	1.82	4.00	3.61	-5.94	-0.78	2.41	4.26
15	-1.29	2.70	5.00	5.00	-5.03	-0.05	3.11	5.00

Interest rate, %	N = 50, T = 50 degree of indexation, % of inflation				N = 50, T = 25 degree of indexation, % of inflation			
	0%	50%	100%	150%	0%	50%	100%	150%
5	NA	-5.00	-5.00	NA	NA	-5.00	-0.88	-0.22
6	NA	-5.33	-4.00	NA	NA	-5.80	-0.92	-0.30
7	NA	-5.42	-3.00	NA	NA	-6.59	-0.87	-0.28
8	NA	-5.14	-2.00	NA	NA	-7.13	-0.72	-0.11
9	NA	-4.50	-1.00	NA	NA	-7.00	-0.43	0.22
10	NA	-3.41	0.00	NA	NA	-5.70	0.00	0.64
11	NA	-2.64	1.00	NA	NA	-4.97	0.56	1.39
12	NA	-1.61	2.00	-4.82	NA	-3.69	1.22	2.17
13	NA	-0.57	3.00	0.36	NA	-2.47	1.96	3.05
14	NA	0.45	4.00	2.98	NA	-1.31	2.77	4.00
15	NA	1.46	5.00	5.00	NA	-0.20	3.62	5.00

Inflation rate: $\gamma = 10\%$ p.a. Tax system: System with indexation: $MI1 : \varepsilon_1 = \varepsilon_2 = \varepsilon$. Survival function: Simultaneous retirement after N years. Depreciation allowance schedule: Linear over T years. Income tax rate: $u = 0.508$. Capital value tax rate: $v = 0$.

Table 9.12: (cont.) Tax equivalent real rate of return as a function of nominal interest rate.

B. Full taxation of (indexed) capital gains: $n = 1$
Full deductibility of (indexed) interest cost: $m = 1$

Interest rate, %	N = 6, T = 6 degree of indexation, % of inflation				N = 6, T = 3 degree of indexation, % of inflation			
	0%	50%	100%	150%	0%	50%	100%	150%
5	3.82	1.40	-5.00	-10.17	2.30	3.17	1.08	0.30
6	4.56	1.60	-4.00	-14.66	2.84	3.02	2.40	0.72
7	5.31	2.44	-3.00	-13.18	3.32	3.49	2.85	1.15
8	6.07	3.27	-2.00	-11.74	3.82	3.96	3.31	1.61
9	6.84	4.11	-1.00	-10.34	4.33	4.45	3.78	2.08
10	7.62	4.28	0.00	-11.67	4.85	4.28	4.28	0.41
11	8.41	5.83	1.00	-7.54	5.40	5.50	4.79	3.13
12	9.21	6.68	2.00	-6.27	5.95	6.02	5.31	3.61
13	10.01	7.55	3.00	-4.96	6.52	6.57	5.85	4.14
14	10.83	8.42	4.00	-3.67	7.10	7.13	6.40	4.70
15	11.65	9.30	5.00	0.26	7.69	7.71	6.97	7.64

Interest rate, %	N = 20, T = 20 degree of indexation, % of inflation				N = 20, T = 10 degree of indexation, % of inflation			
	0%	50%	100%	150%	0%	50%	100%	150%
5	2.07	1.64	-5.00	NA	1.33	2.85	2.94	1.18
6	2.57	2.05	-4.00	NA	1.67	3.01	3.14	1.24
7	3.10	2.62	-3.00	NA	2.05	3.34	3.38	1.34
8	3.67	3.22	-2.00	NA	2.47	3.70	3.66	1.50
9	4.27	3.86	-1.00	NA	2.93	4.10	3.98	1.71
10	4.91	4.34	0.00	NA	3.43	4.34	4.34	1.31
11	5.58	5.24	1.00	NA	3.96	5.01	4.74	2.32
12	6.28	5.96	2.00	NA	4.53	5.52	5.19	2.68
13	7.01	6.72	3.00	NA	5.14	6.06	5.67	3.11
14	7.76	7.49	4.00	-18.78	5.77	6.64	6.20	3.59
15	8.53	8.29	5.00	-8.07	6.43	7.25	6.75	5.05

Interest rate, %	N = 50, T = 50 degree of indexation, % of inflation				N = 50, T = 25 degree of indexation, % of inflation			
	0%	50%	100%	150%	0%	50%	100%	150%
5	0.61	1.95	-5.00	NA	0.45	2.34	3.05	0.86
6	0.86	2.21	-4.00	NA	0.65	2.55	3.15	0.25
7	1.19	2.55	-3.00	NA	0.91	2.82	3.27	-0.44
8	1.60	2.95	-2.00	NA	1.26	3.15	3.43	-1.19
9	2.10	3.43	-1.00	NA	1.69	3.53	3.64	-1.95
10	2.68	3.91	0.00	NA	2.20	3.91	3.91	-3.18
11	3.34	4.58	1.00	NA	2.78	4.48	4.24	-3.03
12	4.06	5.25	2.00	NA	3.44	5.04	4.65	-3.03
13	4.83	5.97	3.00	NA	4.15	5.66	5.13	-2.57
14	5.65	6.74	4.00	NA	4.91	6.33	5.68	-1.76
15	6.50	7.54	5.00	NA	5.70	7.04	6.29	0.11

Inflation rate: $\gamma = 10\%$ p.a. Tax system: System with indexation: $MI1 : \varepsilon_1 = \varepsilon_2 = \varepsilon$. Survival function: Simultaneous retirement after N years. Depreciation allowance schedule: Linear over T years. Income tax rate: $u = 0.508$. Capital value tax rate: $v = 0$.

Table 9.13: Tax equivalent real rate of return as a function of inflation rate.

A. No taxation of capital gains: $n = 0$
Full deductibility of (indexed) interest cost: $m = 1$

Inflation rate, %	N = 6, T = 6 degree of indexation, % of inflation				N = 6, T = 3 degree of indexation, % of inflation			
	0%	50%	100%	150%	0%	50%	100%	150%
0	10.00	10.00	10.00	10.00	6.28	6.28	6.28	6.28
2	7.56	7.80	8.00	8.16	3.95	4.45	4.92	5.38
4	5.12	5.64	6.00	6.20	1.60	2.65	3.61	4.50
6	2.67	3.51	4.00	4.08	-0.76	0.89	2.35	3.63
8	0.19	1.42	2.00	1.77	-3.15	-0.83	1.15	2.76
10	-0.77	0.12	0.00	-1.53	-3.94	-1.73	0.00	1.20
12	-4.78	-2.61	-2.00	-3.64	-7.97	-4.11	-1.08	1.08
14	-7.31	-4.55	-4.00	-6.92	-10.42	-5.67	-2.10	0.27
16	-9.86	-6.44	-6.00	-10.76	-12.92	-7.18	-3.04	-0.54
18	-12.44	-8.25	-8.00	-15.44	-15.45	-8.62	-3.91	-1.34
20	-15.07	-10.00	-10.00	-21.47	-18.04	-10.00	-4.69	-2.13

Inflation rate, %	N = 20, T = 20 degree of indexation, % of inflation				N = 20, T = 10 degree of indexation, % of inflation			
	0%	50%	100%	150%	0%	50%	100%	150%
0	10.00	10.00	10.00	10.00	7.02	7.02	7.02	7.02
2	7.13	7.59	8.00	8.34	4.29	4.86	5.39	5.88
4	4.20	5.23	6.00	6.46	1.44	2.74	3.84	4.76
6	1.17	2.92	4.00	4.21	-1.61	0.67	2.41	3.68
8	-2.08	0.66	2.00	1.32	-5.01	-1.34	1.12	2.66
10	-4.98	-1.26	0.00	-3.17	-8.12	-2.96	0.00	1.50
12	-10.29	-3.63	-2.00	-11.59	-15.62	-5.07	-0.91	0.88
14	-18.42	-5.59	-4.00	NA	NA	-6.70	-1.59	0.15
16	NA	-7.36	-6.00	NA	NA	-8.11	-2.04	-0.47
18	NA	-8.86	-8.00	NA	NA	-9.22	-2.27	-0.95
20	NA	-10.00	-10.00	NA	NA	-10.00	-2.31	-1.31

Inflation rate, %	N = 50, T = 50 degree of indexation, % of inflation				N = 50, T = 25 degree of indexation, % of inflation			
	0%	50%	100%	150%	0%	50%	100%	150%
0	10.00	10.00	10.00	10.00	8.21	8.21	8.21	8.21
2	6.70	7.38	8.00	8.56	5.12	5.75	6.33	6.84
4	3.31	4.80	6.00	6.83	1.79	3.31	4.50	5.39
6	-0.72	2.23	4.00	4.44	-2.90	0.78	2.77	3.86
8	NA	-0.47	2.00	-0.09	NA	-2.06	1.22	2.28
10	NA	-3.41	-0.00	NA	NA	-5.70	-0.00	0.64
12	NA	-9.85	-2.00	NA	NA	NA	-0.72	-0.63
14	NA	NA	-4.00	NA	NA	NA	-0.92	-1.60
16	NA	NA	-6.00	NA	NA	NA	-0.79	-2.00
18	NA	NA	-8.00	NA	NA	NA	-0.55	-1.90
20	NA	-10.00	-10.00	NA	NA	-10.00	-0.32	-1.56

Interest rate: $i = 10\%$ p.a. Tax system: System with indexation: $MI1 : \varepsilon_1 = \varepsilon_2 = \varepsilon$. Survival function: Simultaneous retirement after N years. Depreciation allowance schedule: Linear over T years. Income tax rate: $u = 0.508$. Capital value tax rate: $v = 0$.

Table 9.13: (cont.) Tax equivalent real rate of return as a function of inflation rate.

B. Full taxation of (indexed) capital gains: $n = 1$
Full deductibility of (indexed) interest cost: $m = 1$

Inflation rate, %	N = 6, T = 6 degree of indexation, % of inflation				N = 6, T = 3 degree of indexation, % of inflation			
	0%	50%	100%	150%	0%	50%	100%	150%
0	10.00	10.00	10.00	10.00	6.28	6.28	6.28	6.28
2	9.50	8.80	8.00	7.11	5.98	5.86	5.71	5.51
4	9.02	7.68	6.00	3.89	5.69	5.52	5.21	4.76
6	8.54	6.67	4.00	0.22	5.40	5.26	4.81	3.99
8	8.08	5.77	2.00	-3.94	5.13	5.07	4.50	3.30
10	7.62	4.28	0.00	-11.67	4.85	4.28	4.28	0.41
12	7.18	4.27	-2.00	-15.18	4.59	4.93	4.15	1.86
14	6.75	3.69	-4.00	-23.59	4.34	4.96	4.12	1.16
16	6.34	3.22	-6.00	-37.63	4.09	5.07	4.18	0.45
18	5.94	2.86	-8.00	NA	3.85	5.22	4.33	-0.25
20	5.55	3.59	-10.00	NA	3.62	6.38	4.57	-0.98

Inflation rate, %	N = 20, T = 20 degree of indexation, % of inflation				N = 20, T = 10 degree of indexation, % of inflation			
	0%	50%	100%	150%	0%	50%	100%	150%
0	10.00	10.00	10.00	10.00	7.02	7.02	7.02	7.02
2	8.89	8.52	8.00	7.31	6.24	6.18	6.07	5.87
4	7.82	7.21	6.00	3.87	5.47	5.52	5.30	4.77
6	6.79	6.10	4.00	-1.07	4.75	5.03	4.75	3.73
8	5.82	5.21	2.00	-11.70	4.06	4.70	4.43	2.80
10	4.91	4.34	0.00	NA	3.43	4.34	4.34	1.31
12	4.09	4.08	-2.00	NA	2.85	4.50	4.45	1.29
14	3.35	3.84	-4.00	NA	2.34	4.56	4.74	0.76
16	2.70	3.76	-6.00	NA	1.90	4.69	5.15	0.39
18	2.15	3.83	-8.00	NA	1.53	4.87	5.66	0.17
20	1.70	4.10	-10.00	NA	1.23	5.16	6.20	0.08

Inflation rate, %	N = 50, T = 50 degree of indexation, % of inflation				N = 50, T = 25 degree of indexation, % of inflation			
	0%	50%	100%	150%	0%	50%	100%	150%
0	10.00	10.00	10.00	10.00	8.21	8.21	8.21	8.21
2	8.41	8.30	8.00	7.47	6.92	6.90	6.75	6.47
4	6.85	6.80	6.00	3.77	5.64	5.80	5.51	4.57
6	5.34	5.56	4.00	NA	4.40	4.95	4.58	2.46
8	3.93	4.61	2.00	NA	3.23	4.35	4.04	0.12
10	2.68	3.91	-0.00	NA	2.20	3.91	3.91	-3.18
12	1.69	3.60	-2.00	NA	1.38	3.74	4.08	-6.04
14	0.98	3.39	-4.00	NA	0.81	3.59	4.39	-8.93
16	0.55	3.27	-6.00	NA	0.46	3.45	4.67	-6.19
18	0.32	3.17	-8.00	NA	0.28	3.30	4.85	-3.65
20	0.20	3.07	-10.00	NA	0.19	3.16	4.93	-1.90

Interest rate: $i = 10\%$ p.a. Tax system: System with indexation: $MI1 : \varepsilon_1 = \varepsilon_2 = \varepsilon$. Survival function: Simultaneous retirement after N years. Depreciation allowance schedule: Linear over T years. Income tax rate: $u = 0.508$. Capital value tax rate: $v = 0$.

CHAPTER 10

USER COSTS AND NEUTRALITY INDICATORS FOR NORWEGIAN MANUFACTURING

10.1 Introduction

This chapter presents and discusses empirical results for the user cost of capital, neutrality indicators, and related variables based on an actual set of time series of Norwegian tax and investment data for the aggregate manufacturing sector for the years 1965–1984. The purpose of the investigation is four-fold, first, to illustrate empirically some of the theoretical results obtained in the previous chapters, mainly chapters 6 and 9, second, to describe the development of the user cost over the last two decades, third, to describe the tax distortions and analyze factors which bring the tax system to depart from neutrality, and fourth, to explore possible tax reforms, *inter alia* reforms replacing the existing nominal income tax system with systems containing an indexation of the tax base.

Unfortunately, the empirical information needed for this multi-purpose investigation is far from complete. Reliable estimates of some of the crucial parameters in the theoretical model are either non-existing, or the information available is of less than acceptable quality. This is a particular problem for the parameters describing the survival function of the capital and those representing the taxation of capital gains, and makes the calculation of the user cost and variables related to it subject to uncertainty. It spite of this, the results will illustrate essential features of the Norwegian system of corporate taxation over the last 20 years.

The material is organized as follows. Section 10.2 presents the basic data set, assumptions, and simplifications. The calculated series for the user cost and the implied neutrality indicators for the existing tax system are presented and discussed in some detail in section 10.3. In view of the uncertainty about parameter values, particular emphasis is given on illustrating the *sensitivity* of the results with respect to the assumed maximal life time of the capital, the form of the survival function up to this life time, and the parameters characterizing the taxation of capital gains. Possible tax reforms, including an indexation of the components of the income tax base, are discussed in section 10.4, in terms of user costs, neutrality indicators, and effective tax rates.

10.2   Data and assumptions

In the empirical calculations, two kinds of capital, machinery and equipment, including transport equipment (abbreviated M) and buildings and structures (abbreviated B), are specified. The following results refer to *total manufacturing*, the input data have been constructed by aggregating national accounts data for the manufacturing subsectors at the two-digit level. For the present purpose, this disaggregation of investment, user cost, and capital by kind, at an aggregate *sectoral* level, is convenient, since it permits us to investigate the distortive effects of the tax system specifically with respect to *short-lived* (M) and *long-lived* (B) goods, without having to be concerned with sectoral details. Jorgenson and Yun (1986a, 1986b) give examples of applications of the user cost of capital in a general equilibrium framework at a similar level of aggregation.

10.2.1 Survival functions and life times

The *simultaneous retirement* (simultaneous exit) assumption is selected as our base specification of the form of the survival function for both kinds of capital. This implies that all capital items are assumed to give a constant flow of services during a specific period and are then taken out of operation completely [cf. subsection 3.6.2]. This life time is set to $N_B = 60$ years for buildings and structures and to $N_M = 20$ years for machinery and equipment, which concur with the values presently used by the Central Bureau of Statistics in the calculation of (net) capital stocks and depreciation (capital consumption) flows in the capital accounts of the manufacturing sectors in the Norwegian national accounts.[1] To examine and illustrate the

---

[1]   Gross capital stocks are not (as yet) integrated with the Norwegian national accounting system, see Fløttum (1981, section 5.4.3) and, for details, Skagseth (1982). Machinery and transport equipment are specified as separate items in the capital accounts of the manufacturing sectors, with life times set equal to 25 years and 7 years, respectively, in most cases [confer also Biørn, Holmøy, and Olsen (1985)], $N_M = 20$ years being a compromise value for the aggregate of these two items. A survey of service

sensitivity of the results to the assumed life time, four alternative sets of values are also selected, two of which are lower and two are higher than in the base specification. [See table 10.1, part A.]

Since we will also be concerned with the sensitivity of the results to the assumed *profile* of the deterioration of the capital up to the final scrapping age, we consider, in addition to the simultaneous retirement pattern, five alternative forms of survival functions. [See table 10.1, part B.] These six functions are generated partly by the *concave* function

$$(10.1.a) \qquad B(s) = 1 - \left(\frac{s}{N}\right)^{\sigma} , \qquad 0 \le s \le N ,$$

and partly by the *convex* function

$$(10.1.b) \qquad B(s) = \left(1 - \frac{s}{N}\right)^{\tau} , \qquad 0 \le s \le N ,$$

σ and τ being constants greater than (or equal to) one. These constants may be denoted as curvature parameters. The six profiles considered are

$$\sigma \to \infty , \qquad \text{"simultaneous retirement",}$$
$$\sigma = 5 , \qquad \text{"highly concave",}$$
$$\sigma = 3 , \qquad \text{"moderately concave",}$$
$$\sigma = \tau = 1 , \quad \text{"linear retirement",}$$
$$\tau = 3 , \qquad \text{"moderately convex", and}$$
$$\tau = 5 , \qquad \text{"highly convex".}$$

The two strictly concave functions are characterized by increasing retirement with age [i.e. $b'(s) = -B''(s) > 0$ for $0 \le s \le N$], the two strictly convex functions are characterized by decreasing retirement [i.e. $b'(s) = -B''(s) < 0$ for $0 \le s \le N$], while the intermediate, linear case implies constant retirement [i.e. $b'(s) = -B''(s) = 0$ for $0 \le s \le N$]. These parametric classes of survival functions will also be considered in chapter 11, and for a further discussion of their properties, see subsections 11.2.1 and 11.2.2.

A change in the form of the survival function, with the maximal life time N kept fixed, will, of course, usually change the *average* life time of the capital, and hence its user cost. Probabilistically interpreted [cf. section 3.4],

---

lives assumed in the calculation of capital stocks for other OECD countries is given in Blades (1983, tables 2–5). See also Paccoud (1983).

Table 10.1: Life times and survival functions assumed in calculations.

A. Simultaneous retirement with different life times.

| | Life time, years | |
	Buildings and structures (N_B)	Machinery and transport equipment (N_M)
Low	40	10
Low–Medium	50	15
Medium*	60	20
High-Medium	70	25
High	80	30

B. Different curvature, fixed maximal life time.

| | Survival function, $B(s)$ | |
	Buildings and structures, $0 \leq s \leq 60$	Machinery and transport equipment, $0 \leq s \leq 20$
Simultaneous retirement*	1	1
Highly concave	$1 - (s/60)^5$	$1 - (s/20)^5$
Moderately concave	$1 - (s/60)^3$	$1 - (s/20)^3$
Linear	$1 - s/60$	$1 - s/20$
Moderately convex	$(1 - s/60)^3$	$(1 - s/20)^3$
Highly convex	$(1 - s/60)^5$	$(1 - s/20)^5$

* Base alternative

this corresponds to a change in the probability distribution generating the retirement of capital. The mean and median values of the life time for the six survival functions are given in table 10.2.

Table 10.2: Mean and median values of the life time.[a]

	Buildings and structures		Machinery and transport equipment	
	Mean[b]	Median[c]	Mean[b]	Median[c]
Simultaneous retirement	60.00[d]	60.00[d]	20.00[d]	20.00[d]
Highly concave	50.00	52.23	16.67	17.41
Moderately concave	45.00	47.62	15.00	15.87
Linear	30.00	30.00	10.00	10.00
Moderately convex	15.00	12.38	5.00	4.13
Highly convex	10.00	7.77	3.33	2.50

[a] For detailed definitions, see table 10.1.B.
[b] The mean life time for the concave class of survival functions is, in general, given by

$$E(S) = \int_0^N sb(s)\,ds = (\sigma/N)\int_0^N s(s/N)^{\sigma-1}\,ds = N\sigma/(\sigma+1),$$

and for the convex class by

$$E(S) = \int_0^N sb(s)\,ds = (\tau/N)\int_0^N s(1-s/N)^{\tau-1}\,ds = N/(\tau+1).$$

[c] The general expression for the median life time is $M = B^{-1}(1/2) = N2^{-1/\sigma}$ for the concave class and $M = B^{-1}(1/2) = N(1 - 2^{-1/\tau})$ for the convex class.
[d] Base alternative.

10.2.2 Prices, inflation rates, and interest rate

The data on *investment prices* for machinery/equipment and buildings/ structures, to be denoted as q_M and q_B respectively, are taken from the Norwegian annual national accounts for the manufacturing sectors. They are Paasche indices, constructed by dividing aggregate values at current prices with aggregate values at constant prices. [See table 10.3, columns 1 and 2.]

For machinery and equipment, the *rate of increase of the investment price* is obtained by converting the pro anno rate $\gamma_{Mt} = q_{Mt}/q_{Mt-1} - 1$

into a continuous rate by means of

$$(10.2.a) \qquad \gamma_M(t) = \ln(1 + \gamma_{Mt}) = \ln(q_{Mt}/q_{Mt-1}).$$

Since these rates have not been smoothed (apart from the smoothing implied by the use of annual time aggregates rather than aggregates over shorter time periods) they fluctuate substantially between years, the largest value of γ_{Mt}, 14.5 per cent, occurring in 1974 and the smallest value, -1.7 per cent, in 1973. [See table 10.3, column 5.] For the long-lived asset type buildings and structures, however, some smoothing of the annual rates has been performed. Its rate of price increase has been constructed by converting the three year moving average rate, $\gamma_{Bt} = (q_{Bt+1}/q_{Bt-2})^{1/3} - 1$, into a continuous rate by means of

$$(10.2.b) \qquad \gamma_B(t) = \ln(1 + \gamma_{Bt}) = \tfrac{1}{3} \sum_{i=-1}^{1} \ln(q_{Bt+i}/q_{Bt+i-1}).$$

This rate fluctuates between $\gamma_{Bt} = 11.4$ per cent (in 1975) and 1.8 per cent (in 1979) [table 10.3, column 4]. The two kinds of capital have been treated differently because of their different service lives. Since the life time of buildings and structures is, on the average, three times as large as that of machinery and equipment [cf. tables 10.1 and 10.2], a sensible assumption is that the firms' price extrapolations when evaluating user costs are based on observations for a period which is three times as long.

The *interest rate*, i_t [table 10.3, column 3], is a pro anno rate on loans from commercial banks to companies, published by the Bank of Norway. It is converted into a continuous rate [table 10.3, column 6] by means of

$$(10.3) \qquad i(t) = \ln(1 + i_t).$$

The associated (continuous) real interest rates related to buildings and structures, and machinery and equipment, respectively, i.e.

$$\rho_B(t) = i(t) - \gamma_B(t) = \ln\{(1 + i_t)/(1 + \gamma_{Bt})\},$$
$$\rho_M(t) = i(t) - \gamma_M(t) = \ln\{(1 + i_t)/(1 + \gamma_{Mt})\},$$

also show considerable year-to-year variations and have negative values at the middle of the 1970's [see table 10.3, columns 7 and 8].

10.2.3 Tax rates and depreciation parameters

The tax rates are constructed from the Norwegian rules for joint-stock companies. The *income tax* is the sum of a proportional tax to central government at the rate u_C and a proportional tax to local authorities (municipal tax) at the rate u_L, i.e.[2]

(10.4) $$u = u_C + u_L .$$

It is given in table 10.4, column 5.[3] The companies also pay a proportional tax (to central government) on their *net wealth*, defined as the difference between the value of their assets and debt. The statutory tax rate, v^*, is given in table 10.4, column 6. Assuming that the companies have no other assets than their capital stock, we can convert this tax into an equivalent *capital value tax* [cf. section 5.3], by defining the tax rate v as

(10.5) $$v = v^*(1 - m^*) ,$$

where m^* is the debt share (the ratio between the outstanding net debt and the value of the capital stock). This share, calculated from accounting statistics for Norwegian manufacturing,[4] has fluctuated between 76 and 83 per cent [table 10.4, column 8], to which corresponds a capital value tax rate between $v = 0.04$ and $v = 0.12$ per cent. Exogeneity of v^* will be equivalent to assuming exogeneity of v when calculating user costs and related variables, since we assume that the firm's financial structure, including its debt share m^*, is predetermined in relation to its decisions about capital accumulation [cf. section 6.4].

The parameter values used to describe the system of *depreciation allowances* are given in the first four columns of table 10.4. *Up to and including the year 1981*, three alternative depreciation schedules could be used:

---

[2] The income bases of the government and the municipal taxes are not strictly the same, since — as remarked in footnote 4 to chapter 5 — dividends are treated differently. This has implications for the definition of the effective share of the cost of finance deductible, a point to which we return in subsection 10.2.4.

[3] These data are taken from CBS (1985) (and earlier issues), which also provides more detailed definitions.

[4] See CBS (1984) and earlier issues for detailed definitions. Since data for the years 1983 and 1984 were not available when the series for m^* were compiled, the estimates for these two years are set equal to the 1982 value. For the years before 1967, when the publication of official accounting statistics started in Norway, the 1967 value of m^* has been used.

Table 10.3: Investment price indices and interest rates.

Year	q_{Bt}	q_{Mt}	i_t	γ_{Bt}	γ_{Mt}	$i(t)$	$\rho_B(t)$	$\rho_M(t)$
1965	0.4094	0.4155	0.0541	0.0576	0.0266	0.0527	−0.0033	0.0264
1966	0.4332	0.4238	0.0555	0.0544	0.0201	0.0540	0.0010	0.0341
1967	0.4413	0.4289	0.0565	0.0373	0.0120	0.0550	0.0183	0.0430
1968	0.4570	0.4298	0.0577	0.0383	0.0020	0.0561	0.0185	0.0541
1969	0.4850	0.4478	0.0654	0.0605	0.0418	0.0633	0.0046	0.0224
1970	0.5264	0.5014	0.0667	0.0689	0.1197	0.0646	−0.0021	−0.0485
1971	0.5581	0.5286	0.0668	0.0656	0.0544	0.0647	0.0011	0.0117
1972	0.5868	0.5532	0.0676	0.0654	0.0464	0.0654	0.0020	0.0200
1973	0.6366	0.5441	0.0690	0.0952	−0.0165	0.0667	−0.0242	0.0833
1974	0.7331	0.6229	0.0754	0.1140	0.1449	0.0727	−0.0353	−0.0627
1975	0.8113	0.6946	0.0804	0.1143	0.1151	0.0774	−0.0308	−0.0316
1976	0.8807	0.7615	0.0849	0.0896	0.0963	0.0815	−0.0044	−0.0105
1977	0.9484	0.8267	0.0894	0.0544	0.0855	0.0856	0.0327	0.0035
1978	0.9509	0.9081	0.1072	0.0209	0.0985	0.1019	0.0812	0.0079
1979	0.9369	0.9003	0.1095	0.0178	−0.0086	0.1039	0.0862	0.1126
1980	1.0000	1.0000	0.1130	0.0424	0.1108	0.1071	0.0656	0.0020
1981	1.0770	1.0375	0.1215	0.0772	0.0375	0.1147	0.0403	0.0779
1982	1.1712	1.1220	0.1295	0.0731	0.0814	0.1218	0.0512	0.0435
1983	1.2357	1.1524	0.1304	0.0657	0.0271	0.1225	0.0589	0.0958
1984	1.3034	1.1515	0.1254	0.0549	−0.0007	0.1181	0.0647	0.1188

q_{Bt}: Investment price, buildings and structures, manufacturing, 1980 = 1.
q_{Mt}: Investment price, machinery and equipment, manufacturing, 1980 = 1.
i_t: Interest rate, pro anno.
γ_{Bt}: Rate of increase of investment price, buildings and structures, pro anno rate (3 year moving average).
γ_{Mt}: Rate of increase of investment price, machinery and equipment, pro anno rate.
$i(t) = \ln(1 + i_t)$: Nominal interest rate, continuous time.
$\rho_B(t) = \ln\{(1+i_t)/(1+\gamma_{Bt})\}$: Real interest rate, buildings and structures, continuous time.
$\rho_M(t) = \ln\{(1 + i_t)/(1 + \gamma_{Mt})\}$: Real interest rate, machinery and equipment, continuous time.

Table 10.4: Tax rates and depreciation allowance parameters.

Year	T_B	T_M	α_B	α_M	u	v^*	m	m^*	d
1965	40	10	0.08	0.30	0.5325	0.0020	0.8271	0.7646	0.1235
1966	40	10	0.08	0.30	0.5325	0.0020	0.8271	0.7646	0.1235
1967	40	10	0.08	0.30	0.5325	0.0020	0.8271	0.7646	0.1235
1968	40	10	0.08	0.30	0.5425	0.0020	0.7986	0.7714	0.0544
1969	40	10	0.08	0.30	0.5450	0.0020	0.8141	0.7672	0.0938
1970	40	10	0.08	0.30	0.5050	0.0000	0.8514	0.7963	0.1146
1971	40	10	0.08	0.30	0.5060	0.0030	0.8479	0.7969	0.1058
1972	40	10	0.08	0.30	0.5080	0.0030	0.8429	0.8061	0.0753
1973	40	10	0.08	0.30	0.5080	0.0070	0.8393	0.8047	0.0740
1974	40	10	0.08	0.30	0.5080	0.0070	0.8652	0.8095	0.1183
1975	40	10	0.08	0.30	0.5080	0.0070	0.8627	0.8266	0.0753
1976	40	10	0.08	0.30	0.5080	0.0070	0.8782	0.8338	0.0940
1977	40	10	0.08	0.30	0.5080	0.0070	0.8339	0.8100	0.0521
1978	40	10	0.08	0.30	0.5080	0.0070	0.8425	0.8180	0.0527
1979	40	10	0.08	0.30	0.5080	0.0070	0.8340	0.8087	0.0533
1980	40	10	0.08	0.30	0.5080	0.0070	0.8914	0.7995	0.1961
1981	40	10	0.08	0.30	0.5080	0.0070	0.9063	0.8009	0.2244
1982	40	10	0.08	0.30	0.5080	0.0060	0.8738	0.8023	0.1518
1983	40	10	0.08	0.30	0.5080	0.0050	0.8738	0.8023	0.1518
1984	40	10	0.09	0.35	0.5080	0.0050	0.8738	0.8023	0.1518

T_B: Life time, buildings and structures, linear schedule.
T_M : Life time, machinery and equipment, linear schedule.
α_B: Rate of depreciation (pro anno rate), buildings and structures, declining balance
schedule.
α_M : Rate of depreciation (pro anno rate), machinery and equipment, declining balance schedule.
$u = u_C + u_L$: Income tax rate.
v^*: Net wealth tax rate.
$m = m^*[1 + (u_C/u)d]$: Share of cost of finance effectively deductible in income tax
base.
m^*: Debt share.
d: Dividend ratio.

linear depreciation (L),

linear depreciation combined with accelerated depreciation (LA) ,

linear depreciation combined with initial allowances (LI).

Linear depreciation is characterized by one parameter, the tax permitted life time, denoted as T_B for buildings and structures and as T_M for machinery and equipment. The detailed tax code specified a wide variety of life times for different sectors and asset types. The values we have assumed, $T_B = 40$ and $T_M = 10$ for the entire period, should be regarded as average estimates for the aggregate sector total manufacturing.[5] These tax permitted life times are considerably shorter than the corresponding technical life times. In the base alternative [cf. table 10.1], their ratio is 2/3 for buildings and structures and 1/2 for machinery and equipment.

Accelerated depreciation and initial allowances[6] permitted a faster deduction of the investment cost in the firm's tax accounts, and hence (with a positive interest rate) a larger present value of depreciation allowances and a lower user cost, than ordinary, linear depreciation. We can, somewhat simplified,[7] formalize the rules for the *combined linear/accelerated depreciation schedule* (LA) as follows: Let T be the life time prescribed in the linear schedule, T^A the number of years during which accelerated depreciation is in effect , T^L the number of years during which linear depreciation is in effect $(T^A < T^L < T)$, and let $a^A(s)$ and $a^L(s)$ be the per unit depreciation rates at age s for these two schedules. We then have, with continuous time,[8]

(10.6) $$a(s) = a^L(s) + a^A(s), \qquad 0 \le s \le T,$$

---

[5] The same values are assumed in CBS (1981), tables E.5 and E.6.

[6] The official Norwegian terms are "tilleggsavskrivninger" and "åpningsavskrivninger".

[7] This simplification consists, *inter alia*, in approximating the discrete time (pro anno) formulation in the tax code by the analytically more convenient continuous time formulation.

[8] See Biørn (1975) for details.

where the depreciation rates are subject to the restrictions

$$(10.7) \quad \begin{cases} a^A(s) = \begin{cases} \min\,(1/2T\,,0.05) & \text{for } 0 \le s \le T^A\,, \\ 0 & \text{for } T^A < s \le T\,, \end{cases} \\[2mm] \displaystyle\int_0^{T^A} a^A(s)\,ds \le 0.15\,, \qquad T^A \le 5\,, \\[4mm] a^L(s) = \begin{cases} 1/T & \text{for } 0 \le s \le T^L\,, \\ 0 & \text{for } T^L < s \le T\,, \end{cases} \\[2mm] \displaystyle\int_0^{T^L} a^L(s)\,ds + \int_0^{T^A} a^A(s)\,ds = 1\,. \end{cases}$$

For buildings and structures, i.e. $T = T_D = 40$, we find

$$a^L(s) = a^L = 0.025\,, \qquad 0 \le s \le T^L = 37.5\,,$$
$$a^A(s) = a^A = 0.0125\,, \qquad 0 \le s \le T^A = 5\,,$$

which implies a depreciation rate equal to

$$a(s) = \begin{cases} 0.0375 & \text{for } 0 \le s \le 5, \\ 0.025 & \text{for } 5 < s \le 37.5, \\ 0 & \text{for } 37.5 < s \le 40, \end{cases}$$

whereas machinery and equipment, i.e. $T = T_M = 10$, is characterized by

$$a^L(s) = a^L = 0.10\,, \qquad 0 \le s \le T^L = 8.5\,,$$
$$a^A(s) = a^A = 0.05\,, \qquad 0 \le s \le T^A = 3\,,$$

which implies a depreciation rate equal to

$$a(s) = \begin{cases} 0.15 & \text{for } 0 \le s \le 3, \\ 0.10 & \text{for } 3 < s \le 8.5, \\ 0 & \text{for } 8.5 < s \le 10. \end{cases}$$

The present value of the depreciation rates defined by (10.6)–(10.7) for an arbitrary interest rate ρ is

$$z_\rho^{LA} = \frac{1}{\rho T}(1 - e^{-\rho T^L}) + \frac{a^A}{\rho}(1 - e^{-\rho T^A})\,,$$

which is an increasing function of a^A and T^A when $\rho > 0$.

The rules for the *combined linear/initial allowance schedule* (LI) can be formalized as follows: Let T be the life time prescribed in the linear schedule, a^I the share of the investment cost which can be written off as an initial allowance over the first service year, and $a^L(s)$ the corresponding per unit depreciation rate at age s. We then have[9]

$$(10.8) \qquad a(s) = a^L(s) + a^I(s), \qquad 0 \le s \le T,$$

where the depreciation rates are subject to the restrictions

$$(10.9) \qquad \begin{cases} a^I(s) = \begin{cases} a^I \le 0.25 & \text{for } 0 \le s \le 1, \\ 0 & \text{for } 1 < s \le T, \end{cases} \\ a^L(s) = \begin{cases} 1/T & \text{for } 0 \le s \le T^L, \\ 0 & \text{for } T^L < s \le T, \end{cases} \\ \int_0^{T^L} a^L(s)\,ds + \int_0^1 a^I(s)\,ds = 1. \end{cases}$$

This gives a depreciation rate equal to

$$a(s) = \begin{cases} 1/T + 0.25 & \text{for } 0 \le s \le 1, \\ 1/T & \text{for } 1 < s \le 0.75T, \\ 0 & \text{for } 0.75T < s \le T, \end{cases}$$

whose present value is approximately[10] equal to

$$z_\rho^{LI} = 0.25 + \frac{1}{\rho T}(1 - e^{-0.75\rho T}).$$

From the year 1982, these depreciation systems have all been replaced by the declining balance schedule.[11] Two broad classes of asset types are specified in the tax code for the manufacturing sectors, buildings/structures

---

[9] The initial allowances should not exceed 50 per cent of the assessed income based on ordinary linear depreciation and could only be applied for capital assets with a purchase cost above a certain value. For simplicity, we assume that these restrictions are not binding and that the firm is not otherwise tax-exhausted.

[10] When neglecting the discounting of the first-year initial allowance.

[11] The declining balance schedule is compulsory from the year 1984, however, after a transition period during which both the old and the new system could be used. In most cases, the new system is more favourable than the old one [cf. table 10.6], and for this reason the new system is assumed to be effective from 1982.

and machinery/equipment, with depreciation rates $\alpha_B = 8$ per cent and $\alpha_M = 30$ per cent pro anno, respectively. In 1984, they were increased to 9 per cent and 35 per cent.[12] In our calculations, assuming continuous time, these rates are represented by $\ln(1 + \alpha_B)$ and $\ln(1 + \alpha_M)$, respectively, which is similar to the transformation of the inflation and interest rates [cf. subsection 10.2.2].

10.2.4 Interest deduction and capital gain taxation parameters

The values of the interest deduction parameter m and the capital gains taxation parameter n cannot be read off from the tax code. They are calculated, under simplifying assumptions, from accounting statistics for Norwegian manufacturing (CBS (1984)) as follows:

In chapter 5, the income tax was specified as [cf. (5.23)]

$$T_I(t) = u[X(t) - S_D(t) - S_I(t) + S_G(t)],$$

where $X(t)$ is profit before allowance for capital costs, $S_D(t)$ is the depreciation allowances, $S_I(t)$ is the interest cost deductible in the income tax base, and $S_G(t)$ is the capital gains included in the income tax base. We represent the actual Norwegian tax system, in the terminology of subsection 5.4.2, as a *MNO system*, with interest deductions and capital gains calculated on a nominal basis from market values:

$$S_I(t) = miV(t) = miq(t) \int_0^\infty G(s)J(t-s)\,ds,$$

$$S_G(t) = n\gamma V(t) = n\dot{\gamma}q(t) \int_0^\infty G(s)J(t-s)\,ds,$$

and with depreciation allowances based on the accounting capital at original cost:

$$S_D(t) = E_O(t) = q(t) \int_0^\infty a(s)e^{-\gamma s}J(t-s)\,ds.$$

The tax function then becomes

(10.10) $$T_I(t) = u[X(t) - E_O(t) - miV(t) + n\gamma V(t)].$$

---

[12] See CBS (1985), tables E.4 and E.5.

Dividends paid by the Norwegian joint-stock companies to their owners are partly deductible in the income tax base: they are deductible in the tax base of the central government tax, but not in the tax base of the local (municipal) tax.[13] Debt interests are always fully deductible. The interest deduction component $S_I(t)$ can then be defined in two alternative ways: either narrowly, as containing strictly the interests paid on outstanding debt, or widely, as reflecting also the deduction of dividend payments in the central government income tax base. The narrow interpretation would imply m to be equal to the firm's debt share, m^*, so that $mV(t)$ would represent the debt at time t. The wide interpretation would imply m to depend also on the dividend policy of the firm. We shall adopt the latter, wide interpretation in this study.

Let d denote the ratio between the dividend and the debt interest payment, i.e.

$$\text{Dividends } = d \cdot \text{Debt interests } = dm^*iV(t).$$

Writing the income tax as the sum of the central government tax and the local tax, we have

$$T_I(t) = u_C[X(t) - E_O(t) - m^*iV(t) - dm^*iV(t) + n\gamma V(t)]$$
$$+ u_L[X(t) - E_O(t) - m^*iV(t) + n\gamma V(t)]$$

(10.11)
$$= (u_C + u_L)\left[X(t) - E_O(t)\right.$$

$$\left. - m^*\left(1 + \frac{u_C d}{u_C + u_L}\right)iV(t) + n\gamma V(t)\right].$$

Since $u = u_C + u_L$ [cf. (10.4)], a comparison of (10.10) with (10.11) shows that the effective share deductible of the interests on the market value of the capital is related to the debt share, the dividend/debt interest ratio, and the income tax rates in the following way

(10.12)
$$m = m^*\left(1 + \frac{u_C d}{u}\right).$$

---

[13] Strictly, this rule has been in effect from the year 1969 only. In the years 1965–1968, deductibility of dividend payments in the central government income tax base was permitted for new equity capital only. For simplicity, we assume that the present system has been fully effective since 1965.

Ceteris paribus, m is larger the larger is the debt share, the dividend/ interest payment ratio, and the tax rate for the central government income tax relative to the local tax rate. If, in particular, the dividend/interest payment ratio is equal to the equity/debt ratio, i.e. $d = (1 - m^*)/m^*$, and if all income tax is imposed as a central government tax, i.e. $u_C = u$, then $m = 1$. In practice, we usually have $d < (1 - m^*)/m^*$ — since a fraction of the profit of the firm will be held as retained earnings — and $u_C < u$. Then m will be larger than the debt share m^* and less than unity. Values of m^*, d, and m for the years 1965–1984, calculated from accounting statistics, are given in table 10.4.[14] The debt share m^* has fluctuated between 76 and 83 per cent, the dividend/debt interest ratio d has fluctuated between 5 and 22 per cent, and the resulting value of the effective interest deduction parameter has fluctuated between 80 and 91 per cent.

We treat m^* and d, and hence m, as exogenously given parameters. The interpretation of this is that the *financial structure* and the *dividend policy* of the typical Norwegian manufacturing firm are *predetermined* in relation to its optimal capital accumulation. Hence, our measures of the user cost of capital and related variables will be conditional on the firm's financial position.[15]

The parameter n, representing the share of the capital gains which is included in the income tax base, can be calculated from

$$n_t = \frac{\text{Net value of realized capital gains, year } t}{\text{Capital value, end of year } t - 1 \cdot \text{Rate of inflation, year } t},$$

with the net value of the realized gains and the value of the capital stock taken from the accounting statistics,[16] and the rate of inflation set equal

---

[14] The tax rate for the central government tax is about 60 per cent of the total corporate tax rate. The estimates of d for the years 1983 and 1984 are set equal to the 1982 value. For the years 1965 and 1966, in which data on d are also unavailable, the 1967 value is used, cf. footnote 4.

[15] Confer section 6.4. As remarked in that section, we cannot from a neo-classical model, assuming linear budget constraints in the financial markets and full certainty, explain a debt and dividend behaviour leading to values of m^* and d both larger than zero and less than unity. In this model, a full optimization — including simultaneously the firm's capital accumulation, borrowing and share issuing policy, as well as its dividend behaviour — based on the owners' rate of discount would normally lead to a boundary solution for these variables, for instance $m^* = 1$, $d = 0$. As far as the Norwegian tax system is concerned, this is due to the different treatment of debt interests and dividends as expenditures for the corporate sector and as incomes for the personal sector (including the difference between the tax rates), on the one hand, and the asymmetrical treatment of retained earnings and capital gains, on the other.

[16] See CBS (1985) (and earlier issues). The procedure followed in converting book

to the annual rate of increase of the investment price index for total manufacturing (aggregate of buildings and machinery) according to the national accounts. This procedure is an approximative way of calculating capital gains on an *accrual* basis, but it seems to be the best way of extracting information on realized gains from the data available. The resulting series of n fluctuates considerably from year to year (between 6 and 24 per cent over the period 1969–1982), which may to some extent reflect real fluctuations in the *realized* gains, but may also be due to errors of measurement. In any case, we do not want fluctuations of this order of magnitude to affect our user cost measures — they might in fact dominate its year to year variation — and we decided to set $n = 0.20$ for the entire period, which is close to the average for the years 1969–1982.

10.3 Results for the existing nominal system

In this section, we present series for the user cost and the neutrality indicators for the years 1965–1984, based on the nominal tax system (MNO) existing in this period. Formally, it is the member of the M class of tax systems in which the indexation parameters for the accounting capital and for interest deductions and capital gains are equal to zero ($\varepsilon_1 = \varepsilon_2 = 0$) [cf. subsection 5.4.2]. For this tax system, we (i) compare different depreciation allowance schedules, (ii) examine the effect of the form of the survival function, and (iii) investigate the sensitivity of the results to the assumed value of the technical service life for a given form of the survival function.

10.3.1 Comparison of different depreciation allowance schedules

Four alternative depreciation schedules were permitted in the Norwegian tax system in the period under consideration: linear depreciation, linear depreciation combined with accelerated depreciation, linear depreciation combined with initial allowances, and declining balance, the last one having been effective from 1982 only; see subsection 10.2.3. The associated user costs, with the survival function specified as simultaneous retirement, are given in table 10.5, columns a through d. In addition, we consider two "synthetic" depreciation schedules, denoted as 'degressive' and 'progressive',

---

values of the capital stock at original cost to corresponding values at replacement cost is described in Andersen (1977).

respectively, in columns e and f. The degressive schedule is parametrized as

$$A(s) = \left(1 - \frac{s}{T}\right)^2, \qquad 0 \le s \le T.$$

It is the continuous time counterpart to the sum-of-the-years'-digits schedule, since it implies

$$a(s) = \frac{2}{T}\left(1 - \frac{s}{T}\right), \qquad 0 \le s \le T,$$

i.e. the relative depreciation function decreases linearly over T years from $2/T$ to zero [see e.g. Hall and Jorgenson (1967, p. 394)]. The progressive schedule is parametrized as

$$A(s) - 1 - \left(\frac{s}{T}\right)^2, \qquad 0 \le s \le T,$$

which implies a depreciation function increasing linearly from zero to $2/T$,

$$a(s) = \frac{2}{T}\left(\frac{s}{T}\right), \qquad 0 \le s \le T.$$

Linear depreciation leads to a higher user cost than linear and accelerated depreciation in combination, which again gives a higher user cost than linear depreciation combined with initial allowances. This reflects the different present value of depreciation allowances implied by the three schedules [see table 10.6, columns a–c]. The declining balance schedule permits a faster deduction of the investment cost — i.e. a higher present value of the deductions — than linear and accelerated depreciation, but a somewhat slower deduction than linear depreciation combined with initial allowances (compare column d with b and c). Table 10.7 gives the corresponding present values of the *total* net deductions in the income tax base, λ. The introduction of the declining balance schedule in the Norwegian tax system in 1982 led to an estimated reduction in the user cost, as compared with linear and accelerated depreciation, from 3.18 to 2.27 per cent of the 1980 investment price for buildings and structures and from 5.44 to 5.19 per cent for machinery and equipment.

The degressive schedule is (not surprisingly) more favourable than the linear one, and it is also more favourable than the linear and accelerated depreciation in combination. The progressive schedule, on the other hand, is clearly less favourable that either of the others. These conclusions hold for both kinds of capital. The ranking of the declining balance and the degressive schedule, however, is not unique; the former gives the lowest user cost in all the years for buildings and structures, for machinery and equipment, the latter is the most favourable deprecation schedule in all years but one (1984) [compare table 10.5, columns d and e].

Buildings and structures has a negative user cost in the years 1973–1975 for all the six depreciation schedules considered, and it is negative in 1976 as well for all schedules except the progressive one. This indicates that the Norwegian tax system, under a simultaneous retirement survival function, implied a substantial subsidizing of capital in buildings in the middle of the 1970's. This can also be seen from table 10.8, which shows the relative distortion of the user cost, β, a negative distortion being equivalent to a subsidy by more than 100 per cent. The first part of the 1980's, however, has seen a sharp increase in the user cost for both kinds of capital, and in 1984, it was more than three times as large as in 1981 for buildings and structures and about four times as large as in 1980 for machinery and equipment. This increase primarily reflects the increase in the interest rate along with the decline in the rate of inflation during this period [see table 10.3].

The user cost has been negatively distorted by the tax system in the entire period 1965–1984 for all the four depreciation schedules which have been in effect, but after 1980, the degree of distortion has been reduced [cf. table 10.8]. Even the progressive schedule [column f] would have implied a more favourable tax system than the neutral one in the majority of years (the exceptions being 1979 for both kinds of capital and 1978 for buildings and structures).

The distortive effect of the tax system in the years 1981–1984 is illustrated in terms of the tax equivalent internal rate of return in table 10.9 and in terms of the effective tax rate in table 10.10. (The two latter concepts are defined in subsections 9.4.2 and 9.4.3.) A comparison of table 10.9 with the last two columns of table 10.3 shows that the tax equivalent real rate of return, ρ^*, is less than the pre-tax real interest rate ρ for both kinds of capital in the years 1981–1984, regardless of the depreciation schedule. This is consistent with the conclusion, obtained from table 10.7 and 10.8, that the tax system is more favourable than a neutral one ($\beta < 0$, $\lambda > 1$) for all the depreciation schedules in all the years [cf. (9.13)]. For a given tax rate and a given form of the survival function, the parameters β, λ, and ρ^* define a unique ranking of the tax systems with regard to their departure from neutrality.

Compare, for instance, linear depreciation with the declining balance schedule for buildings and structures in 1984. The per unit present value of the net deductions in income tax base, λ, is 1.269 for the former schedule and 1.484 for the latter [table 10.7]. This can be "translated" into an implicit rate of subsidy of $-\beta = 27.7$ per cent and 50.0 per cent, respectively [table 10.8]. Furthermore, the tax system is equivalent to a reduction in the internal rate of return from 6.47 per cent (continuous rate) [table 10.3] to 4.31 per cent when linear depreciation allowances are permitted and to 2.51 when the declining balance schedule is in effect [table 10.9].

Table 10.10 reports two alternative measures of the effective tax rate. The first, denoted as the *net* rate, excludes the part of the tax rate which represents the "surtax" implied by the nominal, rather than a fully indexed, taxation of the interest income of the saver.[17] The second, denoted as the *gross* rate, is the rate u^* defined in (9.17), which includes the effect of this "surtax". The net rate is smaller than the statutory income tax rate, $u = 0.508$ [cf. table 10.4], for all depreciation schedules and both kinds of capital in all the four years. This, again, is consistent with the observation that these tax systems are more favourable than a neutral system, since

$$\text{net rate } = u + \frac{\rho^* - \rho}{\rho} \begin{matrix}<\\=\\>\end{matrix} u \qquad \text{according as } \quad \rho^* - \rho \begin{matrix}<\\=\\>\end{matrix} 0,$$

provided that the market real interest rate is positive (as is the case in all the years considered). The gross rate, which is larger than the net rate in all years with positive inflation, is smaller than the statutory income tax rate for the linear depreciation schedule combined with initial allowances and for the declining balance schedule. This holds for both kinds of capital. For machinery and equipment, the combined schedule with linear and accelerated depreciation also gives a gross tax rate which is lower than the statutory rate in the years considered. The same holds for buildings and structures in 1981 only. Linear depreciation alone, however, leads to a gross tax rate which exceeds the statutory tax rate in all the years 1981–1984 for buildings and structures and in 1982 for machinery and equipment.

10.3.2 Sensitivity to curvature of the survival function

The results presented above all assume that the survival function has the simultaneous retirement form. Table 10.11 shows the impact on the user cost of changing the form of the survival function $B(s)$ with a given maximal life time and with linear depreciation allowances. Not surprisingly,

---

[17] I.e. the term $u(\gamma - \varepsilon) = u\gamma$ in the expression for the tax wedge; cf. subsection 9.4.3.

the level of the user cost series is substantially different for the six survival functions considered, which primarily reflects their different *mean* life times [cf. table 10.2].[18] It is not always the case, however, that a change in the form of the survival function which entails a reduced mean life time, leads to an increased user cost. The years 1978 and 1979 for buildings and structures are notable examples. The user cost for the highly concave ($\sigma = 5$) and the moderately concave ($\sigma = 3$) survival function are lower than for the simultaneous retirement function ($\sigma \to \infty$) even if the mean life time for the two former are lower than for the latter (50 and 45 years, vs. 60 years). These two years were characterized by very high real interest rates for buildings and structures [cf. table 10.3], and the "interaction" between these interest rates and the survival function through the terms $\Phi_\rho(0)$ and Y_ρ in the user cost formula contributes to the above result.

From table 10.12, giving the corresponding relative distortion of the user cost, it is seen that both the simultaneous retirement and the highly and the moderately concave survival functions allowances (columns a, b and c) imply — under linear depreciation allowances — a tax system which is more favourable than a neutral system ($\beta < 0$) in all the years. The two convex functions (columns e and f) imply a less favourable tax system (the exception being buildings and structures in 1974 and 1975). A linear survival function combined with linear depreciation allowances is a more favourable constellation than a neutral tax system in about two thirds of the years.

10.3.3 Sensitivity to value of technical life time

In table 10.13 is shown the effect on the user cost of changing the technical life time for a simultaneous retirement survival function under linear depreciation allowances. Not surprisingly, we find that the user cost is a decreasing function of the life time in all the years. Particularly interesting is the case where the tax permitted life time coincides with the technical

---

[18] In the absence of taxes and with a zero real interest rate, the user cost would be inversely proportional to the mean life time. This follows from (3.23) and (4.1), which for $\rho = 0$ imply $c(t) = q(t)/E(S)$. With zero interest and tax rates this would give $c(t) = q(t)(\sigma + 1)/(\sigma N)$ for the concave class of survival functions and $c(t) = q(t)(\tau + 1)/N$ for the convex class. Then the user cost in alternatives a–f would increase as the sequence 1, 6/5, 4/3, 2, 4, and 6.

Table 10.5: User cost of capital in manufacturing, per cent of 1980 investment price, for different depreciation allowance schedules.

I. Buildings and structures, $N = 60$

Year	a	b	c	d	e	f
1965	0.304	0.270	0.154	0.178	0.206	0.402
1966	0.404	0.363	0.221	0.250	0.285	0.522
1967	0.917	0.851	0.618	0.666	0.724	1.110
1968	0.981	0.909	0.655	0.707	0.771	1.190
1969	0.430	0.376	0.180	0.222	0.273	0.586
1970	0.268	0.227	0.080	0.112	0.151	0.385
1971	0.389	0.341	0.165	0.203	0.250	0.529
1972	0.431	0.378	0.186	0.228	0.279	0.583
1973	-0.151	-0.176	-0.266	-0.246	-0.222	-0.081
1974	-0.439	-0.458	-0.526	-0.511	-0.492	-0.386
1975	-0.527	-0.551	-0.643	-0.621	-0.596	-0.458
1976	-0.119	-0.185	-0.440	-0.379	-0.307	0.068
1977	2.467	2.281	1.557	1.735	1.943	2.991
1978	5.829	5.520	4.260	4.606	4.981	6.677
1979	5.039	4.775	3.690	3.992	4.315	5.763
1980	5.121	4.792	3.431	3.819	4.226	6.016
1981	1.936	1.701	0.702	1.001	1.301	2.571
1982	3.487	3.181	1.858	2.273	2.672	4.302
1983	4.742	4.381	2.817	3.310	3.782	5.703
1984	6.103	5.691	3.925	4.224	4.998	7.209

II. Machinery and equipment, $N = 20$

Year	a	b	c	d	e	f
1965	2.377	2.233	2.092	2.205	2.167	2.587
1966	2.600	2.439	2.281	2.408	2.365	2.834
1967	2.850	2.672	2.497	2.638	2.591	3.110
1968	3.178	2.971	2.768	2.930	2.876	3.479
1969	2.402	2.223	2.044	2.183	2.140	2.664
1970	1.187	1.106	1.024	1.087	1.068	1.306
1971	2.535	2.369	2.202	2.332	2.292	2.779
1972	2.892	2.701	2.508	2.657	2.612	3.172
1973	5.104	4.774	4.441	4.699	4.621	5.588
1974	1.126	1.029	0.930	1.005	0.983	1.268
1975	1.853	1.692	1.527	1.651	1.617	2.088
1976	2.554	2.327	2.092	2.266	2.220	2.887
1977	3.402	3.109	2.803	3.028	2.971	3.834
1978	3.621	3.253	2.856	3.137	3.077	4.165
1979	10.327	9.470	8.540	9.195	9.058	11.596
1980	3.318	2.927	2.499	2.798	2.738	3.899
1981	8.153	7.342	6.443	7.062	6.948	9.357
1982	6.117	5.437	4.672	5.191	5.105	7.130
1983	10.825	9.777	8.596	9.396	9.265	12.386
1984	13.249	12.047	10.705	11.179	11.462	15.036

Survival function: simultaneous retirement. No inflation adjustment: $\varepsilon_1 = \varepsilon_2 = 0$. Depreciation allowance schedule: a = linear; b = linear with accelerated depreciation; c = linear with initial allowances; d = declining balance; e = degressive; f = progressive.

Table 10.6: Present value of depreciation allowances per unit of investment outlay, z, for different depreciation allowance schedules.

I. Buildings and structures, $N = 60$

Year	a	b	c	d	e	f
1965	0.417	0.464	0.627	0.594	0.553	0.280
1966	0.409	0.457	0.621	0.588	0.547	0.272
1967	0.404	0.452	0.617	0.583	0.542	0.267
1968	0.398	0.446	0.613	0.578	0.536	0.261
1969	0.363	0.412	0.586	0.549	0.503	0.224
1970	0.358	0.406	0.581	0.544	0.497	0.219
1971	0.358	0.406	0.581	0.543	0.497	0.218
1972	0.354	0.403	0.578	0.541	0.494	0.215
1973	0.349	0.397	0.574	0.536	0.488	0.209
1974	0.325	0.374	0.555	0.514	0.464	0.186
1975	0.309	0.357	0.541	0.499	0.447	0.170
1976	0.295	0.344	0.530	0.486	0.433	0.158
1977	0.283	0.331	0.520	0.473	0.419	0.146
1978	0.241	0.289	0.484	0.430	0.372	0.110
1979	0.237	0.284	0.480	0.426	0.367	0.106
1980	0.230	0.278	0.474	0.418	0.359	0.101
1981	0.216	0.263	0.461	0.402	0.342	0.090
1982	0.204	0.250	0.450	0.387	0.327	0.081
1983	0.202	0.249	0.449	0.386	0.325	0.080
1984	0.210	0.256	0.456	0.422	0.335	0.085

II. Machinery and equipment, $N = 20$

Year	a	b	c	d	e	f
1965	0.777	0.824	0.870	0.833	0.845	0.709
1966	0.773	0.820	0.867	0.829	0.842	0.703
1967	0.769	0.817	0.865	0.827	0.839	0.699
1968	0.765	0.814	0.862	0.824	0.837	0.694
1969	0.741	0.794	0.847	0.806	0.818	0.663
1970	0.737	0.791	0.844	0.802	0.815	0.658
1971	0.736	0.790	0.844	0.802	0.815	0.658
1972	0.734	0.788	0.843	0.800	0.813	0.655
1973	0.730	0.785	0.840	0.797	0.810	0.649
1974	0.711	0.769	0.828	0.783	0.796	0.625
1975	0.696	0.757	0.819	0.772	0.785	0.607
1976	0.684	0.746	0.811	0.763	0.776	0.592
1977	0.672	0.736	0.803	0.754	0.767	0.577
1978	0.627	0.698	0.774	0.720	0.732	0.522
1979	0.622	0.693	0.771	0.716	0.728	0.516
1980	0.614	0.686	0.766	0.710	0.721	0.506
1981	0.595	0.670	0.753	0.696	0.706	0.484
1982	0.578	0.655	0.742	0.683	0.693	0.464
1983	0.576	0.654	0.741	0.682	0.691	0.462
1984	0.587	0.663	0.748	0.718	0.700	0.474

Survival function: simultaneous retirement. No inflation adjustment: $\varepsilon_1 = \varepsilon_2 = 0$. Depreciation allowance schedule: a = linear; b = linear with accelerated depreciation; c = linear with initial allowances; d = declining balance; e = degressive; f = progressive.

Table 10.7: Present value of net deductions in tax base per unit of investment outlay, λ, for different depreciation allowance schedules.

I. Buildings and structures, $N = 60$

Year	a	b	c	d	e	f
1965	1.446	1.493	1.659	1.625	1.585	1.307
1966	1.402	1.450	1.617	1.583	1.541	1.262
1967	1.214	1.262	1.430	1.395	1.353	1.074
1968	1.187	1.236	1.405	1.370	1.327	1.048
1969	1.447	1.496	1.672	1.635	1.588	1.306
1970	1.661	1.710	1.885	1.847	1.801	1.522
1971	1.581	1.630	1.809	1.770	1.723	1.439
1972	1.567	1.616	1.795	1.756	1.708	1.425
1973	2.280	2.330	2.514	2.474	2.425	2.135
1974	3.170	3.221	3.408	3.366	3.314	3.026
1975	3.062	3.112	3.302	3.258	3.204	2.919
1976	2.058	2.108	2.300	2.254	2.200	1.917
1977	1.306	1.356	1.550	1.503	1.447	1.165
1978	1.045	1.094	1.294	1.239	1.179	0.911
1979	1.038	1.086	1.287	1.231	1.171	0.904
1980	1.210	1.259	1.460	1.403	1.343	1.078
1981	1.575	1.623	1.826	1.765	1.704	1.446
1982	1.431	1.478	1.682	1.618	1.557	1.306
1983	1.352	1.399	1.602	1.538	1.477	1.227
1984	1.269	1.316	1.518	1.484	1.395	1.142

II. Machinery and equipment, $N = 20$

Year	a	b	c	d	e	f
1965	1.097	1.145	1.191	1.154	1.166	1.028
1966	1.097	1.145	1.193	1.155	1.168	1.027
1967	1.095	1.144	1.192	1.154	1.167	1.024
1968	1.081	1.131	1.179	1.140	1.153	1.009
1969	1.113	1.167	1.221	1.179	1.192	1.034
1970	1.196	1.250	1.304	1.262	1.275	1.117
1971	1.141	1.196	1.251	1.208	1.222	1.061
1972	1.134	1.189	1.245	1.202	1.215	1.053
1973	1.084	1.141	1.199	1.154	1.168	1.000
1974	1.270	1.330	1.391	1.345	1.358	1.181
1975	1.248	1.310	1.375	1.326	1.340	1.156
1976	1.246	1.310	1.377	1.327	1.340	1.151
1977	1.199	1.265	1.334	1.283	1.296	1.101
1978	1.254	1.327	1.405	1.350	1.362	1.147
1979	1.085	1.159	1.238	1.182	1.194	0.977
1980	1.338	1.413	1.494	1.437	1.449	1.228
1981	1.197	1.274	1.359	1.300	1.311	1.083
1982	1.263	1.341	1.430	1.370	1.380	1.146
1983	1.159	1.237	1.326	1.266	1.276	1.042
1984	1.118	1.195	1.281	1.251	1.233	1.003

Survival function: simultaneous retirement. No inflation adjustment: $\varepsilon_1 = \varepsilon_2 = 0$. Depreciation allowance schedule: a = linear; b = linear with accelerated depreciation; c = linear with initial allowances; d = declining balance; e = degressive; f = progressive.

Table 10.8: Relative distortion of user cost, β, for different depreciation allowance schedules.

I. Buildings and structures, $N = 60$

Year	a	b	c	d	e	f
1965	-0.508	-0.562	-0.751	-0.712	-0.666	-0.349
1966	-0.458	-0.512	-0.703	-0.664	-0.616	-0.299
1967	-0.243	-0.298	-0.490	-0.450	-0.402	-0.084
1968	-0.222	-0.279	-0.480	-0.439	-0.388	-0.056
1969	-0.535	-0.594	-0.805	-0.760	-0.704	-0.366
1970	-0.675	-0.724	-0.903	-0.864	-0.817	-0.533
1971	-0.595	-0.646	-0.828	-0.789	-0.741	-0.450
1972	-0.585	-0.636	-0.821	-0.781	-0.731	-0.439
1973	-1.321	-1.373	-1.563	-1.522	-1.471	-1.172
1974	-2.241	-2.293	-2.487	-2.443	-2.390	-2.092
1975	-2.129	-2.181	-2.377	-2.331	-2.276	-1.981
1976	-1.093	-1.144	-1.342	-1.295	-1.239	-0.947
1977	-0.316	-0.368	-0.568	-0.519	-0.461	-0.171
1978	-0.046	-0.097	-0.303	-0.246	-0.185	0.092
1979	-0.039	-0.089	-0.296	-0.238	-0.177	0.099
1980	-0.217	-0.267	-0.475	-0.416	-0.354	-0.080
1981	-0.593	-0.643	-0.853	-0.790	-0.727	-0.460
1982	-0.445	-0.494	-0.704	-0.638	-0.575	-0.315
1983	-0.364	-0.412	-0.622	-0.556	-0.493	-0.235
1984	-0.277	-0.326	-0.535	-0.500	-0.408	-0.146

II. Machinery and equipment, $N = 20$

Year	a	b	c	d	e	f
1965	-0.111	-0.165	-0.218	-0.175	-0.190	-0.032
1966	-0.111	-0.166	-0.220	-0.176	-0.191	-0.031
1967	-0.109	-0.164	-0.219	-0.175	-0.190	-0.027
1968	-0.096	-0.155	-0.213	-0.167	-0.182	-0.011
1969	-0.135	-0.200	-0.264	-0.214	-0.230	-0.041
1970	-0.200	-0.255	-0.310	-0.267	-0.280	-0.120
1971	-0.145	-0.201	-0.257	-0.213	-0.227	-0.062
1972	-0.138	-0.195	-0.253	-0.208	-0.222	-0.055
1973	-0.087	-0.146	-0.206	-0.160	-0.173	-0.000
1974	-0.278	-0.341	-0.404	-0.356	-0.370	-0.187
1975	-0.256	-0.321	-0.387	-0.337	-0.351	-0.162
1976	-0.254	-0.320	-0.389	-0.338	-0.351	-0.156
1977	-0.205	-0.274	-0.345	-0.293	-0.306	-0.104
1978	-0.263	-0.337	-0.418	-0.361	-0.373	-0.152
1979	-0.088	-0.164	-0.246	-0.188	-0.200	0.024
1980	-0.349	-0.426	-0.510	-0.451	-0.463	-0.235
1981	-0.203	-0.283	-0.370	-0.310	-0.321	-0.086
1982	-0.272	-0.353	-0.444	-0.382	-0.392	-0.151
1983	-0.164	-0.245	-0.336	-0.274	-0.285	-0.044
1984	-0.122	-0.201	-0.290	-0.259	-0.240	-0.003

Survival function: simultaneous retirement. No inflation adjustment: $\varepsilon_1 = \varepsilon_2 = 0$. Depreciation allowance schedule: a = linear; b = linear with accelerated depreciation; c = linear with initial allowances; d = declining balance; e = degressive; f = progressive.

Table 10.9: Tax equivalent net real rate of return, ρ^*, for different depreciation allowance schedules. Per cent (continuous rate).

I. Buildings and structures, $N = 60$

Year	a	b	c	d	e	f
1981	0.25	-0.18	-2.69	-1.75	-1.00	1.26
1982	2.14	1.77	-0.16	0.51	1.09	3.08
1983	3.29	2.91	1.09	1.71	2.26	4.23
1984	4.31	3.94	2.19	2.51	3.28	5.28

II. Machinery and equipment, $N = 20$

Year	a	b	c	d	e	f
1981	4.75	3.56	2.16	3.14	2.96	6.42
1982	0.84	-0.30	-1.68	-0.73	-0.88	2.40
1983	6.94	5.67	4.15	5.19	5.02	8.73
1984	9.70	8.36	6.80	7.36	7.69	11.60

Survival function: simultaneous retirement. No inflation adjustment: $\varepsilon_1 = \varepsilon_2 = 0$. Depreciation allowance schedule: a = linear; b = linear with accelerated depreciation; c = linear with initial allowances; d = declining balance; e = degressive; f = progressive.

one. This constellation is more favourable than a neutral tax system for buildings and structures in all years except 1968, 1978, and 1979 (confer the column for $N_B = T_B = 40$ in table 10.14). The corresponding parameter constellation for machinery and equipment (i.e. $N_M = T_M = 10$) is less favourable than neutrality in all the 20 years under consideration. This shows that the incomplete interest deductibility ($0 < m < 1$, cf. table 10.4, column 7), the net wealth taxation ($v^* > 0$, cf. table 10.4, column 6), the incomplete taxation of capital gains ($n = 0.2$), and the lack of indexation of the income tax base ($\varepsilon_1 = \varepsilon_2 = 0$) in combination have a different distortive effect on the two kinds of capital assets in the Norwegian tax system. For buildings and structures, the break-even point for the technical life time N, i.e. the point at which $\beta = 0$ (and hence belongs to the neutrality locus), is less than 40 years in all the years except 1968 (break-even point between 40 and 50 years) and 1978 and 1979 (break-even point between 50 and 60 years). For machinery and equipment, the break-even point for the life time N is between 10 and 15 years over the entire period.

In tables 10.15 and 10.16, the distortive effect of the tax system is illustrated in terms of the tax equivalent net real rate of return and the (net and gross) effective tax rate. In the alternative where the technical and tax

Table 10.10: Effective tax rate for different depreciation allowance schedules.

I. Buildings and structures, $N = 60$

Net rate $= u + (\rho^* - \rho)/\rho$

Year	a	b	c	d	e	f
1981	-0.429	-0.536	-1.159	-0.926	-0.740	-0.178
1982	-0.074	-0.147	-0.523	-0.392	-0.279	0.108
1983	0.066	0.002	-0.307	-0.202	-0.109	0.226
1984	0.175	0.117	-0.153	-0.104	0.016	0.324

Gross rate $= u + u\gamma/\rho + (\rho^* - \rho)/\rho = u^*$

Year	a	b	c	d	e	f
1981	0.509	0.403	-0.221	0.012	0.198	0.760
1982	0.625	0.552	0.176	0.308	0.421	0.808
1983	0.614	0.551	0.241	0.347	0.440	0.775
1984	0.595	0.537	0.267	0.316	0.436	0.744

II. Machinery and equipment, $N = 20$

Net rate $= u + (\rho^* - \rho)/\rho$

Year	a	b	c	d	e	f
1981	0.119	-0.034	-0.215	-0.089	-0.112	0.333
1982	-0.299	-0.560	-0.879	-0.659	-0.695	0.060
1983	0.232	0.099	-0.059	0.049	-0.032	0.419
1984	0.324	0.212	0.081	0.128	0.155	0.485

Gross rate $= u + u\gamma/\rho + (\rho^* - \rho)/\rho = u^*$

Year	a	b	c	d	e	f
1981	0.359	0.206	0.026	0.151	0.129	0.573
1982	0.616	0.355	0.036	0.255	0.220	0.975
1983	0.373	0.241	0.083	0.191	0.174	0.561
1984	0.321	0.209	0.078	0.125	0.152	0.482

Survival function: simultaneous retirement. No inflation adjustment: $\varepsilon_1 = \varepsilon_2 = 0$. Depreciation allowance schedule: a = linear; b = linear with accelerated depreciation; c = linear with initial allowances; d = declining balance; e = degressive; f = progressive.

permitted life times coincide, the effective gross tax rate may be very high, in 1982 for instance 84.6 per cent for buildings and structures and 151 per cent for machinery and equipment. From this we can conclude that for

Table 10.11: User cost of capital in manufacturing, per cent of 1980 investment price, for different forms of survival function.

I. Buildings and structures, $N = 60$

Year	a	b	c	d	e	f
1965	0.304	0.503	0.621	1.149	3.194	5.377
1966	0.404	0.625	0.757	1.354	3.574	5.914
1967	0.917	1.166	1.325	2.086	4.514	6.974
1968	0.981	1.243	1.411	2.219	4.787	7.387
1969	0.430	0.696	0.853	1.558	4.183	6.945
1970	0.268	0.520	0.666	1.308	3.881	6.643
1971	0.389	0.669	0.833	1.564	4.369	7.347
1972	0.431	0.729	0.905	1.685	4.660	7.811
1973	-0.151	0.056	0.170	0.650	3.355	6.574
1974	-0.439	-0.278	-0.194	0.139	2.861	6.418
1975	-0.527	-0.323	-0.218	0.196	3.361	7.391
1976	-0.119	0.295	0.523	1.472	5.813	10.607
1977	2.467	3.030	3.397	5.203	10.736	16.292
1978	5.829	4.529	4.744	10.396	16.645	22.510
1979	5.039	2.613	2.754	10.611	17.099	22.922
1980	5.121	5.456	5.835	8.423	14.645	20.775
1981	1.936	2.620	3.048	5.036	11.454	17.951
1982	3.487	4.192	4.669	7.069	14.236	21.408
1983	4.742	5.390	5.887	8.642	16.289	23.892
1984	6.103	6.592	7.096	10.363	18.489	26.518

II. Machinery and equipment, $N = 20$

Year	a	b	c	d	e	f
1965	2.377	2.897	3.238	4.925	10.099	15.303
1966	2.600	3.134	3.489	5.256	10.594	15.941
1967	2.850	3.394	3.760	5.600	11.060	16.506
1968	3.178	3.729	4.106	6.029	11.616	17.160
1969	2.402	2.982	3.358	5.190	10.955	16.789
1970	1.187	1.702	2.015	3.470	9.061	15.093
1971	2.535	3.191	3.612	5.648	12.185	18.838
1972	2.892	3.589	4.040	6.243	13.173	20.187
1973	5.104	5.789	6.280	8.905	16.153	23.277
1974	1.126	1.732	2.096	3.767	10.658	18.273
1975	1.853	2.637	3.115	5.330	13.591	22.385
1976	2.554	3.482	4.054	6.735	16.173	26.031
1977	3.402	4.460	5.123	8.271	18.860	29.770
1978	3.621	4.823	5.571	9.096	21.078	33.448
1979	10.327	11.510	12.386	17.214	30.289	43.114
1980	3.318	4.626	5.425	9.138	22.249	35.919
1981	8.153	9.627	10.627	15.702	30.630	45.497
1982	6.117	7.727	8.759	13.730	29.550	45.584
1983	10.825	12.452	13.592	19.561	36.532	53.326
1984	13.249	14.796	15.936	22.195	39.261	56.033

Depreciation allowances: linear. No inflation adjustment: $\varepsilon_1 = \varepsilon_2 = 0$. Survival function: a = simultaneous retirement; b = highly concave; c = moderately concave; d = linear; e = moderately convex; f = highly convex.

Table 10.12: Relative distortion of user cost, β, for different forms of survival function.

I. Buildings and structures, $N = 60$

Year	a	b	c	d	e	f
1965	-0.508	-0.330	-0.260	-0.100	0.218	0.351
1966	-0.458	-0.297	-0.232	-0.081	0.223	0.353
1967	-0.243	-0.142	-0.097	0.015	0.250	0.363
1968	-0.222	-0.120	-0.075	0.039	0.278	0.392
1969	-0.535	-0.361	-0.289	-0.119	0.226	0.378
1970	-0.675	-0.479	-0.401	-0.222	0.134	0.285
1971	-0.595	-0.417	-0.346	-0.178	0.158	0.304
1972	-0.585	-0.410	-0.339	-0.172	0.163	0.308
1973	-1.321	-0.912	-0.770	-0.472	0.089	0.293
1974	-2.241	-1.545	-1.321	-0.868	-0.044	0.231
1975	-2.129	-1.494	-1.283	-0.851	-0.054	0.221
1976	-1.093	-0.812	-0.703	-0.452	0.044	0.251
1977	-0.316	-0.221	-0.176	-0.057	0.201	0.333
1978	-0.046	-0.268	-0.247	0.100	0.263	0.362
1979	-0.039	-0.506	-0.486	0.117	0.275	0.370
1980	-0.217	-0.188	-0.157	-0.033	0.180	0.305
1981	-0.593	-0.482	-0.427	-0.277	0.053	0.228
1982	-0.445	-0.361	-0.316	-0.187	0.096	0.253
1983	-0.364	-0.300	-0.262	-0.139	0.118	0.264
1984	-0.277	-0.240	-0.207	-0.079	0.151	0.285

II. Machinery and equipment, $N = 20$

Year	a	b	c	d	e	f
1965	-0.111	-0.065	-0.045	0.002	0.098	0.141
1966	-0.111	-0.066	-0.047	0.000	0.097	0.141
1967	-0.109	-0.065	-0.047	-0.000	0.096	0.141
1968	-0.096	-0.055	-0.037	0.009	0.105	0.150
1969	-0.135	-0.078	-0.054	0.004	0.121	0.174
1970	-0.200	-0.115	-0.084	-0.017	0.112	0.161
1971	-0.145	-0.088	-0.065	-0.010	0.101	0.149
1972	-0.138	-0.084	-0.062	-0.008	0.101	0.150
1973	-0.087	-0.051	-0.035	0.008	0.100	0.146
1974	-0.278	-0.165	-0.124	-0.039	0.124	0.185
1975	-0.256	-0.159	-0.123	-0.042	0.116	0.179
1976	-0.254	-0.165	-0.130	-0.050	0.108	0.174
1977	-0.205	-0.127	-0.096	-0.023	0.125	0.188
1978	-0.263	-0.172	-0.136	-0.049	0.125	0.200
1979	-0.088	-0.048	-0.029	0.024	0.138	0.198
1980	-0.349	-0.242	-0.199	-0.098	0.104	0.191
1981	-0.203	-0.142	-0.114	-0.041	0.114	0.190
1982	-0.272	-0.189	-0.154	-0.066	0.117	0.203
1983	-0.164	-0.110	-0.085	-0.017	0.129	0.203
1984	-0.122	-0.078	-0.056	0.003	0.132	0.200

Depreciation allowances: linear. No inflation adjustment: $\varepsilon_1 = \varepsilon_2 = 0$. Survival function: a = simultaneous retirement; b = highly concave; c = moderately concave; d = linear; e = moderately convex; f = highly convex.

Table 10.13: User cost of capital in manufacturing, per cent of 1980 investment price, for different service lives, N.

I. Buildings and structures

Year	$N = 40$	$N = 50$	$N = 60$	$N = 70$	$N = 80$
1965	0.866	0.528	0.304	0.145	0.028
1966	1.014	0.648	0.404	0.229	0.097
1967	1.555	1.174	0.917	0.732	0.591
1968	1.654	1.251	0.981	0.785	0.636
1969	1.161	0.724	0.430	0.218	0.057
1970	0.985	0.554	0.268	0.065	-0.087
1971	1.171	0.702	0.389	0.165	-0.003
1972	1.260	0.763	0.431	0.193	0.013
1973	0.559	0.115	-0.151	-0.318	-0.423
1974	0.229	-0.205	-0.439	-0.565	-0.628
1975	0.275	-0.239	-0.527	-0.690	-0.778
1976	1.123	0.374	-0.119	-0.465	-0.720
1977	3.884	3.036	2.467	2.058	1.749
1978	8.589	7.712	5.829	2.370	0.247
1979	9.068	7.960	5.039	1.343	-0.135
1980	6.563	5.747	5.121	4.227	2.540
1981	3.687	2.646	1.936	1.418	1.019
1982	5.294	4.213	3.487	2.947	2.468
1983	6.580	5.489	4.742	4.079	3.143
1984	8.020	6.921	6.103	5.055	3.137

II. Machinery and equipment

Year	$N = 10$	$N = 15$	$N = 20$	$N = 25$	$N = 30$
1965	5.000	3.253	2.377	1.850	1.497
1966	5.280	3.494	2.600	2.062	1.703
1967	5.559	3.752	2.850	2.311	1.952
1968	5.902	4.081	3.178	2.641	2.289
1969	5.364	3.392	2.402	1.804	1.402
1970	4.181	2.155	1.187	0.641	0.305
1971	5.921	3.666	2.535	1.853	1.396
1972	6.451	4.082	2.892	2.174	1.692
1973	8.453	6.196	5.104	4.476	4.076
1974	4.834	2.303	1.126	0.486	0.110
1975	6.289	3.305	1.853	1.012	0.477
1976	7.593	4.226	2.554	1.560	0.904
1977	8.991	5.267	3.402	2.281	1.531
1978	9.987	5.749	3.621	2.337	1.475
1979	16.143	12.195	10.327	9.271	8.585
1980	10.376	5.673	3.318	1.903	0.958
1981	15.489	10.587	8.153	6.704	5.747
1982	14.340	8.878	6.117	4.437	3.299
1983	18.870	13.465	10.825	9.284	8.281
1984	20.883	15.706	13.249	11.851	10.905

Depreciation allowances: linear. No inflation adjustment: $\varepsilon_1 = \varepsilon_2 = 0$. Survival function: simultaneous retirement.

Table 10.14: Relative distortion of user cost, β, for different service lives, N.

I. Buildings and structures

Year	$N = 40$	$N = 50$	$N = 60$	$N = 70$	$N = 80$
1965	-0.096	-0.299	-0.508	-0.721	-0.938
1966	-0.082	-0.271	-0.458	-0.643	-0.828
1967	-0.001	-0.129	-0.243	-0.346	-0.438
1968	0.023	-0.107	-0.222	-0.326	-0.419
1969	-0.125	-0.333	-0.535	-0.731	-0.922
1970	-0.219	-0.445	-0.675	-0.907	-1.143
1971	-0.180	-0.388	-0.595	-0.801	-1.005
1972	-0.175	-0.381	-0.585	-0.786	-0.984
1973	-0.408	-0.825	-1.321	-1.915	-2.627
1974	-0.725	-1.383	-2.241	-3.365	-4.845
1975	-0.732	-1.351	-2.129	-3.110	-4.354
1976	-0.443	-0.763	-1.093	-1.432	-1.783
1977	-0.086	-0.211	-0.316	-0.403	-0.477
1978	0.071	0.013	-0.046	-0.188	-0.718
1979	0.092	0.035	-0.039	-0.283	-1.279
1980	-0.072	-0.154	-0.217	-0.275	-0.366
1981	-0.320	-0.471	-0.593	-0.692	-0.774
1982	-0.231	-0.352	-0.445	-0.519	-0.581
1983	-0.182	-0.285	-0.364	-0.427	-0.493
1984	-0.120	-0.209	-0.277	-0.338	-0.427

II. Machinery and equipment

Year	$N = 10$	$N = 15$	$N = 20$	$N = 25$	$N = 30$
1965	0.058	-0.030	-0.111	-0.185	-0.253
1966	0.056	-0.032	-0.111	-0.181	-0.245
1967	0.053	-0.033	-0.109	-0.175	-0.233
1968	0.061	-0.024	-0.096	-0.157	-0.210
1969	0.073	-0.035	-0.135	-0.229	-0.316
1970	0.073	-0.052	-0.200	-0.377	-0.587
1971	0.057	-0.046	-0.145	-0.240	-0.332
1972	0.057	-0.044	-0.138	-0.227	-0.310
1973	0.054	-0.025	-0.087	-0.136	-0.175
1974	0.079	-0.080	-0.278	-0.528	-0.844
1975	0.065	-0.087	-0.256	-0.445	-0.657
1976	0.051	-0.099	-0.254	-0.415	-0.581
1977	0.069	-0.069	-0.205	-0.340	-0.473
1978	0.057	-0.105	-0.263	-0.416	-0.566
1979	0.076	-0.019	-0.088	-0.140	-0.179
1980	0.027	-0.162	-0.349	-0.536	-0.721
1981	0.037	-0.097	-0.203	-0.289	-0.357
1982	0.036	-0.128	-0.272	-0.397	-0.507
1983	0.053	-0.070	-0.164	-0.236	-0.292
1984	0.061	-0.045	-0.122	-0.178	-0.220

Depreciation allowances: linear. No inflation adjustment: $\varepsilon_1 = \varepsilon_2 = 0$. Survival function: simultaneous retirement.

Table 10.15: Tax equivalent net real rate of return, ρ^*, for different service lives, N. Per cent (continuous rate).

I. Buildings and structures

Year	$N = 40$	$N = 50$	$N = 60$	$N = 70$	$N = 80$
1981	1.63	0.84	0.25	-0.23	-0.66
1982	3.27	2.60	2.14	1.79	1.43
1983	4.36	3.73	3.29	2.83	2.04
1984	5.40	4.80	4.31	3.54	1.85

II. Machinery and equipment

Year	$N = 10$	$N = 15$	$N = 20$	$N = 25$	$N = 30$
1981	8.04	5.86	4.75	4.09	3.65
1982	4.73	2.22	0.84	-0.09	-0.79
1983	10.14	8.00	6.94	6.31	5.90
1984	12.60	10.65	9.70	9.13	8.69

Depreciation allowances: linear. No inflation adjustment: $\varepsilon_1 = \varepsilon_2 = 0$. Survival function: simultaneous retirement.

the Norwegian nominal tax system, with incomplete deductibility of the financial cost and incomplete taxation of capital gains, a difference between the life time underlying the depreciation allowances and the technical life time of the capital gives a significant contribution to reducing the effective income tax rate below its statutory value.

10.4   Results for systems with indexation of the income tax base

In this section, we discuss the user cost and the neutrality indicators for a tax reform in which the present fully nominal Norwegian corporate tax system is replaced by a system with full or partial indexation of the income tax base. This system is formally obtained from the M class of tax systems by varying the indexation parameter for the accounting capital, ε_1, alone or in combination with the indexation parameter for interest deductions and capital gains, ε_2. The values of the interest deduction parameter m and the capital gains taxation parameter n are assumed to be the same as under the existing nominal system, i.e. the effect of the indexation will not be shifted, for instance via the financial markets, into the values of these two parameters.

Table 10.16: Effective tax rate for different service lives, N.

I. Buildings and structures

Net rate $= u + (\rho^* - \rho)/\rho$

Year	$N = 40$	$N = 50$	$N = 60$	$N = 70$	$N = 80$
1981	-0.087	-0.284	-0.429	-0.548	-0.655
1982	0.147	0.016	-0.074	-0.143	-0.213
1983	0.248	0.141	0.066	-0.011	-0.146
1984	0.344	0.250	0.175	0.055	-0.206

Gross rate $= u + u\gamma/\rho + (\rho^* - \rho)/\rho = u^*$

Year	$N = 40$	$N = 50$	$N = 60$	$N = 70$	$N = 80$
1981	0.851	0.654	0.509	0.390	0.283
1982	0.846	0.715	0.625	0.556	0.487
1983	0.796	0.689	0.614	0.537	0.402
1984	0.764	0.671	0.595	0.475	0.215

II. Machinery and equipment

Net rate $= u + (\rho^* - \rho)/\rho$

Year	$N = 10$	$N = 15$	$N = 20$	$N = 25$	$N = 30$
1981	0.541	0.261	0.119	0.033	-0.023
1982	0.596	0.019	-0.299	-0.512	-0.674
1983	0.566	0.343	0.232	0.167	0.123
1984	0.568	0.404	0.324	0.277	0.240

Gross rate $= u + u\gamma/\rho + (\rho^* - \rho)/\rho = u^*$

Year	$N = 10$	$N = 15$	$N = 20$	$N = 25$	$N = 30$
1981	0.781	0.501	0.359	0.274	0.217
1982	1.510	0.934	0.616	0.403	0.241
1983	0.708	0.484	0.373	0.308	0.265
1984	0.565	0.401	0.321	0.274	0.237

Depreciation allowances: linear. No inflation adjustment: $\varepsilon_1 = \varepsilon_2 = 0$. Survival function: simultaneous retirement.

Five indexation schemes are considered, and for ease of comparison, we also include the case with no indexation in the tables below. The alternatives are (the terminology is explained in subsection 5.4.2):

a: MNO, i.e. $\varepsilon_1 = \varepsilon_2 = 0$,

b: MNR, i.e. $\varepsilon_1 = \gamma, \varepsilon_2 = 0$,

c: MI with 50 per cent indexation, i.e. $\varepsilon_1 = \varepsilon_2 = 0.5\gamma$,

d: MI with 100 per cent indexation, i.e. $\varepsilon_1 = \varepsilon_2 = \gamma$,

e: MI with 150 per cent indexation, i.e. $\varepsilon_1 = \varepsilon_2 = 1.5\gamma$,

f: MI1 with 100 per cent indexation, i.e. $\varepsilon_1 = \varepsilon_2 = \gamma$.

Consider first table 10.18, which shows the present value of the per unit depreciation allowances, z_ρ. When the rate of inflation is positive, this present value is larger the higher is the degree of indexation — i.e. it is larger in alternative e than in d (and b and f), larger in alternative d than in c, which in turn exceeds the present value in the absence of indexation (alternative a). In the three years with negative inflation, i.e. 1973, 1979, and 1984 for machinery and equipment, these inequalities are reversed. In years with high inflation, a system with full indexation or over-indexation of the depreciation allowances (alternatives d and e) may give very high present values of depreciation allowances, in particular for the long-lived asset type. Compare the result for buildings and structures in the years 1973–1976. In 1974, for instance, the present value for a fully indexed system would be nearly seven times as large as for the present nominal system.

Table 10.17, containing the corresponding user cost series, shows that an indexation of the tax base is not always advantageous to the firm. In years with positive inflation, an indexation of the depreciation allowances only will always bring a reduction in the user cost (compare columns a and b), whereas indexation of the interest deductions and capital gains will have the joint effect of increasing the user cost. In all the years (again excepting 1973, 1979, and 1984 for machinery) the user cost is higher under full indexation than with no indexation (compare columns a and d). This is due to the fact that — with a value of m in the range of 0.8–0.9 and a value of n as low as 0.2 — the positive effect on the user cost of the indexation of the interest deductions by far outweighs the negative effect of the indexation of the capital gains.[19] There exists, however, no monotone relationship between the user cost and the degree of indexation, and in all the years 1965–1977, the user cost for buildings and structures implied by a 150 per cent indexation is lower than that obtained by a 100 per cent indexation (compare columns d and e).

---

[19] Confer (5.61).

Table 10.17: User cost of capital, per cent of 1980 investment price, for different indexation schemes.

I. Buildings and structures, $N = 60$

Year	a	b	c	d	e	f
1965	0.304	-0.148	0.551	0.643	0.417	0.731
1966	0.404	-0.073	0.656	0.755	0.552	0.842
1967	0.917	0.503	1.096	1.184	1.132	1.241
1968	0.981	0.526	1.164	1.247	1.170	1.309
1969	0.430	-0.171	0.782	0.925	0.630	1.037
1970	0.268	-0.308	0.665	0.834	0.472	0.954
1971	0.389	-0.210	0.798	0.980	0.655	1.100
1972	0.431	-0.207	0.862	1.052	0.709	1.179
1973	-0.151	-0.778	0.441	0.686	-0.214	0.893
1974	-0.439	-1.100	0.359	0.724	-0.709	1.005
1975	-0.527	-1.303	0.399	0.823	-0.818	1.136
1976	-0.119	-1.138	0.892	1.393	0.399	1.656
1977	2.467	1.491	3.195	3.639	3.562	3.784
1978	5.829	5.504	6.104	6.346	6.549	6.383
1979	5.039	4.816	5.236	5.414	5.570	5.443
1980	5.121	4.338	5.923	6.561	6.953	6.652
1981	1.936	0.631	3.535	4.628	4.596	4.846
1982	3.487	2.122	5.121	6.273	6.429	6.478
1983	4.742	3.404	6.314	7.467	7.831	7.650
1984	6.103	4.870	7.467	8.508	9.004	8.662

II. Machinery and equipment, $N = 20$

Year	a	b	c	d	e	f
1965	2.377	2.069	2.442	2.493	2.529	2.555
1966	2.600	2.352	2.647	2.687	2.718	2.735
1967	2.850	2.693	2.878	2.902	2.923	2.930
1968	3.178	3.148	3.181	3.185	3.188	3.190
1969	2.402	1.887	2.525	2.612	2.660	2.721
1970	1.187	0.354	1.650	1.938	2.005	2.221
1971	2.535	1.908	2.734	2.874	2.950	3.017
1972	2.892	2.297	3.062	3.186	3.259	3.315
1973	5.104	5.397	5.066	5.019	4.965	4.975
1974	1.126	0.040	1.878	2.346	2.448	2.768
1975	1.853	0.629	2.523	2.947	3.067	3.335
1976	2.554	1.256	3.196	3.622	3.788	3.983
1977	3.402	2.042	3.944	4.288	4.401	4.638
1978	3.621	1.942	4.373	4.846	4.986	5.287
1979	10.327	10.579	10.283	10.235	10.184	10.199
1980	3.318	1.357	4.412	5.132	5.397	5.675
1981	8.153	7.110	8.534	8.850	9.097	9.038
1982	6.117	4.117	6.999	7.610	7.907	8.056
1983	10.825	9.939	11.098	11.332	11.524	11.479
1984	13.249	13.275	13.243	13.236	13.230	13.232

Survival function: simultaneous retirement. Depreciation allowances: linear. Indexation scheme: a = no inflation adjustment ($\varepsilon_1 = \varepsilon_2 = 0$); b = full inflation adjustment of depreciation allowances ($\varepsilon_1 = \gamma$, $\varepsilon_2 = 0$); c = 50 per cent inflation adjustment of depreciation allowances, interest deductions and capital gains ($\varepsilon_1 = \varepsilon_2 = 0.5\gamma$, $\alpha_G = 1$); d = 100 per cent inflation adjustment of depreciation allowances, interest deductions and capital gains ($\varepsilon_1 = \varepsilon_2 = \gamma$, $\alpha_G = 1$); e = 150 per cent inflation adjustment of depreciation allowances, interest deductions and capital gains ($\varepsilon_1 = \varepsilon_2 = 1.5\gamma$, $\alpha_G = 1$); f = as d, but with alternative definition of capital gains ($\varepsilon_1 = \varepsilon_2 = \gamma$, $\alpha_G = 0$).

Table 10.18: Present value of depreciation allowances per unit of investment, z, for different indexation schemes.

I. Buildings and structures, $N = 60$

Year	a	b	c	d	e	f
1965	0.417	1.069	0.639	1.069	1.940	1.069
1966	0.409	0.980	0.610	0.980	1.698	0.980
1967	0.404	0.709	0.526	0.709	1.000	0.709
1968	0.398	0.707	0.521	0.707	1.000	0.707
1969	0.363	0.914	0.551	0.914	1.661	0.914
1970	0.358	1.043	0.576	1.043	2.121	1.043
1971	0.358	0.978	0.561	0.978	1.896	0.978
1972	0.354	0.960	0.553	0.960	1.853	0.960
1973	0.349	1.686	0.685	1.686	5.026	1.686
1974	0.325	2.198	0.722	2.198	8.570	2.198
1975	0.309	1.972	0.667	1.972	7.533	1.972
1976	0.295	1.092	0.517	1.092	2.780	1.092
1977	0.283	0.558	0.385	0.558	0.869	0.558
1978	0.241	0.296	0.266	0.296	0.331	0.296
1979	0.237	0.281	0.257	0.281	0.308	0.281
1980	0.230	0.354	0.281	0.354	0.461	0.354
1981	0.216	0.497	0.311	0.497	0.905	0.497
1982	0.204	0.425	0.282	0.425	0.716	0.425
1983	0.202	0.384	0.270	0.384	0.596	0.384
1984	0.210	0.358	0.207	0.358	0.507	0.358

II. Machinery and equipment, $N = 20$

Year	a	b	c	d	e	f
1965	0.777	0.879	0.826	0.879	0.935	0.879
1966	0.773	0.847	0.809	0.847	0.888	0.847
1967	0.769	0.813	0.791	0.813	0.835	0.813
1968	0.765	0.773	0.769	0.773	0.776	0.773
1969	0.741	0.896	0.814	0.896	0.987	0.896
1970	0.737	1.287	0.969	1.287	1.724	1.287
1971	0.736	0.944	0.833	0.944	1.072	0.944
1972	0.734	0.906	0.815	0.906	1.010	0.906
1973	0.730	0.678	0.704	0.678	0.654	0.678
1974	0.711	1.390	0.986	1.390	1.981	1.390
1975	0.696	1.176	0.900	1.176	1.549	1.176
1976	0.684	1.054	0.846	1.054	1.322	1.054
1977	0.672	0.983	0.810	0.983	1.198	0.983
1978	0.627	0.961	0.773	0.961	1.203	0.961
1979	0.622	0.600	0.611	0.600	0.590	0.600
1980	0.614	0.990	0.776	0.990	1.274	0.990
1981	0.595	0.695	0.643	0.695	0.752	0.695
1982	0.578	0.811	0.683	0.811	0.968	0.811
1983	0.576	0.643	0.609	0.643	0.680	0.643
1984	0.587	0.585	0.586	0.585	0.584	0.585

Survival function: simultaneous retirement. Depreciation allowances: linear. Indexation scheme: a = no inflation adjustment ($\varepsilon_1 = \varepsilon_2 = 0$); b = full inflation adjustment of depreciation allowances ($\varepsilon_1 = \gamma$, $\varepsilon_2 = 0$); c = 50 per cent inflation adjustment of depreciation allowances, interest deductions and capital gains ($\varepsilon_1 = \varepsilon_2 = 0.5\gamma$, $\alpha_G = 1$); d = 100 per cent inflation adjustment of depreciation allowances, interest deductions and capital gains ($\varepsilon_1 = \varepsilon_2 = \gamma$, $\alpha_G = 1$); e = 150 per cent inflation adjustment of depreciation allowances, interest deductions and capital gains ($\varepsilon_1 = \varepsilon_2 = 1.5\gamma$, $\alpha_G = 1$); f = as d, but with alternative definition of capital gains ($\varepsilon_1 = \varepsilon_2 = \gamma$, $\alpha_G = 0$).

Table 10.19: Relative distortion of user cost, β, for different indexation schemes.

I. Buildings and structures, $N = 60$

Year	a	b	c	d	e	f
1965	-0.508	-1.240	-0.107	0.042	-0.325	0.184
1966	-0.458	-1.099	-0.118	0.015	-0.258	0.131
1967	-0.243	-0.585	-0.096	-0.023	-0.066	0.024
1968	-0.222	-0.583	-0.077	-0.011	-0.072	0.038
1969	-0.535	-1.185	-0.155	0.000	-0.319	0.121
1970	-0.675	-1.374	-0.192	0.013	-0.427	0.159
1971	-0.595	-1.218	-0.170	0.018	-0.319	0.144
1972	-0.585	-1.199	-0.170	0.013	-0.317	0.135
1973	-1.321	-2.650	-0.065	0.455	-1.453	0.894
1974	-2.241	-4.108	0.014	1.046	-3.003	1.838
1975	-2.129	-3.791	-0.145	0.763	-2.752	1.433
1976	-1.093	-1.886	-0.305	0.084	-0.689	0.289
1977	-0.316	-0.586	-0.114	0.009	-0.012	0.049
1978	-0.046	-0.100	-0.001	0.038	0.071	0.044
1979	-0.039	-0.081	-0.001	0.033	0.062	0.038
1980	-0.217	-0.337	-0.095	0.003	0.063	0.017
1981	-0.593	-0.867	-0.258	-0.028	-0.035	0.018
1982	-0.445	-0.662	-0.185	-0.002	0.023	0.031
1983	-0.364	-0.543	-0.153	0.002	0.051	0.027
1984	-0.277	-0.423	-0.116	0.008	0.066	0.026

II. Machinery and equipment, $N = 20$

Year	a	b	c	d	e	f
1965	-0.111	-0.226	-0.087	-0.068	-0.054	-0.044
1966	-0.111	-0.196	-0.094	-0.081	-0.070	-0.064
1967	-0.109	-0.158	-0.100	-0.093	-0.086	-0.084
1968	-0.096	-0.105	-0.095	-0.094	-0.093	-0.093
1969	-0.135	-0.321	-0.091	-0.060	-0.042	-0.020
1970	-0.200	-0.762	0.112	0.306	0.351	0.497
1971	-0.145	-0.356	-0.078	-0.031	-0.005	0.018
1972	-0.138	-0.316	-0.088	-0.051	-0.029	-0.012
1973	-0.087	-0.035	-0.094	-0.102	-0.112	-0.110
1974	-0.278	-0.974	0.203	0.504	0.569	0.774
1975	-0.256	-0.747	0.013	0.183	0.231	0.339
1976	-0.254	-0.633	-0.066	0.058	0.107	0.164
1977	-0.205	-0.523	-0.079	0.002	0.028	0.083
1978	-0.263	-0.605	-0.109	-0.013	0.015	0.077
1979	-0.088	-0.066	-0.092	-0.096	-0.101	-0.100
1980	-0.349	-0.734	-0.135	0.006	0.058	0.113
1981	-0.203	-0.305	-0.166	-0.135	-0.111	-0.117
1982	-0.272	-0.510	-0.167	-0.094	-0.058	-0.041
1983	-0.164	-0.233	-0.143	-0.125	-0.110	-0.114
1984	-0.122	-0.120	-0.122	-0.122	-0.123	-0.123

Survival function: simultaneous retirement. Depreciation allowances: linear. Indexation scheme: a = no inflation adjustment ($\varepsilon_1 = \varepsilon_2 = 0$); b = full inflation adjustment of depreciation allowances ($\varepsilon_1 = \gamma$, $\varepsilon_2 = 0$); c = 50 per cent inflation adjustment of depreciation allowances, interest deductions and capital gains ($\varepsilon_1 = \varepsilon_2 = 0.5\gamma$, $\alpha_G = 1$); d = 100 per cent inflation adjustment of depreciation allowances, interest deductions and capital gains ($\varepsilon_1 = \varepsilon_2 = \gamma$, $\alpha_G = 1$); e = 150 per cent inflation adjustment of depreciation allowances, interest deductions and capital gains ($\varepsilon_1 = \varepsilon_2 = 1.5\gamma$, $\alpha_G = 1$); f = as d, but with alternative definition of capital gains ($\varepsilon_1 = \varepsilon_2 = \gamma$, $\alpha_G = 0$).

Table 10.20: Tax equivalent net real rate of return, ρ^*, for different indexation schemes. Per cent (continuous rate).

I. Buildings and structures, $N = 60$

Year	a	b	c	d	e	f
1981	0.25	-2.95	2.56	3.85	3.82	4.09
1982	2.14	0.28	3.94	5.08	5.23	5.28
1983	3.29	1.82	4.80	5.84	6.16	6.00
1984	4.31	3.16	5.50	6.37	6.77	6.49

II. Machinery and equipment, $N = 20$

Year	a	b	c	d	e	f
1981	4.75	3.21	5.29	5.73	6.07	5.99
1982	0.84	-2.78	2.21	3.10	3.52	3.73
1983	6.94	5.87	7.26	7.53	7.76	7.70
1984	9.70	9.73	9.69	9.68	9.68	9.68

Survival function: simultaneous retirement. Depreciation allowances: linear. Indexation scheme: a = no inflation adjustment ($\varepsilon_1 = \varepsilon_2 = 0$); b = full inflation adjustment of depreciation allowances ($\varepsilon_1 = \gamma$, $\varepsilon_2 = 0$); c = 50 per cent inflation adjustment of depreciation allowances, interest deductions and capital gains ($\varepsilon_1 = \varepsilon_2 = 0.5\gamma$, $\alpha_G = 1$); d = 100 per cent inflation adjustment of depreciation allowances, interest deductions and capital gains ($\varepsilon_1 = \varepsilon_2 = \gamma$, $\alpha_G = 1$); e = 150 per cent inflation adjustment of depreciation allowances, interest deductions and capital gains ($\varepsilon_1 = \varepsilon_2 = 1.5\gamma$, $\alpha_G = 1$); f = as d, but with alternative definition of capital gains ($\varepsilon_1 = \varepsilon_2 = \gamma$, $\alpha_G = 0$).

In alternative d (with α_G set to unity) no taxable capital gains emerge, since a 100 per cent indexation of the market value reduces the gain to zero [cf. alternative MI in subsection 5.3.3]. When the inflation adjusted gain is redefined (by setting α_G to zero) as the difference between the gain according to the market value and the gain implicit in the accounting capital, i.e. as $S_G(t) = n\gamma\{V(t) - V_T(t)\}$ [cf. alternative MI* in subsection 5.3.3], a positive gain will be recorded since the assumed life times of the two capital types imply that their market values will exceed their accounting values in all the years $\big(V(t) > V_T(t)\big)$. This explains why the user cost in alternative f exceeds that in alternative d in all years with positive inflation.

The relative distortion of the user cost tends to diminish when the (uniform) degree of indexation of the tax base increases from 0 to 100 per cent [compare columns a, c, and d of table 10.19]. At the same time, the wedge between the effective gross and net tax rates disappears [table 10.21], and with a 100 per cent indexation, the gross and net rates coincide. These results confirm that a fully indexed system is more robust towards changes

Table 10.21: Effective tax rate for different indexation schemes.

I. Buildings and structures, $N = 60$

Net rate $= u + (\rho^* - \rho)/\rho$

Year	a	b	c	d	e	f
1981	-0.429	-1.225	0.145	0.465	0.455	0.525
1982	-0.074	-0.438	0.277	0.500	0.529	0.538
1983	0.066	-0.183	0.323	0.500	0.554	0.527
1984	0.175	-0.004	0.358	0.493	0.555	0.512

Gross rate $= u + u\gamma/\rho + (\rho^* - \rho)/\rho = u^*$

Year	a	b	c	d	e	f
1981	0.509	-0.287	0.605	0.465	0.011	0.525
1982	0.625	0.261	0.621	0.500	0.197	0.538
1983	0.614	0.366	0.593	0.500	0.292	0.527
1984	0.595	0.416	0.566	0.493	0.354	0.512

II. Machinery and equipment, $N = 20$

Net rate $= u + (\rho^* - \rho)/\rho$

Year	a	b	c	d	e	f
1981	0.119	-0.080	0.188	0.244	0.288	0.277
1982	-0.299	-1.132	0.015	0.220	0.317	0.365
1983	0.232	0.120	0.265	0.294	0.317	0.312
1984	0.324	0.327	0.324	0.323	0.322	0.323

Gross rate $= u + u\gamma/\rho + (\rho^* - \rho)/\rho = u^*$

Year	a	b	c	d	e	f
1981	0.359	0.161	0.307	0.244	0.171	0.277
1982	0.616	-0.217	0.464	0.220	-0.115	0.365
1983	0.373	0.262	0.336	0.294	0.248	0.312
1984	0.321	0.324	0.322	0.323	0.324	0.323

Survival function: simultaneous retirement. Depreciation allowances: linear. Indexation scheme: a = no inflation adjustment ($\varepsilon_1 = \varepsilon_2 = 0$); b = full inflation adjustment of depreciation allowances ($\varepsilon_1 = \gamma$, $\varepsilon_2 = 0$); c = 50 per cent inflation adjustment of depreciation allowances, interest deductions and capital gains ($\varepsilon_1 = \varepsilon_2 = 0.5\gamma$, $\alpha_G = 1$); d = 100 per cent inflation adjustment of depreciation allowances, interest deductions and capital gains ($\varepsilon_1 = \varepsilon_2 = \gamma$, $\alpha_G = 1$); e = 150 per cent inflation adjustment of depreciation allowances, interest deductions and capital gains ($\varepsilon_1 = \varepsilon_2 = 1.5\gamma$, $\alpha_G = 1$); f = as d, but with alternative definition of capital gains ($\varepsilon_1 = \varepsilon_2 = \gamma$, $\alpha_G = 0$).

in nominal interest and inflation rates than nonindexed or partially indexed systems.

CHAPTER 11

PRICE — QUANTITY RELATIONS: EMPIRICAL ILLUSTRATIONS FOR MACHINERY IN NORWEGIAN MANUFACTURING

11.1 Introduction

The duality that exists between the capital stock and its service price is basic to the measurement of the user cost of capital and has been touched upon earlier in this study (notably in chapter 1 and section 4.5). The purpose of this chapter is to illustrate some consequences of this duality empirically by using data from the same source as in chapter 10, i.e. annual tax data and investment data for machinery in Norwegian manufacturing for the years 1965–1984. These data are combined with a selection of parametric survival functions with different curvature (concave, linear, convex).

The chapter is organized as follows. The survival functions are defined and their properties are stated in section 11.2. Section 11.3 presents the investment data, the derived series for gross and net capital stock, retirement and depreciation rates, as well as related variables. The numerical computation of the discounted per unit service flow function Φ, which is a crucial element in the calculation of the net capital stock and the user cost [cf. chapters 3 and 4], raises specific problems which are discussed in section 11.4. Next, section 11.5 illustrates empirically, for the concave, linear, and convex survival functions, the price-quantity duality. The service value of the capital stock, i.e. the product of its price and quantity component, is decomposed into a depreciation component and an interest component, similar to the decomposition which holds under exponential decay. This is elaborated further in the next two sections. In section 11.6, the focus is on a similar additive decomposition of the price component of the service value, i.e. the user cost of capital. Two alternative interpretations of the implicit retirement rate, one derived from prices and one derived from quantities, are compared in section 11.7. Finally, the relationship between the form of the survival function and the estimated elasticity of substitution between capital in machinery and labour is investigated in section 11.8.

11.2   The two-parametric survival functions and their properties

The survival functions to be considered in this chapter, belong to the two-parametric concave and convex classes briefly presented in subsection 10.2.1. Below we discuss their properties in some more detail.

11.2.1 The concave class

The concave class of survival functions is defined by

$$(11.1) \qquad B(s) = B^C(s; N, \sigma) = 1 - \left(\frac{s}{N}\right)^\sigma, \qquad 0 \leq s \leq N,$$

where N is the maximal life time of the capital and σ is a positive integer constant. The notation $B^C(s; N, \sigma)$ is used to indicate the two-parametric nature of the function, the superscript C denoting concave. Its retirement (density) function is

$$(11.2)
\begin{aligned}
b(s) = b^C(s; N, \sigma) &= \frac{\sigma}{N}\left(\frac{s}{N}\right)^{\sigma-1} \\
&= \frac{\sigma}{N}\{1 - B^C(s; N, \sigma - 1)\}, \qquad 0 \leq s \leq N.
\end{aligned}$$

This function is increasing with age, i.e. the survival function is strictly concave, whenever $\sigma > 1$. The limiting case $\sigma = 1$ implies linear retirement (constant relative retirement function), and $\sigma \to \infty$ corresponds to simultaneous retirement, since $\lim_{\sigma \to \infty}(s/N)^\sigma = 0$ for $s < N$ and 1 for $s = N$. The age specific retirement rates, as generally defined in (3.10), become

$$(11.3) \qquad b^*(s) = \frac{\sigma}{N}\frac{\left(\frac{s}{N}\right)^{\sigma-1}}{1 - \left(\frac{s}{N}\right)^\sigma} = \sigma\frac{s^{\sigma-1}}{N^\sigma - s^\sigma}, \qquad 0 \leq s < N.$$

These rates are, like $b(s)$, increasing with age.
    Since (11.1) implies

$$
\begin{aligned}
\int_s^N B(z)\, dz &= N - s - \frac{N}{\sigma + 1}\left(1 - \left(\frac{s}{N}\right)^{\sigma+1}\right) \\
&= \frac{\sigma N}{\sigma + 1}(1 - \frac{s}{N}) - \frac{s}{\sigma + 1}\left(1 - \left(\frac{s}{N}\right)^\sigma\right),
\end{aligned}
$$

it follows from (3.23) that

$$(11.4) \quad \Phi_0(s) = \Phi_0^C(s; N, \sigma) = \frac{N}{\sigma + 1} \left(\frac{\sigma(1 - \frac{s}{N})}{1 - (\frac{s}{N})^\sigma} - \frac{s}{N} \right), \quad 0 \leq s < N,$$

so that the weighting function for net capital, (3.28), becomes

$$(11.5) \quad \begin{aligned} G_0(s) = G_0^C(s; N, \sigma) &= 1 - \frac{s}{N} - \frac{s}{\sigma N}\left(1 - \left(\frac{s}{N}\right)^\sigma \right) \\ &= \frac{\sigma + 1}{\sigma} B^C(s; N, 1) - \frac{1}{\sigma} B^C(s; N, \sigma + 1), \quad 0 \leq s \leq N. \end{aligned}$$

Similarly, from (3.35) we get

$$(11.6) \quad \begin{aligned} g_0(s) = g_0^C(s; N, \sigma) &= \frac{\sigma + 1}{\sigma N} \left(1 - \left(\frac{s}{N}\right)^\sigma \right) \\ &= \frac{\sigma + 1}{\sigma N} B^C(s; N, \sigma), \quad 0 \leq s \leq N. \end{aligned}$$

The weighting functions (11.5) and (11.6) are derived under the assumption of a zero discounting rate for future capital services ($\rho = 0$). The general case with a non-zero discounting rate is considered in appendix C.

11.2.2 The convex class

The convex class of survival functions is defined by

$$(11.7) \quad B(s) = B^V(s; N, \tau) = \left(1 - \frac{s}{N} \right)^\tau, \quad 0 \leq s \leq N,$$

where τ is a non-negative integer constant, N, as before, is the maximal life time of the capital, and the superscript V denotes convex. Its retirement (density) function is[1]

(11.8)
$$b(s) = b^V(s; N, \tau) = \frac{\tau}{N}\left(1 - \frac{s}{N}\right)^{\tau-1}$$
$$= \frac{\tau}{N}B^V(s; N, \tau - 1), \quad 0 \le s \le N.$$

The retirement will be decreasing with age, i.e. the survival function is strictly convex, whenever $\tau > 1$. The limiting case $\tau = 0$ corresponds to simultaneous retirement, in which case $b(s)$ is undefined, and $\tau = 1$ gives linear retirement (constant relative retirement function). To this parametrization corresponds the following age specific retirement rates

(11.9) $$b^*(s) = \frac{\tau}{N}\frac{(1 - \frac{s}{N})^{\tau-1}}{(1 - \frac{s}{N})^{\tau}} = \frac{\tau}{N - s}, \quad 0 \le s < N,$$

i.e. these rates are increasing in inverse proportion to the remaining life time, $N - s$, τ being the factor of proportionality. A basic difference between the concave and the convex class is thus that for the former, $b(s)$ and $b^*(s)$ are both increasing with age (when $\sigma > 1$), whereas for the latter, $b(s)$ is decreasing and $b^*(s)$ is increasing (when $\tau > 1$).

Since (11.7) implies

$$\int_s^N B(z)\,dz = \frac{N}{\tau+1}\left(1 - \frac{s}{N}\right)^{\tau+1},$$

it follows from (3.23), (3.28), and (3.35) that

(11.10) $$\Phi_0(s) = \Phi_0^V(s; N, \tau) = \frac{N - s}{\tau + 1}, \quad 0 \le s \le N,$$

and hence

(11.11) $$G_0(s) = G_0^V(s; N, \tau) = \left(1 - \frac{s}{N}\right)^{\tau+1} = B^V(s; N, \tau + 1),$$

---

[1] Note that there is the following symmetry between the specified convex and concave survival functions:

$$B^V(s; N, \tau) = 1 - B^C(N - s; N, \tau),$$

and between the corresponding retirement (density) functions:

$$b^V(s; N, \tau) = b^C(N - s; N, \tau).$$

$$(11.12) \quad g_0(s) = g_0^V(s; N, \tau) = \frac{\tau + 1}{N} \left(1 - \frac{s}{N} \right)^\tau = \frac{\tau + 1}{N} B^V(s; N, \tau) ,$$

$$0 \leq s \leq N .$$

There is thus a remarkably simple relationship between the survival function and the weighting function for net capital in the convex case: increase the parameter τ by one to get from the former to the latter. The weighting functions (11.11) and (11.12) are derived under assumption of a zero discounting rate for future capital services. The general case with an arbitrary discounting rate is considered in appendix C.

11.3 Investment data and derived gross and net capital stocks

The procedure for constructing time series for gross and net capital stocks, formally defined in chapter 3, consists in cumulating gross investment series over a period as long as the assumed maximal life time, N, of the capital. The weights are defined once the parameters of the survival function, σ or τ, and the rate of discount, ρ, have been specified [cf. (3.3), (3.51), (3.52), (11.1), and (11.7)], and once an algorithm which converts the continuous time weighting functions $B(s)$ and $G_\rho(s)$ to the discrete time periodicity of the investment data, has been established.

The results to be presented below are based on data on gross investment in machinery in Norwegian manufacturing taken from the national accounts. The data base is the same as in chapter 10, except that here, to ensure homogeneity of the quantity series, machinery is defined exclusive of transport equipment.[2] The maximal life time is set to $N = 25$ years

---

[2] Gross investment (gross fixed capital formation) includes, according to the United Nations' "System of National Accounts" (1968) (SNA),

"The outlays of industries and general government on additions of new durable goods to their stocks of fixed assets less their net sales of similar second-hand and scrapped goods ... The item also includes work in progress on construction projects, significant capital repairs ... The general rule is that acquisitions of assets with a lifetime of at least one year shall be included in gross fixed capital formation. Repair and maintenance expenses are generally counted as intermediate consumption, but are considered gross fixed capital formation if the repairs or maintenance work are so sizeable that the life time of the asset is expected to be extended or result in higher productivity." (Fløttum (1981, pp. 14 and 65).)

This definition is not ideal to the present purpose. In particular, its treatment of transactions in second hand goods and of repairs and maintenance, may violate our assumption that the the survival function is time invariant and independent of the investment flow. With respect to repairs, an additional problem is created by the fact that the investment series have been calculated according to the SNA definition

Table 11.1: Gross investment in machinery in manufacturing, million 1980 kroner.

Year	Gross investment	Year	Gross investment
1937	1107.4	1961	2873.5
1938	1107.4	1962	2942.5
1939	1205.4	1963	3125.1
1940	879.3	1964	2763.4
1941	515.4	1965	2760.6
1942	199.5	1966	3347.4
1943	55.9	1967	4171.6
1944	55.9	1968	3500.6
1945	199.5	1969	2956.6
1946	584.8	1970	3689.2
1947	1190.3	1971	4123.4
1948	1495.2	1972	3743.0
1949	1471.9	1973	4014.5
1950	1337.0	1974	584.9
1951	1122.2	1975	5578.2
1952	1923.6	1976	5743.5
1953	2146.3	1977	6859.2
1954	2230.1	1978	5520.6
1955	1797.7	1979	4892.1
1956	1783.0	1980	5881.3
1957	1886.1	1981	6563.2
1958	1970.1	1982	5129.0
1959	1702.6	1983	4046.2
1960	2229.1	1984	4814.0

which is the value used for machinery in manufacturing in the Norwegian national accounts.[3] The investment data for the years 1937–1984 (which, with $N = 25$, permit the calculation of capital stocks to start in 1962) are given in table 11.1. The investment has been dominated by an upward trend with cyclical variations, except for a sharp drop in the war years.

The aggregation of the capital stock formulae in continuous time to the annual periodicity of the data is carried out as follows. Let year t (in discrete time) be defined as the interval between time $t - 1$ and time t, measured continuously, and let J_t be the gross investment effectuated during year t and K_t be the gross capital stock at the end of year t. We then

---

back to 1967 only, so that figures for earlier years include repairs and maintenance to a larger extent than do figures for later years. On the other hand, the SNA recommendations for transactions in second hand markets have not been fully adopted. In most cases, no adjustment for sales and purchases of old capital goods has been made, i.e. only investment in new equipment is included.

[3] Confer footnote 1 to chapter 10.

have from (3.3), for any integer value of t,

$$(11.13) \quad K_t = \int_0^N B(s)J(t-s)\,ds = \sum_{i=0}^{N-1} \int_0^1 B(i+\tau)J(t-i-\tau)\,d\tau.$$

By definition,

$$J_t = \int_0^1 J(t-\tau)\,d\tau.$$

Assuming that the investment is effectuated at a constant rate during each year, i.e. $J(t-\tau) = J_t$ for all t and $0 \le \tau < 1$, (11.13) can be rewritten as

$$(11.14) \qquad\qquad K_t = \sum_{i=0}^{N-1} B_i J_{t-i},$$

where B_i are the discrete time survival rates, given by

$$(11.15) \qquad B_i = \int_0^1 B(i+\tau)\,d\tau, \qquad i = 0, 1, \ldots, N-1.$$

Similarly, the net capital stock at the end of year t in discrete time notation is

$$(11.16) \qquad\qquad K_{Nt} = \sum_{i=0}^{N-1} G_{\rho i} J_{t-i},$$

where $G_{\rho i}$ are the discrete time weights, given by [cf. (3.51)]

$$(11.17) \qquad
\begin{aligned}
G_{\rho i} &= \int_0^1 G_\rho(i+\tau)\,d\tau \\[2mm]
&= \frac{\int_0^1 \int_{i+\tau}^N e^{-\rho(z-i-\tau)} B(z)\,dz\,d\tau}{\int_0^N e^{-\rho z} B(z)\,dz}, \qquad i = 0, 1, \ldots, N-1.
\end{aligned}$$

Eqs. (11.14) and (11.16), with B_i and $G_{\rho i}$ calculated numerically by means of Simpson's formula, enable us to compute annual series for the end of the year gross and net capital stocks from annual investment data for any survival function specified.[4] Table 11.2 gives the gross capital stock for the years 1965–1984 thus computed for four (strictly) concave (σ = 5, 4, 3, and 2) and four (strictly) convex (τ = 2, 3, 4, and 5) survival functions, as well as under simultaneous retirement ($\sigma \to \infty$ or $\tau = 0$) and linear retirement ($\sigma = 1$ or $\tau = 1$). The corresponding net capital stocks, assuming a zero discounting rate ($\rho = 0$), are reported in table 11.3. The net stocks for τ = 0, 1, 2, 3, and 4 coincide (apart from numerical inaccuracy in the sixth digit) with the gross stocks for τ = 1, 2, 3, 4, and 5, respectively, which is a consequence of the relationship which exists between the two sets of weighting functions, (11.11). In any year, the capital stocks are lower the lower is the value of σ for the concave class, and the higher is the value of τ for the convex class.

The net/gross stock ratio, given in table 11.4, is time dependent and its mean value over the period considered varies from around 0.60 under simultaneous retirement, via 0.73 under linear retirement ($\tau = 1$), to 0.87 for the strongly convex survival function ($\tau = 5$). Its fluctuations reflect the cyclical variations in gross investment [cf. table 11.1]. Consider, as a benchmark, a sitation with constant investment, i.e. stationarity. From (11.1), (11.4), and (11.5) it follows that the value of the net/gross stock ratio in this situation for the *concave* class is equal to

$$
\begin{aligned}
\frac{K_N}{K} &= \frac{\int_0^N G_0^C(s; N, \sigma)\, ds}{\int_0^N B^C(s; N, \sigma)\, ds} \\
(11.18) \qquad &= \frac{\frac{\sigma+1}{\sigma}\, \Phi_0^C(0; N, 1) - \frac{1}{\sigma}\, \Phi_0^C(0; N, \sigma + 1)}{\Phi_0^C(0; N, \sigma)} \\
&= \frac{(\sigma + 1)^2}{2\sigma(\sigma + 2)} .
\end{aligned}
$$

The corresponding ratio for the *convex* class under stationarity, obtained

---

[4] Note that, in the zero discounting case ($\rho = 0$), (11.15) and (11.17) imply the following exact discrete time relationship between the weighting functions for gross and net capital

$$
G_{0i} = \frac{B_i + B_{i+1} + \cdots + B_{N-1}}{B_0 + B_1 + \cdots + B_{N-1}}, \qquad i = 0, \ldots, N-1.
$$

With a non-zero interest rate, no such exact relationship holds in general.

Table 11.2: Gross capital stock, machinery in manufacturing, million 1980 kroner, for different survival functions. $N = 25$ years.

Year	Concave				
	$\sigma \to \infty$	$\sigma = 5$	$\sigma = 4$	$\sigma = 3$	$\sigma = 2$
1965	40359.4	38311.9	37509.1	36091.1	33281.6
1966	43191.4	41066.0	40141.3	38548.8	35468.5
1967	47163.5	44567.4	43507.1	41729.7	38370.8
1968	50609.1	47249.3	46053.8	44095.2	40462.7
1969	53510.6	49189.2	47870.0	45745.0	41853.7
1970	57000.3	51637.5	50214.6	47944.3	43815.9
1971	60538.9	54306.5	52801.1	50406.4	46060.4
1972	63091.6	56445.2	54868.2	52358.3	47800.7
1973	65610.9	58777.5	57125.8	54495.2	49717.5
1974	68724.0	61619.0	59884.9	57123.5	52113.4
1975	72965.2	65361.9	63542.1	60645.5	55395.5
1976	77586.6	69120.3	67223.6	64198.1	58708.9
1977	82522.2	73865.9	71897.8	68745.2	63009.3
1978	85896.5	77235.4	75181.0	71883.8	65870.4
1979	88558.5	79962.4	77800.7	74331.0	68003.8
1980	92642.1	83624.3	81336.1	77673.2	71005.2
1981	97422.3	87844.6	85422.8	81557.7	74535.6
1982	100665.0	90486.7	87927.3	83854.0	76467.7
1983	102741.0	91890.4	89190.8	84904.6	77149.9
1984	105853.0	93856.3	91023.8	86530.7	78418.7

Year	Convex				
	$\tau = 1$	$\tau = 2$	$\tau = 3$	$\tau = 4$	$\tau = 5$
1965	26440.3	19599.0	15567.1	12926.8	11062.5
1966	28121.4	20774.3	16507.6	13728.6	11769.8
1967	30492.5	22614.2	18094.8	15156.9	13083.4
1968	32043.4	23624.1	18837.4	15724.7	13523.0
1969	32922.4	23991.1	18951.1	15677.3	13363.8
1970	34407.2	24998.5	19718.2	16295.9	13884.4
1971	36185.6	26310.9	20782.2	17204.7	14689.3
1972	37460.3	27119.9	21337.0	17601.9	14981.4
1973	38905.0	28092.5	22057.7	18170.1	15450.3
1974	40808.4	29503.3	23208.3	19162.0	16337.2
1975	43559.9	31724.3	25138.6	20906.2	17950.1
1976	46300.1	33891.3	26971.7	22515.7	19394.4
1977	49965.4	36921.5	29613.6	24889.1	21563.4
1978	52123.3	38376.1	30642.3	25623.7	22076.1
1979	53530.8	39057.7	30911.7	25623.1	21883.7
1980	55794.9	40584.4	32042.1	26504.9	22598.2
1981	58564.7	42593.9	33645.2	27853.7	23776.1
1982	59737.4	43007.0	33662.9	27631.7	23399.3
1983	59718.9	42287.9	32611.6	26404.0	22078.5
1984	60366.3	42313.8	32373.2	26051.4	21687.9

Table 11.3: Net capital stock, machinery in manufacturing, million 1980 kroner, for different survival functions. Discounting rate : $\rho = 0$. $N = 25$ years.

Year	Concave				
	$\sigma \to \infty$	$\sigma = 5$	$\sigma = 4$	$\sigma = 3$	$\sigma = 2$
1965	26440.3	23968.0	23472.4	22750.7	21614.9
1966	28121.4	25416.9	24885.2	24114.8	22907.7
1967	30492.5	27541.1	26973.8	26154.3	24873.9
1968	32043.4	28844.4	28241.9	27373.3	26017.5
1969	32922.4	29491.5	28855.7	27939.9	26511.1
1970	34407.2	30767.3	30099.6	29138.0	27638.6
1971	36185.6	32355.4	31655.4	30647.1	29075.3
1972	37460.3	33447.5	32714.1	31657.7	30011.3
1973	38905.0	34704.5	33936.9	32831.4	31109.9
1974	40808.4	36408.8	35605.7	34449.6	32650.8
1975	43559.9	38950.2	38109.4	36899.2	35017.2
1976	46300.1	41476.8	40595.0	39325.6	37351.1
1977	49965.4	44917.9	43990.2	42654.6	40575.5
1978	52123.3	46823.0	45845.2	44437.1	42243.0
1979	53530.7	47952.2	46922.8	45440.7	43130.6
1980	55794.8	49918.7	48837.4	47281.0	44855.6
1981	58564.7	52379.2	51244.7	49611.9	47068.2
1982	59737.4	53237.9	52050.0	50340.7	47679.1
1983	59718.8	52914.4	51676.0	49894.9	47126.0
1984	60366.2	53279.2	51993.7	50147.0	47284.1

Year	Convex				
	$\tau = 1$	$\tau = 2$	$\tau = 3$	$\tau = 4$	$\tau = 5$
1965	19598.9	15567.1	12926.7	11062.4	9672.1
1966	20774.2	16507.5	13728.6	11769.7	10310.0
1967	22614.1	18094.7	15156.9	13083.4	11535.3
1968	23624.0	18837.3	15724.6	13523.0	11875.9
1969	23991.0	18951.0	15677.2	13363.8	11635.8
1970	24998.4	19718.1	16295.9	13884.3	12089.7
1971	26310.8	20782.0	17204.6	14689.2	12821.9
1972	27119.8	21336.9	17601.8	14981.4	13040.4
1973	28092.4	22057.6	18170.0	15450.3	13441.1
1974	29503.2	23208.2	19161.9	16337.2	14253.5
1975	31724.2	25138.5	20906.1	17950.0	15766.2
1976	33891.2	26971.6	22515.6	19394.4	17079.5
1977	36921.3	29613.4	24888.9	21563.4	19083.1
1978	38375.9	30642.1	25623.6	22076.1	19419.4
1979	39057.5	30911.5	25623.0	21883.6	19085.3
1980	40584.3	32041.9	26504.8	22598.2	19684.3
1981	42593.6	33645.0	27853.6	23776.1	20742.9
1982	43006.8	33662.7	27631.5	23399.3	20263.2
1983	42287.7	32611.4	26403.9	22078.5	18897.5
1984	42313.6	32373.0	26051.3	21687.9	18509.2

Table 11.4: Net/gross stock ratio, machinery in manufacturing, for different survival functions. Discounting rate : $\rho = 0$. $N = 25$ years.

Year	Concave				
	$\sigma \to \infty$	$\sigma = 5$	$\sigma = 4$	$\sigma = 3$	$\sigma = 2$
1965	0.65512	0.62560	0.62578	0.63037	0.64946
1966	0.65109	0.61893	0.61994	0.62557	0.64586
1967	0.64653	0.61797	0.61999	0.62675	0.64825
1968	0.63316	0.61047	0.61324	0.62078	0.64300
1969	0.61525	0.59955	0.60279	0.61077	0.63342
1970	0.60363	0.59583	0.59942	0.60775	0.63079
1971	0.59773	0.59579	0.59952	0.60800	0.63124
1972	0.59374	0.59257	0.59623	0.60463	0.62784
1973	0.59296	0.59044	0.59407	0.60246	0.62573
1974	0.59380	0.59087	0.59457	0.60307	0.62653
1975	0.59699	0.59592	0.59975	0.60844	0.63213
1976	0.59675	0.60007	0.60388	0.61257	0.63621
1977	0.60548	0.60810	0.61184	0.62047	0.64396
1978	0.60681	0.60624	0.60979	0.61818	0.64130
1979	0.60447	0.59968	0.60312	0.61133	0.63424
1980	0.60226	0.59694	0.60044	0.60872	0.63172
1981	0.60114	0.59627	0.59989	0.60830	0.63149
1982	0.59343	0.58835	0.59197	0.60034	0.62352
1983	0.58125	0.57584	0.57939	0.58766	0.61084
1984	0.57029	0.56767	0.57121	0.57953	0.60297
Stationarity	0.500	0.514	0.521	0.533	0.563

Year	Convex				
	$\tau = 1$	$\tau = 2$	$\tau = 3$	$\tau = 4$	$\tau = 5$
1965	0.74125	0.79428	0.83038	0.85578	0.87432
1966	0.73873	0.79461	0.83165	0.85731	0.87597
1967	0.74163	0.80015	0.83764	0.86319	0.88167
1968	0.73725	0.79737	0.83476	0.85999	0.87820
1969	0.72871	0.78992	0.82725	0.85243	0.87070
1970	0.72655	0.78877	0.82644	0.85201	0.87074
1971	0.72711	0.78986	0.82785	0.85379	0.87288
1972	0.72396	0.78676	0.82494	0.85112	0.87044
1973	0.72208	0.78518	0.82375	0.85032	0.86996
1974	0.72297	0.78663	0.82565	0.85258	0.87246
1975	0.72829	0.79240	0.83163	0.85860	0.87834
1976	0.73199	0.79583	0.83479	0.86137	0.88064
1977	0.73894	0.80206	0.84046	0.86638	0.88497
1978	0.73625	0.79847	0.83622	0.86155	0.87966
1979	0.72963	0.79143	0.82891	0.85406	0.87213
1980	0.72738	0.78951	0.82719	0.85260	0.87105
1981	0.72729	0.78990	0.82786	0.85360	0.87243
1982	0.71993	0.78273	0.82083	0.84683	0.86597
1983	0.70811	0.77118	0.80965	0.83618	0.85592
1984	0.70095	0.76507	0.80472	0.83250	0.85344
Stationarity	0.667	0.750	0.800	0.833	0.857

Table 11.5: Retirement rate (retirement/gross capital stock), machinery in manufacturing, for different survival functions. Per cent. $N = 25$ years.

Year	Concave				
	$\sigma \to \infty$	$\sigma = 5$	$\sigma = 4$	$\sigma = 3$	$\sigma = 2$
1965	2.179	1.556	1.844	2.329	3.270
1966	1.193	1.445	1.782	2.308	3.272
1967	0.423	1.504	1.852	2.374	3.308
1968	0.109	1.733	2.071	2.574	3.482
1969	0.103	2.067	2.382	2.857	3.741
1970	0.350	2.403	2.678	3.107	3.941
1971	0.966	2.678	2.911	3.296	4.079
1972	1.887	2.842	3.054	3.421	4.190
1973	2.279	2.862	3.076	3.446	4.219
1974	2.142	2.829	3.049	3.425	4.200
1975	1.832	2.808	3.023	3.391	4.145
1976	1.446	2.872	3.067	3.413	4.139
1977	2.331	2.861	3.039	3.363	4.061
1978	2.499	2.785	2.975	3.314	4.037
1979	2.518	2.708	2.922	3.289	4.057
1980	1.940	2.654	2.884	3.269	4.056
1981	1.830	2.667	2.899	3.284	4.069
1982	1.874	2.748	2.985	3.378	4.181
1983	1.918	2.876	3.120	3.528	4.360
1984	1.609	3.035	3.275	3.684	4.521
Stationarity	4.000	4.800	5.000	5.333	6.000

Year	Convex				
	$\tau = 1$	$\tau = 2$	$\tau = 3$	$\tau = 4$	$\tau = 5$
1965	5.952	10.506	14.755	18.847	22.880
1966	5.925	10.456	14.581	18.542	22.431
1967	5.905	10.311	14.282	18.099	21.844
1968	6.085	10.543	14.641	18.651	22.635
1969	6.310	10.794	15.001	19.161	23.315
1970	6.407	10.728	14.819	18.842	22.821
1971	6.480	10.684	14.721	18.684	22.591
1972	6.589	10.819	14.942	19.009	23.035
1973	6.605	10.828	14.933	18.967	22.948
1974	6.571	10.758	14.798	18.750	22.636
1975	6.489	10.583	14.511	18.339	22.091
1976	6.487	10.553	14.498	18.360	22.167
1977	6.392	10.371	14.241	18.023	21.751
1978	6.452	10.595	14.659	18.678	22.685
1979	6.510	10.781	14.955	19.095	23.235
1980	6.483	10.730	14.827	18.863	22.863
1981	6.477	10.691	14.742	18.721	22.650
1982	6.623	10.965	15.184	19.366	23.530
1983	6.806	11.269	15.631	19.974	24.309
1984	6.902	11.316	15.607	19.833	23.998
Stationarity	8.000	12.000	16.000	20.000	24.000

Table 11.6: Depreciation rate (depreciation/net capital stock), machinery in manufacturing, for different survival functions. Per cent. Discounting rate : $\rho = 0$. $N = 25$ years.

Year	Concave				
	$\sigma \to \infty$	$\sigma = 5$	$\sigma = 4$	$\sigma = 3$	$\sigma = 2$
1965	5.952	7.432	7.745	8.209	8.976
1966	5.925	7.470	7.774	8.225	8.969
1967	5.905	7.434	7.723	8.152	8.866
1968	6.085	7.618	7.905	8.335	9.059
1969	6.310	7.831	8.119	8.554	9.290
1970	6.407	7.844	8.124	8.549	9.268
1971	6.480	7.835	8.111	8.530	9.240
1972	6.589	7.926	8.206	8.631	9.353
1973	6.605	7.946	8.226	8.653	9.373
1974	6.571	7.912	8.190	8.612	9.323
1975	6.489	7.797	8.068	8.479	9.172
1976	6.487	7.756	8.025	8.435	9.128
1977	6.392	7.610	7.875	8.276	8.958
1978	6.452	7.722	7.996	8.412	9.121
1979	6.510	7.847	8.129	8.557	9.285
1980	6.483	7.842	8.122	8.547	9.266
1981	6.477	7.833	8.110	8.531	9.243
1982	6.623	8.021	8.307	8.741	9.476
1983	6.806	8.258	8.554	9.003	9.760
1984	6.902	8.351	8.648	9.097	9.847
Stationarity	8.000	9.333	9.600	10.000	10.667

Year	Convex				
	$\tau = 1$	$\tau = 2$	$\tau = 3$	$\tau = 4$	$\tau = 5$
1965	10.506	14.755	18.847	22.880	26.893
1966	10.456	14.581	18.542	22.431	26.281
1967	10.311	14.282	18.099	21.844	25.542
1968	10.543	14.641	18.651	22.635	26.608
1969	10.794	15.001	19.161	23.316	27.472
1970	10.728	14.819	18.842	22.821	26.761
1971	10.684	14.721	18.685	22.591	26.448
1972	10.819	14.942	19.009	23.035	27.028
1973	10.828	14.933	18.967	22.948	26.886
1974	10.758	14.798	18.751	22.636	26.467
1975	10.583	14.511	18.340	22.091	25.786
1976	10.553	14.498	18.360	22.167	25.939
1977	10.371	14.242	18.024	21.751	25.445
1978	10.595	14.660	18.678	22.685	26.697
1979	10.780	14.954	19.095	23.235	27.383
1980	10.730	14.827	18.863	22.863	26.836
1981	10.691	14.742	18.721	22.650	26.537
1982	10.965	15.184	19.366	23.530	27.680
1983	11.269	15.631	19.973	24.309	28.638
1984	11.316	15.607	19.833	23.998	28.106
Stationarity	12.000	16.000	20.000	24.000	28.000

from (11.7), (11.10), and (11.11), is

$$
(11.19) \qquad \frac{K_N}{K} = \frac{\int_0^N G_0^V(s;N,\tau)\,ds}{\int_0^N B^V(s;N,\tau)\,ds} = \frac{\Phi_0^V(0;N,\tau+1)}{\Phi_0^V(0;N,\tau)} = \frac{\tau+1}{\tau+2}.
$$

These "theoretical" ratios are given in the bottom line of table 11.4. With one exception (the year 1984 for the two most strongly convex survival functions, i.e. $\tau = 4$ and $\tau = 5$), they are smaller than the net/gross stock ratios based on actual data, e.g. 0.5 under simultaneous retirement ($\sigma \to \infty$ or $\tau = 0$), 0.67 under linear retirement ($\sigma = 1$ or $\tau = 1$), and 0.86 for the most strongly convex survival function ($\tau = 5$).

Corresponding series for retirement and depreciation in year t are obtained from the discrete time counterpart to the 'exact' formulae in continuous time, (3.4) and (3.53), i.e.

$$
(11.20) \qquad D_t = J_t - (K_t - K_{t-1}),
$$

and

$$
(11.21) \qquad D_{Nt} = J_t - (K_{Nt} - K_{Nt-1}),
$$

respectively. The implied values of the retirement rate D_t/K_t and the depreciation rate D_{Nt}/K_{Nt} are reported in tables 11.5 and 11.6. These rates also vary cyclically, reflecting the fluctuations in past investments. The retirement rate increases from an average of around 1.5 per cent under simultaneous retirement, via 6–7 per cent under linear retirement, to 22–23 per cent for the strongly convex survival function ($\tau = 5$). The corresponding average values of the depreciation rates are about 6 per cent, 10 per cent, and 26 per cent, respectively.

Under stationarity, retirement and depreciation both coincide with the (constant) gross investment flow ($D = D_N = J$). The implied retirement and depreciation rates, for the *concave* class of survival functions, are

$$
(11.22) \qquad \frac{D}{K} = \frac{1}{\int_0^N B^C(s;N,\sigma)\,ds} = \frac{1}{\Phi_0^C(0;N,\sigma)} = \frac{\sigma+1}{\sigma}\frac{1}{N},
$$

$$
\frac{D_N}{K_N} = \frac{1}{\int_0^N G_0^C(s;N,\sigma)\,ds}
$$

$$
(11.23) \qquad = \frac{1}{\frac{\sigma+1}{\sigma}\Phi_0^C(0;N,1) - \frac{1}{\sigma}\Phi_0^C(0;N,\sigma+1)}
$$

$$= \frac{\sigma + 2}{\sigma + 1} \frac{2}{N},$$

respectively, and for the *convex* class,

$$(11.24) \quad \frac{D}{K} = \frac{1}{\int_0^N B^V(s; N, \tau)\, ds} = \frac{1}{\Phi_0^V(0; N, \tau)} = \frac{\tau + 1}{N},$$

$$(11.25) \quad \frac{D_N}{K_N} = \frac{1}{\int_0^N G_0^V(s; N, \tau)\, ds} = \frac{1}{\Phi_0^V(0; N, \tau + 1)} = \frac{\tau + 2}{N},$$

respectively. These "theoretical" rates — given in the bottom line of tables 11.5 and 11.6 — are decreasing in σ and increasing in τ, and take their lowest value, $D/K = 1/N$ and $D_N/K_N = 2/N$, respectively, under simultaneous retirement. Both rates are, with two exceptions (the years 1083 and 1984 for the two most strongly convex survival functions, i.e. $\tau = 4$ and $\tau = 5$), larger than the rates based on actual data.

11.4 Numerical computation of the discounted per unit service function

In this section, we discuss procedures for efficiently computing the discounted per unit service flow function $\Phi_\rho(s)$, and the discounted per unit retirement flow function $\Psi_\rho(s)$ for the concave and the convex classes of survival functions with an arbitrary discounting rate ρ. These functions are basic elements in the calculation of time series for the user cost, the net capital stock, and the depreciation. Below, only the case $s = 0$ will be considered. Generalizations valid for any value of s between 0 and N are discussed in appendix C. The algorithms will be useful, inter alia, in decomposing the user cost into interest and depreciation terms.

11.4.1 An auxiliary function

Consider an auxiliary function defined by the integral

$$(11.26) \quad D(i, x) = \int_0^1 e^{x\theta}(1 - \theta)^i\, d\theta,$$

where i is a non-negative integer constant and x is an arbitrary real (positive or negative) variable. For $x = 0$, we have in particular

$$(11.27) \qquad D(i, 0) = \frac{1}{i + 1}, \qquad i = 0, 1, 2, \dots .$$

When $i = 0$, (11.26) implies

$$D(0, x) = \frac{1}{x}(e^x - 1),$$

$(11.28.a)$

$$D(0, -x) = \frac{1}{x}(1 - e^{-x}), \qquad x \neq 0.$$

Otherwise, the function satisfies the recursion

$$D(i, x) = \frac{1}{x}[iD(i - 1, x) - 1],$$

$(11.28.b)$

$$D(i, -x) = \frac{1}{x}[1 - iD(i - 1, -x)], \qquad i = 1, 2, \dots, \quad x \neq 0,$$

which is easily proved by means of integration by parts.

Differentiating (11.26) with respect to x, while using the fact that $\theta(1 - \theta)^i = (1 - \theta)^i - (1 - \theta)^{i+1}$, yields

$$\frac{\partial D(i, x)}{\partial x} = D(i, x) - D(i + 1, x),$$

(11.29)

$$\frac{\partial D(i, -x)}{\partial x} = -[D(i, -x) - D(i + 1, -x)], \qquad i = 0, 1, \dots .$$

By differentiating (11.26) with respect to i we get

$$(11.30) \qquad \frac{\partial D(i, x)}{\partial i} = \int_0^1 e^{x\theta}(1 - \theta)^i \ln(1 - \theta)\, d\theta < 0,$$

$$(11.31) \qquad \frac{\partial^2 D(i, x)}{\partial i^2} = \int_0^1 e^{x\theta}(1 - \theta)^i \{\ln(1 - \theta)\}^2\, d\theta > 0.$$

This shows that $D(i, x)$ *is increasing in x, decreasing in i, and convex in i.*

11.4.2 A recursion procedure

Consider the per unit discounted service flow function of a new capital unit, $\Phi_\rho(0)$, defined in (3.12), and the corresponding per unit discounted retirement flow function, $\Psi_\rho(0)$, defined in (3.14). For the *concave* class [cf. (11.1) and (11.2)], we have

$$\Phi_\rho(0) = \int_0^N e^{-\rho s} \left(1 - \left(\frac{s}{N}\right)^\sigma\right) ds = \frac{1}{\rho}(1 - e^{-\rho N}) - \int_0^N e^{-\rho s} \left(\frac{s}{N}\right)^\sigma ds,$$

$$\Psi_\rho(0) = \frac{\sigma}{N} \int_0^N e^{-\rho s} \left(\frac{s}{N}\right)^{\sigma-1} ds.$$

Substituting $x = \rho N$ and $\theta = 1 - s/N$, i.e. $\rho = x/N$ and $s = N(1 - \theta)$, while using (11.26) and (11.28), these functions can be expressed in terms of $D(i, x)$ as[5]

(11.32) $\quad \Phi_\rho(0) = N e^{-\rho N}[D(0, \rho N) - D(\sigma, \rho N)], \qquad \sigma = 1, 2, \ldots,$

(11.33) $\quad \Psi_\rho(0) = \sigma e^{-\rho N} D(\sigma - 1, \rho N), \qquad \sigma = 1, 2, \ldots.$

For the *convex* class [cf. (11.7) and (11.8)], we have

$$\Phi_\rho(0) = \int_0^N e^{-\rho s} \left(1 - \frac{s}{N}\right)^\tau ds,$$

$$\Psi_\rho(0) = \frac{\tau}{N} \int_0^N e^{-\rho s} \left(1 - \frac{s}{N}\right)^{\tau-1} ds.$$

---

[5] From the recursion (11.28) it is easy to verify that (11.32) and (11.33) satisfy (3.16). Using x as a shorthand for ρN, we find

$$\Psi_\rho(0) + \rho \Phi_\rho(0) = \sigma e^{-x} D(\sigma - 1, x) + e^{-x} x \left[\frac{1}{x}(e^x - 1) - D(\sigma, x)\right]$$

$$= \sigma e^{-x} D(\sigma - 1, x) + 1 - e^{-x} - e^{-x}[\sigma D(\sigma - 1, x) - 1] = 1.$$

By substituting $x = \rho N$ and $\theta = s/N$, i.e. $\rho = x/N$ and $s = N\theta$, we find, in a similar way[6]

(11.34) $\qquad \Phi_\rho(0) = ND(\tau, -\rho N), \qquad \tau = 0, 1, 2, \ldots,$

(11.35) $\qquad \Psi_\rho(0) = \tau D(\tau - 1, -\rho N), \qquad \tau = 1, 2, \ldots.$

Eqs. (11.32)–(11.35), in combination with (11.28), define an algorithm by means of which $\Phi_\rho(0)$ and $\Psi_\rho(0)$ can be computed recursively for any real interest rate ρ and any value of the curvature parameter σ or τ.

11.4.3 An algorithm based on Taylor expansions

If ρ is small and the value of σ or τ is large, the above recursion procedure may, however, be numerically inaccurate since the errors in the successive steps may accumulate.[7] A better way of keeping the accuracy under control, is to represent $D(i, x)$ by its Taylor expansion. Expanding e^x in (11.28.a) by means of Taylor's formula, we get

$$D(0, x) = \frac{1}{x}(1 + x + \frac{x^2}{2!} + \frac{x^3}{3!} + \cdots - 1)$$

$$= 1 + \frac{x}{1 \cdot 2} + \frac{x^2}{1 \cdot 2 \cdot 3} + \frac{x^3}{1 \cdot 2 \cdot 3 \cdot 4} + \cdots.$$

Inserting this expression into (11.28.b), it follows that

$$D(1, x) = \frac{1}{x}[1 \cdot D(0, x) - 1] = \frac{1}{2} + \frac{x}{2 \cdot 3} + \frac{x^2}{2 \cdot 3 \cdot 4} + \frac{x^3}{2 \cdot 3 \cdot 4 \cdot 5} + \cdots,$$

$$D(2, x) = \frac{1}{x}[2 \cdot D(1, x) - 1] = \frac{1}{3} + \frac{x}{3 \cdot 4} + \frac{x^2}{3 \cdot 4 \cdot 5} + \frac{x^3}{3 \cdot 4 \cdot 5 \cdot 6} + \cdots,$$

---

[6] Again, using the recursion (11.28), we can check that (11.34) and (11.35) satisfy (3.16). Using x as a shorthand for ρN, we have

$$\Psi_\rho(0) + \rho \Phi_\rho(0) = \tau D(\tau - 1, -x) + x D(\tau, -x)$$

$$= \tau D(\tau - 1, -x) + 1 - \tau D(\tau - 1, -x) = 1.$$

[7] How serious this problem will be, depends on the numerical accuracy of the computer and the computer program. The calculations in this study were performed by means of the TROLL system on the IBM computer of the Bank of Norway.

and in general

$$D(i, x) = \frac{1}{i+1} + \frac{x}{(i+1)(i+2)} + \frac{x^2}{(i+1)(i+2)(i+3)} + \cdots$$

(11.36)

$$= i! \sum_{j=1}^{\infty} \frac{x^{j-1}}{(i+j)!}, \qquad i = 0, 1, 2, \ldots,$$

which can be verified by induction. This expression generalizes (11.27).

By truncating (11.36) after a suitable number of terms, the numerical accuracy of the computation of $\Phi_\rho(0)$ and $\Psi_\rho(0)$, and hence of the user cost, the net capital stock, and the depreciation, can be kept under control. Similar algorithms can be used for numerical computation of Y_ρ and Z_ρ in the general user cost formula [cf. (6.14)–(6.17)].

11.5 Relations between the capital stock and its user cost. Decomposition of the service value

Table 11.7 contains the service value (user value) of the stock of machinery in Norwegian manufacturing, defined as the product of the user cost of capital and the gross capital stock, for the years 1965–1984. The price component contains the effect of the tax system, which is represented as a MNO system [cf. subsection 5.4.2], with depreciation allowances based on the combined linear and accelerated schedule up to 1981 and the declining balance schedule thereafter [cf. table 10.4]. This tax corrected service value shows substantial year-to-year variations, which mainly reflect the fluctuations in its price component, its quantity component follows a fairly stable growth path [cf. table 11.2].

As shown in table 11.2, the estimated gross capital stock is an increasing function of σ for the concave class of survival functions and a decreasing function of τ for the convex class. The user cost shows the opposite variation, and the latter effect dominates over the former in most of the years. In all the years except 1979 and 1984, the user value of the stock of machinery is a decreasing function of σ and an increasing function of τ.

Table 11.8 shows the value of depreciation, defined as the product of the tax corrected investment price and the volume of depreciation. Table 11.9 gives the corresponding value of the capital stock, defined as the product of the tax corrected investment price and the net capital stock.

Table 11.7: User value of capital stock (tax corrected user cost × gross capital stock), machinery in manufacturing, million 1980 kroner, for different survival functions. $N = 25$ years.

Year	Concave				
	$\sigma \to \infty$	$\sigma = 5$	$\sigma = 4$	$\sigma = 3$	$\sigma = 2$
1965	697.14	814.02	833.56	860.38	900.11
1966	830.96	958.04	977.18	1003.40	1042.37
1967	1016.43	1145.74	1163.92	1189.13	1227.53
1968	1243.74	1359.08	1374.02	1394.92	1427.17
1969	884.55	1029.76	1053.05	1086.41	1138.26
1970	333.43	486.92	514.42	554.35	617.61
1971	1039.15	1202.78	1232.38	1275.16	1342.00
1972	1270.49	1436.49	1466.79	1510.44	1578.06
1973	2736.14	2751.15	2752.38	2753.93	2755.31
1974	289.89	506.54	546.07	603.56	694.76
1975	652.85	949.12	1003.03	1081.13	1204.31
1976	1073.05	1427.20	1493.18	1588.60	1738.90
1977	1686.95	2093.73	2170.47	2281.61	2457.66
1978	1750.08	2265.84	2361.30	2499.26	2716.96
1979	7488.67	7448.57	7432.67	7408.19	7370.02
1980	1471.57	2134.92	2254.36	2426.59	2696.37
1981	5804.25	6212.24	6280.96	6379.87	6533.89
1982	3649.75	4363.79	4489.57	4670.01	4948.21
1983	8160.45	8393.43	8423.05	8462.97	8514.81
1984	10450.30	10281.50	10241.10	10177.50	10062.10

Year	Convex				
	$\tau = 1$	$\tau = 2$	$\tau = 3$	$\tau = 4$	$\tau = 5$
1965	966.55	1101.65	1183.16	1239.26	1280.72
1966	1108.41	1241.25	1322.96	1380.63	1424.20
1967	1296.22	1433.23	1523.80	1591.93	1646.39
1968	1484.88	1600.05	1676.19	1732.33	1775.73
1969	1228.40	1413.47	1531.90	1613.32	1671.41
1970	732.43	1019.21	1225.53	1377.55	1492.47
1971	1459.73	1705.75	1866.94	1980.11	2063.77
1972	1695.00	1934.95	2087.34	2191.32	2266.21
1973	2754.81	2773.81	2784.55	2789.55	2791.62
1974	861.88	1304.04	1632.79	1881.06	2073.97
1975	1428.91	1964.64	2347.25	2634.36	2859.99
1976	2012.79	2628.57	3060.56	3384.30	3639.75
1977	2783.21	3489.92	3990.57	4372.79	4679.91
1978	3112.57	3967.77	4558.63	4996.47	5335.87
1979	7311.86	7282.99	7281.30	7282.88	7279.97
1980	3175.27	4224.06	4924.82	5421.26	5786.85
1981	6802.13	7343.84	7690.43	7929.32	8101.69
1982	5421.58	6365.64	6944.39	7324.50	7584.92
1983	8562.54	8715.10	8751.13	8723.05	8660.41
1984	9827.39	9508.03	9252.82	9027.44	8826.69

Table 11.8: Value of depreciation (tax corrected investment price × volume of depreciation), machinery in manufacturing, million 1980 kroner, for different survival functions. $\rho = 0$. $N = 25$ years.

Year	Concave				
	$\sigma \to \infty$	$\sigma = 5$	$\sigma = 4$	$\sigma = 3$	$\sigma = 2$
1965	497.46	602.80	622.29	649.71	691.47
1966	539.31	655.72	675.66	703.67	746.48
1967	594.32	718.10	738.42	767.27	812.07
1968	656.95	782.61	803.06	832.48	878.95
1969	657.42	800.56	824.45	858.92	913.24
1970	628.20	837.57	871.43	919.26	992.15
1971	872.54	1034.98	1064.02	1106.12	1172.14
1972	977.64	1143.54	1174.39	1219.18	1289.56
1973	1125.77	1262.26	1288.61	1327.25	1388.56
1974	684.11	1047.79	1106.70	1189.03	1312.46
1975	963.04	1315.89	1376.57	1462.78	1594.83
1976	1187.32	1551.95	1618.02	1712.98	1860.89
1977	1562.33	1944.08	2016.45	2121.18	2286.56
1978	1553.72	2032.35	2122.69	2253.83	2461.85
1979	2461.74	2787.94	2853.05	2949.23	3105.93
1980	1401.31	2038.43	2153.95	2320.63	2582.14
1981	2488.41	2959.17	3049.87	3183.94	3400.59
1982	2186.50	2797.91	2913.44	3082.69	3352.79
1983	3061.78	3561.02	3656.44	3797.13	4022.11
1984	3287.23	3722.58	3806.66	3929.97	4124.34

Year	Convex				
	$\tau = 1$	$\tau = 2$	$\tau = 3$	$\tau = 4$	$\tau = 5$
1965	763.99	919.49	1019.90	1091.43	1145.51
1966	821.22	981.10	1085.15	1159.65	1215.93
1967	892.58	1064.65	1181.46	1268.23	1335.96
1968	964.23	1146.18	1273.17	1368.87	1444.07
1969	1010.66	1220.35	1362.35	1464.77	1541.36
1970	1116.08	1384.73	1552.56	1665.17	1744.07
1971	1288.85	1538.81	1704.31	1820.36	1905.20
1972	1414.06	1680.26	1856.86	1980.93	2072.03
1973	1498.40	1730.43	1887.02	1998.55	2081.43
1974	1518.45	1967.30	2239.82	2420.08	2547.44
1975	1823.57	2321.73	2643.23	2868.35	3036.45
1976	2125.16	2702.19	3092.60	3377.66	3598.41
1977	2589.39	3249.97	3712.39	4060.34	4336.19
1978	2844.04	3685.79	4279.22	4725.68	5076.81
1979	3402.56	4033.16	4489.47	4836.30	5107.28
1980	3046.97	4069.95	4755.23	5240.46	5596.39
1981	3801.65	4668.43	5280.76	5732.41	6075.48
1982	3841.65	4905.45	5633.98	6155.61	6541.41
1983	4424.52	5282.32	5855.84	6251.50	6530.15
1984	4465.44	5176.42	5628.43	5922.39	6116.41

Since the fiscal factor depends on the form of the survival function assumed (via the interest deduction component and the capital gains component in the income tax base), both the price and the quantity components of these two variables will be functions of σ or τ. The tax corrected value of depreciation is larger the smaller is σ and the larger is τ, in all the years under investigation. The tax corrected value of the capital stock does not show a uniform variation with changes in the curvature parameters: a decrease in σ leads to a decrease in the value of the capital in about half of the years and to an increase in the other half, an increase in τ leads to a decrease in the capital value in all the years.

In section 4.5, the following decomposition of the user value of the capital services was shown to hold with continuous time and in the absence of taxes [cf. (4.25)]

$$
\begin{aligned}
& \textit{User value of capital services} \quad [c(t)K(t)] \\
=\ & \textit{Real interest on capital value} \quad [\rho q(t)K_N(t)] \\
+\ & \textit{Gross value of depreciation} \quad [q(t)D_N(t)].
\end{aligned}
$$

Of course, its validity will not be changed if all the prices are multiplied by a common fiscal factor. An underlying assumption is that the same (real) interest rate ρ is used in the construction of the net capital, the depreciation, and the user cost. This simple decomposition cannot be expected to hold *exactly* in the case we are considering here, in which we (i) have made an approximation to discrete time, and (ii) have constructed the series for net capital and depreciation on the basis of a zero rate of discount ($\rho = 0$), instead of using the time dependent real market interest rate on which the user cost is based. It will, however, hold as an approximation.

Let c_t and q_t denote the (tax corrected) user cost and the investment price in year t, respectively, and let K_t, K_{Nt}, and D_{Nt} be defined as in (11.14), (11.16), and (11.21). The real interest rates implied by the service value series in table 11.7 ($c_t K_t$), the depreciation value series in table 11.8 ($q_t D_{Nt}$), and the capital value series in table 11.9 ($q_t K_{Nt}$), i.e.

$$
(11.37) \qquad\qquad \rho_t = \frac{c_t K_t - q_t D_{Nt}}{q_t K_{Nt}},
$$

are reported for selected values of σ and τ in the upper part of table 11.10, along with the real interest rates observed. In the lower part of the table are given the corresponding implicit real interest rates when net capital and

Table 11.9: Value of capital stock (tax corrected investment price × net capital stock), machinery in manufacturing, million 1980 kroner, for different survival functions. $\rho = 0$. $N = 25$ years.

Year	Concave				
	$\sigma \to \infty$	$\sigma = 5$	$\sigma = 4$	$\sigma = 3$	$\sigma = 2$
1965	8358.36	8110.68	8034.87	7914.50	7703.71
1966	9101.71	8778.49	8691.34	8555.74	8322.89
1967	10065.30	9659.84	9561.92	9412.13	9158.96
1968	10796.80	10273.40	10159.40	9987.63	9702.23
1969	10417.90	10222.90	10154.50	10041.00	9830.10
1970	9805.21	10677.90	10726.50	10752.80	10704.60
1971	13464.80	13208.90	13118.50	12967.20	12685.00
1972	14836.90	14428.10	14312.20	14124.90	13787.40
1973	17043.00	15886.00	15664.60	15339.00	14814.30
1974	10411.10	13243.20	13513.00	13807.30	14078.00
1975	14840.60	16877.30	17062.80	17252.10	17387.10
1976	18304.10	20010.20	20161.30	20307.80	20385.80
1977	24440.70	25546.80	25607.10	25629.20	25524.20
1978	24082.90	26320.20	26547.90	26792.30	26990.30
1979	37816.80	35526.90	35095.50	34464.70	33452.40
1980	21615.00	25992.70	26519.10	27152.40	27866.80
1981	38418.30	37779.80	37606.90	37322.90	36790.30
1982	33014.20	34881.40	35072.50	35267.10	35381.30
1983	44984.20	43122.80	42746.80	42176.70	41212.00
1984	47624.50	44576.80	44018.40	43200.20	41884.90

Year	Convex				
	$\tau = 1$	$\tau = 2$	$\tau = 3$	$\tau = 4$	$\tau = 5$
1965	7271.96	6231.56	5411.37	4770.16	4259.55
1966	7854.36	6728.48	5852.38	5169.74	4626.69
1967	8656.64	7454.35	6527.62	5805.78	5230.52
1968	9145.64	7828.28	6826.16	6047.64	5427.19
1969	9363.32	8135.09	7109.92	6282.40	5610.64
1970	10403.40	9344.03	8239.74	7296.53	6517.30
1971	12063.90	10452.90	9121.46	8057.86	7203.60
1972	13070.30	11245.20	9768.47	8599.78	7666.26
1973	13837.90	11588.10	9948.88	8708.88	7741.56
1974	14114.00	13294.40	11945.20	10691.50	9624.92
1975	17231.50	15999.20	14412.70	12984.00	11775.40
1976	20138.10	18638.00	16843.80	15237.50	13872.70
1977	24967.70	22820.40	20597.20	18667.30	17041.40
1978	26842.50	25142.60	22910.60	20831.90	19016.60
1979	31562.40	26969.50	23511.10	20815.00	18651.20
1980	28397.80	27449.10	25209.80	22920.70	20854.40
1981	35558.50	31666.60	28208.00	25308.40	22894.40
1982	35034.20	32306.90	29092.40	26161.10	23632.70
1983	39263.50	33794.40	29318.20	25717.10	22802.20
1984	39461.60	33166.80	28379.30	24678.40	21761.60

Table 11.10: Implicit real interest rate = (user value − value of depreciation)/ value of capital stock, per cent (continuous rate). $N = 25$ years.

Year	$\rho = 0$				
	$\sigma \to \infty$	$\sigma = 3$	$\tau = 1$	$\tau = 3$	observed
1965	2.389	2.662	2.785	3.017	2.640
1966	3.204	3.503	3.656	4.064	3.410
1967	4.194	4.482	4.663	5.244	4.301
1968	5.435	5.631	5.693	5.904	5.405
1969	2.180	2.266	2.325	2.385	2.240
1970	−3.006	−3.394	−3.688	−3.969	−4.853
1971	1.237	1.304	1.416	1.783	1.169
1972	1.974	2.062	2.149	2.359	2.002
1973	9.449	9.301	9.080	9.021	8.335
1974	−3.787	−4.240	−4.652	−5.082	−6.266
1975	−2.090	−2.212	−2.290	−2.054	−3.159
1976	−0.624	−0.612	−0.558	−0.190	−1.049
1977	0.510	0.626	0.776	1.351	0.353
1978	0.815	0.916	1.000	1.220	0.793
1979	13.293	12.938	12.386	11.875	11.258
1980	0.325	0.390	0.452	0.673	0.199
1981	8.631	8.563	8.438	8.542	7.785
1982	4.432	4.501	4.510	4.504	4.348
1983	11.334	11.063	10.539	9.875	9.585
1984	15.041	14.462	13.588	12.771	11.882

Year	$\rho = 0.10$				
	$\sigma \to \infty$	$\sigma = 3$	$\tau = 1$	$\tau = 3$	observed
1965	3.487	3.318	3.175	3.126	2.640
1966	4.125	3.933	3.895	4.104	3.410
1967	4.858	4.708	4.778	5.256	4.301
1968	5.748	5.630	5.682	5.897	5.405
1969	3.044	2.768	2.649	2.518	2.240
1970	−1.157	−1.960	−2.700	−3.532	−4.853
1971	2.032	1.884	1.786	1.911	1.169
1972	2.547	2.498	2.425	2.452	2.002
1973	8.320	8.407	8.496	8.732	8.335
1974	−1.939	−2.711	−3.587	−4.606	−6.266
1975	−0.629	−1.042	−1.502	−1.719	−3.159
1976	0.504	0.313	0.058	0.083	−1.049
1977	1.402	1.383	1.274	1.579	0.353
1978	1.707	1.665	1.502	1.469	0.793
1979	11.472	11.547	11.522	11.517	11.258
1980	1.345	1.159	0.954	0.870	0.199
1981	7.796	7.867	7.982	8.314	7.785
1982	4.486	4.481	4.485	4.462	4.348
1983	9.675	9.694	9.653	9.427	9.585
1984	12.338	12.292	12.188	12.061	11.882

depreciation are constructed on the basis of a 10 per cent rate of discount ($\rho = 0.10$). The two sets of implicit real interest rates have the same order of magnitude as those observed in the majority of years, 1977 and 1980 being the most notable exceptions.

11.6 Additive decomposition of the user cost

The textbook formula

$$user\ cost = investment\ price \times (real\ interest\ rate + retirement\ rate),$$

which implicitly assumes the survival function to be exponentially declining $[B(s) = e^{-\delta s}]$, splits the user cost into an interest component (investment price × real interest rate) and a retirement component (investment price × retirement rate), the retirement rate being the parameter δ of the survival function [see subsection 4.4.1]. In this section, we discuss a similar decomposition for the convex class of survival functions.

From (11.34), by using the recursion (11.28), it follows that the inverse of the per unit discounted service flow function for a convex survival function can be decomposed in two alternative ways

$$\frac{1}{\Phi_\rho(0)} = \frac{1}{ND(\tau, -\rho N)}$$

(11.38.a) $$= \rho + \frac{\tau}{N} \frac{D(\tau - 1, -\rho N)}{D(\tau, -\rho N)}, \quad \tau = 1, 2, \ldots,$$

or

$$\frac{1}{\Phi_\rho(0)} = \frac{1}{ND(\tau, -\rho N)}$$

(11.38.b) $$= \rho \frac{D(\tau + 1, -\rho N)}{D(\tau, -\rho N)} + \frac{\tau + 1}{N}, \quad \tau = 0, 1, \ldots,$$

This implies that the relative user cost in the absence of taxes [cf. (4.1)] can be interpreted either as the sum of the actual real interest rate and a modified retirement rate,

$$\delta' = \frac{\tau}{N} \frac{D(\tau - 1, -\rho N)}{D(\tau, -\rho N)}, \quad \tau = 1, 2, \ldots,$$

or as the sum of a retirement rate equal to $(\tau + 1)/N$ [cf. (11.24)] and a modified real interest rate,

$$\rho' = \rho \frac{D(\tau + 1, -\rho N)}{D(\tau, -\rho N)}, \qquad \tau = 0, 1, \ldots .$$

The user cost will *not* be the sum of a "pure" interest component and a "pure" retirement component. Since δ' depends on the interest rate ρ, and ρ' depends on the parameters characterizing the retirement process, i.e. τ and N, there will be an *interaction* between the two components.

Since $D(i, x)$ is decreasing in i for all x, we know that

$$\delta' > \frac{\tau}{N} \text{ and } |\rho'| < |\rho| \text{ for all } \rho, \tau, \text{ and } N.$$

Consequently, the relative user cost will always, whenever $\rho > 0$, satisfy the inequality

(11.39)
$$\rho + \frac{\tau}{N} < \frac{\bar{c}}{q} < \rho + \frac{\tau + 1}{N} .$$

This shows that the retirement rate obtained by deducting the real interest rate from the relative user cost, has τ/N as its lower and $(\tau + 1)/N$ as its upper bound. This interval for the implicit retirement rate is $(0, 1/N)$ under simultaneous retirement, $(1/N, 2/N)$ under linear retirement, etc. More precisely, we have

$$\frac{\bar{c}}{q} = \rho + \frac{\tau}{N} + \kappa_1 = \rho + \frac{\tau + 1}{N} + \kappa_2 ,$$

where κ_1 and κ_2 are interaction terms given by

$$\kappa_1 = \delta' - \frac{\tau}{N} = \frac{\tau}{N} \left(\frac{D(\tau - 1, -\rho N)}{D(\tau, -\rho N)} - 1 \right) > 0 ,$$

$$\kappa_2 = \rho' - \rho = -\rho \left(1 - \frac{D(\tau + 1, -\rho N)}{D(\tau, -\rho N)} \right) < 0 , \qquad \text{when } \rho > 0 .$$

The following question arises: how is (11.39) related to the additive decomposition of the user cost ensured in the case of exponential retirement and assumed in the textbook formula? Let, for the convex survival function (11.7), $\tau = \delta N$, where δ is a positive constant, and let N go to infinity. This gives, when we recall the definition $e = \lim_{n \to \infty}(1 + 1/n)^n$,

$$\lim_{\substack{\tau/N=\delta \\ N \to \infty}} B(s) = \lim_{N \to \infty} \left(1 - \frac{s}{N}\right)^{\delta N} = e^{-\delta s},$$

i.e. the convex survival function converges to the simple exponential survival function. Since (11.26), or (11.36), implies

$$\lim_{\substack{\tau/N=\delta \\ N \to \infty}} \frac{D(\tau - 1, -\rho N)}{D(\tau, -\rho N)} = 1, \qquad \text{for alle } \rho,$$

we know that κ_1 will always converge to zero from above and that κ_2 will converge to zero from below or from above according as $\rho > 0$ or $\rho < 0$. This shows that the case with an exponential survival function, in which there exists a strictly additive decomposition of the user cost, can be interpreted as the limiting case of the convex function in which the interval (11.39) for the relative user cost collapses into $\bar{c}/q = \rho + \tau/N = \rho + \delta$.

11.7 The retirement rate. Interpretations based on prices and on quantities

Let us pursue the argument somewhat further. Corresponding to a given retirement process, a retirement rate can be defined in two alternative ways, either on the basis of the implied user cost, i.e. as

$$\text{retirement rate} = \frac{\text{user cost}}{\text{investment price}} - \text{real interest rate,}$$

or on the basis on the volume of the capital flow retired, i.e. as

$$\text{retirement rate} = \frac{\text{retirement}}{\text{gross capital stock}}.$$

We shall call these two definitions the *price related* and the *quantity related* definitions, respectively. They are *not* equivalent in general. This contrasts with the common practice of using estimated time series based on the latter definition as inputs in user cost calculations, by letting

$$user\ cost = investment\ price \times (real\ interest\ rate + \frac{retirement}{gross\ capital\ stock}).$$

The latter would be a valid formula *only if the survival function is exponential*, in which case both definitions would imply a constant retirement rate, equal to the rate of decline of the survival function, δ. Let us now, for the convex class of survival functions, compare the two definitions in a more formal way.

11.7.1 Retirement rate derived from the user cost

From (4.1), (11.28), (11.34), and (11.38) it follows that the price related retirement rate can be written as

$$(11.40.a) \quad \delta_P = \delta_P(\rho, 0, N) = \frac{\bar{c}}{q} - \rho = \frac{1}{N\,D(0, -\rho N)} - \rho = \frac{1}{N\,D(0, \rho N)}$$

for the simultaneous retirement case ($\tau = 0$) and as

$$(11.40.b) \quad \delta_P = \delta_P(\rho, \tau, N) = \frac{\bar{c}}{q} - \rho = \frac{\tau}{N}\frac{D(\tau - 1, -\rho N)}{D(\tau, -\rho N)}, \quad \tau = 1, 2, \dots,$$

for a general strictly convex survival function. The equivalent expressions based on Taylor expansions, obtained by inserting for $D(i, x)$ from (11.36), are

$$(11.41.a) \quad \delta_P = \delta_P(\rho, 0, N)$$

$$= \frac{1}{N}\frac{1}{1 + \frac{\rho N}{2!} + \frac{(\rho N)^2}{3!} + \cdots} = \frac{1}{N}\frac{1}{\sum_{j=1}^{N}\frac{(\rho N)^{j-1}}{j!}},$$

$$(11.41.b) \quad \delta_P = \delta_P(\rho, \tau, N)$$

$$= \frac{\tau}{N}\frac{\frac{1}{\tau} + \frac{(-\rho N)}{\tau(\tau+1)} + \frac{(-\rho N)^2}{\tau(\tau+1)(\tau+2)} + \cdots}{\frac{1}{\tau+1} + \frac{(-\rho N)}{(\tau+1)(\tau+2)} + \frac{(-\rho N)^2}{(\tau+1)(\tau+2)(\tau+3)} + \cdots}$$

$$= \frac{\tau+1}{N}\frac{1 + \frac{(-\rho N)}{\tau+1} + \frac{(-\rho N)^2}{(\tau+1)(\tau+2)} + \cdots}{1 + \frac{(-\rho N)}{\tau+2} + \frac{(-\rho N)^2}{(\tau+2)(\tau+3)} + \cdots}, \quad \tau = 1, 2, \dots$$

The latter formulae can be used to control the numerical accuracy of the calculations.

Since $D(i, x)$ is convex in i [cf. (11.31)], it follows from (11.40) that δ_P is a decreasing function of the real interest rate ρ, i.e.

(11.42) $$\frac{\partial \delta_P(\rho, \tau, N)}{\partial \rho} < 0, \qquad \text{for all } \tau \text{ and } N.$$

11.7.2 Retirement rate derives from quantities

It was shown in subsection 3.2.3 that the vintage specific retirement rates $D(t, s)/K(t, s)$ are, in general, age dependent, so that the overall retirement rate $D(t)/K(t)$ will not be invariant to changes in the age distribution of the capital stock [cf. eqs. (3.9)–(3.11)]. We now assume, for simplicity, that investment has been growing at a constant rate g from time $t - N$ to the current time t, i.e.

$$J(t - s) = e^{-gs} J(t), \qquad 0 \le s \le N.$$

The (relative) age distribution of the (gross) capital stock will then be uniquely determined by g and the form of the survival function. [The demographic analogue to this is that the age distribution of a population depends on the rate of increase of its number of births, which in turn depends on the age specific net reproduction coefficients, and on the age specific death rates.] The gross capital at time t now becomes the following function of the gross investment, its growth rate, the maximal life time, and the curvature parameter of the survival function

$$K(t) = \int_0^N e^{-gs} \left(1 - \frac{s}{N}\right)^\tau J(t)\, ds = ND(\tau, -gN)\, J(t),$$

where the function D is defined as in (11.26). The corresponding expression for the retirement, obtained by inserting (11.8) in (3.4), is

$$D(t) = \begin{cases} J(t - N) = e^{-gN} J(t), & \text{for } \tau = 0, \\ \frac{\tau}{N} \int_0^N e^{-gs} (1 - \frac{s}{N})^{\tau-1} J(t)\, ds \\ \quad = \tau D(\tau - 1, -gN) J(t), & \text{for } \tau = 1, 2, \ldots. \end{cases}$$

Hence, the quantity related retirement rate can be written as

$$(11.43.a) \qquad \delta_Q = \delta_Q(g,0,N) = \frac{D(t)}{K(t)} = \frac{e^{-gN}}{ND(0,-gN)} = \frac{1}{ND(0,gN)}$$

for the simultaneous retirement case ($\tau = 0$) and as

$$(11.43.b) \quad \delta_Q = \delta_Q(g,\tau,N) = \frac{D(t)}{K(t)} = \frac{\tau}{N} \frac{D(\tau-1,-gN)}{D(\tau,-gN)}, \qquad \tau = 1,2,\ldots,$$

otherwise. Owing to the convexity of $D(i,x)$ in i, this retirement rate will be a decreasing function of the growth rate g, i.e.

$$(11.44) \qquad \frac{\partial \delta_Q(g,\tau,N)}{\partial g} < 0, \qquad \text{for all } \tau \text{ and } N.$$

11.7.3 Comparison of the two interpretations

There is a striking similarity between the price related expression for the retirement rate, (11.40), and the quantity related expression, (11.43). Their mathematical form is the same, with the parameters τ and N occupying similar places in the two expressions. The real interest rate ρ plays the same role in the price related expression as does the growth rate of investment g in the quantity related expression. The implication of this result, in combination with (11.42) and (11.44), can be summarized as follows:

Proposition 11.A Assume that the survival function belongs to the convex class, (11.7), and that the real interest rate and the rate of growth of investment are constants equal to ρ and g, respectively. Then

(i) the price related retirement rate δ_P will be a decreasing function of ρ, and the quantity related retirement rate δ_Q will be a decreasing function of g.

(ii) equality of the two retirement rates will be ensured only if the real interest rate is equal to the growth rate of investment ($\rho = g$).

(iii) When ρ is less than/greater than g, then δ_P will be greater than/less than δ_Q.

An illustration is given in table 11.12. During the period of observation, the mean growth rate of investment was slightly less than the mean value of the real interest rate, $g = 0.0293$ and $\rho = 0.0302$ (continuous rates),

Table 11.11: Retirement rates, machinery in manufacturing. Values derived from prices $(\delta_P = c/q - \rho)$ and from quantities $(\delta_Q = D/K)$. Per cent.

Year	$\tau = 0$		$\tau = 1$		$\tau = 3$	
	δ_P	δ_Q	δ_P	δ_Q	δ_P	δ_Q
1965	2.824	2.179	7.212	5.952	15.516	14.755
1966	2.534	1.193	7.015	5.925	15.390	14.581
1967	2.228	0.423	6.804	5.905	15.252	14.282
1968	1.888	0.109	6.565	6.085	15.092	14.641
1969	2.984	0.103	7.320	6.310	15.584	15.001
1970	6.905	0.350	9.968	6.407	17.144	14.819
1971	3.444	0.966	7.629	6.480	15.775	14.721
1972	3.082	1.887	7.386	6.589	15.625	14.942
1973	1.185	2.279	6.040	6.605	14.721	14.933
1974	7.919	2.142	10.681	6.571	17.552	14.798
1975	5.785	1.832	9.198	6.489	16.703	14.511
1976	4.548	1.446	8.365	6.487	16.217	14.498
1977	3.826	2.331	7.884	6.392	15.930	14.241
1978	3.617	2.499	7.744	6.452	15.846	14.659
1979	0.718	2.518	5.648	6.510	14.414	14.955
1980	3.901	1.940	7.934	6.483	15.961	14.827
1981	1.297	1.830	6.128	6.477	14.785	14.742
1982	2.212	1.874	6.793	6.623	15.245	15.184
1983	0.960	1.918	5.858	6.806	14.582	15.631
1984	0.642	1.609	5.580	6.902	14.355	15.607
Mean	3.125	1.571	7.388	6.423	15.585	14.817
St. deviation	1.990	0.786	1.378	0.271	0.862	0.359
Coeff. of corr.	-0.083		-0.072		-0.447	

Table 11.12: Approximate retirement rates, machinery in manufacturing, based on mean values of ρ and g, 1965–1984.[a] Per cent. Mean$(\rho) = 0.03019$. Mean$(g) = 0.02927$.

	$\tau = 0$	$\tau = 1$	$\tau = 2$	$\tau = 3$	$\tau = 4$	$\tau = 5$
δ_P based on mean real interest rate ρ	2.679	7.114	11.33	15.45	19.54	23.60
δ_Q based on mean rate of growth of investment, g	2.714	7.137	11.34	15.47	19.55	23.61
Stationarity[b]	4.000	8.000	12.00	16.00	20.00	24.00

[a] Cf. (11.40) and (11.43).
[b] Cf. table 11.5.

respectively. The corresponding mean values of the retirement rates have the same order of magnitude, δ_P being less than δ_Q for the convex survival functions considered, and also less than the value under stationarity. This is consistent with Proposition 11.A.

The year specific values of the price related and the quantity related retirement rates, defined as $\delta_P = c/q - \rho$ and $\delta_Q = D/K$, respectively, and reported in table 11.11, differ substantially. The former has a larger mean value and a larger standard deviation than the latter, i.e. the quantity related retirement rate is a more smoothly changing time series than its counterpart implied by the (exact) user cost formula. Further, their coefficient of correlation is *negative*. Almost dramatic are the differences for the simultaneous retirement survival function, ($\tau = 0$) (confer in particular the years 1970 and 1974), with a mean value of δ_P which is twice as large as the mean value of δ_Q. These mean values differ significantly from those in table 11.12, and both are smaller than the values under stationarity (i.e. based on $\rho = 0$ and $g = 0$, respectively). On the whole, the results in tables 11.11 and 11.12 demonstrate that the standard treatment of the retirement component in the user cost of capital may be inadequate.

This conclusion is elaborated in tables 11.13 and 11.14, which show the exact and the approximate user cost in the absence of taxes for selected values of τ. The user cost based on the approximate formulae, i.e. on the additive textbook formula $c = q(\rho + \delta_Q)$ with the retirement rate set equal to the retirement/gross capital ratio ($\delta_Q = D/K$), may take negative values. The exact formula $c = q/\Phi_\rho(0)$ always gives positive values. This holds regardless of whether δ_Q is set equal to its year specific value (approximation 1) or equal to its sample mean (approximation 2). Both the absolute (c) and the relative user cost (c/q) show larger dispersion, as measured by their standard deviation, when the approximate, linear formula is used than when using the exact, nonlinear one, the approximate formulae tend to exaggerate the annual changes in the user cost. The exact user cost is a *highly non-linear* function of the real interest rate. In periods with fluctuating interest and inflation rates, as Norway and several other countries have experienced during the last 15 years, the linear approximation may be far too rough for practical purposes. This may be important for macroeconometric model building and corporate tax simulation studies. On the whole, the departure between the exact and the approximate user cost is smaller in the linear case ($\tau = 1$) than under simultaneous retirement ($\tau = 0$). Their correlation, however, is high, in particular under the linear and the strictly convex ($\tau = 3$) survival functions.

Table 11.13: Exact and approximate user cost of capital, machinery in manufacturing. No taxes. Per cent of 1980 investment price
Approx. (1) : Based on year specific retirement rates δ_Q
Approx. (2) : Based on mean of retirement rates δ_Q.

Year	$\tau = 0$			$\tau = 1$		
	Exact	Approx. (1)	Approx. (2)	Exact	Approx. (1)	Approx. (2)
1965	2.27	2.00	1.75	4.09	3.56	3.76
1966	2.52	1.95	2.11	4.42	3.96	4.17
1967	2.80	2.03	2.52	4.76	4.38	4.60
1968	3.13	2.37	3.00	5.14	4.94	5.08
1969	2.34	1.05	1.71	4.28	3.83	3.88
1970	1.03	-2.26	-1.65	2.56	0.78	0.79
1971	2.44	1.13	1.45	4.65	4.04	4.01
1972	2.81	2.15	1.98	5.19	4.75	4.66
1973	5.18	5.77	5.39	7.82	8.13	8.03
1974	1.03	-2.57	-2.92	2.75	0.19	0.10
1975	1.82	-0.92	-1.10	4.20	2.31	2.27
1976	2.66	0.30	0.40	5.57	4.14	4.09
1977	3.45	2.22	1.59	6.81	5.58	5.60
1978	4.00	2.99	2.15	7.75	6.58	6.55
1979	10.78	12.40	11.55	15.22	16.00	15.92
1980	4.10	2.14	1.77	8.13	6.68	6.62
1981	9.42	9.98	9.71	14.43	14.80	14.74
1982	7.36	6.98	6.64	12.50	12.31	12.08
1983	12.15	13.25	12.86	17.80	18.89	18.45
1984	14.42	15.54	15.49	20.11	21.63	21.08

Table 11.14: Exact and approximate user costs, machinery in manufacturing. Summary statistics, 1965–1984.

A. Standard deviation × 100*

	$\tau = 0$	$\tau = 1$	$\tau = 3$
Absolute user cost			
Exact	3.90	5.21	7.44
Approx. (1)	5.13	6.06	8.06
Approx. (2)	4.97	5.92	7.80
Relative user cost			
Exact	3.15	3.69	4.17
Approx. (1)	5.18	5.08	5.21
Approx. (2)	5.02	5.02	5.02

B. Coefficient of correlation*

	$\tau = 0$	$\tau = 1$	$\tau = 3$
Absolute user cost			
Exact vs. approx.(1)	0.986	0.994	0.997
Exact vs. approx.(2)	0.981	0.993	0.998
Relative user cost			
Exact vs. approx.(1)	0.979	0.997	0.999
Exact vs. approx.(2)	0.985	0.996	0.999

* See table 11.13.

11.8   The survival function and the degree of substitution between capital and labour

In;substitution this final section, we reconsider the duality between the capital stock and the user cost from another point of view. Consider a firm with a neo-classical technology, whose output Q can be expressed as a function of the labour input L (measured in manhours), the input of capital in machinery K_M, and the input of capital in buildings and structures K_B, in the following way

$$Q = F[\,G(L, K_M), K_B\,]\,,$$

i.e. we assume a separability between K_B on the one hand and L and K_M on the other. The firm pursues a cost minimizing strategy. The first-order conditions for this are

$$\frac{\dfrac{\partial Q}{\partial L}}{\dfrac{\partial Q}{\partial K_B}} = \frac{\dfrac{\partial F}{\partial G}\dfrac{\partial G}{\partial L}}{\dfrac{\partial F}{\partial K_B}} = \frac{w}{c_B}\,, \qquad \frac{\dfrac{\partial Q}{\partial K_M}}{\dfrac{\partial Q}{\partial K_B}} = \frac{\dfrac{\partial F}{\partial G}\dfrac{\partial G}{\partial K_M}}{\dfrac{\partial F}{\partial K_B}} = \frac{c_M}{c_B}\,,$$

where w is the (hourly) wage rate and c_M and c_B are the user costs of machinery and buildings/structures, respectively. It follows that the marginal rate of substitution between machinery and labour is

(11.45)
$$\frac{\dfrac{\partial G}{\partial L}}{\dfrac{\partial G}{\partial K_M}} = \frac{w}{c_M}\,.$$

   Assume that the substitution between labour and machinery can be described by the linear homogeneous CES function,

(11.46) $G(L, K_M) = (\mu L^{-\rho} + (1-\mu)K_M^{-\rho})^{-1/\rho}\,, \qquad \rho > -1,\quad 0 < \mu < 1\,,$

while F may be any function satisfying neo-classical assumptions. From (11.45) and (11.46) it follows that

$$\frac{\mu}{1-\mu}\left(\frac{L}{K_M}\right)^{-\rho-1} = \frac{w}{c_M}\,.$$

From this we derive

(11.47) $\ln(K_M/L) = k - \sigma_{ML}\ln(c_M/w)\,,$

where $\sigma_{ML} = 1/(1 + \rho)$ is the elasticity of substitution between machinery and labour, and k is a constant. If the price ratio c_M/w is treated as exogenous and is assumed to be *measured without error*, an ordinary least squares regression on (11.47) will give unbiased and consistent estimates of k and σ_{ML}, provided its (additive) disturbance term satisfies the classical assumptions. The assumption of an error free measurement of c_M/w implies, *inter alia*, that the survival function $B(s)$ is measured without error, since the present value of $B(s)$ is a component in the user cost formula.

This simple property of the CES technology under cost minimization and classical assumptions about the disturbances can be utilized to investigate empirically the sensitivity of the degree of substitution between labour and machinery to the assumed form of the survival function, provided the latter has been correctly specified. A change in the survival function, as noted in section 11.5, will change the gross capital stock and the user cost of capital, i.e. it will affect both the left hand side and the right hand side variable of (11.47).

The statistical model used for this investigation is a dynamic version of (11.47), in which lagged values of the left and right hand variables are included along with the current ones, i.e. it has the form

$$
\begin{aligned}
\ln(K_M/L)_t = C &+ a_0 \ln(c_M/w)_t + a_1 \ln(c_M/w)_{t-1} \\
&+ b_1 \ln(K_M/L)_{t-1} + u_t ,
\end{aligned}
$$

(11.48)

where C, a_0, a_1, and b_1 are constants and u_t is a disturbance assumed to be a zero mean white noise. To facilitate its economic interpretation, this equation is reparametrized into an *error correction equation* [cf. Hendry, Pagan, and Sargan (1984, pp. 1048–1049), Hendry (1986), and Engle and Granger (1987)] in the following way

$$
\begin{aligned}
\ln(K_M/L)_t &- \ln(K_M/L)_{t-1} \\
&= -\alpha_{ML}[\ln(c_M/w)_t - \ln(c_M/w)_{t-1}] \\
&\quad + \gamma[k - \sigma_{ML} \ln(c_M/w)_{t-1} \\
&\quad - \ln(K_M/L)_{t-1}] + u_t ,
\end{aligned}
$$

(11.49)

where $\alpha_{ML} > 0$, $\sigma_{ML} > 0$, $0 < \gamma < 1$, and where the one-to-one correspondence between the coefficients is given by

$$
-\alpha_{ML} = a_0 , \quad \gamma = 1 - b_1 , \quad k = \frac{C}{1 - b_1} , \quad -\sigma_{ML} = \frac{a_0 + a_1}{1 - b_1} ,
$$

i.e.,

$$a_0 = -\alpha_{ML}, \quad b_1 = 1 - \gamma, \quad C = \gamma k, \quad a_1 = \alpha_{ML} - \gamma\sigma_{ML}.$$

This equation says that the (logarithmic) increase in the capital/labour ratio has two components. The first, which may be denoted as the short run effect, is represented by the (logarithmic) increase in the relative user cost/wage rate. Its coefficient, α_{ML}, may be denoted as the short run elasticity of substitution between machinery and labour. The second component represents the error correction. Consider (11.47) as the long run relationship between the capital/labour ratio and the corresponding price ratio. If the value of $\ln(K_M/L)$ in the previous year is too low (high) in comparison with its long run value, the difference will generate a positive (negative) adjustment in $\ln(K_M/L)$ in the current year. Eq. (11.49) gives the net result of the short run adjustment to the current price increase and the error correction, γ being the speed of error correction.

This error correction equation is estimated by means of ordinary least squares (OLS) for the same concave and convex survival functions $B(s)$ and the same value of the maximal life time ($N = 25$ years) as considered in sections 11.3–11.7. The data on L and w are, like the data on J and q, taken from the national accounts. The user cost of capital contains a tax factor representing a MNO system [cf. subsection 5.4.2], with depreciation allowances based on the combined linear and accelerated schedule up to 1981 and the declining balance schedule thereafter [cf. table 10.4].[8] Results for three versions of the model are reported below. The static version, in which no distinction is made between the short run and the long run elasticity of substitution ($\alpha_{ML} = \sigma_{ML}$) and with a speed of adjustment set equal to one ($\gamma = 1$),[9] is considered in table 11.15.

The estimated elasticity of substitution is highly sensitive to the assumed form of the survival function. It is increasing with decreasing value of the curvature parameter σ for the concave class, from $\sigma_{ML} = 0.11$ for $\sigma \to \infty$ to $\sigma_{ML} = 0.22$ for $\sigma = 2$, and is increasing with increasing value of the curvature parameter τ for the convex class, from $\sigma_{ML} = 0.28$ under linearity ($\tau = 1$) to $\sigma_{ML} = 0.84$ for $\tau = 5$. The low values of the Durbin-Watson statistic (DW), however, indicate that the equation is dynamically misspecified.

---

[8] These assumptions agree with those in table 11.7.

[9] This relation is static since when $\alpha_{ML} = \sigma_{ML}$ and $\gamma = 1$, all terms containing lagged variables cancel against each other.

Table 11.15: Estimates of elasticity of substitution between machinery and labour (σ_{ML}), based on different survival functions. CES function. Standard errors in parenthesis.
Econometric model: Static ($\alpha_{ML} = \sigma_{ML}, \gamma = 1$).
No error of measurement.
Period of estimation: 1966–1984

	σ_{ML}	k	SER	DW	R^2
$\sigma \to \infty$	0.1056 (0.1092)	4.0082 (0.8014)	0.3552	0.1345	0.0663
$\sigma = 5$	0.1546 (0.1281)	3.5954 (0.9021)	0.3366	0.1759	0.0317
$\sigma = 4$	0.1663 (0.1321)	3.4954 (0.9225)	0.3341	0.1856	0.0296
$\sigma = 3$	0.1844 (0.1368)	3.3376 (0.9435)	0.3305	0.2032	0.0289
$\sigma = 2$	0.2159 (0.1442)	3.0622 (0.9738)	0.3245	0.2328	0.0325
$\tau = 1$	0.2809 (0.1557)	2.4754 (1.0002)	0.3119	0.2958	0.0539
$\tau = 2$	0.4742 (0.1752)	1.1448 (1.0408)	0.2779	0.4738	0.1052
$\tau = 3$	0.6347 (0.1777)	0.1628 (0.9969)	0.2469	0.6072	0.1602
$\tau = 4$	0.7534 (0.1717)	−0.5057 (0.9220)	0.2205	0.6880	0.2025
$\tau = 5$	0.8371 (0.1628)	−0.9466 (0.8408)	0.1989	0.7273	0.2314

The results in table 11.16 show that the unrestricted error correction model gives a better dynamic specification of the capital/labour adjustment process. We get a substantially lower standard error of residuals (SER) and a DW statistic closer to the acceptable interval. Again, the long run elasticity of substitution is highly sensitive to the assumed curvature of the survival function. The estimate increases from $\sigma_{ML} = 0.38$ for $\sigma \to \infty$, via $\sigma_{ML} = 0.81$ for $\tau = 1$ to $\sigma_{ML} = 0.91$ for $\tau = 5$. The estimated short run and long run elasticities of substitution differ widely, and in no case is the former significantly different from zero. The speed of error correction, γ, is also low. Both the estimate of the short run elasticity and the speed of error correction are increasing with increasing σ over the range from 5 to 1 for the concave class and is increasing with increasing τ over the entire range for the convex class. These conclusions about the long run and short run

Table 11.16: Estimates of elasticity of substitution between machinery and labour (σ_{ML}), based on different survival functions. CES function. Standard errors in parenthesis.
Econometric model: Error correction (σ_{ML}, α_{ML}, γ unrestricted).
No error of measurement.
Period of estimation: 1966–1984

	σ_{ML}	α_{ML}	γ	k	SER	DW	R^2
$\sigma \to \infty$	0.3777 (0.3337)	−0.0032 (0.0077)	0.0285 (0.0220)	4.1429 (2.5416)	0.02351	1.431	0.2400
$\sigma = 5$	0.5860 (0.5268)	−0.0037 (0.0099)	0.0270 (0.0266)	2.6883 (2.9508)	0.02430	1.322	0.2253
$\sigma = 4$	0.6372 (0.5668)	−0.0034 (0.0102)	0.0275 (0.0273)	2.2822 (2.9945)	0.02426	1.318	0.2325
$\sigma = 3$	0.6958 (0.6040)	−0.0029 (0.0108)	0.0289 (0.0281)	1.7742 (3.0687)	0.02429	1.308	0.2437
$\sigma = 2$	0.7567 (0.5609)	−0.0022 (0.0119)	0.0321 (0.0278)	1.1402 (2.9256)	0.02451	1.280	0.2640
$\tau = 1$	0.8062 (0.4125)	0.0000 (0.0143)	0.0426 (0.0261)	0.3639 (2.2949)	0.02518	1.211	0.3129
$\tau = 2$	0.8895 (0.4520)	0.0052 (0.0206)	0.0690 (0.0408)	−0.5913 (2.3225)	0.02730	1.115	0.3793
$\tau = 3$	0.9041 (0.3223)	0.0099 (0.0292)	0.0980 (0.0441)	−0.8581 (1.6422)	0.03010	1.062	0.4101
$\tau = 4$	0.9090 (0.2635)	0.0139 (0.0397)	0.1270 (0.0497)	−0.9769 (1.3152)	0.03327	1.041	0.4219
$\tau = 5$	0.9110 (0.2309)	0.0168 (0.0520)	0.1551 (0.0562)	−1.0404 (1.1279)	0.03662	1.041	0.4229

elasticities of substitution are confirmed for the partial adjustment version of the model (table 11.17), in which the restriction $\alpha_{ML} = \gamma\sigma_{ML}$, i.e. $a_1 = 0$, is imposed a priori.

The coefficients of correlation between the three coefficient estimates in the error correction version of the model are given in table 11.18. Regardless of which survival function is assumed, the estimated long run elasticity of substitution is positively correlated with the short run elasticity and is negatively correlated with the speed of error correction. There is also a positive correlation between the estimated short run elasticity and the estimated speed of error correction, but it is relatively weak in most cases.

Errors of measurement in the survival function may affect the above conclusions. Below is given an illustration of this. Assume that the form of $B(s)$ has been erroneously specified. This error, which may be systematic or random, will affect the series for both the gross capital stock and the

Table 11.17: Estimates of elasticity of substitution between machinery and labour (σ_{ML}), based on different survival functions. CES function. Econometric model: Partial adjustment ($\alpha_{ML} = \gamma\sigma_{ML}$). No error of measurement. Period of estimation: 1966–1984

	σ_{ML}	$\alpha_{ML} - \sigma_{ML}\gamma$	γ	k	SER	DW	R^2
$\sigma \to \infty$	−0.0595	−0.0011	0.0180	8.5912	0.02511	1.551	0.0750
$\sigma = 5$	0.0074	0.0001	0.0136	8.8785	0.02627	1.454	0.0341
$\sigma = 4$	0.0618	0.0008	0.0133	8.5362	0.02640	1.455	0.0308
$\sigma = 3$	0.1420	0.0019	0.0134	7.8658	0.02664	1.452	0.0290
$\sigma = 2$	0.2611	0.0038	0.0147	6.5269	0.02720	1.439	0.0327
$\tau = 1$	0.4252	0.0089	0.0209	4.1204	0.02858	1.411	0.0565
$\tau = 2$	0.6583	0.0242	0.0367	1.4113	0.03162	1.384	0.1116
$\tau = 3$	0.7423	0.0421	0.0567	0.3881	0.03470	1.361	0.1634
$\tau = 4$	0.7909	0.0620	0.0784	−0.1402	0.03782	1.341	0.2030
$\tau - 5$	0.8239	0.0828	0.1005	−0.4601	0.04092	1.324	0.2315

user cost of capital and hence will distort the estimate of the elasticity of substitution. To indicate the nature of this potential bias more precisely, consider the static relationship (11.47) and let the "true", unobserved values of $\ln(K_M/L)$ and $\ln(c_M/w)$ be denoted as η and ξ, while the values measured are Y and X, respectively. With this simplified notation, we have

$$\eta = k - \sigma_{ML}\xi,$$

(11.50) $$\qquad Y = \eta + \varepsilon,$$

$$X = \xi + \delta,$$

where ε and δ are the errors of measurement in Y and X, respectively.[10] For our illustrative purpose, these errors are treated as random, although they will probably also contain a systematic component. Assume that ε and δ have zero means and are uncorrelated with the true value of the (logarithm of the) price ratio ξ. Their variances are $\mu_{\varepsilon\varepsilon}$, $\mu_{\delta\delta}$, and $\mu_{\xi\xi}$, respectively, when we let from now on μ, with appropriate subscripts, denote second order population moments. Allowance is, however, made for correlation between ε and δ, since the errors of measurement in the gross capital stock and its user cost will have errors in the survival function as a common component. A positive shift in $B(s)$ will affect K_M positively and

---

[10] The disturbance term in (11.47) is also included in ε.

Table 11.18: Correlation coefficients of coefficient estimates for different survival functions.
CES function. Error correction model.
Period of estimation: 1966–1984

	σ_{ML}, α_{ML}	σ_{ML}, γ	α_{ML}, γ
$\sigma \to \infty$	0.517	-0.286	0.240
$\sigma = 5$	0.352	-0.603	0.209
$\sigma = 4$	0.318	-0.664	0.192
$\sigma = 3$	0.289	-0.717	0.173
$\sigma = 2$	0.273	-0.695	0.207
$\tau = 1$	0.313	-0.557	0.267
$\tau = 2$	0.275	-0.817	0.023
$\tau = 3$	0.284	-0.725	0.053
$\tau = 4$	0.300	-0.651	0.050
$\tau = 5$	0.317	-0.589	0.031

c_M negatively, so that the error covariance, $\mu_{\varepsilon\delta}$, will usually be negative [cf. section 11.5].

The population covariance between the values of Y and X observed and the variance of the latter will then be given by

$$\mu_{YX} = -\sigma_{ML}\mu_{\xi\xi} + \mu_{\varepsilon\delta},$$

$$\mu_{XX} = \mu_{\xi\xi} + \mu_{\delta\delta}.$$

The probability limit of the OLS estimate of σ_{ML}, i.e. $\sigma_{ML}^{OLS} = -M_{YX}/M_{XX}$, M denoting sample moments, will then (under the usual regularity conditions) be given by

$$\text{plim } \sigma_{ML}^{OLS} = -\frac{\mu_{YX}}{\mu_{XX}} = \frac{\sigma_{ML}\mu_{\xi\xi} - \mu_{\varepsilon\delta}}{\mu_{\xi\xi} + \mu_{\delta\delta}}$$

(11.51)

$$= \sigma_{ML} - \frac{\mu_{\delta\delta}}{\mu_{\xi\xi} + \mu_{\delta\delta}} \left(\sigma_{ML} + \frac{\mu_{\varepsilon\delta}}{\mu_{\delta\delta}} \right).$$

It follows from this that, in the presence of random errors of measurement,

$$\text{plim } \sigma_{ML}^{OLS} \gtreqless \sigma_{ML} \quad \Longleftrightarrow \quad \left(-\frac{\mu_{\varepsilon\delta}}{\mu_{\delta\delta}} \right) \gtreqless \sigma_{ML}.$$

Hence, the OLS estimate of the elasticity of substitution between machinery and labour will be biased unless, by chance, $(-\mu_{\varepsilon\delta}/\mu_{\delta\delta}) = \sigma_{ML}$. A priori, the bias may go in either direction. If, in particular, the errors of measurement in the price and the quantity variable perfectly cancel against each other, so that the value of the capital input, $c_M K_M$, is correctly measured, i.e. if $\delta = -\varepsilon$, so that $\mu_{\varepsilon\delta} = -\mu_{\delta\delta}$, then the estimate will be biased against one. If the errors are uncorrelated, which is the customary textbook assumption for errors-in-variables models [cf. e.g. Kmenta (1986, p. 347)], the bias goes towards zero. Further information about the error structure — which will necessitate a closer empirical analysis of the survival function — will be needed to describe the potential bias in the estimated elasticity of substitution more precisely.

CHAPTER 12

CONCLUDING REMARKS

The primary concern of this study has been the concept of the price of capital services — the user cost of capital — and its measurement. The setting has, in several ways, been more general than what is common in the literature. Throughout, we have emphasized the relationship between the user cost of capital, the properties of the corporate income tax system, and the specification of the production technology of the firm. We have parametrized the corporate tax system in a flexible way, with respect to the treatment of interest deductions, depreciation allowances, and capital gains, and with respect to indexation of the income tax base. Concerning the technology, two aspects have been in focus: the form of the retirement process of the capital and the degree of input substitution. In this concluding chapter, we summarize briefly the main results.

First, the study has highlighted the role that ex post substitution between capital and other inputs plays in the analysis of the user cost of capital, by giving a parallel treatment of the neo-classical and the putty-clay technology. The user cost of capital can be given either a service price or a shadow price interpretation, and its 'dimension' under a putty-clay technology is different from what it is when the full capital malleability assumption of the neo-classical model is adopted. The variables motivating the producers' output and investment decisions under the former technology are life cycle prices for output and non-capital inputs, and the investment price. Under the latter technology, the relevant prices are the instantaneous prices of output and non-capital inputs, and the user cost of capital. Furthermore, under the putty-clay technology, the relevant price variables depend on the firms' plans for scrapping of the capital equipment.

Second, the study has shown how to represent, in a flexible way, the effect of the corporate tax system on the user cost of capital for both kinds of production technologies. With this representation of the user cost, the study has discussed the conditions for neutrality of the tax system and has compared different indicators of its departure from neutrality. These indicators can all be expressed as functions of the present value of the net deductions allowed in the income tax base per unit invested, and the income tax rate. The present value of the net deductions in the income tax base per unit invested is in fact a basic parameter characterizing the effect of the tax system on the user cost of capital. The relative distortion of the user cost of capital is one neutrality indicator which is useful for empirical applications, and it is related in a fairly simple way to the effective rate of corporate taxation according to the more familiar definition. By using the concept of a 'neutrality locus', the study has shown how to distinguish between uniformly neutral tax systems and systems ensuring neutrality for certain values of tax parameters and market variables (interest rate, inflation rate, survival function etc.) only.

Third, one of the principal objectives of the study has been to show how to operationalize, in user cost calculatons, retirement patterns for capital which depart from the well-known and frequently used exponential decay assumption. This extension of the model has made it necessary, when describing the effect of the tax system, to specify two distinct capital concepts, one representing the capital's capacity dimension — the gross capital stock — and the other representing its wealth dimension — the net capital stock. These two concepts coincide numerically under exponential decay, but differ for other retirement patterns.

Fourth, the study has, by exploiting the duality which exists between the capital stock and its user cost, thrown light on some measurement problems which arise at the interface between the two variables. One conclusion is that the estimated effect on the capital/labour ratio induced by corresponding relative input price changes may be very sensitive to the assumed form (concave, linear, convex) of the retirement pattern of the capital. Another conclusion is that if the true survival function departs from exponential decay, then the frequently used linear approximation formulae for the user cost of capital, relating the user cost of capital to the investment price, the real interest rate, and the retirement rate, may be highly misleading. This may in particular be a problem if the correct survival function is concave.

Fifth, the study has given, in the form of time series for a period of 20 years, empirical illustrations of the user cost of capital, neutrality indicators etc., related to the current Norwegian tax system and to potential tax reforms. The data has been taken from the Norwegian manufacturing sector and has, inter alia for the purpose of sensitivity analysis, made use of a flexible parametrization of the retirement process in the form of concave and convex survival functions. Even if certain features of the tax system had to be sacrificed, the results indicate that time series information is essential for this kind of investigation. The results also support the conclusion that the relative distortion of the user cost of capital diminishes as the degree of indexation of the tax base increases from zero to 100 per cent. A fully indexed corporate tax system is more robust towards changes in nominal interest and inflation rates than non-indexed or partially indexed systems.

Without doubt, there is a strong need for empirical evidence on the shape of the survival functions by means of which we could constrain the class of specifications relevant to empirical work on the user cost of capital, gross capital, net capital, and related variables, and on capital accumulation in general. Such information could, at least for the neo-classical technology, be obtained along two lines of research: (i) by observing the actual age distribution of the existing capital stock and the actual scrapping behaviour of the investing firms, or (ii) by observing the development of prices in second hand markets for sufficiently homogeneous types of capital assets and exploiting the arbitrage condition between vintages.

A NOTE ON THE MYOPIC CAPITAL SERVICE PRICE IN THE NEO-CLASSICAL MODEL

In chapter 4, two alternative expressions for the cost of capital services for a neo-classical technology, eqs. (4.1) and (4.3), were derived. The purpose of this appendix is to show that these expressions admit a myopic interpretation of the capital service price and state the assumptions needed.

Let t denote current time, s the age of the capital good, and $t + z$ (where z may be different from s) the time to which the price expectations of the firm refer. We then have, with triple subscripts on the price variables,

$q(t + z, s, t)$: market price expected at time t to prevail at time $t + z$
for a capital unit of age s,

$c(t + z, s, t)$: price expected at time t to prevail at time $t + z$ for a
unit of capital services from capital of age s.

This generalizes the notation in the main text, $q(t + s, s, t)$ corresponding to $q(t + s, s)$, $c(t + z, s, t)$ corresponding to $c(t + z)$, etc.

Consider a firm at time t, planning at time $t + s$ to invest in a capital unit of age s. Its expected price is $q(t + s, s, t)$. The time path of the expected per unit service price from this unit over its remaining service period is given by $\{c(t + z, s, t), z \geq s\}$. We first state the relationship between q and the time path of c. For this purpose we need

Assumption A. Consistency of expectations for capital prices and service prices for any given age.

Assume that the expected capital purchase price for a given age s is consistent with the expected service prices for a commodity bought at age s, in the following sense

Expected purchase price = Present value of expected service cost.

This can be expressed as follows

$$(A.1) \quad q(t+s,s,t) = \int_s^\infty e^{-r(t)(z-s)} c(t+z,s,t) \frac{B(z)}{B(s)} \, dz, \quad \text{for all } s \geq 0,$$

where $r(t)$ is the interest rate at time t and $B(z)/B(s)$ is the share of one unit of capital purchased at age s which will survive at age $z \geq s$. This expression generalizes eq. (4.3) in the main text.

The second assumption is

Assumption B. Age independence of expected future service price.

If a perfect second hand market for capital goods (or a perfect market for capital services) is assumed to exist, the expected price per unit of capital services will be independent of the age of the capital from which the services are obtained. Formally,

$$(A.2) \qquad c(t+z,s,t) = c(t+z,t), \qquad \text{for all } s \geq 0.$$

From (A.1) and (A.2) it follows that

$$(A.3) \quad q(t+s,s,t) = \int_s^\infty e^{-r(t)(z-s)} c(t+z,t) \frac{B(z)}{B(s)} \, dz, \qquad \text{for all } s \geq 0.$$

Since (A.3) holds for any non-negative s, it follows for any θ and $s \geq \theta$ that

$$(A.4) \quad \begin{aligned} &\int_\theta^s e^{-r(t)z} c(t+z,t) B(z) \, dz \\ &= e^{-r(t)\theta} B(\theta) q(t+\theta,\theta,t) - e^{-r(t)s} B(s) q(t+s,s,t), \quad s \geq \theta. \end{aligned}$$

Eq. (A.4) can be interpreted as follows. Consider a new capital unit at time t. The *expected* service cost of this unit from age θ to age s, i.e. from time $t+\theta$ to time $t+s$, shall be equal to the decline in its discounted *expected* resale value between ages θ and s, when taking account of the fact that only a share of the original unit equal to $B(\theta)$ and $B(s)$, respectively, remains at these two ages.

If $\theta = 0$, (A.4) implies in particular, since, by assumption, $B(0) = 1$ and $q(t,0,t) = q(t)$, where $q(t)$, as before, is the market price of a new capital good at time t,

$$\int_0^s e^{-r(t)z} c(t+z,t) B(z) \, dz = q(t) - e^{-r(t)s} B(s) q(t+s,s,t).$$

Differentiating with respect to s, we obtain

$$e^{-r(t)s}c(t+s,t)B(s) = [r(t)B(s) - B'(s)]e^{-r(t)s}q(t+s,s,t)$$
$$- e^{-r(t)s}B(s)\frac{dq(t+s,s,t)}{ds},$$

i.e.

$$c(t+s,t) = q(t+s,s,t)\left[r(t) + \frac{b(s)}{B(s)}\right] - \frac{dq(t+s,s,t)}{ds}$$

(A.5)
$$= q(t+s,s,t)[r(t) + b^*(s)] - \frac{dq(t+s,s,t)}{ds},$$

$$\text{for all } s \geq 0,$$

where $b^*(s)$ is defined as in (3.10). The interpretation of this equation is the following. The service price of capital at time $t+s$ as expected at time t is equal to the corresponding expected vintage price multiplied by the sum of the current interest rate and the age specific retirement rate at age s [cf. subsection 3.2.3] minus the rate of increase of the expected vintage price at age s. For the instantaneous service price at time t, i.e. when $s = 0$, (A.5) gives in particular

$$c(t,t) = q(t,0,t)\left[r(t) + \frac{b(0)}{B(0)}\right] - \frac{dq(t+s,s,t)}{ds}\bigg|_{s=0}$$

$$= q(t)[r(t) + b(0)] - \frac{dq(t+s,s,t)}{ds}\bigg|_{s=0}.$$

This equation says that the service price of capital at time t is known once the firm knows the price of a new capital unit, the interest rate, the age specific retirement rate at age 0, *and the price at which the same unit can be sold at time $t+ds$*, i.e. when it is ds years old. In this sense, we get a 'myopic' expression for the capital service price.

We now go one step further. The (total) derivative of the expected resale price with respect to age in (A.5) has two components, a *time effect* — representing the change in the general price level over time — and a *cohort effect* — representing the ageing, i.e. the effect of the declining expected remaining service flow. This can be expressed as

(A.6)
$$\frac{dq(t+s,s,t)}{ds} = \frac{\partial q(t+s,s,t)}{\partial(t+s)} + \frac{\partial q(t+s,s,t)}{\partial s}.$$

For age $s = 0$, the decomposition reads

$$\frac{dq(t+s,s,t)}{ds}\bigg|_{s=0} = \dot{q}(t) + \frac{\partial q(t+s,s,t)}{\partial s}\bigg|_{s=0},$$

since $\dot{q}(t)$ represents the time effect for a new capital good.

Assume that the firm at time t observes the price of a new capital good, $q(t)$, and its rate of increase, $\dot{q}(t)/q(t) = \gamma(t)$. It forecasts the price of a corresponding new capital unit at time $t + s$ by means of

Assumption C. Exponential price forecasts for new capital goods.

$(A.7)$ $$q(t+s,0,t) = q(t)e^{\gamma(t)s}.$$

At time t, the firm, on the basis of this price forecast, also makes forecasts for the expected remaining service flows per capital unit of age s, discounted at the prevailing real interest rate,

$(A.8)$ $$\rho(t) = r(t) - \gamma(t),$$

i.e. it forecasts [cf. (3.12)]

$(A.9)$ $$\Phi_\rho(s;t) = \frac{\int_s^\infty e^{-\rho(t)(z-s)} B(z)\,dz}{B(s)} = \frac{\int_s^\infty e^{-\rho(t)z} B(z)\,dz}{e^{-\rho(t)s} B(s)}.$$

On this basis we assume that the "structure" of the price forecasts for the vintage prices satisfies

Assumption D. Consistency of vintage price forecasts across vintages at a given time.

$(A.10)$ $$\frac{q(t+s,s,t)}{q(t+s,0,t)} = \frac{\Phi_\rho(s;t)}{\Phi_\rho(0;t)}, \qquad \text{for all } s \geq 0.$$

This assumption says that the ratio between the price of an old and a new capital unit at time $t+s$, as expected at time t, is equal to the ratio between their expected discounted service flows [cf. (3.48)].

Using assumptions C and D, we can find *explicit expressions* for the time effect and the cohort effect, i.e. for the partial derivatives in (A.6). From (A.7) and (A.10) it follows that the time effect is

(A.11)
$$\frac{\partial q(t+s,s,t)}{\partial(t+s)} = \frac{\partial q(t+s,0,t)}{\partial(t+s)} \frac{\Phi_\rho(s;t)}{\Phi_\rho(0;t)}$$

$$= q(t+s,0,t)\gamma(t)\frac{\Phi_\rho(s;t)}{\Phi_\rho(0;t)} = q(t+s,s,t)\gamma(t).$$

The cohort effect is

$$\frac{\partial q(t+s,s,t)}{\partial s} = \frac{q(t+s,0,t)}{\Phi_\rho(0;t)}\frac{\partial\Phi_\rho(s;t)}{\partial s} = \frac{q(t+s,s,t)}{\Phi_\rho(s;t)}\frac{\partial\Phi_\rho(s;t)}{\partial s}.$$

Since it can be shown from (A.9) that

(A.12)
$$\frac{\partial\Phi_\rho(s;t)}{\partial s} = -1 + \left[\rho(t) + \frac{b(s)}{B(s)}\right]\Phi_\rho(s;t),$$

the expression for the cohort effect can be simplified to

(A.13)
$$\frac{\partial q(t+s,s,t)}{\partial s} = q(t+s,s,t)\left[\rho(t) + \frac{b(s)}{B(s)} - \frac{1}{\Phi_\rho(s;t)}\right].$$

Inserting (A.11) and (A.13) in (A.5), while using (A.8) and (A.10), it follows that the capital service price at time $t+s$ as expected at time t is

(A.14)
$$c(t+s,t) = \frac{q(t+s,s,t)}{\Phi_\rho(s;t)} = \frac{q(t+s,0,t)}{\Phi_\rho(0;t)}.$$

The instantaneous service price $(s=0)$ is, in particular,

$$c(t,t) = \frac{q(t,0,t)}{\Phi_\rho(0;t)} = \frac{q(t)}{\Phi_\rho(0;t)}.$$

From this we can conclude that the formulae for the capital service price derived in the main text, i.e. (4.1) and (4.3), agree with (A.5) under assumptions A–D. The four assumptions, however, play different roles. Only A and B are needed for the myopic formula (A.5), whereas C and D are required for obtaining an explicit decomposition of $dq(t+s,s,t)/ds$ into a time effect and a cohort effect.

A GENERALIZATION: TIME VARYING INTEREST AND INFLATION RATES

In this appendix, the user cost formula for the neo-classical model in the presence of taxes, derived in chapter 6, is generalized to account for changes in the interest and inflation rates over time. The tax rates, however, are still assumed to be constant. For simplicity, only the indexed tax system with a common indexation parameter for all components, i.e. system *MI*, is considered.

Let $i(t)$ be the interest rate at time t. The discounting factor for discounting nominal payment streams from time θ to time t is then

$$(B.1) \qquad \beta(\theta, t) = \exp\left\{ -\int_\theta^t i(\tau)\, d\tau \right\},$$

which implies

$$(B.2) \qquad i(t) = -\frac{\partial \ln \beta(\theta, t)}{\partial t}.$$

The rate of increase of the investment price q at time t is

$$(B.3) \qquad \gamma(t) = \frac{d \ln q(t)}{dt},$$

so that the inflation cumulated from time 0 to time t can be written as

$$(B.4) \qquad \frac{q(t)}{q(0)} = \exp\left\{ \int_0^t \gamma(\tau)\, d\tau \right\}.$$

Similarly, let $\varepsilon(t)$ be the rate of inflation adjustment allowed in the tax base at time t. The inflation adjustment cumulated from time θ to time t can then be written as

$$(B.5) \qquad \pi(\theta, t) = \exp\left\{ \int_0^t \varepsilon(\tau)\, d\tau \right\},$$

which implies

$$(B.6) \qquad \varepsilon(t) = \frac{\partial \ln \pi(\theta, t)}{\partial t}.$$

Eqs. (5.25), (5.26), (5.28), and (5.30) can then for tax system MI (i.e. $\alpha_I = \alpha_G = 1$) be generalized to

$$V_T(t) = \int_0^\infty A(s)\pi(t-s,t)q(t-s)J(t-s)\,ds,$$

$$S_D(t) = \int_0^\infty a(s)\pi(t-s,t)q(t-s)J(t-s)\,ds,$$

$$S_I(t) = m[i(t) - \varepsilon(t)]q(t)\int_0^\infty G(s)J(t-s)\,ds,$$

$$S_G(t) = n[\gamma(t) - \varepsilon(t)]q(t)\int_0^\infty G(s)J(t-s)\,ds.$$

We assume, for simplicity, that the weighting function for net capital, $G(s)$, is defined as in subsection 3.5.4, i.e. on the basis of a time invariant rate of discount, for instance the average value of the real interest rate $i(t) - \gamma(t)$. More generally, it could have been defined in terms of the time varying rate of discount, which would have made G a time dependent function. The tax function (5.23) then becomes

$$(B.7) \qquad \begin{aligned} T(t) &= u[X(t) - S_D(t) - S_I(t) + S_G(t)] + vV_T(t) \\ &= u[X(t) - q(t)\int_0^\infty \mu(s,t)J(t-s)ds], \end{aligned}$$

where

$$(B.8) \qquad \begin{aligned} \mu(s,t) &= \frac{q(t-s)}{q(t)}\pi(t-s,t)\left\{a(s) - \frac{v}{u}A(s)\right\} \\ &\quad + \{m[i(t) - \varepsilon(t)] - n[\gamma(t) - \varepsilon(t)]\}G(s). \end{aligned}$$

The latter function is, as before, the net deduction in the income tax base at age s per unit of initial investment cost at replacement value. But now this function it is not only age dependent, it also depends on the current time t.

The net cash-flow of the firm, discounted from time 0 to ∞ with the discounting factor β, is

$$W_T = \int_0^\infty \beta(0,t)[X(t) - q(t)J(t) - T(t)]\,dt.$$

Inserting from (B.7), this can be written as

$$
\begin{aligned}
W_T = (1-u)W - u\int_0^\infty \beta(0,t)q(t)J(t)\,dt \\
\end{aligned}
$$

(B.9)

$$+ u\int_0^\infty \beta(0,t)q(t)\int_0^t \mu(s,t)J(t-s)\,ds\,dt + W_{T_0},$$

where

(B.10) $$W = \int_0^\infty \beta(0,t)[X(t) - q(t)J(t)]\,dt$$

is the present value of the pre-tax cash-flow and

(B.11) $$W_{T_0} = u\int_0^\infty \beta(0,t)q(t)\int_t^\infty \mu(s,t)J(t-s)\,ds\,dt$$

is the predetermined part of W_T.

Substituting $\theta = t - s$, $\tau = s$, i.e. $t = \theta + \tau$, $s = \tau$, while using the fact that $\beta(0,\theta+\tau) = \beta(0,\theta)\beta(\theta,\theta+\tau)$ for any θ and τ, we find that

$$
\begin{aligned}
&\int_0^\infty \beta(0,t)q(t)\int_0^t \mu(s,t)J(t-s)\,ds\,dt \\
&= \int_0^\infty \int_0^\infty \beta(0,\theta+\tau)q(\theta)\frac{q(\theta+\tau)}{q(\theta)}\mu(\tau,\theta+\tau)J(\theta)\,d\tau\,d\theta \\
&= \int_0^\infty \beta(0,\theta)q(\theta)\lambda(\theta)J(\theta)\,d\theta,
\end{aligned}
$$

where

(B.12)
$$
\begin{aligned}
\lambda(\theta) &= \int_0^\infty \beta(\theta,\theta+\tau)\frac{q(\theta+\tau)}{q(\theta)}\mu(\tau,\theta+\tau)\,d\tau \\
&= \int_0^\infty \exp\left\{-\int_\theta^{\theta+\tau}[i(x)-\gamma(x)]\,dx\right\}\mu(\tau,\theta+\tau)\,d\tau.
\end{aligned}
$$

Then W_T can be expressed as

$$(B.13) \quad \begin{aligned} W_T &= (1-u)W - u \int_0^\infty \beta(0,t)q(t)[\,1-\lambda(t)\,]J(t)\,dt + W_{T_0} \\ &= (1-u) \int_0^\infty \beta(0,t)\left[X(t) - q(t)\frac{1-\lambda(t)u}{1-u}J(t) \right]dt + W_{T_0}. \end{aligned}$$

Eqs. (B.12) and (B.13) generalize eqs. (6.5) and (6.6) in the main text. The income deduction parameter λ and the fiscal factor $(1-\lambda u)/(1-u)$ now become time dependent functions. As before, they are predetermined in relation to the firm's investment decisions. The tax corrected investment price is

$$(B.14) \qquad\qquad q^*(t) = q(t)\frac{1-\lambda(t)u}{1-u},$$

which generalizes (6.7).

A GENERALIZATION: RECURSION FORMULAE FOR THE WEIGHTING FUNCTIONS WITH NON-ZERO DIS-COUNTING RATES

The purpose of this appendix is to derive formulae which can be used for recursive calculationrecursion formula of the weighting functions $G_\rho(s)$ and $g_\rho(s)$ for the concave and the convex class of survival functions in chapters 10 and 11 when the rate of discount is different from zero ($\rho \neq 0$). Corresponding formulae for the case with zero discounting ($\rho = 0$) are given in section 11.2.

Define the functions

$$(C.1) \; D_1(v; i, x) = \int_v^1 e^{x(\theta - v)} \theta^i \, d\theta , \qquad 0 \leq v \leq 1, \; i = 0, 1, 2, \ldots ,$$

$$(C.2) \; D_2(v; i, x) = \int_v^1 e^{x(\theta - v)} (1 - \theta)^i \, d\theta , \; 0 \leq v \leq 1, \; i = 0, 1, 2, \ldots ,$$

where x is an arbitrary real variable, $x \neq 0$. These functions are auxiliary functions for the concave and the convex class of survival functions, respectively [cf. eqs. (11.1)–(11.2) and (11.7)–(11.8)]. In particular, we have $D_2(0; i, x) = D(i, x)$, where the latter is the auxiliary function defined in section 11.4 [cf. eq. (11.26)].

Using integration by parts, we obtain

$$D_1(v; i, x) = \frac{1}{x} \left[e^{x(1-v)} - v^i \right] - \frac{i}{x} \int_v^1 e^{x(\theta - v)} \theta^{i-1} \, d\theta , \; i = 1, 2, \ldots ,$$

which implies the following recursion

$$(C.3) \qquad D_1(v; i, x) = \frac{1}{x} \left[e^{x(1-v)} - v^i - iD_1(v; i - 1, x) \right], \; i = 1, 2, \ldots .$$

Its initial value is

$$(C.4) \qquad\qquad D_1(v; 0, x) = \frac{1}{x} \left[e^{x(1-v)} - 1 \right].$$

Likewise, using integration by parts on (C.2), we find

$$D_2(v; i, x) = -\frac{1}{x}(1-v)^i + \frac{i}{x} \int_v^1 e^{x(\theta-v)}(1-\theta)^{i-1}d\theta, \quad i = 1, 2, \ldots .$$

which implies the following recursion

$$(C.5) \qquad D_2(v; i, x) = \frac{1}{x}\left[iD_2(v; i-1, x) - (1-v)^i\right], \quad i = 1, 2, \ldots .$$

Its initial value is the same as for D_1, i.e.

$$(C.6) \qquad\qquad\qquad D_2(v; 0, x) = \frac{1}{x}\left[e^{x(1-v)} - 1\right].$$

The recursion (C.5)–(C.6) generalizes (11.28a–b) in the main text.

The concave class

From eqs. (11.1), (C.1), and (C.4) it follows that

$$\int_s^N e^{-\rho(z-s)} B(z)\, dz = \frac{1}{\rho}\left[1 - e^{-\rho(N-s)}\right] - \int_s^N e^{-\rho(z-s)}(z/N)^\sigma\, dz$$

$$= ND_1(s/N; 0, -\rho N) - ND_1(s/N; \sigma, -\rho N),$$

after substituting $x = -\rho N$, $\theta = z/N$, and $v = s/N$. Inserting this expression in (3.12) and (3.51), we obtain, for $\sigma = 1, 2, \ldots$,

$$(C.7) \qquad \Phi_\rho(s) = \Phi_\rho^C(s; N, \sigma)$$

$$= \frac{ND_1(s/N; 0, -\rho N) - ND_1(s/N; \sigma, -\rho N)}{B^C(s; N, \sigma)},$$

$$(C.8) \qquad G_\rho(s) = G_\rho^C(s; N, \sigma)$$

$$= \frac{D_1(s/N; 0, -\rho N) - D_1(s/N; \sigma, -\rho N)}{D_1(0; 0, -\rho N) - D_1(0; \sigma, -\rho N)}.$$

From eqs. (11.2) and (C.1) it follows that

$$\int_s^N e^{-\rho(z-s)} b(z)\, dz = \frac{\sigma}{N} \int_s^N e^{-\rho(z-s)} (z/N)^{\sigma-1}\, dz$$

$$= \sigma D_1(s/N; \sigma - 1, -\rho N),$$

after substituting $x = -\rho N$, $\theta = z/N$, and $v = s/N$. Inserting this expression in (3.14) and (3.55), we obtain, for $\sigma = 1, 2, \ldots$,

$$(C.9) \quad \Psi_\rho(s) = \Psi_\rho^C(s; N, \sigma) = \frac{\sigma D_1(s/N; \sigma - 1, -\rho N)}{B^C(s; N, \sigma)},$$

$$(C.10) \quad g_\rho(s) = g_\rho^C(s; N, \sigma) = \frac{\sigma D_1(s/N; \sigma - 1, -\rho N)}{N D_1(0; 0, -\rho N) - N D_1(0; \sigma, -\rho N)}.$$

The convex class

From eqs. (11.7) and (C.6) it follows that

$$\int_s^N e^{-\rho(z-s)} B(z)\, dz = \int_s^N e^{-\rho(z-s)} (1 - z/N)^\tau\, dz$$

$$= N D_2(s/N; \tau, -\rho N),$$

after substituting $x = -\rho N$, $\theta = z/N$, and $v = s/N$. Inserting this expression in (3.12) and (3.51), we obtain, for $\tau = 0, 1, 2, \ldots$,

$$(C.11) \qquad \Phi_\rho(s) = \Phi_\rho^V(s; N, \tau) = \frac{N D_2(s/N; \tau, -\rho N)}{B^V(s; N, \tau)},$$

$$(C.11) \qquad G_\rho(s) = G_\rho^V(s; N, \tau) = \frac{D_2(s/N; \tau, -\rho N)}{D_2(0; \tau, -\rho N)}.$$

From eqs. (11.8) and (C.2) it follows that

$$\int_s^N e^{-\rho(z-s)} b(z)\, dz = \frac{\tau}{N} \int_s^N e^{-\rho(z-s)} (1 - z/N)^{\tau-1}\, dz$$

$$= \tau D_2(s/N; \tau - 1, -\rho N),$$

after substituting $x = -\rho N$, $\theta = z/N$, and $v = s/N$. Inserting this expression in (3.14) and (3.55), we obtain, for $\tau = 1, 2, \ldots,$

$(C.12)$ $\qquad \Psi_\rho(s) = \Psi_\rho^V(s; N, \tau) = \dfrac{\tau D_2(s/N; \tau - 1, -\rho N)}{B^V(s; N, \tau)},$

$(C.13)$ $\qquad g_\rho(s) = g_\rho^V(s; N, \tau) = \dfrac{\tau D_2(s/N; \tau - 1, -\rho N)}{N D_2(0; \tau, -\rho N)}.$

LIST OF SYMBOLS AND NOTATIONAL CONVENTIONS

Important variables and parameteres have a common notation throughout this study. In the following list, reference is made to the section in which the symbol defined first occurs.

A	Cost of an investment project (2.2)
A^*	Critical value of the cost of an investment project (2.3)
$A(s)$	Survival function of the accounting capital; proportion of the volume of an investment still included in the accounting capital at age s (5.2.1)
$a(s) = -A'(s)$	Depreciation allowance function; proportion of the volume of an investment allowed to be depreciated at age s (5.2.1)
$a^*(s) = a(s)/A(s)$	Age specific rate of depreciation allowance (5.2.1)
$a^L(s), a^A(s), a^I(s)$	Depreciation allowance functions, linear depreciation, accelerated depreciation, initial allowances (10.2.3)
$B(s)$	Survival function; proportion of an investment still included in the gross capital stock at age s (3.2.1)
B_i	Survival rate, discrete time notation (11.3)
$B(\tau\|s) = B(\tau + s)/B(s)$	Survival probability of a capital unit of age s (3.4.2)
$B_L(s)$	Age profile of vintage specific labour input in putty-clay model (7.3.1)
$B_X(s)$	Age profile of vintage specific output in putty-clay model (7.3.1)
$b(s) = -B'(s)$	Retirement function; proportion of the volume of an investment retired at age s (3.2.3)
$b^*(s) = b(s)/B(s)$	Age specific retirement rate; failure rate function (3.2.3)

$b(\tau\|s) = b(\tau + s)/B(s)$	Conditional density of remaining life time at age s (3.4.2)
$C^*(t)$	Ex ante life cycle cost of vintage t, putty-clay model (7.5.2)
$c(s)$	Implicit cost of an investment project at age s (2.4)
$c(t)$	User cost of capital at time t (4.2)
c_t	User cost of capital in year t (11.5)
$c_A(t), c_M(t)$	User cost of capital for a tax system in class A, class M (6.5.1)
$c_K(t + s, t)$	Capital service price normalized against capital purchase cost, putty-clay model (7.4.2)
$c_L(t + s, t)$	Capital service price normalized against labour cost, putty-clay model (7.4.3)
$c_X(t + s, t)$	Capital service price normalized against output value, putty-clay model (7.4.4)
$\bar{c}(t)$	User cost of capital for a neutral tax system (9.2.1)
$D(t)$	Volume of retirement at time t (3.2.3)
$D(t, s)$	Volume of capital of age s retired at time t (3.2.3)
$D(i, x)$	Auxiliary function used in computing the discounted per unit service function (11.4)
D_t	Volume of retirement in year t (11.3)
$D_H(t)$	Depreciation allowances in volume terms at time t (5.2.1)
$D_H(t, s)$	Depreciation allowances in volume terms for capital of age s at time t (5.2.1)
$D_N(t)$	Volume of depreciation at time t (3.5.3)
$D_N(t, s)$	Volume of depreciation of capital of age s at time t (3.5.3)
D_{Nt}	Volume of depreciation in year t (11.3)
d	Dividend/interest payment ratio (10.2.4)
$E(t)$	Net value of depreciation at time t (3.5.3)
$E(t, s)$	Net value of depreciation of capital of age s at time t (3.5.3)

$E_o(t)$	Net value of depreciation of accounting capital at time t, based on original cost (5.2.2)
$E_o(t,s)$	Net value of depreciation of accounting capital of age s at time t, based on original cost (5.2.2)
$E_R(t)$	Net value of depreciation of accounting capital at time t, based on replacement cost (5.2.2)
$E_R(t,s)$	Net value of depreciation of accounting capital of age s at time t, based on replacement cost (5.2.2)
$E(S)$	Expected life time of a new capital unit (3.5.2)
$E(T|s)$	Expected remaining life time of a capital unit of age s (3.4.3)
$F(K(t))$	Restricted profit function in neo-classical model (4.3)
$F(L,K)$	Ex ante production function in putty-clay model (7.2.1)
f_A, f_M	Fiscal factor of class A, class M of tax systems (6.5.1)
$G_\rho(s)$	Weighting function of net capital; proportion of the volume of an investment still included in the net capital at age s (3.5.4)
$G_{\rho i}$	Weighting function of net capital, discrete time notation (11.3)
$g_\rho(s) = -G'_\rho(s)$	Depreciation function; proportion of the volume of an investment depreciated at age s (3.5.5)
g	Growth rate of investment (11.7.2)
$H(t)$	Volume of accounting capital at age t (5.2.1)
$H(t,s)$	Volume of accounting capital of age s at time t (5.2.1)
$H_a(M) = (1 - e^{-aM})/a$	Annuity factor; value of a constant annuity of 1 discounted over M years at the rate a (3.6.2)
$h(s)$	Labour/capital requirement function (7.2.2)
i	Nominal market interest rate (2.2)
i^*	Rate of return from an investment project (2.2)

$J(t)$	Volume of investment at time t (3.2.1)
J_t	Volume of investment in year t (11.3)
$K(t)$	Volume of gross capital stock at time t (3.2.2)
$K(t,s)$	Volume of gross capital of age s at time t (3.2.1)
K_t	Volume of gross capital stock at the end of year t (11.3)
$K_N(t)$	Volume of net capital stock at time t (3.5.2)
$K_N(t,s)$	Volume of net capital of age s at time t (3.5.2)
K_{Nt}	Volume of net capital stock at the end of year t (11.3)
k	Share of the cost of a project written off immediately (2.6)
$L(t+s,s)$	Labour input allocated to vintage t at time $t+s$, putty-clay model (7.2.1)
$M(t)$	Debt outstanding at time t (6.4)
m	Proportion of imputed interests on the capital value deductible in income tax base (2.6)
m^*	Debt share (10.2.3)
N	Maximal life time (3.6.2)
$N(t)$	Ex ante life time of vintage t, putty-clay model (7.3.2)
n	Proportion of (accrued) capital gains included in income tax base (5.3.3)
$p(t)$	Output price at time t (7.4.4)
$p^*(t+s,t)$	Output price at time $t+s$ as expected at time t (7.3.1)
$q(t)$	Investment price, price per unit of new capital, at time t (3.5.1)
$q(t,s)$	Price per (efficiency) unit of capital of age s at time t (3.5.1)
$q^*(t)$	Tax corrected investment price at time t (6.2)
q_t	Investment price in year t (11.5)

q_{Bt}	Investment price, buildings and structures in manufacturing, year t (10.2.2)
q_{Mt}	Investment price, machinery and equipment in manufacturing, year t (10.2.2)
$R(t)$	Net cash-flow before tax at time t (4.3)
$R^*(t+s,t)$	Ex ante quasi rent before tax from vintage t at time $t+s$, putty clay model (7.3.1)
$R_T(t)$	Net cash-flow after tax at time t (6.2)
$R_T^*(t+s,t)$	Ex ante quasi rent after tax from vintage t at time $t+s$, putty-clay model (8.2)
r	Rate of interest used in discounting of cash-flow (4.3)
S	Life time of a new capital unit, stochastically interpreted (3.4)
$S_D(t)$	Depreciation allowances deductible in income tax base at time t (5.3)
$S_I(t)$	Interest cost deductible in income tax base at time t (5.3)
$S_G(t)$	Capital gains included in income tax base at time t (5.3)
s	Age of capital (3.2.1)
$T = S - s$	Remaining life time at age s, stochastically interpreted (In chapter 3 only) (3.4.2)
T	Maximal life time of capital prescribed in tax code (6.5.2)
$T(t)$	Tax payment at time t (5.3)
$T^*(t+s,t)$	Ex ante tax payment from vintage t at time $t+s$, putty-clay model (8.2)
t	Time (3.2.1)
U	Lagrangian of neo-classical optimization problem (4.3)
u	Income tax rate (2.6)
u^*	Effective tax rate (9.4.3)

u_C	Income tax rate, central government tax (10.2.3)
u_L	Income tax rate, local (municipal) tax (10.2.3)
$V(s)$	Value of an investment project at age s (2.4)
$V(t)$	Market value of capital at time t (3.5.1)
$V(t,s)$	Market value of capital of age s at time t (3.5.1)
$V_o(t)$	Value of accounting capital at time t, at original cost (5.2.2)
$V_o(t,s)$	Value of accounting capital of age s at time t, at original cost (5.2.2)
$V_R(t)$	Value of accounting capital at time t, at replacement cost (5.2.2)
$V_R(t,s)$	Value of accounting capital of age s at time t, at replacement cost (5.2.2)
$V_T(t)$	Value of accounting capital implicit in definition of depreciation allowances and capital value tax at time t (5.3)
v	Capital value tax rate (5.3)
v^*	Wealth tax rate (10.2.3)
W	Present value of net cash-flow before tax (4.3)
W_T	Present value of net cash-flow after tax (6.2)
$w(i)$	Present value of normalized revenue function (2.2)
$w(t)$	Wage rate at time t (7.4.3)
$w^*(t+s,t)$	Wage rate at time $t+s$ as expected at time t (7.3.1)
$X(t)$	Profit before deduction of capital cost at time t (4.3)
$X(t+s,s)$	Output from vintage t at time $t+s$ (7.2.1)
$x(s)$	Relative cash-flow from an investment project at age s (2.2)
Y_ρ	Present value of the weighting function of net capital, discounted at the rate ρ (5.5.1)
$y(s)$	Cash-flow from a project at age s (2.2)
y^*	Critical value of $y(0)$ (2.3)

Z_ρ	Present value of the weighting function of (the volume component of) accounting capital, discounted at the rate ρ (5.5.1)
z_ρ	Present value of depreciation allowance function, discounted at the rate ρ (5.5.1)
α	Rate of decline (rate of depreciation), declining balance schedule (6.5.1)
α_G	Parameter defining method of indexation of capital gains (5.3.3)
α_I	Parameter defining method of indexation of interest deduction (5.3.2)
β	Elasticity of labour in Cobb-Douglas kernel of ex ante putty-clay technology (In chapter 7 only) (7.2.3)
β	Relative distortion of user cost (9.4.1)
γ	Rate of increase of investment price (4.2)
γ_L	Rate of increase of wage rate (7.4.3)
γ_X	Rate of increase of output price (7.4.4)
δ	Rate of decline of exponential yield function (2.5)
δ_P	Price related retirement rate (11.7.1)
δ_Q	Quantity related retirement rate (11.7.2)
ε	Scale elasticity of ex ante putty-clay technology (In chapter 7 only) (7.2.3)
ε	Inflation adjustment parameter, class A of tax systems (5.3.1)
$\varepsilon_1, \varepsilon_2$	Inflation adjustment parameters, class M of tax systems (5.4.1)
$\Lambda_K(t)$	Factor of annualization related to capital, in putty-clay model (7.4.2)
$\Lambda_L(t)$	Factor of annualization related to labour, in putty-clay model (7.4.3)
$\Lambda_X(t)$	Factor of annualization related to output, in putty-clay model (7.4.4)

λ	Income deduction parameter; present value of net deductions in income tax base allowed per unit of investment outlay (6.2)
λ_A	Value of λ, class A of tax systems (5.5)
λ_M	Value of λ, class M of tax systems (5.5)
$\mu(s)$	Net deduction in income tax base at age s per unit of investment outlay at replacement value (6.2)
$\mu_A(s)$	Value of $\mu(s)$, class A of tax systems (5.4.1)
$\mu_M(s)$	Value of $\mu(s)$, class M of tax systems (5.4.1)
ν	Rate of increase of labour input per capital unit, putty-clay model (7.6)
$\xi(t)$	Lagrange parameter, neo-classical optimization problem (4.3)
Π	Life cycle profit from an investment project (2.2)
$\Pi^*(t)$	Ex ante life cycle profit from vintage t before tax, putty-clay model (7.3.2)
$\Pi_T^*(t)$	Ex ante life cycle profit from vintage t after tax, putty-clay model (8.2)
$\pi(s)$	Profit from investment project at age s (2.4)
ρ	Real rate of discount (3.3.1)
ρ^*	Internal real rate of return (9.4.2)
ρ_T	After tax real rate of return to saver (9.4.3)
σ	Curvature parameter of concave class of survival functions (10.2.1)
σ_{ML}	Elasticity of substitution between machinery and labour (11.8)
τ	Curvature parameter of convex class of survival functions (10.2.1)
$\Phi_\rho(s)$	Per unit discounted service flow at age s (3.3.1)
$\varphi(\rho)$	Abbreviated notation for $\Phi_\rho(0)$ (9.4.2)
$\Psi_\rho(s)$	Per unit discounted retirement flow at age s (3.3.2)
$\Psi[K(t), J(t), t]$	Hamiltonian of neo-classical optimization problem (4.3)

REFERENCES

Ackley G. (1961): *Macroeconomic Theory.* (New York: Macmillan.)

Allen R.G.D. (1967): *Macro-Economic Theory. A Mathematical Treatment.* (London: Macmillan Press.)

Andersen S. (1977): *Prisnivåjusterte regnskaper. Bergverksdrift og industri. (Price-Level Accounting. Mining and Manufacturing.)* Articles No. 103, Central Bureau of Statistics. (Oslo: Central Bureau of Statistics.)

Anderson G.J. (1981): A New Approach to the Empirical Investigation of Investment Expenditures. *Economic Journal* 91, 88–103.

Ando A.K., Modigliani F., Rasche R., and Turnovsky S.J. (1974): On the Role of Expectations of Price and Technological Change in an Investment Function. *International Economic Review* 15, 384–414.

Arrow K.J. (1964): Optimal Capital Policy, the Cost of Capital, and Myopic Decision Rules. *Annals of the Institute of Statistical Mathematics* 16, 21–30.

Arrow K.J. (1968): Optimal Capital Policy with Irreversible Investment. In *Value, Capital, and Growth. Papers in Honour of Sir John Hicks*, ed. by J.N. Wolfe. (Edinburgh: Edinburgh University Press), 1–19.

Arrow K.J., and Levhari D. (1969): Uniqueness of the Internal Rate of Return with Variable Life of Investment. *Economic Journal* 79, 560–566.

Artus P., and Muet P.A. (1980): Un retour sur la comparaison des hypothèses "putty-putty" et "putty-clay" dans l'estimation des demandes effectives d'investissement. *Annales de l'INSEE*, 38–39, 193–206.

Artus P., Muet P.A., Palinkas P., and Pauly P. (1981): Economic Policy and Private Investment Since the Oil Crisis: A Comparative Study of France and Germany. *European Economic Review* 16, 7–51.

Atkinson A.B., and Stiglitz J.E. (1980): *Lectures on Public Economics.* (Maidenhead, Berkshire: McGraw-Hill.)

Auerbach A.J. (1983a): Taxation, Corporate Financial Policy and the Cost of Capital. *Journal of Economic Literature* 21, 905–940.

Auerbach A.J. (1983b): *The Taxation of Capital Income.* (Cambridge, Mass.: Harvard University Press.)

Barlow R.E., and Proschan F. (1975): *Statistical Theory of Reliability and Life Testing.* (New York: Holt, Rinehart and Winston.)

Bartle R.G. (1964): *The Elements of Real Analysis.* (New York: John Wiley & Sons.)

Bergström V., and Södersten J. (1982): Taxation and Real Cost of Capital. *Scandinavian Journal of Economics* 84, 443–456.

Bierman H., and Smidt S. (1980): *The Capital Budgeting Decision*. (New York: Macmillan.)

Biørn E. (1975): *Avskrivningsregler og prisen på bruk av realkapital. (Depreciation Rules and the User Cost of Capital.)* Articles No. 74, Central Bureau of Statistics. (Oslo: Central Bureau of Statistics.)

Biørn E. (1984): Inflation, Depreciation, and the Neutrality of the Corporate Income Tax. *Scandinavian Journal of Economics* 86, 214–228.

Biørn E. (1986): Energy Price Changes and Induced Scrapping and Revaluation of Capital — a Putty-Clay Approach. Discussion Paper No. 16, Central Bureau of Statistics, Oslo.

Biørn E., and Frenger P. (1986): Expectations, Substitution, and Scrapping in a Putty-Clay Model. Paper presented at the European Meeting of the Econometric Society, Budapest, 1986. Discussion Paper No. 17, Central Bureau of Statistics, Oslo.

Biørn E., Holmøy E., and Olsen Ø. (1985): Gross and Net Capital, Productivity, and the Form of the Survival Function — Some Norwegian Evidence. Paper presented at the Fifth World Congress of the Econometric Society, Boston, 1985. Discussion Paper No. 11, Central Bureau of Statistics, Oslo.

Blades D. (1983): Service Lives of Fixed Assets. Working Paper No. 4, OECD Economics and Statistics Department, Paris, March 1983.

Boadway R. (1978): Investment Incentives, Corporate Taxation, and Efficiency in the Allocation of Capital. *Economic Journal* 88, 470–481.

Boadway R. (1980): Corporate Taxation and Investment: A Synthesis of the Neo-classical Theory. *Canadian Journal of Economics* 13, 250–267.

Boadway R., and Bruce N. (1979): Depreciation and Interest Deductions and the Effect of the Corporate Income Tax on Investment. *Journal of Public Economics* 11, 93–105.

Boadway R., Bruce N., and Mintz J. (1983): On the Neutrality of Flow-of-funds Corporate Taxation. *Economica* 50, 49–61.

Bradford D.F., and Fullerton D. (1981): Pitfalls in the Construction and Use of Effective Tax Rates. In *Depreciation, Inflation, and the Taxation of Income from Capital*, ed. by C.R. Hulten. (Washington: The Urban Institute Press), 251–279.

Burmeister E. (1980): *Capital Theory and Dynamics*. (Cambridge: Cambridge University Press.)

Burmeister E., and Turnovsky S.J. (1976): The Specification of Adaptive Expectations in Continuous Time Dynamic Econometric Models. *Econometrica* 44, 879–905.

CBS (1981): *Aktuelle skattetall (Current Tax Data)*. Report 81/26, Central Bureau of Statistics. (Oslo: Central Bureau of Statistics.)

CBS (1984): *Regnskapsstatistikk 1982. Oljeutvinning, bergverksdrift og industri. (Statistics of Accounts 1982. Oil Extraction, Mining and Manufacturing.)* (Oslo: Central Bureau of Statistics.)

CBS (1985): *Aktuelle skattetall (Current Tax Data).* Report 85/2, Central Bureau of Statistics. (Oslo: Central Bureau of Statistics.)

Davidson R., and MacKinnon J.G. (1981): Several Tests for Model Specification in the Presence of Alternative Hypotheses. *Econometrica* 49, 781–793.

Dorfman R. (1969): An Economic Interpretation of Optimal Control Theory. *American Economic Review* 59, 817–831.

Eisner R. (1972): Components of Capital Expenditure: Replacement and Modernization versus Expansion. *Review of Economics and Statistics* 54, 297–305.

Engle R.F., and Granger C.W.J. (1987): Co-integration and Error Correction: Representation, Estimation, and Testing. *Econometrica* 55, 251–276.

Feldstein M.S., and Foot D.K. (1971): The Other Half of Gross Investment: Replacement and Modernization Expenditures. *Review of Economics and Statistics* 53, 49–58.

Feldstein M., and Green J. (1983): Why Do Companies Pay Dividends? *American Economic Review* 73, 17–30.

Feldstein M.S., and Rothschild M. (1974): Towards an Economic Theory of Replacement Investment. *Econometrica* 42, 393–423.

Feller W. (1966): *An Introduction to Probability Theory and Its Applications. Volume II.* (New York: John Wiley & Sons.)

Fisher I. (1930): *The Theory of Interest.* (New York: Macmillan.)

Fløttum E.J. (1981): *National Accounts of Norway. System and Methods of Estimation.* Report 81/1, Central Bureau of Statistics. (Oslo: Central Bureau of Statistics, 1981.)

Fullerton D. (1987): The Indexation of Interest, Depreciation, and Capital Gains and Tax Reform in The United States. *Journal of Public Economics* 32, 25–51.

Fuss M. (1977): The Structure of Technology over Time: A Model for Testing the 'Putty-Clay' Hypothesis. *Econometrica* 45, 1797–1821.

Fuss M. (1978): Factor Substitution in Electricity Generation. A Test of the Putty-Clay Hypothesis. In *Production Economics. A Dual Approach to Theory and Applications, vol. 2*, ed. by M. Fuss and D. McFadden. (Amsterdam: North-Holland Publishing Company), 187–213.

Førsund F.R., and Hjalmarsson L. (1987): *Analyses of Industrial Structure: A Putty-Clay Approach.* (Stockholm: Almqvist & Wiksell International.)

Gould J.P. (1968): Adjustment Costs in the Theory of Investment of the Firm. *Review of Economic Studies* 35, 47–55.

Griliches Z. (1963): Capital Stock in Investment Functions: Some Problems of Concept and Measurement. In *Measurement in Economics: Studies in*

Mathematical Economics and Econometrics in Memory of Yehuda Grunfeld, ed. by C.F. Christ et al. (Stanford: Stanford University Press), 115–137.

Haavelmo T. (1960): *A Study in the Theory of Investment*. (Chicago: University of Chicago Press.)

Hall R.E. (1968): Technical Change and Capital from the Point of the Dual. *Review of Economic Studies* 35, 35–46.

Hall R.E. (1971): The Measurement of Quality Change from Vintage Price Data. In *Price Indexes and Quality Change*, ed. by Z. Griliches. (Cambridge, Mass.: Harvard University Press), 240–271.

Hall R.E., and Jorgenson D.W. (1967): Tax Policy and Investment Behavior. *American Economic Review* 57, 391–414.

Hall R.E., and Jorgenson D.W. (1971): Application of the Theory of Optimal Capital Accumulation. In *Tax Incentives and Capital Spending*, ed. by G. Fromm. (Amsterdam: North-Holland Publishing Company), 9–60.

Hartman R. (1978): Investment Neutrality of Business Income Taxes. *Quarterly Journal of Economics* 92, 245–260.

Hendry D.F. (1986): Econometric Modelling with Cointegrated Variables: An Overview. *Oxford Bulletin on Economics and Statistics* 48, 201–228.

Hendry D.F., Pagan A., and Sargan J.D. (1984): Dynamic Specification. In *Handbook of Econometrics, vol. II*, ed. by Z. Griliches and M.D. Intriligator. (Amsterdam: North-Holland Publishing Company), ch. 18.

Hicks J.R. (1969): The Measurement of Capital. *Bulletin de l'Institut International de la Statistique* 43, 253–264.

Hicks J.R. (1973): *Capital and Time*. (Oxford: Oxford University Press.)

Hirshleifer J. (1958): On the Theory of Optimal Investment Decision. *Journal of Political Economy* 66, 329–352.

Hotelling H. (1925): A General Mathematical Theory of Depreciation. *Journal of the American Statistical Association* 20, 340–353.

Hulten C.R., and Wykoff F.C. (1980): Economic Depreciation and Taxation of Structures in the United States Manufacturing Industries: An Empirical Analysis. In *The Measurement of Capital*, ed. by D. Usher. (Chicago: The University of Chicago Press), 83–109.

Hulten C.R., and Wykoff F.C. (1981a): The Estimation of Economic Depreciation Using Vintage Asset Prices: An Application of the Box-Cox Power Transformation. *Journal of Econometrics* 15, 367–396.

Hulten C.R., and Wykoff F.C. (1981b): The Measurement of Economic Depreciation. In *Depreciation, Inflation, and the Taxation of Income from Capital*, ed. by C.R. Hulten. (Washington: The Urban Institute Press), 81–125.

Johansen L. (1959): Substitution versus Fixed Production Coefficients in the Theory of Economic Growth: A Syntheses. *Econometrica* 27, 157–176.

Johansen L. (1960): *A Multi-Sectoral Study of Economic Growth*. (Amsterdam: North-Holland Publishing Company.)

Johansen L. (1972): *Production Functions.* (Amsterdam: North Holland Publishing Company.)

Johansen L., and Sørsveen Å. (1967): Notes on the Measurement of Real Capital in Relation to Economic Planning Models. *Review of Income and Wealth* 13, 175–197.

Jorgenson D.W. (1963): Capital Theory and Investment Behavior. *American Economic Review* 53, 247–259.

Jorgenson D.W. (1965): Anticipations and Investment Behavior. In *The Brookings Quarterly Econometric Model of the United States*, ed. by J.S. Duesenberry, E. Kuh, G. Fromm, and L.R. Klein. (Chicago: Rand McNally 1965), 35–92.

Jorgenson D.W. (1967): The Theory of Investment Behaviour. In *Determinants of Investment Behaviour*, ed. by R. Ferber. (New York: National Bureau of Economic Research), 129–155.

Jorgenson D.W. (1974): The Economic Theory of Replacement and Depreciation. In *Econometrics and Economic Theory. Essays in Honour of Jan Tinbergen*, ed. by W. Sellekaerts. (London: Macmillan Press), 189–221.

Jorgenson D.W. (1986): Econometric Methods for Modeling Producer Behavior. In *Handbook of Econometrics, vol. III*, ed. by Z. Griliches and M.D. Intriligator. (Amsterdam: North-Holland Publishing Company), ch. 31.

Jorgenson D.W., and Stephenson J.A. (1967): Investment Behavior in U.S. Manufacturing, 1947–1960. *Econometrica* 35, 169–220.

Jorgenson D.W., and Sullivan M.A. (1981): Inflation and Corporate Capital Recovery. In *Depreciation, Inflation, and the Taxation of Income from Capital*, ed. by C.R. Hulten. (Washington: The Urban Institute Press), 171–238.

Jorgenson D.W., and Yun K.Y. (1986a): Tax Policy and Capital Allocation. *Scandinavian Journal of Economics* 88, 355–377.

Jorgenson D.W., and Yun K.Y. (1986b): The Efficiency of Capital Allocation. *Scandinavian Journal of Economics* 88, 85–107.

Kalbfleisch J.D., and Prentice R.L. (1980): *The Statistical Analysis of Failure Time Data.* (New York: John Wiley & Sons.)

King M.A. (1974): Taxation and the Cost of Capital. *Review of Economic Studies* 41, 21–35.

King M.A. (1975): Taxation, Corporate Financial Policy, and the Cost of Capital. A Comment. *Journal of Public Economics* 4, 271–279.

King M.A. (1977): *Public Policy and the Corporation.* (London: Chapman and Hall.)

King M.A., and Fullerton D. (1984): *The Taxation of Income From Capital.* (Chicago: The University of Chicago Press.)

Kmenta J. (1986): *Elements of Econometrics. 2nd edition.* (New York: Macmillan Publishing Company.)

Koskenkylä H. (1985): *Investment Behaviour and Market Imperfections with an Application to the Finnish Corporate Sector.* (Helsinki: Bank of Finland.)

Lucas R.E. (1967): Optimal Investment Policy and the Flexible Accelerator. *International Economic Review* 8, 78–85.

Malcomson J.M. (1975): Replacement and the Rental Value of Capital Equipment Subject to Obsolescence. *Journal of Economic Theory* 10, 24–41.

Malcomson J.M. (1979): Optimal Replacement Policy and Approximate Replacement Rules. *Applied Economics* 11, 405–414.

Malcomson J.M., and Prior M.J. (1979): The Estimation of a Vintage Model of Production for U.K. Manufacturing. *Review of Economic Studies* 46, 719–736.

Malinvaud E. (1971): Peut-on mesurer l'évolution du coût d'usage du capital productif? *Economie et Statistique* 22, 5–20.

Malinvaud E. (1972): *Lectures on Microeconomic Theory.* (Amsterdam: North-Holland Publishing Company.)

Moene K.O. (1985): Fluctuations and Factor Proportions: Putty-Clay Investments Under Uncertainty. In *Production, Multi-Sectoral Growth and Planning*, ed. by F.R. Førsund, M. Hoel, and S. Longva. (Amsterdam: North-Holland Publishing Company), 87–108.

Musgrave R.A. (1959): *The Theory of Public Finance.* (New York: McGraw-Hill.)

Muzondo T.R. (1979): The Corporation Income Tax and Depreciation Policy in the Short Run. *Canadian Journal of Economics* 12, 15–28.

Nickell S.J. (1978): *The Investment Decisions of Firms.* (Cambridge: Cambridge University Press.)

NOU (1984): *Personbeskatning. (Personal Taxation.).* Report from the Norwegian Tax Commission, NOU 1984:22. (Oslo: Universitetsforlaget.)

Paccoud T. (1983): *Stock of Fixed Assets in Industry in the Community Member States: Towards Greater Comparability.* (Luxembourg: Eurostat.)

Pesaran M.H., and Deaton A.S. (1978): Testing Non-Nested Nonlinear Regression Models. *Econometrica* 46, 677–694.

Phelps E.S. (1963): Substitution, Fixed Proportions, Growth and Distribution. *International Economic Review* 4, 265–288.

Ross S.A., Spatt C.S., and Dybvig P.H. (1980): Present Values and Internal Rates of Return. *Journal of Economic Theory* 23, 66–81.

Samuelson P.A. (1964): Tax Deductibility of Economic Depreciation to Insure Invariant Valuation. *Journal of Political Economy* 72, 604–606.

Sandmo A. (1974): Investment Incentives and the Corporate Income Tax. *Journal of Political Economy* 82, 287–302.

Sandmo A. (1979): A Note on the Neutrality of the Cash-Flow Corporation Tax. *Economics Letters* 4, 173–176.

Seierstad A. (1985): Properties of Production and Profit Functions Arising from the Aggregation of a Capacity Distribution of Micro Units. In *Production, Multi-Sectoral Growth and Planning*, ed. by F.R. Førsund, M. Hoel, and S. Longva. (Amsterdam: North-Holland Publishing Company), 65–85.

Sen A. (1975): Minimal Conditions for Monotonicity of Capital Value. *Journal of Economic Theory* 11, 340–355.

Skagseth P. (1982): *Det norske nasjonalregnskapet. Dokumentasjonsnotat nr. 12. Beregning av investering, realkapital og kapitalslit.* Report 82/12, Central Bureau of Statistics. (Oslo: Central Bureau of Statistics.)

Smith V.L. (1963): Tax Depreciation Policy and Investment Theory. *International Economic Review* 4, 80–91.

Steele G.R. (1980): The Relationship Between Gross Capital Stock and Net Capital Stock: An Assessment of the U.K. Time Series. *Oxford Bulletin on Economics and Statistics* 42, 227–234.

Steigum E. (1983): A Financial Theory of Investment Behavior. *Econometrica* 5, 637–645.

Stiglitz J.E. (1973): Taxation, Corporate Financial Policy, and the Cost of Capital. *Journal of Public Economics* 2, 1–34.

Stiglitz J.E., and Weiss A. (1981): Credit Rationing in Markets with Imperfect Information. *American Economic Review* 71, 393–410.

Takayama A. (1985): *Mathematical Economics, 2nd edition.* (Cambridge: Cambridge University Press.)

Treadway A.B. (1971): The Rational Multivariate Flexible Accelerator. *Econometrica* 39, 845–855.

Varian H.R. (1978): *Microeconomic Analysis.* (New York: W.W. Norton & Company.)

Young A.H., and Musgrave J.C. (1980): Estimation of Capital Stock in the United States. In *The Measurement of Capital*, ed. by D. Usher. (Chicago: The University of Chicago Press), 23–68.

AUTHOR INDEX